AN INTRODUCTORY BIBLIOGRAPHY FOR JAPANESE STUDIES

Vol. II
Part 2

UNIVERSITY OF TOKYO PRESS

UTP No. 3300–09236–5149
ISBN 0–86008–210–5

Copyright © 1977
The Japan Foundation
3–7–1, Kasumigaseki, Chiyoda-ku, Tokyo, Japan 100
Prepared by the Center for Social Science Communication
Printed in Japan

PREFACE

This is the fourth in an annual bibliography series published by the Japan Foundation. The series aims to provide non-Japanese scholars with an outline of the most noteworthy Japanese research in the major disciplines. Social sciences and humanities are dealt with in alternate years. Volume I, Part 1 (1974) surveyed publications in the social sciences primarily from 1969 through 1972; Volume I, Part 2 (1975) presented works in the humanities from 1970 through 1973; Volume II, Part 1 (1976) contains important books and articles in the social sciences published between January 1973 and December 1974. Accordingly, this volume continues bibliographical information on works in the humanities published from 1974 through 1975.

Volume II, Part 2 covers seven disciplines; history, intellectual history (*shisōshi*), language, literature, religion, art and archaeology. Each section begins with an introduction providing general background on works in the field and annotation on content, followed by a list of representative studies that came out during 1974–75. We have included substantive comment on as many selections as possible, but unfortunately not all the titles in the bibliographical list could be touched upon in the text. The names of authors have been romanized according to the Hepburn system, and a tentative English translation has been made for each title to facilitate use for non-Japanese researchers. The purpose of these volumes is to present works published by Japanese authors in the Japanese language; for detailed coverage of English language materials on Japan, we recommend the bibliography published by the Association for Asian Studies in the United States.

Seventeen scholars, each an outstanding specialist in his field, selected the publications for inclusion in the bibliography and wrote the introductions. They are: Professors Akiyama Terukazu, Arima Manabu, Chijiwa Itaru, Imaizumi Toshio, Ishii Susumu, Itō Takashi, Kanai Seiichi, Kubota Jun, Mayuzumi Hiromichi, Mikami Tsugio, Nomoto Kikuo, Ōishi Shinzaburō, Shiraishi Yoshihiko, Taguchi Eiichi, Tamaru Noriyoshi, Tamura Kōichi, Yamamoto Takeo, and Yoshida Shōichirō.

We wish to express our appreciation for their devoted efforts in writing the text. We also extend our warmest thanks to Mr. Kano Tsutomu and his staff for their translations and editorial work. Final responsibility, however, rests with the Japan Foundation. Any opinions or views expressed herein are those of the individual authors, and are not necessarily those of the Foundation.

As this series continues, we urge our readers to make known to us their suggestions for improving the presentation or format of the bibliography so that it might best serve them.

May 1977
The Japan Foundation

CONTENTS

EDITORIAL NOTES

1. Romanization: The Hepburn system with minor modifications has been employed in the Romanization of Japanese words.
2. Personal names: In accordance with Japanese practice, the family names precede the given names.
3. Brackets in the bibliographical listings indicate series title.

JAPANESE HISTORY
——ANCIENT PERIOD

MAYUZUMI Hiromichi
Gakushūin University

Translated by Lynne E. Riggs

I. PRE-SEVENTH CENTURY

Since the end of World War II research in ancient history has progressed rapidly, but at the same time the field has begun to reflect the fragmentation and confusion which often accompanies a period of reexamination. There have been numerous attempts to systematize the research that has been done until now and to define the problems and prospects for the future. What is noteworthy among recent developments is the recognition that ancient Japanese history should be seen as part of the ancient history of East Asia, with the history of Japan-Korea relations at the center of focus. This trend has developed in several different directions. In addition, there has emerged growing resistance to the old centric view of domestic history as revolving around the Kinai district.

A notable feature of the research of 1974–75 is the attempt to review theoretical assumptions underlying research in ancient history, and even to offer new perspectives. Summarizing both prewar and postwar theory and controversy around the "Asiatic mode of production," Kawaguchi Katsuyasu, Harashima Reiji and others [I-01(1), (2); I-02(1)–(4)] define the communal society of ancient Japan as an Asiatic *Hörige* (bondsman) system, which differed from slavery or serfdom patterns in the West. Hara Hidesaburō, Naoki Kōjirō and Yamao Yukihisa [I-03 (1); I-04 (1), (2)] discuss the position, nature and formation of the ancient Japanese state in world history in terms of social structure, history of social development and international relations.

Numerous works have been published and several special editions of journals put together concerning the connection between Japanese and East Asian history as a whole. A volume on the history of Japanese-Korean relations edited by Inoue Hideo and Hatada Takashi [I-05] contains translations of the work of several North and South Korean historians who have tried to revise the Japan-centered historical view and to raise issues of which Japanese scholars have not even been aware. Hatada's study [I-06] is a collection of essays from the Japanese side written in response to the challenge of Korean scholars.

The long years of Japanese colonial domination of Korea before the war, and the complexity of political relations between Japan and both North and South Korea at present, however, have contributed to a wide gap between Japanese scholars and Korean, with regard to the analysis and interpretation of historical materials. Taking into account these conditions, Murayama Kōichi [I-07] and Kitō Kiyoaki [I-08] survey and attempt to systematize the history of research on Japan-Korea relations.

As always, treatises on the Yamatai state and the *Wajin* (people of Wa) are flourishing. Egami Namio's "Higashi Ajia ni okeru Wajin no kigen to katsudō" (The Origin and Movements of the Wa People in East Asia) [I-09] presents an argument against the popular *Wajin*-equals-Japanese thesis, asserting that the *Wajin* mentioned occasionally in the Chinese and Korean records were fishermen residing on islands off Southern China, who in due course migrated to various locations along the coast of the East China Sea. Tanaka Yoshiaki in "Yama-taikoku-ron" [I-02 (2)] broadly surveys the history of research on the state of Yamatai, and points out that recent archaeological findings make it necessary to revise the hypothesis that *dōken* and *dōtaku* (bronze sword and bronze bell) formed a large culture sphere. Archaeologists have also come up with new ideas regarding the highland settlements with fortifications scattered along the coastline of the Inland Sea. Tanaka urges fellow historians to take heed of these developments. Yamao Yukihisa's "Seiji kenryoku no hassei" (The Emergence of Political Power) [I-04 (2)] offers an excellent introduction to the state of Yamatai.

Research on the tomb of the Koguryo king, Kwanggaet'o (Kōkaidoō, in Japanese) (r. 392–413), has progressed rapidly. This tomb has long been considered a basic source of evidence for Japanese advances into Korea in the fourth century, but Lee Chin-hŭi, Korean historian living in Japan, presents the shocking opinion in his *Kōkaidoōryōhi no kenkyū* (Research on the Kwanggaet'o Stele) (Yoshikawa Kōbunkan, 1972) that the inscription was altered by applying lime as part of a Japanese army plot just before the Russo-Japanese War. His "alteration theory" has produced much heated debate over both the reading of the inscription and the authenticity of the alteration theory itself. Naka-tsuka Akira [I-06 (3)] and Saeki Arikiyo [I-06 (4)] both attempt to clarify the distorted image of Korean history which dominated Meiji period research on the inscription that was carried out by General Staff Headquarters, as well as Japan's modern historiography as a whole. Hamada Kōsaku investigates the logical structure of the epitaph and discusses the suitability of the established reading in his article, "Kōkuri Kōkaidoōryō hibun no kenkyū: hibun no kōzō to shishin no hippō o chūshin toshite" (Koguryo King Kwanggaet'o's Tomb Inscription: Its Structure and the Writing Style of Official Historians) [I-06 (2)]. Even if the alterations in the inscription were not intentional, the application of lime as pointed out by Mr. Lee is now undisputed. Hatada Takashi [I-06 (1)] and Hoshino Ryōsaku [I-10] provide some clarification of the problems in research on the Kwanggaet'o tomb inscription in recent years.

In the area of dynastic theory and historical emperors, Naoki Kōjirō's "Ōjin tennō no jitsuzaisei o megutte" (Did Emperor Ōjin Actually Exist?) [I-11] advocates that Emperor Ōjin, heretofore thought to be the earliest historical emperor, is actually fictional, created in the image of his successor, Nintoku. On the other hand, Ōishi Ryōzai [I-12] declares that Ōjin's father, Chūai (r. 192–200), long considered one of the legendary emperors, was actually the earliest historical emperor. In addition, Harashima Reiji in *Jimmu tennō no tanjō* (Birth of Emperor Jimmu) [I-13] holds that the creation of Jimmu in the image of a founding emperor occurred around the sixth century and was influenced by the example of the founding emperors of the Koguryo, Silla and Paekche kingdoms and their creation of royal genealogies. Ōtani Eiji has produced a good synthesis of theories on the Sujin dynasty in "Irikei keifu no fukugen ni kansuru ichi shiron" (Restoration of the Ili Genealogy: A Hypothesis) [*Shishō*, No. 3, Risshō Daigaku-in Shishōkai, 1974], and Maekawa Akihisa discusses the appearance of Emperor Keitai in "Keitai tennō yōritsu no seiryoku kiban ni tsuite" (The Power Base of Emperor Keitai's Assumption of the Throne) [*Kodai bunka*, Vol. 26:1, Kodaigaku Kyōkai, 1974]. Hirano Kunio, "Yamato ōken to Chōsen" (Korea and the Sovereignty of Yamato) [I-04 (3)] is an excellent survey of the formation of the imperial dynasty and sanction of its power. Somehow the research in this area tends to be influenced by arbitrary considerations of individual scholars, however.

Yamao and Hirano support the general view that stable sovereign power and the ancient state were established during the sixth century [I-04 (2, 3)]. Kitō Kiyoaki [I-03 (2)] and Yoshida Akira [I-14 (2)] push this view further and emphasize that establishment of a strongly unified state came about through a process of subjugation by the imperial court of the strong local chiefdoms in Tsukushi (Kyushu), Kenu (the provinces of Shimotsuke and Kōzuke), and elsewhere. Making the widespread emergence of a new social class of village chieftains in the sixth century the focus of their study, Kawaguchi Katsuyasu [I-15] and Sasaki Ken'ichi [I-16] offer a fresh perspective on this topic by showing that the characteristics and development of this class created the fundamental conditions for the emerging centralized state. Kishi Masahiro, "Yōmei-Sushunki no seiji katei" (Political Processes during the Reigns of Emperors Yōmei and Sushun) [I-17] is but one of many works dealing with the reigns of these two emperors in context of the political history of the sixth century. Others include Honiden Kikushi, "Yōmei-Sushunki no nairan ni tsuite" (Civil Wars during the Reigns of Emperors Yōmei and Sushun) [*Shigen*, 19, Shigenkai, 1975] and Noda Reishi, "Sūbutsu ronsō no saikentō" (Controversy on Buddhism Reconsidered) [*Jinbunkenkyū*, 3, Kobe Yakka Daigaku, 1975].

The repudiation by Hara Hidesaburō and others of the Taika Reform as recorded in the *Nihon shoki* is already ten years past, but Mr. Hara has recently refortified his argument in "Josetsu: Nihon kodai kokka kenkyū no rironteki zentei" (The Theoretical Premises of Research on the Ancient Japanese State: An Introduction) [I-03 (1)], and Kitō Kiyoaki, having reviewed all the several theories, concludes that denial of the occurrence of the Taika Reform is the most reasonable [I-02 (4)]. On the other hand, in an essay supporting the historical event of the reform, Inoue Mitsusada proposes the existence of the original decree which served as the basis for the imperial decree promulgating the reform [I-14 (3)].

Yagi Atsuru, "Nanaseiki chūki ni okeru seiken kōsō" (Power Struggle in the Mid-Seventh Century) [I-18] presents bold new theories on the political history of the period; Emperor Kōtoku did not ascend the throne in the first year of Taika (645), for example, but succeeded at the abdication of Empress Kōgyoku in the fifth year of Taika (650); that Nakanoōe-no-ōji (later Emperor Tenji) and Emperor Kōtoku disagreed over diplomatic policy; and after Kōtoku's death the Naniwa court was maintained by Empress Hashihito.

Controversy regarding the Taika Reform continues unabated, but the belief that the *ritsuryō* system was rapidly established in the thirty-odd years between the reigns of Tenji (688–71) and Tenmu-Jitō (673–96) is now generally accepted in the academic world. Nonetheless it has become gradually clearer that the course of the reform was neither direct nor smooth. Yoshie Akiko, *Taihō izen no koseki seido* ('The Household Registry System Prior to the Taihō Reform) [I-19] and Hayakawa Shōhachi, *Ritsuryō kokka* (The *Ritsuryō* State) [II-02] generally confirm two points: that in the process of development of the penal and administrative codes known as the *ritsuryō* system, considerable variation occurred from the Tenji reign to the Tenmu-Jitō period, and between that time and the formation of the Taihō Code; and that during the Tenmu reign and thereafter a centralized system of rule extending over subjects throughout the country was effected, particularly after the compilation of the *Kōinnenjaku* (Registry of the year 690) under Empress Jitō.

Research focusing on another, completely different area has also contributed to unraveling the developmental process of the *ritsuryō* system after the mid-seventh century. There have been a number of commendable studies recently on the layout of the ancient capital centering on the imperial palace (*tojōsei*), one of which, edited by Tsuboi Kiyotari and Suzuki Kakichi [I-20], attempts to demonstrate how the capital cities were constructed to embody requirements generated by establishment of the *ritsuryō* system and how changes in the layout reflected the formative process of the system.

So far we have been dealing with scholarly material largely by period; now let us look at developments in several areas of specialization. In the first place, Yagi Atsuru's discussion of the *kuni-no-miyatsuko* and *agata-nushi* (types of district and provincial officials) draws parallels between the history of the local forms of government, from their emergence to their decline, and the evolution of a centralized state. It also provides concrete explanation of how the *kuni-no-miyatsuko* controlled the people under their jurisdiction [I-14 (1)]. The work of Honiden Kikushi, "Kokuzōsei 'atai' ni kansuru ichi-ni no mondai" (Questions Concerning the *'Atai'* in the Ranking of Provincial Officials) (*Shoku Nihongi kenkyū*, 172, Shoku Nihongi Kenkyūkai, 1974), is a consideration of the rank of *atai* in the *kabane* hierarchy.

There has been vigorous research on specific *uji* (clans) and numerous essays have been published. Among them is Katō Kenkichi's study [I-21] on the sixth and seventh century Hata clan, which, by pointing to the territorial coincidence of the areas where the clan people resided, the center of production of mercury and cinnabar, and the distribution of the Mibu-be, clarifies the character of the industrial clan once so close to imperial power during the reign of Empress Suiko (592–628). A related work of interest is Saeki Arikiyo, *Kodai shizoku no keizu* (A Diagram of the Ancient Clans) [I-22], which outlines the history of powerful local clans (*gōzoku*) through an analysis of genealogies of the Ioki-be, Kamo, and other *uji*.

With regard to the system of *be*, which are occupational service groups, and the *miyake* (sovereign estates), Yoshida Akira, "Taika zendai no shakai kōzō" (Social Structure of Japan before the Taika Reform) [I-02 (3)] provides a well-organized outline of the system of *be*, and Harashima Reiji, in "Minashiro ni tsuite" (The Minashiro: *Be* of the Imperial Estates) [I-01 (2)] stresses that *be* working on the private estates of the imperial clan (*minashiro*) were economic and military in their function and that large numbers of such *be* were formed during the reign of Emperor Kinmei (539–71). Not to be overlooked on this subject is Senda Minoru's article [I-23], which demonstrates by geographical methodology the close relationship between the *miyake* and the names of Inukai and Tabe, as well as the special grid system of land allotment in ancient Japan.

The participation of scholars from many disciplines has much enriched research on Japanese mythology, which has tended to divide into two main types, one approaching the study as cultural anthropology or comparative mythology, and the other laying emphasis on the rites and historical background. Great contributions have been made to the study of mythology by several recent works. Among them are: Ōbayashi Taryō, ed., *Nihon shinwa no hikaku kenkyū* (Comparative Study of Japanese Myths) [I-24], which draws on material from cultures outside but surrounding Japan; Yoshida Atsuhiko, *Nihon shinwa to In-Ō shinwa* (Japanese and Indo-European Mythology) [I-25], in which the structure and course of diffusion of Japanese myths are likened to and compared with Greek and Indo-European myths; and Ōbayashi's *Nihon shinwa no kōzō* (Structure of Japanese Mythology), which is likewise a structural analysis [I-26].

Okada Seishi, however, in "Kiki shinwa no seiritsu" (Birth of *Nihon-shoki* and *Kojiki* Myths) [I-14(5)] which represents the second of these two types of approach, asserts that *Kojiki* and *Nihon shoki* are essentially political, no more than historically formulated ritual myths of the imperial court. Also worthy of mention is Mizuno Yū, *Kodai shakai to Urashima densetsu* (Ancient Society as Reflected in the Legend of Urashima Tarō) (2 vols.) [I-27], which deals not only with the genealogy of the Urashima Tarō tale and the fisherfolk who transmitted the legend, but also with the origins of the Ise Shrine.

Following the trend mentioned earlier toward broadening the perspective on historical research to embrace East Asia as a whole, work on the history of Buddhism also reflects the serious attention being given to the connection of Buddhism with the international relations of East Asia and the extensive sphere of Buddhist culture. Studies have appeared which reconsider the long-neglected existence and role of the Buddhist culture of Silla and Paekche (1–28, 29, 30). Saeki Arikiyo's "Kizoku bunka no hassei" (Emergence of an Aristocratic Culture) [I-14 (4)] places Buddhism of the Asuka period as Japan's first affluent and aristocratic culture of a cosmopolitan character.

Coinciding with this reconsideration of the Japan-centered historical approach is a growing tendency to question and reevaluate the central place that the Yamato court has been given in domestic historical studies until recently. Scholars have increasingly felt that the ancient history of local regions should be appraised in terms of the individual, independent qualities of each region, as in the study on Izumo. Now we are beginning to find studies on the so-called uncivilized tribes, including the Ezo, Kumaso and Hayato peoples.

One such work analyzing Ezo society on its own merits and treating its history from the point of view of Ezo people themselves is Takahashi Tomio, *Kodai Ezo—sono shakai kōzō* (Structure of Ancient Ezo Society) [I-31]. Another is Inoue Tatsuo, *Hayato to Yamato seiken* (The Hayato People and the Government in Yamato) [I-32], which is a careful inquiry into the unique culture, mores and social structure of the Kumaso and Hayato peoples, and an investigation of their relations with the Yamato court and the *ritsuryō* state.

The feverish pace of research on the Takamatsuzuka tomb excavated in 1972, which so ignited national interest and curiosity, seems to have died down. One of the more thought-provoking publications is Aboshi Yoshinori, et al., *Takamatsuzuka-ron hihan* (Critiques of Studies on the Takamatsuzuka Tomb) [I-33], which attempts to correct certain erroneous hypotheses and offers basic, factual information about the tomb and its historical background.

Research with regard to Shōtoku Taishi is not widespread at the moment, but Ienaga Saburō, et al. have conducted careful revision and detailed commentary on the basic documents relating to the prince's life story and thought, now out in *Nihon shisō taikei II: Shōtoku Taishishū* (The Iwanami Library of Japanese Thought, Vol. 2, The Complete Works of Shōtoku Taishi) [I-34].

In addition to the above, I should also like to mention the volumes in the Shōgakkan Japanese History series by Naoki Kōjirō, Ueda Masaaki and Inoue Mitsusada [I-35, 36, 37]. Though written simply in a style meant for a general readership, they nevertheless incorporate the results of recent scholarly efforts and research.

Endō Motoo, ed. [I-38] presents an exhaustive index by period of the majority of works relating to Japanese historical research published between the Meiji period and 1972, with bibliographical notes added for the principal citations; almost all the writings on early history are found in the glossary of this convenient work. *Nihon kodaishi jiten* (Encyclopaedia of Ancient Japanese History) [I-39] by the same author is a well-prepared and very useful basic reference tool.

II. NARA PERIOD

The themes in historical research on the Nara period that marked 1974–75 fall into the following broad categories: 1) characteristics and configurations of the *ritsuryō* state; 2) peasant control; 3) the early *shōen*; 4) the powerful families of the ancient period; and 5) ancient capitals and their planning and layout.

One work that touches on all five areas is Naoki Kōjirō, "Genshi, kodaishi josetsu" (Introduction to Prehistoric and Ancient Japanese History) [I-04 (1)], published in the first volume of the new Iwanami Japanese history series. Naoki's essay provides an indication of overall trends in the field, on such topics as the implications for Japanese society and culture of a geographic and climatic location on the eastern edge of Asia; the political configurations of the various periods; changes in ancient society, the rise of the medieval state and the enduring legacy of the ancient state in terms of the development of landownership and perspectives on the manor system, as well as issues concerning historical materials.

In contrast to this is Kadowaki Teiji and Amakasu Ken, *Minshushi no kiten* (The Starting Point of Popular History) [II-01], which seeks to provide an overall view of the *ritsuryō* society from the perspective of folk history. Encompassing the vast time-span between Palaeolithic and Heian times, the authors discuss such varied issues as the characteristics of the three social categories of peasant, craftsman, and *be* member; the impact on the people of the formation and consolidation of the ancient unified state with regard to taxes, military service and land development; city and countryside in the ancient period; changes in the system of taxation and the outbreak of popular disturbances and civil wars.

An excellent work on the *ritsuryō* state is that by Hayakawa Shōhachi, *Ritsuryō kokka* [II-02]. This work includes detailed reconstructions of the laws and institutions of the *ritsuryō* state, as well as a discussion of the nature of the imperial institution in that era, and a presentation of the author's opinions concerning research methodology on ancient history. Satō Sōjun, "Ritsuryō daijōkansei to tennō" (Administration of the

Ritsuryō State: Emperor and the Minister System) [II-03] is a noteworthy study of the emperor system as it functioned in ancient times.
Inspired by the realization that research on the emperor system so far
has provided too little concrete detail on the structure and function of
the *daijōkan* system, this work probes the nature of the *ritsuryō daijōkan*
and the process through which it was established. Before the Taihō
Code was promulgated the *daijōkan* was not functionally differentiated,
and the imperial household institutions remained outside the framework of the official government structure as they had since ancient
times. With the Taihō Code, the Nakatsukasa (Ministry of the
Center) and the Kunaishō (Ministry of the Imperial Household) were
formulated under the purview of the *daijōkan* structure and a clear
division of duties emerged within the *daijōkan* as an institution, between
administrative and consultative functions. This made the *daijōkan*
office into a central administrative body with jurisdiction over all
eight ministries, a development that paralleled the institutionalization
of the imperial system as an element of the *ritsuryō* government framework.

With regard to the historical character of the *ritsuryō daijōkan*, Satō
rejects the view that it can be understood as a concrete manifestation
of aristocratic rule. In his view the unfolding of the *ritsuryō* state policy
shows a preponderance of imperial authority, which militates against
characterizing the system as rule by the aristocracy. In terms of this
argument, the *daijōkan* functioned as a consultative organ in possession
of authority only to the extent that it did not infringe upon imperial
prerogatives. This suggests an overall conception of a centralized state
under the supreme power of the emperor in the ancient period.

Hayashi Noriaki, "Ritsuryō kokka no seiritsu" (Establishment of the
Ritsuryō State) [II-04] delves into the international aspects of the
ritsuryō system by tracing the process through which it was received
from China, and comparing that process to a similar one experienced
by the Korean kingdom of Silla. He goes on to discuss the nature of the
ancient state in its preservation of the communal functions of the rural
village, even as it adopted the *ritsuryō* codes. Here the focus is on the
observance of *koki*, the anniversary of the preceding emperor's death,
and the methods used to extend central control directly over each
individual.

Nomura Tadao has published his accumulated research results in a volume entitled *Kanjinsei-ron* (Government Bureaucracy under the *Ritsuryō* System) [II-05]. This is an investigation of the fundamental and collateral Taihō court ranks, from which he singles out the lowest of the eight official rankings, *soi*, as most pertinent. On the system of inner and outer ranks (*naige kaisei*), Nomura refines the definition of *kanjin* with reference to the criteria of formation of the *ritsuryō* bureaucracy, which marked a departure from the Chinese ideals of virtue and talent. He emphasizes the fundamental importance of the fact that the bureaucracy consisted of two separate worlds—inner and outer—each with its own hierarchy and criteria for appointment and promotion. He points out that adjustment of one's social origins and the path of bureaucratic advancement was completed between 708 and 715, and then incorporated into the Taihō Code on that subject.

On peasant control and the land system, Yoshimura Takehiko [II-06] examines the nature of systems of landownership by the state in an attempt to better understand the applicability to Japan of the concept of "Asiatic mode of production," and goes on to an analysis of Japanese despotism and relations between ruler and ruled. After clarifying the point that landholding under the *ritsuryō* system falls under the category of state landownership, he considers how that system relates to types of privately-held land, such as *enchi* (*shōen* lands) and *takuchi* (residential land), as well as to the distinctive characteristics of the *ritsuryō* system of control. In terms of state functions, he identifies the public land system (*kōchisei*) as the variation of state landownership that characterizes Japanese history.

Through a discussion of the actual state of household registers and demographic records, Funao Yoshimasa [II-07] attempts to sketch in the exploitative system of rule which impinged directly upon individuals in the Nara period. He also comments on the role of village leaders and others in the collection of taxes in kind, corvée levies and the practice of *suiko*, or forced high-interest advances of seed-rice.

Fujii Kazuji has skillfully synthesized the current concerns of research on the early *shōen* in "Shoki shōen to chihō gōzoku" (Early Period *Shōen* and the Local Clans) [II-08]. He discusses the role of *zaichi gōzoku* (wealthy landed clans) in the typical early period *shōen* owned by Tōdaiji in the Hokuriku area in terms of formation, management and decline. His investigation on the nature and structure of land management as carried on by the clans, and their political status as village leaders is well backed by solid theory. Niino Naoyoshi's article, "Ritsuryō chihō seido no shomondai" (The Provincial Administration of the *Ritsuryō* System: Some Problems in Research) [II-09], also deals with the clans. It is a discussion of three systems adopted after the Taika Reform: the *koku-gun* system of provincial and district divisions, the *gunji* system of district magistrates, and the *gōri* and *amarube* as units of village administration. He distinguishes "new" *kuni-no-miyatsuko* from the earlier type, and concludes that the *kuni-no-miyatsuko* of the *ritsuryō* era became established as officers in charge of Shintō ceremonies in the provinces. Aoki Kazuo [II-10] discusses diverse aspects of the ancient *gōzoku*, which until now have been studied with emphasis on political and economic dimensions, but can also be seen as a class or social group.

A second area of research, which, like the *ritsuryō* system, has advanced markedly, is the ancient city. Nakao Yoshiharu [II-11] has produced a study of the *tojō* type of city layout based on the latest archaeological finds. Kanō Hisashi [II-12] deals with the ancient capital city as a tangible manifestation of the *ritsuryō* state and the emperor system of that period. By studying the architecture of the *daigokuden* (central audience hall) Kanō shows how knowledge of the Chinese capital city building scheme introduced to Japan in stages culminated in the Heijō palace and presaged the Nagaoka and Heian models. Yagi Atsuru's *Kodai Nihon no miyako* (Capitals of Ancient Japan) [II-13] reveals some of the distinctive characteristics of the ancient capital city through use of the distinction between inner and outer courts.

In conclusion, I should like to introduce some selected specialized works. Takashige Susumu, *Kodai, chūsei no kōchi to sonraku* (Agricultural Lands and Villages in Ancient and Medieval Japan) [II-14] shows the different ways of awarding *enchi* (*shōen* land) and *takuchi* (residential land) in the Kinai, intermediate, and Kyushu regions. It is a monumental work in the area of historical geography. He also discusses such topics as the relation of land transfer procedures to the Taihō Code, and the process of grading land in standardized square units, including both paddy and dry field lands of the *kubunden* and *shōen* fields.

Uemura Junzō's study of the eighth-century labor organizations of painters [II-15] points out that the nucleus of the labor force was not those under the Tōdaiji Construction Bureau, but those affiliated with the Painters' Bureau and those working in the private sector. Since private painters were usually related by consanguinity or geographic proximity to those in the Painters' Bureau, Uemura concludes that they could not be considered truly independent artisans. The volume by Sasayama Haruo [II-16] outlines the development of the military system in the ancient state from the pre-Taika Reform to the Heian periods.

III. HEIAN PERIOD

Research on the Heian period during 1974–75 tended towards recapitulation of earlier findings framed in new analytical terms, which often highlight the interrelationship between political and socio-economic history. However, research in political history has been somewhat languid.

The studies published may be broadly categorized as follows: 1) the disintegration of the *ritsuryō* system in the ninth century; 2) the *kokushi* (provincial governor) system; 3) the tax collection system; 4) the imperial state in transition; and 5) peasant struggles and disturbances. A number of studies have resulted from the efforts to treat the concept of *fugōsō* (wealthy landholders), which was developed in the 1960s, not as a supra-historical or abstract idea, but as a concrete element in the making of the medieval age [III-01]. Those who approach the *kokuhen* system (an attempt at government management of agricultural lands undertaken in the Heian period) from a political perspective seek not merely to explain the circumstances which led to the development of the system, but to define the political orientation of this period of reorganization in the *ritsuryō* state.

Tamai Tsutomu, in "Kyū-jusseiki no kurōdodokoro ni kansuru ichikōsatsu" (A Look at the Bureau of Archivists in the Ninth and Tenth Centuries) [III-02] states that sometime during the Jōwa period (834–48) officials in the Bureau of Archivists (Kurōdodokoro), an organ placed directly under the emperor, acquired concurrent positions in the inner court, thereby gaining control of personnel appointments there. The study traces the process by which this bureau came to function as the pivot of court finances through the periods of Regent government (*sekkan seiji*) and rule by cloistered ex-emperors (*insei*).

Scholarly work on the provincial governor (*kokushi*) system has made remarkable progress during these two years, beginning with the publication of Niino Naoyoshi's "Ritsuryō chihō seido no shomondai" [II-09] (see above). Focusing on the activities of the *kokushi* from the ninth century on, Niino points out that although during the eighth century it was primarily the *gunji* class who became estranged from, or even rebellious against, the central government, after the Jōgan period (858–876), many *kokushi*, too, were subjected to punishment for violating regulations concerning their duties. For example, provincial governors were prohibited from allowing official buildings and storehouses to be destroyed by lightning, operating private agricultural lands in their official area of jurisdiction, extending their tenure beyond the normal period of appointment, or marrying women of their own district or province. The article describes how the *kokushi* gradually became resident officials in the provinces (*zuryō*), and how the government tried to control them.

Izumiya Yasuo explains in "Zuryō kokushi to nin'yō kokushi" (Resident Governors and Appointed *Kokushi* Officials) [III-04] how joint administration of the *kuni* by four ranks of provincial officials (*kuni no kami* or governor, *suke*, *jō*, and *sakan*), typical of the *ritsuryō* period, changed after the turn of the ninth century. He shows that by the Kōnin period (810–823), the authority of the provincial administration became concentrated in the hands of the *zuryō*, as the position of other appointed *kokushi* officials steadily lost importance. By that time, for example, the *geyujō* (a release presented by a new appointee to his predecessor acknowledging the completion of the latter's duties) was no longer subject to auditing by officials other than the *zuryō*. Thus, these provincial government officials came to be responsible only to the *zuryō*, rather than directly to the central government, but since many of these appointed officials were from the wealthy landed class of the local areas, there naturally developed an increasing number of troubles in the ninth and tenth centuries between them and the *zuryō*.

Umemura Takashi [III-05] takes up the subject of the policies intended for the control of the *kokushi* in the form of the Minbushō *kankai* (inspection by the Ministry of Popular Affairs). As the *ritsuryō* system of revenue collection proceeded to its decline, inspection of regional revenue and finances, which had been carried out by the Minbushō until then, now became part of the audit of the *kageyushi* (release commissioners) in preparing a document (*fuyogeyujō*) regarding the reasons a new appointee to a province would not accept the liabilities of his appointed position. The locally appointed *kokushi* officials (*nin'yō kokushi*) played an important role in the preparation of the *fuyogeyujō*, and Umemura states that the *nin'yō kokushi* used this official document to control their superiors in the provincial government, and the central government had no choice but to endorse their charges against unlawful *kokushi*. He also points out that the *fuyogeyujō* and other official paperwork were instituted in a central government effort to gain support of the powerful local landowners.

Hōjō Hideki's work [III-06] is also aimed at treating the tendency to appoint proxy governors (*zuryō*) to administer in the provinces, not by the criterion of the principles of the *ritsuryō* system, but from the perspective of a new system developed to cope with the conflict between the central government and the *kokushi*. He feels it should be pursued as the changes in the nature of administrative paperwork for communication between the central government and the provinces (i.e., the procedures involving payments of tax in kind, such as cloth, inspection of official documents [*kumon kankai*]). The earlier procedure, whereby revenue goods, together with financial records, were subject to *kumon kankai* upon reaching the capital, whereupon an official receipt was issued, changed in the first half of the ninth century. Documentary inspection was severed from actual payment procedures and its responsibilities fell exclusively upon the chief of the inspection office. In the latter part of the century the responsibilities for tax payment shifted in practice to the governor of the province itself. Finally when the system of *kumon kankai* became formalized as a procedure of issuing a general receipt by the inspection chief, it no longer had anything to do with payment of taxes in kind. It was meaningful later only because it provided documents for evaluation of the *kokushi*. Hōjō's description of the shifting relationship between the capital and the provinces in the ninth century is meticulous.

Research on questions concerning the tax collection system are centered around its relationship to the *kueiden* (government and officially managed fields). It is believed that the *kueiden* represent the convergence of all the contradictions of the early Heian period, and that they should be studied not simply in institutional terms but from a much broader perspective. Nakano Hideo's "Ritsuryōsei shakai kaitaiki no zaichi jōsei" (The Land Situation during the Decline of the *Ritsuryō* System) [III-07] pursues the problem of transition involved in the system of taxation from the standpoint of distribution of manufactured or handicrafted goods. Exemption from *chō* and *yō* upon adoption of the *kueiden* system did not mean government purchase of *chō* and *yō* goods with *shōzei* (tax rice preserved in the provincial government), but rather de facto exemption granted in exchange for thirty days per year of labor in the government-managed fields. Nakano goes on to clarify how the provincial government managed to secure *chō* and *yō* goods by trading with local potentates who controlled the handicrafted and manufactured products in their province. There have been many studies of *rinji zōyaku* (extra corvée), but none seems to give sufficient explanation of its historical significance.

It appears that the problems surrounding the imperial state (*ōchō-kokka*) have been brought to a stage of review and synthesis. Scholars have accepted the concept of the imperial state during the transition period in the eleventh and twelfth centuries as being characterized basically by the dissolution of the *koseki*, *keichō*, and *handen* systems, the appearance of a unit of control over public land, known as the *myō*, the designation of cultivators as *fumyō* (lit., possessors of tenure) and the imposition of taxes in place of produce, labor, and woven goods. Yet Sakamoto Shōzō, Nagahara Keiji, and Takahashi Masaaki [III-08, 09, 10] remain divided over the exact place of the imperial state in history. Apparently current research assumes that the development of a state system of exploitation and oppression (i.e., medieval military system) is the key index for determining the historical position of the transitional state.

Sakamoto's study on regency politics of the central government in this period criticizes the dominant theory that the structure of the state, based on *shōen* holdings, strongly reflected the private interests of the Fujiwara family, whose regency rule was conducted from its internal household administrative offices (Mandokoro). He believes it misleading to assume that national affairs were handled in the Mandokoro of the regent family, explaining that public land (estate) control at that time still predominated over private, *shōen*, control. He holds that the concept of regency government or Fujiwara ascendancy cannot fully explain the structure of the state in that period.

Finally, among works dealing with peasant disturbances and civil wars, Toda Yoshizane's folk history approach [III-11] is a concrete and multifaceted inquiry into the local union of the *rōnin* (vagabonds) and the peasants in the Heian period, the character of organized uprisings and subsequent expressions of religious fanaticism of the mid-Heian period, peasant appeals (*hyakushō jōso*), peasant struggle against the governor's office from the *insei* period to the establishment of the Kamakura bakufu, and the status hierarchy among the rural population. The author analyzes these subjects by referring to the state of transportation and city plans, religious consciousness and the nonagricultural population.

Although basically a biographical study, Kitayama Shigeo's *Taira no Masakado* is a fascinating portrayal of the character of the early *bushi*, including a critique of the *Shōmonki* document itself and a historical analysis of the Jōhei-Tengyō rebellions (935–41).

Below is an introduction to some additional monographs and specialized studies. First, treating the Heian period in survey style are Murai Yasuhiko [III-13] and Yasuda Motohisa [III-14]. The first is a discussion of regency politics and cloister government as a political structure of a "familial" (*miuchi*) society, which makes it an interesting treatise on Japanese civilization. Hashimoto Yoshihiko's "Insei-ron" (A Study of Rule by Cloistered Emperors) [III-15] states that the cloister government organization (*in-no-chō*) was not intended as an *insei* mechanism, but brings attention to the fact that the retired emperor appointed personal attendants to the posts of chief archivist, chief of the inner treasury, and *zuryō*, thus grasping control of the existing machinery of government. He states that the policy of reconstructing and buttressing the state in the *insei* period involved much more than the response to *zuryō* demands, contrary to many interpretations. On the political reforms of the late Heian period are Ōishi Naomasa [III-16], and Yoshie Akio [III-17], while Takeuchi Rizō's collection of *shōen* distribution charts [III-18] provides the fundamentals for ongoing research on the *shōen*. Yamanaka Yutaka's volume [III-19] discusses Minamoto no Tōru, Fujiwara no Michinaga, Fujiwara no Kaneie, and Ōe no Masafusa and touches on their respective periods of activity.

文　　献

I–01　川口勝康 Kawaguchi Katsuyasu 日本マルクス主義古代史学研究史序説——戦前篇（上・下）"Introduction to Japanese Marxist Historiography of the Ancient Period—Prewar History" (2 pts.)『原始古代社会研究』1, 2（原始古代社会研究会編）pp. 201–48; pp. 187–241, 校倉書房, 1974, 1975.

原島礼二 Harashima Reiji 御名代について "The Minashiro: *Be* of the Imperial Estates"『原始古代社会研究』1（原始古代社会研究会編）pp. 77–112, 校倉書房, 1974.

02　吉田　晶ほか（編）Yoshida Akira, et al. (eds.)『日本史を学ぶ』1–原始・古代 *Learning Japanese History*, Vol. 1 (Prehistoric and Ancient Periods) [有斐閣選書] 338 pp., 有斐閣, 1975.

吉村武彦 Yoshimura Takehiko アジア的生産様式論 "The Asiatic Mode of Production," pp. 1–16.

田中義昭 Tanaka Yoshiaki 邪馬台国論 "The Yamatai State," pp. 63–85.

吉田　晶 Yoshida Akira 大化前代の社会構造 "The Social Structure of Japan before the Taika Reform," pp. 103–22.

鬼頭清明 Kitō Kiyoaki 「大化改新」論の現状と課題 "The Current Status of Research on the Taika Reform and Future Problems," pp. 123–37.

03　原　秀三郎 Hara Hidesaburō 序説日本古代国家研究の理論的前提 "Theoretical Premises of Research on the Ancient Japanese State: An Introduction"『大系日本国家史』(1 古代), pp. 1–65, 東京大学出版会, 1975.

鬼頭清明 Kitō Kiyoaki 日本民族の形成と国際的契機 "International Factors in the Formation of the Japanese People"『大系日本国家史』(1 古代), pp. 68–119.

04　直木孝次郎ほか Naoki Kōjirō, et al.『岩波講座　日本歴史 1』（原始および古代 1）*Iwanami Lectures on Japanese History*, Vol. 1 (Prehistoric and Ancient Periods, Pt. 1), 401 pp., 岩波書店, 1975.

直木孝次郎 Naoki Kōjirō 原始・古代史序説 "Introduction to Prehistoric and Ancient Japanese History," pp. 1–34.

山尾幸久 Yamao Yukihisa 政治権力の発生 "The Emergence of Political Power"『原始および古代』(1) pp. 183–226.

平野邦雄 Hirano Kunio ヤマト王権と朝鮮 "Korea and Yamato Authority"

『原始および古代』(1) pp. 227–72.

05 井上秀雄・旗田 巍(編) Inoue Hideo and Hatada Takashi (eds.) 『古代日本と朝鮮の基本問題』 *Basic Issues in the Study of Ancient Japan and Korea*, 214 pp., 学生社, 1974.

06 朝鮮史研究会(編), 旗田 巍(監修) Society of Korean History (ed.), Hatada Takashi (supervisory editor) 『古代朝鮮と日本』 *Ancient Korea and Japan*, 352 pp. 龍溪書舎, 1974.

旗田 巍 Hatada Takashi 広開土王陵碑文の諸問題 "Kwanggaet'o Tomb Inscription: Problems and Issues," pp. 3—21.

浜田耕策 Hamada Kōsaku 高句麗広開土王陵碑文の研究 ——碑文の構造と史臣の筆法を中心として—— "Koguryo King Kwanggaet'o's Tomb Inscription: Its Structure and the Writing Style of Official Historians," pp. 47–83.

中塚 明 Nakatsuka Akira 日本近代史の展開と「朝鮮史像」——とくに参謀本部と歴史研究のかかわりについて—— "Modern Japanese History and Images of Korean History: With Special Reference to General Staff Intervention in Historical Research," pp. 267–84.

佐伯有清 Saeki Arikiyo 高句麗広開土王碑文研究と紀年論争——参謀本部の古代日朝関係史観—— "The Study and Debate over the Tomb Inscription of Koguryō's King Kwanggaet'o: The General Staff View of Relations between Ancient Japan and Korea," pp. 285–98.

佐伯有清・鈴木靖民・武田幸男・旗田 巍・原島礼二・李 進熙 Saeki Arikiyo, Suzuki Yasutami, Takeda Yukio, Hatada Takashi, Harashima Reiji, and Lee Chin-hŭi 広開土王陵碑と東アジア (座談会) "East Asia and the Kwanggaet'o Tomb Inscription: A Panel Discussion"

07 村山光一 Murayama Kōichi 古代日朝関係史研究の現状と課題 "The Current Status and Focus of Historical Research on the Relationship between Ancient Japan and Korea" 「歴史評論」302, pp. 1 17 and p. 70, 歴史科学協議会, 1975.

08 鬼頭清明 Kitō Kiyoaki 近年の古代日朝関係史研究の諸問題 "Recent Historical Research on the History of Relations between Ancient Japan and Korea: A Review of the Issues" 「史学雑誌」(東京大学) 84 編 4 号, pp. 60–72, 史学会, 1975.

09 江上波夫 Egami Namio 東アジアにおける倭人の起源と活動 "The Origin and Movements of the Wa People in East Asia" 『続・日本古代史の謎』 *Riddles of Ancient Japanese History*, II, pp. 173–213, 朝日新聞社, 1975.

10 星野良作 Hoshino Ryōsaku 最近における広開土王碑文の研究 "Recent Studies of the Kwanggaet'o Tomb Inscription," 「史元」18, pp. 33–51, 史元会, 1974.

11 直木孝次郎 Naoki Kōjirō 応神天皇の実在性をめぐって "Did Emperor Ōjin Actually Exist?"「人文研究」25 の 10, pp. 88–107, 大阪市立大学文学部, 1973.

12 大石良材 Ōishi Ryōzai『日本王権の成立』*The Establishment of Imperial Authority in Japan* [塙選書] 379 pp., 塙書房, 1975.

13 原島礼二 Harashima Reiji『神武天皇の誕生』*Birth of Emperor Jimmu*, 235 pp., 人物往来社, 1975.

14 井上光貞ほか Inoue Mitsusada, et al.『岩波講座　日本歴史 2』(古代 2) *Iwanami Lectures on Japanese History*, Vol. 2 (The Ancient Period, pt. 2), 377 pp., 岩波書店, 1975.

八木　充 Yagi Atsuru 国造制の構造 "The Structure of the *Kuni-no-miyatsuko* System of Provincial Administration," pp. 1–37.

吉田　晶 Yoshida Akira 古代国家の形成 "The Evolution of the Ancient Japanese State," pp. 39–87.

井上光貞 Inoue Mitsusada 大化改新と東アジア "East Asia and the Taika Reform," pp. 129–74.

佐伯有清 Saeki Arikiyo 貴族文化の発生 "The Emergence of an Aristocratic Culture," pp. 175–212.

岡田精司 Okada Seishi 記紀神話の成立 "The Evolution of the Myths of the *Kojiki* and *Nihon Shoki*," pp. 289–330.

門脇禎二 Kadowaki Teiji 古代社会論 "Ancient Japanese Society," pp. 331–77.

15 川口勝康 Kawaguchi Katsuyasu 在地首長制と日本古代国家 "The System of Territorial Administration and the Ancient Japanese State"「歴史学研究」別冊, pp. 41–52, 歴史学研究会, 1975.

16 佐々木虔一 Sasaki Ken'ichi 律令制成立期の在地の動向と在地首長制 "Residence in the Provinces in the Formative Period of the *Ritsuryō* System and the System of Territorial Administration"「歴史学研究」別冊, pp. 52–60, 歴史学研究会, 1975.

17 岸　雅裕 Kishi Masahiro 用明・崇峻期の政治過程 "Political Processes during the Reigns of Emperors Yōmei and Sushun"「日本史研究」148; pp. 30–50, 日本史研究会, 1975.

18 八木　充 Yagi Atsuru 七世紀中期における政権抗争 "The Struggle for Power in the Mid-Seventh Century"『日本書紀研究　第八冊　──三品先生追悼記念──』(横田健一編) pp. 385–413, 塙書房, 1975.

19 義江明子 Yoshie Akiko 大宝以前の戸籍制度 (上・下) "The Household Registry System Prior to the Taihō Reform" (2 pts.)「続日本紀研究」175 (上), 176 (下), pp. 1–19, 23–32, 続日本紀研究会, 1974.

20 坪井清足・鈴木嘉吉(編) Tsuboi Kiyotari and Suzuki Kakichi (eds.)『埋れた

宮殿と寺』 *Buried Palaces and Temples* [古代史発掘 9] 164 pp., 講談社, 1974.

21 加藤謙吉 Katō Kenkichi ミブ・ニフ二題 "A Study of the *mibu* and the *nifu*" 「続日本紀研究」182, pp. 1–30, 続日本紀研究会, 1975.

22 佐伯有清 Saeki Arikiyo 『古代氏族の系図』 *A Diagram of the Ancient Clans*, 202 pp., 学生社, 1975.

23 千田　稔 Senda Minoru ミヤケの地理的実体 "Geography of *Miyake*" 「史林」(京都大学) 58 の 4, pp. 1–37, 史学研究会, 1975.

24 大林太良(編) Ōbayashi Taryō (ed.) 『日本神話の比較研究』 *Comparative Study of Japanese Myths*, 433 pp., 法政大学出版局, 1974.

25 吉田敦彦 Yoshida Atsuhiko 『日本神話と印欧神話』 *Japanese and Indo-European Mythology*, 262 pp., 弘文堂, 1974.

26 大林太良 Ōbayashi Taryō 『日本神話の構造』 *Structure of Japanese Mythology*, 285 pp., 弘文堂, 1975.

27 水野　祐 Mizuno Yū 『古代社会と浦島伝説』(上・下) *Ancient Society as Reflected in the Legend of Urashima Tarō* (2 vols.), 雄山閣, 1975.

28 中井真孝 Nakai Shinkō 仏教東漸と国際関係 "The Eastward Advance of Buddhism and Japan's International Relations" 『日本史論集』 (時野谷勝教授退官記念事業会編) *A Collection of Essays on Japanese History* (Memorial Lectures in Honor of the Retirement of Professor Tokinoya Masaru), pp. 59–76, 清文堂, 1975.

29 田村圓澄・洪　淳昶(編) Tamura Enchō and Hong Sung-ch'ang (eds.) 『新羅と飛鳥・白鳳の仏教文化』 *Silla and Asuka-Hakuhō Buddhist Culture*, 360 pp., 吉川弘文館, 1975.

30 田村圓澄 Tamura Enchō 『飛鳥・白鳳仏教論』 *A Study of Asuka and Hakuhō Buddhism* [古代史選書 2] 355 pp., 雄山閣, 1975.

31 高橋富雄 Takahashi Tomio 『古代蝦夷 ──その社会構造──』 *Structure of Ancient Ezo Society*, 237 pp., 学生社, 1974.

32 井上辰雄 Inoue Tatsuo 『隼人と大和政権』 *The Hayato People and the Government in Yamato*, 209 pp., 学生社, 1974.

33 網干善教・有坂隆道・奥村郁三・高橋三知雄 Aboshi Yoshinori, Arisaka Takamichi, Okumura Ikuzō and Takahashi Michio 『高松塚論批判』 *Critiques of Studies on the Takamatsuzuka Tomb*, 258 pp., 創元社, 1974.

34 家永三郎・藤枝　晃・早島鏡正・築島　裕 Ienaga Saburō, Fujieda Akira, Hayashima Kyōshō and Tsukishima Hiroshi (eds.) 『日本思想大系 2』(聖徳太子集) *Iwanami Library of Japanese Thought*, Vol. 2 (The Complete Works of Shōtoku Taishi), 592 pp., 岩波書店, 1975.

35 直木孝次郎 Naoki Kōjirō 『倭国の誕生』 *The Birth of the Japanese State*, [日本の歴史 1] 390 pp., 小学館, 1973.

36 上田正昭 Ueda Masaaki 『大王の世紀』 *The Centuries of Great Kings* [日本の

歴史 2] 390 pp., 小学館, 1973.

37　井上光貞　Inoue Mitsusada『飛鳥の朝廷』*The Asuka Court* [日本の歴史 3] 454 pp., 小学館, 1974.

38　遠藤元男(編) Endō Motoo (ed.)『日本史研究書総覧』*A Comprehensive Survey of Research Works on Japanese History*, 402 pp., 名著出版, 1975.

39　遠藤元男(編) Endō Motoo (ed.)『日本古代史辞典』*Encyclopedia of Ancient Japanese History*, 845 pp., 朝倉書店, 1974.

II–01　門脇禎二・甘粕　健 Kadowaki Teiji and Amakasu Ken『民衆史の起点』*The Starting Point of Popular History* [日本民衆の歴史 1] 436 pp., 三省堂, 1974.

02　早川庄八 Hayakawa Shōhachi 『律令国家』*The Ritsuryō State* [日本の歴史 4] 454 pp., 小学館, 1974.

03　佐藤宗諄 Satō Sōjun 律令太政官制と天皇 "Administration of the *Ritsuryō* State: Emperor and the Minister System"『大系日本国家史 1』pp. 169–218, 東京大学出版会, 1975.

04　林　紀昭 Hayashi Noriaki 律令国家の成立 "The Establishment of the *Ritsuryō* State"『日本史を学ぶ 1』pp. 138–59, 有斐閣, 1975.

05　野村忠夫 Nomura Tadao『官人制論』*Government Bureaucracy under the Ritsuryō System*, 271 pp., 雄山閣, 1975.

06　吉村武彦 Yoshimura Takehiko 律令国家と土地所有 "Landownership and the *Ritsuryō* State"『大系日本国家史 1』pp. 257–98, 東京大学出版会, 1975.

07　舟尾好正 Funao Yoshimasa 奈良朝の国家と農民 "Farmer and State in Nara Japan"『日本史を学ぶ 1』[有斐閣選書] pp. 184–205, 有斐閣, 1975.

08　藤井一二 Fujii Kazuji 初期荘園と地方豪族 "Early Period *Shōen* and the Local Clans"『日本史を学ぶ 1』pp. 209–29, 有斐閣, 1975.

09　新野直吉 Niino Naoyoshi 律令地方制度の諸問題 "The Provincial Administration of the *Ritsuryō* System: Some Problems in Research"『日本古代地方制度の研究』吉川弘文館, 1974.

10　青木和夫 Aoki Kazuo『古代豪族』*The Powerful Local Clans in the Ancient Period* [日本の歴史 5] 369 pp., 小学館, 1974.

11　中尾芳治 Nakao Yoshiharu 日本における都城制の成立 "The Establishment of Capital Cities in Japan"『日本史を学ぶ 1』[有斐閣選書] pp. 160–83, 有斐閣, 1975.

12　狩野　久 Kanō Hisashi 律令国家と都市 "The City and the *Ritsuryō* State"『大系日本国家史 1』pp. 219–56, 東京大学出版会, 1975.

13　八木　充 Yagi Atsuru『古代日本の都』*Capitals of Ancient Japan*, 222 pp., 講談社, 1974.

14　高重　進 Takashige Susumu 『古代・中世の耕地と村落』*Agricultural Lands and Villages in Medieval and Ancient Japan*, 332 pp., 大明堂, 1975.

15　上村順造 Uemura Junzō 八世紀における画師の労働編成について "Painter

Labor Organizations of the Eighth Century" 『名古屋大学日本史論集』（上）pp. 173–204, 吉川弘文館, 1975.

16 笹山晴生 Sasayama Haruo 『古代国家と軍隊』 *The Military Forces of the Ancient State* [中公新書] 198 pp., 中央公論社, 1975.

III–01 福岡猛志 Fukuoka Takeshi 弘仁 14 年 2 月 21 日官奏の性格 "The Nature of the February 21, 824 Report to the Throne" 『名古屋大学日本史論集』（上）pp. 233–58, 吉川弘文館, 1975.

02 玉井 力 Tamai Tsutomu 9・10 世紀の蔵人所に関する一考察 "A Look at the Bureau of Archivists in the Ninth and Tenth Centuries" 『名古屋大学日本史論集』（上）pp. 291–324, 吉川弘文館, 1975.

03 福岡猛志 Fukuoka Takeshi 律令国家の解体 "The Disintegration of the *Ritsuryō* State" 『日本史を学ぶ 1』 pp. 230–46, 有斐閣, 1975.

04 泉谷康夫 Izumiya Yasuo 受領国司と任用国司 "Resident Governors and Appointed *Kokushi* Officials" 「日本歴史」316 号, pp. 75–89, 吉川弘文館, 1974 年 9 月.

05 梅村 喬 Umemura Takashi 民部省勘会と勘解由使勘判 "Ministry of Popular Affairs Inspections and *Kageyushi* Reviews" 『名古屋大学日本史論集』（上）pp. 259–90, 吉川弘文館, 1975.

06 北条秀樹 Hōjō Hideki 文書行政より見たる国司受領化 "Expansion of the Proxy Governor System as Evidenced in Administrative Paperwork" 「史学雑誌」84 編 6 号, pp. 1–43. 山川出版社, 1975.

07 中野栄夫 Nakano Hideo 律令制社会解体期の在地情勢 "The Land Situation during the Decline of the *Ritsuryō* System" 「歴史学研究」416, pp. 1–34, 青木書店, 1975.

08 坂本賞三 Sakamoto Shōzō 『摂関時代』 *The Regent Period* [日本の歴史 6] 390 pp., 小学館, 1974.

09 永原慶二 Nagahara Keiji 王朝国家をめぐって "On the Heian State" 『中世国家論』[シンポジウム 日本歴史 7] pp. 13–82, 学生社, 1974.

10 高橋昌明 Takahashi Masaaki 王朝国家論 "A Study of the Heian State" 『日本史を学ぶ 1』 pp. 263–84, 有斐閣, 1975.

11 戸田芳実 Toda Yoshimi 律令制からの解放 "Emancipation from *Ritsuryō* Rule" 『土一揆と内乱』[日本民衆の歴史 2] pp. 2–101, 三省堂, 1975.

12 北山茂夫 Kitayama Shigeo 『平将門』 *Taira no Masakado*, 238 pp., 朝日新聞社, 1975.

13 村井康彦 Murai Yasuhiko 『王朝貴族』 *The Heian Aristocracy* [日本の歴史 8] 369 pp., 小学館, 1974.

14 安田元久 Yasuda Motohisa 『院政と平氏』 *The Insei and the Taira Clan* [日本の歴史 7] 381 pp., 小学館, 1974.

15 橋本義彦 Hashimoto Yoshihiko 院政論 "A Study of Rule by Cloistered

24

Emperors"「日本歴史」327 号，pp. 37–48, 吉川弘文館，1975 年 8 月.

16　大石直正　Ōishi Naomasa 平安時代末期の内乱 "The Civil Wars of the Late Heian Period"『日本史を学ぶ 2』(中世) pp. 42–58, 有斐閣，1975.

17　義江彰夫　Yoshie Akio 転換期としての院政朝 "The *Insei* Period as a Transitional Period"『日本史を学ぶ 2』(中世) pp. 23–41, 有斐閣，1975.

18　竹内理三(編) Takeuchi Rizō (ed.)『荘園分布図』(上) *Shōen Distribution Maps*, Vol. 1, 218 pp., 吉川弘文館，1975.

19　山中　裕　Yamanaka Yutaka『平安人物誌』*Major Personalities of the Heian Period*, 251 pp., 東大出版会，1975.

JAPANESE HISTORY
—MEDIEVAL PERIOD

Ishii Susumu and Chijiwa Itaru
University of Tokyo

Translated by Bernard Susser

I.   General Remarks

1.   Our purpose here is to present a bibliography of the more important works published by Japanese specialists on medieval Japanese history between April 1974 and December 1975, and to review the major trends in research on medieval Japan in that period, as a continuation to the previously published *An Introductory Bibliography for Japanese Studies*, Vol. I, Part 2.

Several different types of multivolume histories of Japan appeared in this period, as did series containing monographs covering the whole of Japanese history. We can begin with the volumes on medieval history from two representative examples. In *Nihon no rekishi* (History of Japan) [I-01], published by Shōgakkan, each period of Japanese history is the subject of a separate volume authored by a single specialist in that period; all together, they form a complete history of Japan. A great many series of this type have already appeared. Since all of the authors in this series are leading scholars who have incorporated the results of the most recent findings into their respective volumes, the contents are quite substantial. This series is recommended to both those interested in the detail of specific periods of the history of the middle ages, and those concerned with the current state of research.

The *Iwanami kōza Nihon rekishi* (Iwanami Lectures on Japanese History) [I-02], like its predecessor of the same name (1962–64), is a series intended to be a comprehensive collection of studies that represent the present level of scholarship; it is a completely new version of the previous series in terms of both content and contributors. Only half of the section on medieval history has been published, but these volumes contain articles on sixteen important subjects, all written by leading specialists. One unique feature of this series is that it includes many articles which are in fact research monographs, so anyone who wants to know the present level of the field and trends in research should look here first.

These series both include among their contributors exponents of the different schools of thought in the academic world, and in this sense they are representative. On the other hand, the mixture of research of different tendencies in a single volume or series can be a source of confusion and disunity. And this is particularly apparent with respect to the points currently at issue among historians of medieval history. For example, as Kuroda Toshio points out in his article, "Chūseishi josetsu" (Introduction to Medieval History), which appears in the above-mentioned Iwanami series, numerous conflicting viewpoints have been advanced by postwar historians regarding such very basic questions as how Japan's middle ages should be treated as a whole or how medieval society should be defined, and that these conflicting views have not yet been reconciled to this very day. In our view, this clash of basic viewpoints and the existence of a variety of theories is in fact a very good thing. But is the present state of the academic world really sound, where exchange and debate is all too rare, and where we have nothing more than each person asserting his own theory over and over? We doubt that it is. These two series were planned to represent the current situation of scholarship, inevitably revealing its obvious defects.

Nihon minshū no rekishi (A History of the Japanese People) [I-03], also an ambitious series, is the result of discussion among specialists, whose intention is to present a general history of Japan from the point of view of the people. Compared to the two series mentioned above we might expect to find a greater meeting of minds, yet here too we find great differences in point of view among the various contributors. The absence of unanimity in the Shōgakkan and Iwanami series, is characteristic of these works as well.

2. Several works, each with some unique features, have appeared in this period which present surveys of the current state of research in

the field. Every year a special annual issue of *Shigaku zasshi*, entitled "Kaiko to tenbō" (Retrospect and Prospects) [I-04], features a comprehensive bibliography of research monographs; the Historical Science Society of Japan (Rekishigaku Kenkyūkai) published a general survey of historiographical trends from 1958 through the 1960s [I-05]; and *Nihonshi kenkyū nyūmon IV* (Introduction to Research on Japanese History, Vol. IV) [I-06] is an introduction to research in the field surveying the trends in research from 1967 through 1972 and discusses prospects for the future. Volume two of the new series, *Nihonshi o manabu* (Learning Japanese History) [I-07] contains a discussion of nineteen key issues which have occupied historians since the war; many of the contributors are comparatively young and they present a clear description of current trends and activities in the field and of the problems which must be confronted in the future. These quite different works, when used together, provide a very adequate picture of the current state of historical research.

3. In the area of diplomatics and the study of source materials in general, proposals such as Kawane Yoshiyasu's [I-08] have led us to anticipate at long last a surge of new research. We have not seen as many works as we should, but among those which have appeared is the second volume of Nakamura Naokatsu's outline treatment of ancient documents [I-09], and Satō Shin'ichi's original article [I-10] on *kaō* (signatures), an important problem in the study of historical documents. Also, *Sho no Nihonshi* (Calligraphy in Japanese History) [I-11] is a well-organized series not to be overlooked; it contains discussions of representative works by prominent personalities in Japanese history, and is supplemented with short articles providing a survey of each period and discussing the major problems of diplomatics.

As usual, there has been much activity in the editing and publication of historical source materials. The Shiryō Hensanjo (Historiographical Research Institute) of the University of Tokyo continued publication of the *Dai-Nippon shiryō* (Historical Materials of Japan), *Dai-Nippon komonjo* (Ancient Documents of Japan) and the *Dai-Nippon kokiroku* (Ancient Diaries of Japan), and there were many important publications in the form of source collections on local history. More detailed information may be found in the bibliographies mentioned above [I-04, etc.]. Among those that are particularly deserving of mention here is the chronologically-ordered collection of Kamakura period documents edited by Takeuchi Rizō [I-12]; nine volumes have appeared so far, displaying almost superhuman efforts on the part of the editor. Another welcome project presently under way is the *Shōen shiryō sōsho* (Collection of *Shōen* Source Materials) [I-13], which will gather together the relevant historical source materials for each of the major *shōen*. Another work [I-14] provides photographs of documents along with a printed version and a detailed analysis, an example of a new direction in the editing and publication of ancient documents. We must also note that, thanks to the labors of Seno Seiichirō, a chronological bibliography of all the documents from the Kamakura and Nambokuchō periods pertaining to the Kyushu region has been published [I-15]. A work of a slightly different character by Takeuchi Rizō [I-16] giving maps showing the distribution of *shōen* throughout Japan is also useful.

This concludes the introductory section; we will now turn to a bibliography of the literature and a description of trends in research during this period, under two headings: II, "Political and Social History;" and III, "Cultural History." Commensurate with the focus of current research, we have combined two sections of the previous *Introductory Bibliography*, "Social and Economic History" and "Political, Legal and Diplomatic History," into a single section entitled "Political and Social History."

II. POLITICAL AND SOCIAL HISTORY

1. Distinctive Trends: First of all, research on comparatively neglected subjects, including such economic and social groups as merchants, artisans, fishermen, townsmen, *shōen* lords and aristocrats, etc., is finally being done in earnest, and a number of excellent works have appeared. Kuroda Toshio has published a collection of his articles [II-01] on a wide range of topics, approaching the medieval state with the "*kenmon* (influential houses) system" theory—which claims that the medieval state was a system in which the influential houses and powerful families of both the imperial court and the bakufu combined forces to rule the country, to control the social structure of

medieval society, and to influence the exoteric and esoteric Buddhist religions of the medieval world. Inoue Hiroshi's bold preliminary article takes almost the same point of view [II-02]. The publication of the symposium *Chūsei kokkaron* (On the Medieval State) [II-03], a discussion among several active scholars including Kuroda and Naga-hara Keiji, and of *Taikei Nihon kokkashi* (Studies in the History of the Japanese State) [II-04], a collection of monographs by six leading specialists, demonstrates that research on the medieval state dealing with the points raised by Kuroda is finally being taken seriously. It is also significant that we now have a collection of works by Shimizu Mitsuo [II-05], who published brilliant studies in the late 1930s and early 1940s, blazing the trail for the above-mentioned trends in re-search. Several works on cities have appeared, including Akiyama Kunizō and Nakamura Ken's research on Kyoto [II-06], articles by Toda Yoshimi [II-07] and Wakita Haruko [II-08], and a survey article by Miura Keiichi [II-09]. Sound monographs on *shōen* lords by Tana-hashi Mitsuo [II-10] and Nagamura Makoto [II-11] have also ap-peared.

The most noteworthy result from this trend of research has been the work of Amino Yoshihiko. Amino has been publishing one article after another on the *kugonin* (monopoly merchants), tradesmen, artisans and fishermen who were connected directly to the imperial house, on the system of control and the pattern of distribution of the Tōji's *shōen*, to mention only a few, and he has brought his ideas together in a book, *Mōko shūrai* (The Mongol Invasions), written for the Shōgakkan series mentioned above [I-01]. There has been comparatively little interest in the history of the period from mid- to late Kamakura, but it is interest-ing how skilfully he introduces this period as one of great social change which marked a turning point in Japan's premodern history. This book is not only a rare masterpiece of historical writing, but is also valuable for the imaginative questions it poses and for its summary of the results of historical research. And, as the title, *Mongol Invasions*, itself shows, this book places Japan's medieval age in the context of East Asian history and further, of world history. It has recently become particularly important to see Japan in the broader context of East Asia, but this book is noteworthy because it applies this approach to the study of Japanese history as a whole, not merely to some specialized discipline such as "history of foreign relations" or "diplomatic history." Incidentally, we should note that Tanaka Takeo has published a book in the field of foreign relations, giving an overview of the whole period [II-12], and that Mori Katsumi's many works on Japanese-Sung trade have been brought together in an edition of selected works [II-13].

The second trend of research to note is that on peasants and farming villages. In this area Inagaki Yasuhiko's monograph [II-14] takes issue with previous research on the subject of independent small-scale farming by peasants, and has incited much debate. Previously, scholars such as Nagahara Keiji asserted that independent small-scale farming by peasants appeared first from the 13th-14th centuries, but Inagaki maintains that it had already come into existence and had spread widely by a much earlier date. In a sense, Inagaki's work can be seen as a development of the theories of Shimizu Mitsuo, and shows, in conjunction with the trend to diversify the study of social groupings noted above, that the direction of postwar research on medieval history is finally changing. A number of works on peasants and farming villages presenting interesting subjects have appeared [II-15, 16, 17], as has a book by Takashige Susumu [II-18] which treats land under cultivation and village settlements from the standpoint of historical geography.

Recently hardly any notable research on the *bushidan* (warrior bands) has appeared, but Ishii Susumu's volume *Chūsei bushidan* (Medieval *Bushidan*) in the above-mentioned series [I-01] treats the *bushidan* as the distinctive group which formed the mainstay of medieval society. He studies them through the results of field surveys of the historical geographical type and of archaeological excavations (discussed in Section III. 2 below), concentrating on their power as the holders of the right to rule the *ie* (household), which was the basis of medieval society.

2. The Late Heian Period: There has not been much noteworthy research concentrating on this period. Sakamoto Shōzō has attempted a narrative of the history of the Fujiwara regency period [I-01], and this is useful for its lucid explications of theories which have recently gained much attention in the academic world but which were much criticized for their complexity, at least in his monographs and articles. Also, we must not neglect the publication of Hashimoto Yoshihiko's own "Inseiron" (Cloister Government) [II-19], coming after the publication of his excellent research on the history of aristocratic society.

Gomi Fumihiko has also raised some new questions in his survey of the *insei* in the late Heian and Kamakura periods [II-20].

3. Kamakura Period: Ōyama Kyōhei, known for his research on the history of village settlements, has written *Kamakura bakufu* (The Kamakura Bakufu), a fresh, readable survey history for the Shōgakkan series [I-01] covering the period from the formation of the bakufu to the mid-Kamakura period. Part of his new theory on the establishment of the *shugo-jitō* system in the Bunji Era (1185–89) has also been published in monographs [II-21,22]. In addition, Yoshie Akio has published a major monograph on the rise of the *jitō* system from a slightly different viewpoint [II-23], so that questions concerning the period which saw the rise of the bakufu are again being highlighted. The above-mentioned *Mōko shūrai* by Amino Yoshihiko [I-01] provides an excellent description of the political history of the mid- and late Kamakura period. Irumada Nobuo, in his essay, "Kamakura jidai no kokka kenryoku" (State Authority in the Kamakura Period) [II-24], answers Kuroda Toshio's "theory of the *kenmon* system" by stressing the role of the bakufu, and in another monograph [II-25], examines a specific area once under the control of the bakufu, but later a holding of the Hōjō family. Seno Seiichirō brings together some of his research on the *gokenin* (direct vassals of the shogun) in the Kyushu region in [II-26], which was done on the basis of previously prepared background research [I-15]. Gomi Fumihiko has clarified the situation of the *zaikyo-nin* warriors who were stationed in Kyoto, and has examined the question of continuity between the Kamakura and Muromachi bakufu [II-27].

In legal history, Isogai Fujio has published an article [II-28] discussing the regulations on slaves in bakufu law, and Kasamatsu Hiroshi makes a penetrating analysis [II-29] of medieval law, taking as his starting point the existence of transactions in land conducted without documents establishing the seller's right to the land.

4. Nambokuchō-Muromachi Periods: There are two symposia volumes centering on the themes indicated by their titles, *Nambokuchō no nairan* (The Civil Wars of the Nambokuchō Period) [II-30] and *Tsuchi ikki* (Medieval Peasant Rebellions) [II-31]; the former records an extremely interesting debate on basic issues of contention among Amino Yoshihiko, Nagahara Keiji and others, and contains some

rather sharp disagreements seldom seen in the academic world. Also, a very welcome publication is *Muromachi seiken* (Muromachi Government) [II-32] which reprints seventeen important monographs published since 1960 on political history from the Nambokuchō through the Sengoku periods, with introductory notes and an appended bibliography.

A good deal of research has been published in the field of political history, concentrating on the bakufu, and the quality of this research has been excellent. Itō Kiyoshi's article [II-33] attempts to clarify the process through which the bakufu usurped authority from the imperial court during the Nambokuchō period; Kawazoe Shōji takes up the Asō family, who were *hōkōshū*, vassals under the direct command of the shogun, in Kyushu [II-34]; Shimosaka Mamoru's research [II-35] has thrown light on the bakufu's policy toward the Enryakuji; and Gomi Fumihiko has attempted to grasp the broad changes in the bakufu system from Yoshimitsu to Yoshinori and beyond [II-36]. Also, some of Imatani Akira's work, mentioned below [II-45 etc.], is relevant here. The *tsuchi ikki* have been receiving a lot of attention recently, and Nakamura Kichiji's well-known monographs have been published in a single volume [II-37], convenient for future research.

Turning to local history, we find that a good deal of work is being done on the *shugo* domain provinces, and the local *kokujin* (provincial warriors) who were active within them. For example, Hatai Hiromu's "Shugo ryōgoku taisei no kenkyū" (Studies on the System of *Shugo* Domain Provinces) [II-38], an ambitious work written almost ten years ago, uses materials drawn for the most part from Ōmi province, and emphasizes the special characteristics of the *shugo* domain province system in or near the Kinai region. Also, Murai Shōsuke has published an excellent article [II-39] on the Matsuura *ikki* (league), one of the leagues of *zaichi ryōshu* (local lords) who lived in every region, known for the model written law they produced.

5.   Sengoku Period: This period marked an important turning point in Japanese history and is very interesting in its own right; research on this period has been especially active recently. *Sengoku shakaishiron* (A Social History of the Sengoku Period) [II-40], offers a collection of important articles by Fujiki Hisashi, currently among the leading scholars in this area and contains monographs on the main

characteristics of Sengoku society, the development of *zaichi ryōshu*, the formation and structure of Sengoku law, the economic structure and the *chigyō* (benefice) system in daimyo domain provinces, among other topics. Fujiki's "Daimyō ryōgokuseiron" (Essay on the Daimyo Domain Provinces) [II-41], together with his "Tōitsu seiken no keisei" (The Formation of a Unified Regime) written for the new Iwanami series [I-02], shows the current focus of his research on this transitional period.

On the other hand, Nagahara Keiji has taken a position opposing the views held by Fujiki and others who see the Sengoku period as the last stage of the *shōen* system. Nagahara's excellent book, *Sengoku no dōran* (The Wars of Sengoku) [I-01], presents his view of the history of the whole Sengoku period, emphasizing the decisive importance of the *zaichi ryōshu* system. He has also published an article [II-42] summarizing his basic historical stance. Through a case study of a cadastral survey done by one Sengoku daimyo [II-43], Katsumata Shizuo has made clear that the daimyo sought to establish a *kanmon* system (in which the value of land is expressed in units of money) to serve as the foundation for his authority, and has raised the important question of how to determine the character of Sengoku period daimyo. Concerning the *Ikkō ikki* rebellions against the daimyo, Shingyō Norikazu's book [II-44] makes a detailed examination of the relationship between the uprisings and the Matsudaira family in Mikawa province.

Up to now, research on the Sengoku period has concentrated on the daimyo in the provinces while the Muromachi bakufu in Kyoto has been almost completely neglected. The importance of research in this area is obvious, as is apparent also from the recent trends mentioned at the beginning of Section II.1. Imatani Akira's dynamic work should receive a great deal of attention for what he has done in shedding light on this topic, until now a virtual blind spot [II-45, 46, 47].

III. Cultural History

1. The works that come under this heading represent such fields as the history of religion, art history, and intellectual history. The reason for this is that many people think of "cultural history" as

a general concept which includes all these disciplines rather than as an independent subject. Unfortunately, of the many works which could be mentioned here, we shall have to content ourselves with brief and selected notice. For example, the two most outstanding achievements in recent years are those by Kuroda Toshio and Yokoi Kiyoshi. Kuroda's book [II-01] and monograph [III-01] assert that the Buddhism characteristic of medieval times was exoteric and esoteric, not the so-called "new Kamakura Buddhism," and argues that the relationship between exoteric and esoteric shrines and temples and the state, which has usually been regarded as characteristic of the ancient period, was in fact basic to medieval religion. Yokoi illuminates the life and consciousness of people of medieval times in a collection of articles [III-02] depicting the conflicts and contradictions which preoccupied people of that period, and further indicates that Buddhism and other dominant ideologies concealed within their very doctrines the concept of discrimination. These works will be discussed in greater detail in the relevant sections of this bibliography.

In the field of the history of Buddhism we also have Kasahara Kazuo's work [III-03] which goes into how the concept of admitting women to Paradise changed in Buddhism over time and how it differed from sect to sect. Also, monographs on Shugendō and mountain worship, subjects which have been neglected until recently, have been collected in the *Sangaku shūkyō-shi kenkyū sōsho* (Research Series on the History of Mountain Worship) [III-04]. We already have research by Wajima Yoshio and Ueda Sachiko on Eison and Ninshō, two eminent prelates of the Saidaiji (Ritsu sect) who represented ancient Buddhism in the Kamakura period, but Amino Yoshihiko [I-01] has examined their activities from the broad perspective of Kamakura political history. He shows how these monks of the Saidaiji, with close ties to the Hōjō family, traveled on sea routes from the Japan Sea through the Inland Sea to the Kinai region. Their activities, carried on in the name of religion, helped to maintain transportation routes, and contributed to the Hōjō's ability to dominate strategic points. Kawazoe Shōji has also pointed out the role played by Buddhist monks of the Saidaiji and other temples in importing civilization from China [III-05]. Both bring a new perspective to research on the Saidaiji sect. A monograph by Kawakatsu Masatarō focuses on the

Ōkura school of stonemasons, which had a very close relationship with the Saidaiji [III-06].

Kawane Yoshiyasu's article, "Yasurai matsuri no seiritsu" (The Beginnings of the Yasurai Festival) [III-07] takes up a Kyoto festival still celebrated today, and describes how against the political background of the *insei* period the townspeople created this festival and made it their own. Ishida Yoshihito [III-08], Ogasawara Nagakazu [III-09], and others attempt to recreate provincial culture and religious beliefs in medieval times.

It has been possible to mention only a few recent works in the category of history of religions that are concerned in some way with social or political history. Works on doctrine and individual sects, are included in the chapter on religion.

In literature and the performing arts, the previously-published articles of Sakurai Yoshirō have been collected into one volume [III-11]. Sakurai has also undertaken a reevaluation of the *Taiheiki* and later military chronicles. Up to now these have often been considered simply as works of literature, but here he presents an analysis of their structure of expression [III-12, 13]. Kanai Kiyomitsu's books [III-14, 15] on the Jishū priests, who have left a heavy imprint on medieval literature and the performing arts, present a neat arrangement of their historiography. And Morita Yoshinori's work [III-16] portrays the state of the minor performing arts, including *senshū banzei* (a ceremony of dance and prayer, originally performed at court and by temples and aristocratic houses at New Years), *matsubayashi* (a song and dance presentation for New Year's), puppet shows, and so forth, and the mode of existence of the medieval outcastes who took part in such performances.

There are several collections of source materials that are part of the category of cultural history [III-19, 20, 21]. Surveys and research on stone inscriptions and stone remains are also flourishing, concurrent with the recent spate of local histories. If we include articles published in prefectural and city histories devoted to source materials, it would be almost impossible to count them all. To mention just one or two, the works by Aikyō and Tatsumi [III-22] and by Mochizuki Tomoyoshi [III-23] are exhaustive investigations of the stone inscriptions and stone remains in Wakayama (chiefly Kōyasan, Kumano, etc.) and Ōita (mainly the Kunisaki penninsula) respectively, both areas being treasure troves of stone remains. Both books are very readable, the former having lavish illustrations and the latter very detailed commentary.

2. There has been a great deal of excavating in medieval sites everywhere in recent years. In the past only isolated sites tended to be excavated, but in places like the Ichijōdani remains (Fukui prefecture) [III-25, 26], Kusado Sengen (Hiroshima prefectures) and Wakatsukinoshō (Nara prefecture) [III-27], large-scale excavations of an entire town or *shōen* are being carried out. The remains of medieval dwellings have been verified in many cases, and without exception they have yielded various types of contemporary household implements. Ichijōdani, for example, yielded a variety of toys and games, such as *shōgi* pieces, the likes of which are rare even among our art treasures. Such excavations are very important because they add to the number of relics which, as art treasures, are unusual. Those relics that are known as art treasures are generally arrayed separately in museums, isolated from each other, but now the same types of articles are beginning to appear together with others at the very sites where they all once played a part in daily life. These tendencies promise to have a great influence on research on the history of daily life, technology and Buddhism (particularly archaeological research on Buddhist religious implements, etc.), and these relics will be important source materials.

In the case of pottery, for example, the number of ceramic art treasures is large, and even researchers who depend mainly on documentary evidence are comparatively familiar with the subject. Even so, an exhibition called "Chinese Ceramics Excavated in Japan" [III-28], held at the Tokyo National Museum in June 1976, showed that rough Chinese folk pottery (miscellaneous items for daily use) was imported to Japan in large quantities and had come into general use. That destroyed the general notion derived from studies of art treasures that "Chinese pottery" meant just a few, high-quality pieces. It also gave further evidence that pottery was imported from Thailand and other areas as well as from China, and that by the middle ages this imported Chinese pottery had spread through trade as far as the Ainu settlements in Hokkaido. Thus, even in the case of pottery, where there is a large number of art treasures and where we thought research was advanced, a gulf remained between research based on the fine arts and that based on artifacts. The same is true in areas besides pottery, where there are few art treasures, and analysis of the production techniques and the way they were used must be based on just a few examples and on scroll paintings, etc. The history of daily life and cultural history up to now rests on a synthesis of such research, so it is only to be expected that there must be revision.

This applies not only to artifacts but to a site as a whole. For example, when an effort is made to study a whole *shōen*, as in the excavation of Wakatsukinoshō, we can see in detail the layout of the fields, irrigation ditches, etc., and learn much that is new about the technical aspects of agriculture, such as irrigation. If we can grasp the connections among the village settlement, arable land and festivals, our image of the daily life of the medieval village, now formed on the basis of drawings and scroll paintings, can be drawn anew.

文　　献

I-01　坂本賞三 Sakamoto Shōzō『摂関時代』 *The Regent Period* [日本の歴史 6] 390 pp., 小学館, 1974.

安田元久 Yasuda Motohisa『院政と平氏』 *The Insei and the Taira Clan* [日本の歴史 7] 390 pp., 小学館, 1974.

村井康彦 Murai Yasuhiko『王朝貴族』 *The Heian Aristocracy* [日本の歴史 8] 374 pp., 小学館, 1974.

大山喬平 Ōyama Kyōhei『鎌倉幕府』 *The Kamakura Bakufu* [日本の歴史 9] 390 pp., 小学館, 1974.

網野善彦 Amino Yoshihiko『蒙古襲来』 *The Mongol Invasions* [日本の歴史 10] 454 pp., 小学館, 1974.

佐藤和彦 Satō Kazuhiko『南北朝内乱』 *The Civil Wars of the Nanbokuchō Period* [日本の歴史 11] 358 pp., 小学館, 1974.

石井　進 Ishii Susumu『中世武士団』 *Medieval Bushidan* [日本の歴史 12] 390 pp., 小学館, 1974.

佐々木銀弥 Sasaki Gin'ya『室町幕府』 *The Muromachi Bakufu* [日本の歴史 13] 390 pp., 小学館, 1975.

永原慶二 Nagahara Keiji『戦国の動乱』 *The Wars of Sengoku* [日本の歴史 14] 390 pp., 小学館, 1975.

02　朝尾直弘ほか(編) Asao Naohiro, et al. (eds.)『岩波講座 日本歴史 6』(中世 1) *Iwanami Lectures on Japanese History*, Vol. 6 (Medieval Period 1) 350 pp., 岩波書店, 1975.

38

　　朝尾直弘ほか(編) Asao Naohiro, et al. (eds.)『岩波講座　日本歴史 7』(中世 2) *Iwanami Lectures on Japanese History*, Vol. 7 (Medieval Period 2) 350 pp., 岩波書店, 1975.

03　稲垣泰彦・戸田芳実(編) Inagaki Yasuhiko and Toda Yoshimi (eds.)『土一揆と内乱』*Medieval Peasant Rebellions and the Civil Wars* [日本民衆の歴史 2] 429 pp., 三省堂, 1975.

　　佐々木潤之介(編) Sasaki Junnosuke (ed.)『天下統一と民衆』*National Unification and the People* [日本民衆の歴史 3] 355 pp., 三省堂, 1974.

04　石井　進・村井章介・龍福義友・衛藤　駿 Ishii Susumu, Murai Shōsuke, Ryūfuku Yoshitomo and Etō Shun 1974 年の歴史学界 ——回顧と展望—— (中世) "Historical Research in 1974: Retrospect and Prospect" (Medieval)『史学雑誌』84–5, pp. 73–106, 1975.

05　歴史学研究会(編) The Historical Science Society of Japan (ed.)『現代歴史学の成果と課題 2』(共同体・奴隷制・封建制) *The Past Achievements and Future Tasks of Contemporary Historiography*, Vol. 2 (Community, Slavery and Feudalism), 183 pp., 青木書店, 1974.

06　井上光貞・永原慶二(編) Inoue Mitsusada and Nagahara Keiji (eds.)『日本史研究入門 IV』*Introduction to Research on Japanese History*, Vol. IV, 416 pp., 東大出版会, 1975.

07　永原慶二(編) Nagahara Keiji (ed.) 『日本史を学ぶ 2』(中世 1) *Learning Japanese History*, Vol. 2 (Medieval Period 1), 307pp., 有斐閣, 1975.

08　河音能平 Kawane Yoshiyasu 歴史科学運動と史料学の課題 "Historical Scientist Movement and the Task of Historiography"『現代歴史科学の課題』pp. 69–78, 大阪歴史科学協議会, 1974.

09　中村直勝 Nakamura Naokatsu『日本古文書学』(中) *The Study of Japanese Diplomatics*, Vol. 2, 1021 pp., 角川書店, 1974.

10　佐藤進一 Satō Shin'ichi 日本花押史の一節 "A Note on the History of Signatures (*Kaō*) in Japan"『名古屋大学日本史論集』(下) pp. 3–18, 吉川弘文館, 1975.

11　田中　稔(編) Tanaka Minoru (ed.)『書の日本史』第 3 巻, (鎌倉・南北朝) *Calligraphy in Japanese History*, Vol. 3 (The Kamakura and Nanbokuchō Periods), 293 pp., 平凡社, 1975.

　　佐藤進一・羽下徳彦(編) Satō Shin'ichi and Haga Norihiko (eds.)『書の日本史』第 4 巻 (室町・戦国) *Calligraphy in Japanese History*, Vol. 4 (The Muromachi and Sengoku Periods), 287 pp., 平凡社, 1975.

12　竹内理三 Takeuchi Rizō『鎌倉遺文』(6, 7, 8, 9) *Surviving Kamakura Documents*, Vols. 6–9, 東京堂, 1974–75.

13　竹内理三(編) Takeuchi Rizō (ed.)『伊賀国黒田庄史料』*Source Materials on Kuroda-shō, Iga Province*, Vol. 1 [荘園史料叢書 1] 243 pp., 吉川弘文館, 1975.

瀬野精一郎(編) Seno Seiichirō (ed.) 『肥前国神崎荘史料』 *Source Materials on Kanzaki Shōen in Hizen Province* [荘園史料叢書] 243 pp., 吉川弘文館, 1975.

14 佐藤進一・藤木久志・桑山洪然・阿部洋輔・金子 達・中野豈任(編) Satō Shin'ichi, Fujiki Hisashi, Kuwayama Kōnen, Abe Yōsuke, Kaneko Tatsu, and Nakano Kazuhide (eds.) 『影印北越中世文書』 *Reproductions of Medieval Documents of Echigo and Etchū Provinces*, 355 pp., 柏書房, 1975.

15 瀬野精一郎(編) Seno Seiichirō (ed.) 『九州地方中世編年文書目録』鎌倉時代篇, 南北朝時代篇 *Chronological Bibliography of Medieval Documents of Kyushu*, Volumes on Kamakura and Nanbokuchō Periods, 258 pp.; 276 pp., 吉川弘文館, 1974.

16 竹内理三(編) Takeuchi Rizō (ed.) 『荘園分布図』(上巻) *Shōen Distribution Maps*, Vol. 1, 189 pp., 吉川弘文館, 1975.

17 大隅和雄(編) Ōsumi Kazuo (ed.) 『太平記人名索引』 *Personal Name Index to the Taiheiki*, 279 pp., 北海道大学図書刊行会, 1974.

18 戦国文書研究会(編) Society for the Study of Sengoku Documents (eds.) 『戦国文書聚影 長宗我部氏篇』 *Sengoku Documents Collected and Photographed: The Chōsokabe Family*, 24 葉, 柏書房, 1975.

戦国文書研究会(編) Society for the Study of Sengoku Documents (eds.) 『戦国文書聚影 伊達氏篇』 *Sengoku Documents Collected and Photographed: The Date Family*, 35 葉, 柏書房, 1974.

II-01 黒田俊雄 Kuroda Toshio 『日本中世の国家と宗教』 *State and Religion in Medieval Japan*, 574 pp., 岩波書店, 1975.

02 井上寛司 Inoue Hiroshi 日本封建制度研究とアジア的社会構成 ——日本中世封建制論再検討の試み—— "Research on Japanese Feudalism and Asiatic Social Structure—An Attempt to Reexamine the Theory of Japan's Medieval Feudalism" 「歴史評論」292, pp. 6–24, 歴史科学協議会 (校倉書房), 1974 年 8 月.

03 永原慶二 (司会) Nagahara Keiji (moderator) 『中世国家論』 *On the Medieval State* [シンポジウム 日本歴史 7] 256 pp., 学生社, 1974.

04 峰岸純夫(編) Minegishi Sumio (ed.) 『大系日本国家史 2』(中世) *A Systematic History of the Japanese State*, Vol. 2 (Medieval Period) 294 pp., 東大出版会, 1975.

05 清水三男 Shimizu Mitsuo 『上代の土地関係』 *Land Relationships in the Ancient Period* [清水三男著作集 1] 221 pp., 校倉書房, 1975.

清水三男 Shimizu Mitsuo 『日本中世の村落』 *Medieval Villages in Japan* [清水三男著作集 2] 354 pp., 校倉書房, 1974.

清水三男 Shimizu Mitsuo 『中世荘園の基礎構造』 *The Basic Structure of Medieval Shōen* [清水三男著作集 3] 258 pp., 校倉書房, 1975.

06 秋山国三・仲村 研 Akiyama Kunizō and Nakamura Ken 『京都「町」の

研究』 *Research on 'Neighborhoods' in Kyoto*, 373 pp., 法政大学出版局, 1975.

07 戸田芳実 Toda Yoshimi 王朝都市論の問題点 "Issues Concerning Heian Period Cities" 「日本史研究」139-40 合併号, pp. 7-14, 日本史研究会, 1974.

08 脇田晴子 Wakita Haruko 日本中世都市の構造 "The Structure of Medieval Cities in Japan" 「日本史研究」139-40 合併号, pp. 15-35, 日本史研究会, 1974.

09 三浦圭一 Miura Keiichi 中世の分業流通と都市 "Specialized Commodity Distribution and Cities in the Medieval Period" 『大系日本国家史 2』(中世) pp. 157-206, 東京大学出版会, 1975.

10 棚橋光男 Tanahashi Mitsuo 中世伊勢神宮領の形成とその特質 (上) (下) "The Formation and Characteristics of the Holdings of the Ise Shrine in Medieval Times" (Parts 1 and 2) 「日本史研究」155, 156, pp. 1-23; pp. 35-60, 日本史研究会, 1975 年 7 月, 8 月.

11 永村　真 Nagamura Makoto 東大寺大勧進職と油倉の成立 "The Post of Solicitor for Contributions to the Tōdaiji and the Origin of Oil Storehouses" 「民衆史研究」12, pp. 99-132, 民衆史研究会, 1974 年 5 月.

12 田中健夫 Tanaka Takeo 『中世対外関係史』 *A History of Foreign Relations in the Medieval Period* [東大人文科学研究叢書] 424 pp., 東京大学出版会, 1975.

13 森　克巳 Mori Katsumi 『新訂日宋貿易の研究』 *Researches on Japan-Sung Trade* (rev. ed.) [森克巳著作選集 1] 598 pp., 国書刊行会, 1975.
森　克巳 Mori Katsumi 『続日宋貿易の研究』 *Further Research on Japan-Sung China Trade* [森克巳著作選集 2] 427 pp., 国書刊行会, 1975.
森　克巳 Mori Katsumi 『続々日宋貿易の研究』 *Additional Researches on Japan-Sung Trade* [森克巳著作選集 3] 446 pp., 国書刊行会, 1975.
森　克巳 Mori Katsumi 『増補日宋文化交流の諸問題』 *Problems in Cultural Exchange between Japan and Sung China* (Enlarged Edition) [森克巳著作選集 4] 429 pp., 国書刊行会, 1975.

14 稲垣泰彦 Inagaki Yasuhiko 中世の農業経営と収取形態 "Agriculture and the Forms of Collection in Medieval Times" 『岩波講座　日本歴史 6』(中世 2) pp. 167-205, 岩波書店, 1975.

15 富沢清人 Tomisawa Kiyoto 「在家」の身分的性格について ──中世農民論の前進のために── "The Social Status of *Zaike*—Towards an Advance in the Study of Medieval Peasantry" 「歴史学研究」411, pp. 16-26, 歴史学研究会 (青木書店), 1974 年 8 月.

16 河音能平 Kawane Yoshiyasu 丹波国田能庄の百姓とその「縁共」について ──中世前期村落における小百姓の存在形態── "On the Peasants of Tanō *Shōen* in Tamba Province and the Situation of the Lower Peasantry in Early Medieval Village Settlements" 「人文研究」(大阪市大) 26-11, pp. 21-46, 大阪市立大, 1974 年 12 月.

17 森川英純 Morikawa Hidezumi 興福寺領における作主職の成立と郷村制 "The Rise of the Cultivator Rights (*sakushu-shiki*) on Kōfukuji Holdings and the Village System"「ヒストリア」66, pp. 17–39, 大阪歴史学会, 1975 年3月.

18 高重 進 Takashige Susumu 『古代・中世の耕地と村落』 *Arable and Village Settlements in the Ancient and Medieval Periods*, 327 pp., 大明堂, 1975.

19 橋本義彦 Hashimoto Yoshihiko 院政論——古代末期政治形態論の一齣—— "Cloister Government: An Aspect of Political Forms at the End of the Ancient Period"「日本歴史」327, pp. 37–48, 日本歴史学会 (吉川弘文館), 1975 年8月.

20 五味文彦 Gomi Fumihiko 院支配権の一考察 "A Study of the Cloistered Emperors' Governing Authority"「日本史研究」158, pp. 1–22, 日本史研究会, 1975 年10月.

21 大山喬平 Ōyama Kyōhei 文治国地頭の三つの権限について——鎌倉幕府守護制度の歴史的前提—— "On the Three Rights of the *Kuni-jitō* in the Bunji Era—Historical Premises of the *Shugo* System of the Kamakura Bakufu"「日本史研究」158, pp. 48–66, 日本史研究会, 1975 年10月.

22 大山喬平 Ōyama Kyōhei 没官領・謀叛人所帯跡地領の成立——国家恩賞授与権との関連をめぐって—— "The Rise of Holdings of Land Confiscated from Criminals and Traitors—With Respect to Their Relation to the Right to Confer State Rewards"「史林」58–6, pp. 1–34, 史学研究会 (京大) 1975 年11月.

23 義江彰夫 Yoshie Akio 鎌倉幕府地頭職の成立 (上) (下) "The Origin of the Kamakura Bakufu's *Jitō-shiki*" (Parts 1 and 2)「文学部紀要」(北大) 23, XXIV-1 pp. 27–229; pp. 1–134, 1975 年3月.

24 入間田宣夫 Irumada Nobuo 鎌倉時代の国家権力 "State Authority in the Kamakura Period"『大系日本国家史 2』(中世), pp. 107–56, 東京大学出版会, 1975.

25 入間田宣夫 Irumada Nobuo 北条氏と摂津国多田院, 多田庄 "The Hōjō and the Tada-in and the Tada Shōen of Settsu Province"「日本歴史」325, 日本歴史学会 (吉川弘文館), 1975 年6月.

26 瀬野精一郎 Seno Seiichirō 『鎮西御家人の研究』 *Research on the Gokenin of Kyushu* [日本史学研究叢書] 536 pp., 吉川弘文館, 1975.

27 五味文彦 Gomi Fumihiko 在京人とその位置 "*Zaikyōnin* and Their Position"「史学雑誌」83–8, pp. 1–26, 史学会, 1974 年8月.

28 磯貝富士男 Isogai Fujio 日本中世奴隷法の基礎的考察 ——鎌倉幕府法の奴婢規定を中心に—— "A Basic Study of Law on Slaves in Medieval Japan—On the Provisions on Slaves in the Law of the Kamakura Bakufu"「歴史学研究」424, pp. 30–46, 歴史学研究会 (青木書店), 1975.

29 笠松宏至 Kasamatsu Hiroshi 本券無し "Without Title Deeds"「史学雑誌」 84–2, pp. 50–57, 史学会, 1975 年 2 月.

30 網野善彦 (司会) Amino Yoshihiko (moderator)『南北朝の内乱』 The Civil Wars of the Nanbokuchō Period [シンポジウム 日本歴史 8] 学生社, 1974.

31 峰岸純夫 (司会) Minegishi Sumio (moderator)『土一揆』 Medieval Peasant Rebellions [シンポジウム 日本歴史 9] 279 pp., 学生社, 1974.

32 小川 信 (編) Ogawa Makoto (ed.)『室町政権』 Muromachi Government [論集日本歴史 5] 380 pp., 有精堂出版, 1975.

33 伊藤喜良 Itō Kiyoshi 室町幕府と武家執奏 "The Muromachi Bakufu and the Buke Shissō"「日本史研究」145, pp. 23–51, 日本史研究会, 1974 年 9 月.

34 川添昭二 Kawazoe Shōji 室町幕府奉公衆筑前府生氏について "On the Asō Family of Chikuzen, a Hōkōshū of the Muromachi Bakufu"「九州史学」 57, pp. 1–33, 九州史学研究会, 1975 年 7 月.

35 下坂 守 Shimosaka Mamoru 山門使節制度の成立と展開──室町幕府の山門政策をめぐって── "The Rise and Development of the Enryakuji Envoy System—On the Muromachi Bakufu's Policy toward the Enryakuji"「史林」 58–1, pp. 67–114, 史学研究会 (京大), 1975 年 1 月.

36 五味文彦 Gomi Fumihiko 管領制と大名制 ──その転換── "The Kanrei System and the Daimyō System—The Transformation"「紀要」(神戸大) 4, pp. 27–54, 神戸大学, 1975 年 1 月.

37 中村吉治 Nakamura Kichiji『土一揆研究』 Research on Medieval Peasant Rebellions, 694 pp. 校倉書房, 1974.

38 畑井 弘 Hatai Hiromu『守護領国体制の研究──六角氏領国に見る畿内近国的発展の特質──』 Studies on the System of Shugo Domain Provinces—The Special Features of Its Development in Provinces near the Kinai as Seen in the Rokkaku Domain, 495 pp., 吉川弘文館, 1975 年 4 月.

39 村井章介 Murai Shōsuke 在地領主法の誕生 ──肥前松浦一揆── "The Birth of Local Seignorial Law—The Case of the Matsuura Ikki in Hizen"「歴史学研究」419, pp. 18–35, 歴史学研究会 (青木書店), 1975 年 4 月.

40 藤木久志 Fujiki Hisashi『戦国社会史論──日本中世国家の解体──』 Towards a History of Society in the Sengoku Period—The Disintegration of Japan's Medieval State, 404 pp., 東京大学出版会, 1974.

41 藤木久志 Fujiki Hisashi 大名領国制論 "Essay on the Daimyō Domain Provinces"『大系日本国家史 2』(中世) pp. 249–89, 東京大学出版会, 1975.

42 永原慶二 Nagahara Keiji 大名領国制の歴史的位置──中世～近世移行期把握のための覚書── "The Historical Significance of the Daimyō Domain Provinces—A Note for Understanding the Transitional Period between the Medieval and Early Modern Periods"「歴史評論」300, pp. 71–94, 歴史科学協議会 (校倉書房), 1975 年 1 月.

43 勝俣鎮夫 Katsumata Shizuo 遠州浜名神戸大福寺領注進状案について——戦国大名今川氏検地の一事例—— "On the Draft Report on the Daifukuji's Domain in Hamana Kanbe, Tōtōmi Province—An Example of a Cadastral Survey by the Imagawa, A Sengoku *Daimyō*"「日本歴史」320, pp. 102–115, 日本歴史学会 (吉川弘文館), 1975 年 1 月.

44 新行紀一 Shingyō Norikazu『一向一揆の基礎構造 ——三河一向一揆と松平氏——』*The Basic Structure of Ikkō Ikki—The Ikkō Peasant Uprisings in Mikawa and the Matsudaira Family*, 350 pp., 吉川弘文館, 1975.

45 今谷 明 Imatani Akira『戦国期の室町幕府』*The Muromachi Bakufu in the Sengoku Period* [季刊論叢日本文化 2] 230 pp., 角川書店, 1975.

46 今谷 明 Imatani Akira 室町幕府最末期の京都支配 ——発給文書を通じて見た三好政権—— "Control of Kyoto under the Late Muromachi Bakufu—The Miyoshi Regime Seen through their Documents"「史林」58–3, pp. 69–105, 史学研究会 (京大), 1975 年 5 月.

47 今谷 明 Imatani Akira 管領代奉書の成立 "The Origin of the Substitute *Kanrei's* Instructions"「古文書研究」7, 8, pp. 43–64, 日本古文書学会 (吉川弘文館), 1975 年 2 月.

III–01 黒田俊雄 Kuroda Toshio 中世寺社勢力論 "Secular Power of Medieval Temples and Shrines"『岩波講座 日本歴史 6』(中世 2) pp. 245–96, 岩波書店, 1975.

02 横井 清 Yokoi Kiyoshi『中世民衆の生活文化』*Life and Culture of the People in Medieval Times, Popular Culture and Daily Life in Medieval Japan*, 376 pp., 東京大学出版会, 1975.

03 笠原一男 Kasahara Kazuo『女人往生思想の系譜』*The Concept of Enlightenment for Woman: A Historical Study* [日本宗教史研究叢書] 427 pp., 古川弘文館, 1975.

04 和歌森太郎 (編) Wakamori Tarō (ed.)『山岳宗教の成立と展開』*The Emergence and Development of the Mountain Sects* [山岳宗教史研究叢書 1] 388 pp., 名著出版, 1975.
五来 重(編) Gorai Shigeru (ed.)『吉野熊野信仰の研究』*Research on the Yoshino Kumano Creed* [山岳宗教史研究叢書 4] 450 pp., 名著出版, 1975.
戸川安章(編) Togawa Anshō (ed.)『出羽三山と東北修験の研究』*The Dewa Peaks and Shūgendō in Tōhoku* [山岳宗教史研究叢書 5] 444 pp., 名著出版, 1975.

05 川添昭二 Kawazoe Shōji 鎌倉時代の対外関係と文物の移入 "Foreign Relations and the Importation of Culture in the Kamakura Period"『岩波講座日本歴史 6』(中世 2) pp. 41–84, 岩波書店, 1975.

06 川勝政太郎 Kawakatsu Masatarō 大蔵派石大工と関係遺品 "The Ōkura School of Stonemasons and Their Work"「史迹と美術」44–9, pp. 337–45, 史

迹美術同放会，1974 年 11 月．

07 河音能平 Kawane Yoshiyasu やすらい祭の成立（上・下）"The Beginnings of the Yasurai Festival" (Parts 1 and 2)「日本史研究」137, 138, pp. 1-22; pp. 44-72, 日本史研究会，1973-74.

08 石田善人 Ishida Yoshihito 都鄙民衆の生活と宗教 "Religion and Daily Life of City and Country Folk"『岩波講座　日本歴史 6』(中世 2) pp. 297-337, 岩波書店，1975.

09 小笠原長和 Ogasawara Nagakazu 中世の天神信仰と地方文化——安房平群天神縁起絵巻と武蔵小手指村北野天神図絵 "The Tenjin Cult and Provincial Culture in the Middle Ages—The Scroll Painting of the Origins of the Awa Heguri Tenjin and the Painting of the Kitano Tenjin of Kotesashi Village in Musashi"「人文研究」(千葉大) 4, pp. 31-66, 千葉大学，1975 年 3 月．

10 中ノ堂一信 Nakanodō Kazunobu 東大寺大勧進職の成立 ——「俊乗房重源」像の再検討—— "The Origin of the Post of Solicitor for Contributions to the Tōdaiji—A New View of Shunjōbō Chōgen"「日本史研究」152, pp. 28-53, 日本史研究会，1975 年 4 月．

11 桜井好朗　Sakurai Yoshirō 『中世日本の精神史的景観』 *Medieval Japan's Spiritual Landscape*, 380 pp., 塙書房，1974.

12 桜井好朗 Sakurai Yoshirō 太平記の歴史叙述——軍記の表現構造をさぐるための試み—— "Historical Narrative in the *Taiheiki*—An Experiment in Search of the Structure of Expression in Military Chronicies"「文学」43-5, pp. 1-20, 岩波書店，1975 年 5 月．

13 桜井好朗 Sakurai Yoshirō 室町軍記における歴史叙述 "Historical Narration in Military Chronicles of the Muromachi Period"『名古屋大学日本史論集』(上) pp. 429-53, 吉川弘文館，1975.

14 金井清光 Kanai Kiyomitsu『時衆と中世文学』*The Jishū and Medieval Literature*, 568 pp., 東京堂，1975.

15 金井清光 Kanai Kiyomitsu 『一遍と時衆教団』*Ippen and the Jishū Order*, 557 pp., 角川書店，1975.

16 盛田嘉徳 Morita Yoshinori『中世賤民と雑芸能の研究』*Research on Outcastes and the Minor Performing Arts in the Middle Ages*, 397 pp., 雄山閣出版，1974.

17 林屋辰三郎 Hayashiya Tatsusaburō『内乱のなかの貴族——南北朝期「園太暦」の世界——』*The Aristocracy in the Civil Wars—The World of the 'Entaireki,' a Diary of the Nanbokuchō Period* [季刊論叢日本文化 1] 180 pp., 角川書店，1975.

18 水野恭一郎 Mizuno Kyōichirō『武家時代の政治と文化』*Politics and Culture in Japan Under Warrior Rule*, 320 pp., 創元社，1975.

19 桜井徳太郎・萩原龍夫・宮田　登(校注) Sakurai Tokutarō, Hagiwara Tatsuo and Miyata Noboru (eds.) 『寺社縁起』*Accounts of the Origins of Temples and*

Shrines [日本思想大系　第 20 巻] 530 pp., 岩波書店, 1975.

20　高山寺典籍文書綜合調査団(編) The Joint Committee for the Study of the Kōzanji's Books and Documents (eds.) 『高山寺文書』 *Kōzanji Documents*, 534 pp., 東大出版会, 1975.

21　藤田経世 Fujita Tsuneyo 『校刊美術史料』(中・下) *Sources for Art History*, Vol. 2 and 3, 517 pp., 中央公論美術出版, 1975.

22　巽　三郎・愛甲昇寛 Tatsumi Saburō and Aikyō Masuhiro 『紀伊国金石文集成』 *A Collection of Stone Inscriptions in Kii Province*, 南紀考古同好会, 1974.

23　望月友善 Mochizuki Tomoyoshi 『大分の石造美術』 *Stone Art in Ōita*, 木耳社, 1975.

24　庚申懇話会(編) Kōshin Society (ed.) 『日本石仏事典』 *Dictionary of Stone Buddhas in Japan*, 雄山閣, 1975.

25　福井県教育委員会・朝倉氏遺跡調査研究所　Research Institute for the Investigation of the Asakura Remains, Board of Education, Fukui Prefecture 『特別史跡一乗谷朝倉氏遺跡』(V, VI) *Designated Historical Site: The Asakura Remains at Ichijōdani*, Vols. V, VI, 30 pp., 73 pp., 福井県教委, 朝倉氏遺跡調査研究所, 1974–75.

26　福井県教育委員会・朝倉氏遺跡調査研究所 Research Institute for the Investigation of the Asakura Remains, Board of Education, Fukui Prefecture 『一乗谷石造遺物調査報告書 1』(銘文集成) *Reports of the Investigation of Stone Artifacts at Ichijōdani*, Vol. 1 (Collection of Stone Inscriptions), 114 pp., 福井県教委, 朝倉氏遺跡調査研究所, 1975.

27　大和郡山市の古文化財を守る会(編)　The Society for the Protection of Ancient Cultural Properties of Yamato-Kōriyama City (ed.) 『若槻荘の歴史』 *The History of Wakatsuki Shōen*, 46 pp., 大和郡山市の古文化財を守る会, 1975.

28　東京国立博物館 Tokyo National Museum 『日本出土の中国陶磁』 *Chinese Ceramics Excavated in Japan*, 116 pp., 東京国立博物館, 1975.

JAPANESE HISTORY —EARLY MODERN PERIOD

Ōishi Shinzaburō
Gakushūin University

Translated by Wayne Root and Takechi Manabu

I. Introduction

Publications on early modern Japanese history during 1974 and 1975 evidence the appearance of several significant trends. The first is the tendency to view the social system (the *bakuhan taisei shakai*) set up by Oda Nobunaga, Toyotomi Hideyoshi and Tokugawa Ieyasu as an entirety in terms of the concept of *kokka* (state). For years scholars have stressed the position of the *han*—contending that although Tokugawa society consisted of a combination of *bakufu* and *han* control, the driving force of government was the *han*. The shogun stood at the head of the Edo bakufu, but he was first and foremost the lord of the Tokugawa *han*, and it was the overwhelming size of these fief holdings compared to that of other daimyō which guaranteed Tokugawa control over the bakufu. The *han* maintained self-sufficiency through control of political, economic, revenue-gathering and other administrative activities to such an extent that the concept of the State may readily be applied to these local units throughout the early modern period. It is significant that the eventual establishment of the modern Japanese state and the turnover of the entire *bakuhan taisei* society in accordance with Japan's new status in the modern world were not even attempted until the political forces of the Meiji Restoration had succeeded in dismantling the power of the *han*.

However, scholars have recently argued that to apply the concept of State to the *han* and to neglect incisive inquiry into the nature of

Japan as a whole, was to leave too many unanswered questions. For example, in Japan's diplomatic relations with the outside world throughout the Tokugawa period the declared policy was one of seclusion (*sakoku*). Japan did conduct trade and commercial negotiations with other countries through the port of Nagasaki, but the bakufu maintained exclusive control over trade arrangements and negotiations. No *han* was allowed to conduct relations with nations outside Japan.

Concerning the flow of currency too, often thought of as the lifeblood of society and the economy, the bakufu held sole authority over the minting of gold, silver and copper coins, the three types of money in standard use at the time. Paper currency or *hansatsu* was issued by *han* governments to supplement deficiencies which arose in coinage, but such currency was restricted to use within the boundaries of the issuing *han*, could be printed only with bakufu authorization, and could not be used in commerce with other fiefs.

This means that some of the most essential elements in the functioning of any state were denied the *han*. As long as the bakufu maintained its grip over the monetary system and the conduct of foreign affairs, and remained the ultimate coordinator of *han* activity, the *han* could not actually be considered a viable "State." The *han* were granted the prerogative of rule over the people within their domain, and an individual peasant would pay his taxes directly to his daimyo, owing no additional payment to the bakufu. Yet, at least in theory, ultimate power resided in the bakufu, so we may be justified in calling the bakufu the State. A collection written from this conceptual perspective of the early modern state has been compiled under the editorship of Sasaki Junnosuke as *Taikei Nihon kokkashi, 3, kinsei* (Studies in the History of the Japanese State, Vol. 3, The Early Modern Period) [I-01].

Another outstanding feature of research in this period is the valuable work on discrimination against the *burakumin* or *eta* minority. The lingering prejudice against this group is said to have become institutionalized in the social structure of the Tokugawa era, and research on the historical aspects of the problem is part of a general effort to rid Japan of persisting discrimination against these orphans of history. Two leading contributors in this area are Harada Tomohiko in *Hisabetsu buraku no rekishi* (The History of Outcaste Communities) [I-02] and Ishio Yoshihisa, *Hisabetsu buraku kigenron* (The Origin of the *Buraku* Communities) [I-03]. Another important contribution is the Saraike Village Documents Research Association compilation of the *Kawachi no kuni Saraike mura monjo* (Documents of Saraike Village, Kawachi Province, Vol. 3) [I-04].

A third important event is the publication of a great number of general reference works and reprints of primary sources, thus making these materials accessible to a much wider audience than ever before. The quantity of extant primary material on the ancient and medieval periods is rather small, so that most has been printed and published while relatively few of the much larger body of early modern history documents had, until recently, hardly been touched. Many Tokugawa primary sources are in the hands of old and wealthy universities or research institutes, who permit access only to selected individuals; others are in the possession of individuals or families often unaware of their historical value. The publication of these primary resource materials (though printing all would be impossible) would open many new doors for scholarly endeavor. Their release would allow impartial access to a much wider audience, which is perhaps more valuable than the relatively restricted exposure they receive through the publications of a fortunate few.

II. INTRODUCTORY AND GENERAL WORKS

A good introductory work for the newcomer in early modern history should ideally include an outline of issues in the field, information on relevant bibliographies and source materials, and a review of the status of specific areas of research. One of the best arranged general works of this nature is the *Nihon kinseishi nyūmon* (Introduction to Early Modern Japanese History) [II-01] edited by Arai Eiji, designed for the undergraduate Japanese history major. *Rekishi no shiten* (Perspectives on History) [II-02] is a work directed at those with a general interest in history and is a thematic discussion of the field by specialists in dialogue form.

In the past few years, a group of historians have begun to study Tokugawa history using the methods of econometrics. *Sūryō keizaishi nyūmon* (Introduction to Quantitative Economic History) [II-03] is the most informative introduction to these efforts in what may be called "econometric history." While intended as an introductory text, it will prove excellent reading for specialists as well. *Nihonshi kenkyū nyūmon, IV* (Introduction to Research on Japanese History, Vol. 4) [II-04] gives a concise explanation of research trends and issues from 1967 to 1972 for each historical period, from ancient to modern. The book is written in readable style, making it a very useful introductory text. Another helpful reference is the *Nihonshi bunken nenkan 75* (Annual Bibliography of Japanese History, 1975) [II-05] compiled by the Chihōshi Kenkyū Kyōgikai (Council for Research on Local History), and indexing a wide range of fields including history, folklore and archaeology.

In the past there have been numerous attempts to produce a Japanese history series written in nontechnical language for the general public, yet based on the latest, advanced historical research. Three such series, published by Kōdansha [II-06], Shūeisha [II-07] and Shōgakkan are now available. Of the three, the Shōgakkan series is probably the most detailed and up-to-date in content. Nine volumes in the series deal with various phases of the early modern period: Fujiki Hisashi, *Oda-Toyotomi seiken* (The Regimes of Oda Nobunaga and Toyotomi Hideyoshi) [II-08]; Kitajima Masamoto, *Edo bakufu* (The Tokugawa Bakufu) [II-09]; Asao Naohiro, *Sakoku* (National Seclusion) [II-10]; Kodama Kōta, *Daimyō* (Regional Lords of the Tokugawa Period) [II-11]; Bitō Masahide, *Genroku jidai* (The Genroku Period) [II-12]; Ōishi Shinzaburō, *Bakuhansei no tenkan* (Transformation of the *Bakuhan* System) [II-13]; Nakai Nobuhiko, *Chōnin* (The Townspeople of the Tokugawa Period) [II-14]; Tsuda Hideo, *Tenpō kaikaku* (The Tenpō Reforms) [II-15]; and Shibahara Takuji, *Kaikoku* (Japan Opens Its Doors) [II-16].

Other general works include the Japan Art Center edition, *Jinbutsu Nihon no rekishi* (Personalities of Japanese History) [II-17]; Sasaki Junnosuke, ed., *Nihon minshū no rekishi, 3, 4, 5* (A History of the Japanese People) [II-18] and Imai Shōji, et al., *Sho no Nihonshi* (Calligraphy in Japanese History) [II-19] which approach Japanese history from the perspectives of personality, popular disturbances and calligraphy, respectively. All are excellent studies, and Imai's work particularly recommends itself for the numerous plates in each volume with samples of calligraphy by several hundred historical figures, each supplied with background explanation. There is also a discussion of the particular writing styles typical of each period, a history of *sumi* ink, the *suzuri* (ink stone), *terakoya* (temple schools) and other topics related to the art of calligraphy.

A bit more specialized are the volumes of the Iwanami series *Nihon rekishi* (Japanese History) [II-20], nine and ten of which contain a detailed treatment of various topics on the early modern period, whose authors have the more serious researcher in mind.

An important work dealing with the philosophical foundations of popular history is Haga Noboru's *Minshūshi no sōzō* (Creating a Popular History) [II-21]. Born in 1890 in the home of a former samurai of Mito *han*, Yamakawa Kikue has collected anecdotes passed down in her family in *Oboegaki bakumatsu no Mito han* (Reminiscences of Mito-han in the Bakumatsu Period) [II-22], bringing to life the political situation during the final days of the shogunate. Several other excellent and useful biographic studies include Toyama Mikio's *Ōtomo Sōrin* [II-23], Kuwata Tadachika's *Tokugawa Tsunayoshi to Genroku jidai* (Tokugawa Tsunayoshi and the Genroku Era) [II-24], Miyazaki Michio's *Arai Hakuseki no jidai to sekai* (The World and Times of Arai Hakuseki) [II-25], Ōishi Shinzaburō's *Ōoka Echizen no kami Tadasuke* (Ōoka Tadasuke, Lord of Echizen) [II-26], Okamoto Ryōichi's *Ōshio Heihachirō* [II-27], Morita Shirō's *Ninomiya Sontoku* [II-28], Shinobu Seizaburō's *Shōzan to Shōin: kaikoku to jōi no ronri* (Sakuma Shōzan and Yoshida Shōin: The Logic of the "Open the Country" and "Expel the Barbarians" Policies) [II-29], Ishii Takashi's *Katsu Kaishū* [II-30], and Matsuura Rei's *Tokugawa Yoshinobu* [II-31].

Kitajima Masamoto has edited an account of the achievements and lives of the fifteen Tokugawa shoguns in *Tokugawa shōgun retsuden* (Biographies of the Tokugawa Shoguns) [II-32]. *Nihon kagakushi sanpo: Edoki no kagakushatachi* (The History of Science in Japan: A Study of Scientists of the Tokugawa Period) [II-33] discusses the accomplishments of thirty scientists in the early modern era. Author Ōya Shin'ichi visited their homesites and tombs and carried out extensive research on their writings to complete this worthwhile contribution to a little explored field.

III. Specialized Research

Several publications focus on the development of the social structure of the *bakuhan* system. Wakita Osamu's *Oda seiken no kiso kōzō: shokuhō seiken no bunseki, I* (The Basic Structure of the Oda Regime: An Analysis of Nobunaga and Hideyoshi's Power, I) [III-01] is primarily an examination of landholding practices of the period and an explanation of Nobunaga's system of control over rural areas. Yamaguchi Keiji, *Bakuhansei seiritsushi no kenkyū* (Historical Studies on the Establishment of the *Bakuhan* System) [III-02] is a discussion of three specific facets of the *bakuhan* system at the time it was established: Hideyoshi's regime, the creation and structure of the *han,* and the State and its logic under that system.

Shintei bakuhan taiseishi no kenkyū: kenryoku kōzō no kakuritsu to tenkai (History of the *Bakuhan* System: the Establishment and Development of Power Structure, revised edition) [III-03] by Fujino Tamotsu is devoted to an analysis of *bakuhan* power structure and its principles of organization. *Hansei seiritsuki no kenkyū* (A Study of the Period of *Han* Establishment) [III-04] by Kanai Madoka, is a study which drives at an explanation of the *han* system with particular attention to its formative period.

Until recently it was generally accepted that Osaka formed the commercial hub of the Tokugawa economy. However, new theories contend that commerce had two centers, one in Edo serving the Kantō and Tōhoku regions, and the other in Osaka serving the central and western regions of Honshu. The economy of the Edo sphere was based on gold currency, while that of Osaka was based on silver. The dual hub market theory is presented by Ōishi Shinzaburō in *Nihon kinsei shakai no shijō kōzō* (The Market Structure of Early Modern Japanese Society) [III-05], an important contribution to research on the establishment and structure of the *bakuhan* system.

Whether the social system devised by Nobunaga, Hideyoshi and Ieyasu is called "early modern society" or "*bakuhan taisei* society," all the above-mentioned studies share the view that Tokugawa society was feudal. However, some scholars believe that the generally accepted concept of feudalism as it was known in Europe does not adequately describe conditions in Japan during the early modern period, to which the term *hōken* refers. The power of the bakufu was enormous and these scholars contend that both the industrial economy and the bureaucracy had attained such high levels of development that the term "feudal" is inadequate in Japan's case. Iinuma Jirō is one of these, whose *Kokudakasei no kenkyū: Nihongata zettaishugi no kiso kōzō* (A Study of the *Kokudaka* System: The Fundamental Structure of Japanese Absolutism) [III-06] presents a unique approach, which proposes that the nature of the Tokugawa regime was absolutist, a transitional stage from medieval feudalism to modern capitalism. One volume of *Taikei Nihonshi sōsho* (Outline Series on Japanese History), *Tochi seidoshi II* (History of the Land System, Vol. II) [III-07], Kitajima Masamoto, ed., contains several articles on this issue, and those by Ōishi Shinzaburō on early-modern, and Fukushima Masao on post-Meiji period landholding practices merit special attention. Ōishi systematically analyzes the *bakuhan* landownership system from its early Edo period origins and its development over the centuries of Tokugawa rule. Nakabe Yoshiko's *Kinsei toshi shakai keizaishi kenkyū* (Studies of the Socio-Economic History of Early Modern Cities) [III-08] is a collection of some of her essays on urban research. *Edo chōnin no kenkyū, 4* (Research on the Edo Townsmen, Vol. 4) [III-09] edited by Nishiyama Matsunosuke, consists of five articles on town organization in the Edo period: "Machibugyō: Shōtoku izen o chūshin ni" (Town Magistrates before the 1711–1716 Period) by Tokoro Rikio; "Machibugyō: Kyōhō ikō o chūshin ni" (Town Magistrates after the 1716–1735 Period) by Minami Kazuo; "Machidoshiyori" (Town Elders) by Yoshihara Ken'ichiro; "Machi nanushi" (Town Heads) by Mizue Renko; and "Edo no machinanushi Saitō Gesshin" (Saitō Gesshin, Head of a District of Edo) by editor Nishiyama.

Using the wealth of data on commerce in the early modern period, Arai Eiji discusses the principal export items in *Kinsei kaisanbutsu bōekishi no kenkyu* (The History of Trade in Marine Products in the Early Modern Period) [III-10]. A study of economic conditions in rural areas emerges in Saku Takashi's *Kinsei nōson no sūteki kenkyū: Echizennokuni shūmon ninbetsu on'aratamechō no bunseki sōgō* (Quantitative Research on Early Modern Farm Villages: An Analysis of Temple Registration Records of Echizen Province) [III-11], from the records kept by temples of local citizenry. Rice was the staple product of the Tokugawa economy and *Kinsei beikoku kin'yūshi no kenkyū* (History of Rice Finance in the Early Modern Period) [III-12] by Dohi Noritaka, is an examination of the distribution of this crucial commodity.

Kinsei shukueki no kisoteki kenkyū (Basic Research on Post Towns of the Early Modern Period) [III-13] is Maruyama Yasunari's study of the relationship between official post stations and the adjacent farming villages. His research draws upon field work on the Warabi Inn and Toda ferry situated on the Nakasendō in what is now Saitama prefecture. Igarashi Tomio's *Kinsei sekisho seido no kenkyū* (Studies of the Check Station System of the Early Modern Period) [III-14] is a substantive analysis of the *sekisho* (barriers and checking stations) system through the records of Kōzuke province (present Gunma prefecture) and adjacent areas.

The office of commissioner (*bugyō*) at Uraga was set up in 1720 on the Miura peninsula to control traffic entering and leaving Edo Bay. The first authoritative study of this important shogunal office is Takahashi Kyōichi's *Uraga bugyōshi* (History of the Uraga Commissioners) [III-15].

Hayashiya Tatsusaburō's *Kinsei dentō bunka ron* (Traditional Culture of the Early Modern Period) [III-16] is a collection of essays on the lives and careers of cultural leaders of the Tokugawa period. *Kinsei no chika shinkō* (Underground Faiths of Early Modern Japan) [III-17] by Kataoka Yakichi, Tamamuro Fumio and Oguri Junko is a study of relations of *han* to religion, examining the groups of the Christian (*kakure-Kirishitan*), Jōdo Sect (*kakure-Nenbutsu*) and Nichiren Buddhist (*kakure-Daimoku*) followers who practiced their faith in hiding after suppression by *han* authority. (See also Religion, Folk religion, Section IV, p. 8)

Kimura Yōjirō provides an outline of the birth and development of the natural sciences in Japan in *Nihon shizenshi no seiritsu: rangaku to honsōgaku* (The Origins of Natural History Research in Japan: Dutch Learning and Botany) [III-18], bringing to life the personalities and achievements of the scientific world in the Edo period. The late Tokugawa period physician Sugita Genpaku (1733–1817) is the subject of a study by Uchiyama Kōichi which examines several different texts of *Rangaku kotohajime* (Founding Dutch Studies) and discusses the cultural implications of Genpaku's pioneering translation work [III-19].

A series handy for research on Japan's currency system has grown out of a project entitled *Zuroku Nihon no kahei* (Japan's Currency System Illustrated) by the Research Bureau of the Bank of Japan. Specialists have been recruited to contribute to the compilation of this series consisting largely of graphs and charts illustrating the study of monetary systems in Japan. Three titles published in this series are: *Kinsei heisei no tenkai* (The Evolution of Currency Systems in Early Modern Japan) [III-20] and *Kinsei shin'yō kahei no hattatsu* (Development of the Fiduciary Money System in the Early Modern Period), Volumes I and II, [III-21, 22].

Five volumes of *Chihōshi kenkyū sōsho* (Local History Research Series) have been published by the Council on Local Histories under the general editorship of chairman Kodama Kōta, gathering together relevant essays on specific themes and arranged by prefecture. An example of this splendid series is the volume on Aichi prefecture edited by long-time Aichi resident Hayashi Tōichi, *Owarihan kashindan no kenkyū* (Studies of the Retainers of Owari Han) [III-23]. The essays included are:

Part I

"Hansei kaikaku to Meiji ishin [Owari han]" (Han Government Reform and the Meiji Restoration in Owari Han) by Tokoro Mitsuo

"Owari han no zaisei to hansatsu" (The Financial System and Paper Currency of Owari Han) by Tokoro Mitsuo

Part II

"Shoki Owari han no kashin to kyūchi" (Retainers and Stipends in Early Owari Han) by Hata Tatsuya

"Jūnana seiki no Owari han kashindan no kōzō" (The Structure of Vassalage in Owari Han in the Seventeenth Century) by Maeda Kōji

"Kinsei ni okeru jitō no kenkyū" (A Study of *Jitō* in the Early Modern Period) by Funuki Hideo

"Edo jidai chūki Owari hanshi chigyō no kenkyū" (Studies of the Stipendiary Land of Owari Samurai during the Middle Edo Period) by Shinmi Kichiji

"Owari han no jitō to hyakushō" (Farmers and Shōen Managers of Owari Han) by Shinmi Kichiji

"Jitō ryōchiken no ichikōsatsu" (A Study of *Jitō* Rights to Fief) by Hayashi Tōichi

"Shibun no yashiki hairyō, kasaku shinchiku iten, yashikinai fuyōdo no jōto no tetsuzuki" (Procedures for Acceptance of Residences Bestowed by a Daimyo, Moving or Rebuilding of Residences and Transfer of Unused Land within Residence Compounds) by Shinmi Kichiji

"Owari han keihai no naishoku kōnin to rōsokushin ton'ya" (Official Permissions for Lower Grade Samurai in Owari Han to Take Part-time Employment and the Role of Candlewick Wholesalers) by Shinmi Kichiji

"Daikansho shitayakunin nōto" (Notes on Lower Ranking District Deputy Officials) by Kojima Kōji

"Bakumatsuki no kyūchi ni okeru kahei chidai no sonzai keitai" (Forms of Cash Payment of Rent during the Bakumatsu Period) by Kawaura Yasuji

"Hanseki hōkan to Kiso Fukushima Yamamurake" (Return of Lands and People to the Emperor and the Yamamura House of Kiso Fukushima) by Shinmi Kichiji

"Jitō ryōchiken no teppai" (Abolition of *Jitō* Rights to Fief) by Hayashi Tōichi.

A list of primary sources with annotations is appended to part one by Tokoro Mitsuo, "Owari kachū bugenkō" (Status Registry of Owari Retainers), and to part two by Morihara Akira and Shingyō Norikazu "Ōya Shigeharu ichidaiki" (A Biography of Ōya Shigeharu).

Other works on local history of mention are those on the history of Kumamoto prefecture edited by Morita Seiichi, *Higo Hosokawa han no kenkyū* (A Study of Hosokawa *Han*, Province of Higo) [III-24]; on Kanagawa prefecture, by Murakami Tadashi, *Kinsei Kanagawa no kenkyū* (A Study of Early Modern Kanagawa) [III-25]; on Toyama prefecture, by Sakai Seiichi, *Kinsei Etchū no shakai keizai kōzō* (Social and Economic Structure of Etchū Province in the Early Modern Era) [III-26] and on Tokushima prefecture, by Miyoshi Shōichirō, *Tokushima han no shiteki kōzō* (Historical Structure of Tokushima Han) [III-27].

The works of Furushima Toshio, a leading scholar of early modern agricultural history, published prior to World War II and in the confusion of the immediate postwar period, have been very difficult to obtain. Fortunately, altogether six volumes of Furushima's work were republished in 1974–75 in a multivolume set, the *Furushima Toshio chosakushū* (Collection of the Works of Furushima Toshio). The titles in this collection are:

Yōeki rōdōsei no hōkai katei (The Dissolution of the Corvée Labor System) [III-28]

Nihon hōken nōgyō shi (History of Feudal Agriculture in Japan) and *Kazoku keitai to nōgyō no hattatsu* (Familial Patterns and the Development of Agriculture) [III-29]

Kinsei Nihon nōgyō no kōzō (The Structure of Agriculture in Early Modern Japan) [III-30]

Shinshū chūma no kenkyū (A Study of Transport Horses in Shinano Province) [III-31]

Nihon nōgakushi (History of Japanese Agricultural Science), Vol. 1 [III-32]

Nihon nōgyō gijutsushi (History of Agricultural Technology in Japan) [III-33].

IV. DOCUMENTS AND SOURCE MATERIALS

The outstanding feature of publications during the 1974–75 period is the abundance of documents and other source materials dealing with early modern history. Of these only the most important can be included here.

Of all the aspects of historical study in early modern Japan, the least progress has been made in the study of Tokugawa intellectual history, one reason being that relatively few scholars are working in this field. Another reason is the inaccessibility of relevant primary sources. In this sense, *Nihon shisō taikei* (Iwanami Library of Japanese Thought), published by Iwanami Shoten, is a valuable contribution which goes far in filling the gaps in basic tools for further research. In Japan, we do not always assume that publishers will print important manuscripts with quality commentary, but Iwanami has done its utmost to produce a reference work of high standard. Considering that the value of source works differs according to the reader's ability and perspective, it may be thought most desirable to keep explanatory notes to a minimum so as to avoid inconveniencing advanced users. However, from the point of view that, compared to other aspects of history, intellectual history is less blessed with numbers of scholars and quantities of reference materials, the detailed notes included in this series are very helpful.

Another virtue of the series is that the excellent introductory essays for each volume are of such a quality that they can stand on their own. The volumes published during the 1974–75 period are: *Mikawa monogatari, Hagakure* (The Tales of Mikawa, The Hagakure) [IV-01] compiled by Saiki Kazuma, Okayama Yasushi and Sagara Tōru; *Nakae Tōju* (Nakae Tōju, 1608–1648) [IV-02] by Yamanoi Yū, Yamashita Ryūji, Kaji Nobuyuki and Bitō Masahide; *Kinsei buke shisō* (Warrior Class Ideology in the Early Modern Era) [IV-03] by Ishii Shirō; *Seiyō kenbunshū* (Accounts of Travel in the West) [IV-04], eds., Numata Jirō and Matsuzawa Hiroaki; *Arai Hakuseki* [IV-05], edited by Matsumura Akira, Bitō Masahide and Katō Shūichi; *Fujiwara Seika, Hayashi Razan*, edited by Ishida Ichirō and Kanaya Osamu [IV-06]; and *Kinsei chōnin shisō* (Values and Ideals of the Townsmen of Tokugawa Japan) [IV-07] edited by Nakamura Yukihiko.

Until several years ago research on urban history was far behind that on rural or regional history, but this period evidences a greater interest in study of the city in history as shown by the numerous monograph titles as well as the publication of pertinent source materials. Among the latter is the *Nihon toshi seikatsu shiryō shūsei* (Collection of Historical Materials on Japanese Urban Life), edited by Harada Tomohiko, which when complete, will be a definitive reference source in urban history. So far in this series are *Jōkamachi hen I* (Castle Towns, Part I) [IV-08] and *Minatomachi hen I* (Port Towns, Part I) [IV-09]. The first focuses on the activities of merchants and samurai living in castle towns in Shikoku and Kyushu, while the second is a collection of valuable letters and geographical notes and observations made by Shinto priests and government officials in Kyushu, Tsuruga, Mikunihama and Niigata.

During 1974 and 1975, three further volumes on the Tenpō era were published in the *Osaka hennenshi* (The Chronicles of Osaka) collection of documents on this great commercial center of the Edo period. Volume eighteen, [IV-10] deals with the period from January 1834 to February 1837; volume nineteen [IV-11] with February 1837 to December 1839, and volume twenty [IV-12] with January 1840 to September 1843. The *Hakatatsu yōroku* (Record of Hakata Port), Vol. 1, [IV-13] by Hidemura Senzō is a historical chronicle of Hakata (present-day Fukuoka city), the most prosperous port in Kyushu during the late Sengoku and Edo periods. The first volume contains information on the period from 1666 to 1736.

Of special mention is the publication by the Japan Monopoly Corporation of an immense collection of documents on the manufacture of that vital item of human existence, salt. In ancient Japan, earthenware vessels were used in extracting salt from sea water, later *agehama* and *irihama* (methods of dispersion and evaporation in beach ponds) were used, yielding after World War II to the *ryūkashiki* (evaporation in artificially made clay or vinyl ponds) method. These salt fields vanished completely when the ion exchange method of salt production was adopted in 1965, and with the ancient techniques destined to fade into history, the *Engyō taikei* (Outline of Salt Manufacture) is devoted to recording the story of these major salt farming methods of traditional Japan. Volumes one and four of this series, subtitled *Shiryōhen: kinsei* (Historical Materials—Early Modern Period) [IV-14, 15] were published in this period. Volume one contains the household documents of the respective operators of each salt farm, Akō of Harima, Kojima of Bizen, Yūzaki of Bitchū, Tomihama of Bingo, Nagahama of Suō, Hashihama and Takihama of Iyo, and Sakaide and Shōdoshima of Sanuki. Volume four includes the "Takehara endenshi" (Records of Takehara Salt Field) kept by Koyama Hideoki of Takehara, Hiroshima prefecture, an area famous for its salt fields. The records are now at the municipal library in Takehara. This volume is a most valuable historical reference for the study of salt manufacturing as it encompasses the period from the middle of the seventeenth to the beginning of the twentieth century and deals also with management, labor, sale and production.

In *Kyūluku kyūryō torishirabechō* (Records of the Investigations of Tokugawa Period Stipends and Domains), Kimura Motoi has restored old lists of village *kokudaka* (land assessments for taxation) and proprietorship records as surveyed in the first year of the Meiji period. "Kinki hen" (The Kinki Region) [VI-16] in the series, was published during 1974–75 as a continuation of a previously published volume on the Kantō region. The structure and composition of Edo bakufu offices such as *gundai* (district deputy) and *daikan* (local magistrates) in the period after 1839 are described in *Edo bakufu daikan shiryō, kenrei shūran* (Documents on the Bakufu Magistrates Appointed to the Provinces: Directory of Prefectural Governors) [IV-17] edited by Murakami Tadashi and Arakawa Hidetoshi, a convenient source of information on Tokugawa techniques for direct control of shogunal domains.

The last volume of the diary of Ōoka Tadasuke, official of the bakufu administration throughout most of the rule of eighth shogun, Yoshimune, has now been published, covering the period between 1747 and 1751 [IV-18].

A third volume of documents has been published on the Hakone border check station on the Tōkaidō highway, probably the most important of these offices set up in the Edo period for surveillance of persons and goods moving from one province to another [IV-19]. The second [IV-20] and third [IV-21] volumes have been published of *Fuchō yoroku* (Supplementary Genealogical Records), a compilation of documents from the Jōkyō era (1684–1686) that the Tokugawa issued to their daimyo and *hatamoto*. Mention should be made of the publication of the *Oranda shōkanchō nisshi* (Diaries of the Dutch Factors) Part II, Translation, Vols. 1 and 2 [IV-22, 23].

Four major compilations of daimyo family records have been published, including volumes four, five and six of *Date chika kiroku* (Records of the House of Date) [IV-24, 25, 26] compiled by the Date family, formerly lords of the Sendai *han*; the first volume of the *Aizu han kasei jikki* (Genealogy of Aizu *Han*) [IV-27], a chronicle compiled by the Matsudaira of the former Aizu Wakamatsu *han*; the *Kōyoroku* Volume I, [IV-28], a compilation of family records of Lord Abe of Tanakura in Iwaki province, and the *Eiho kijiryaku* (Record for Posterity) [IV-29], a collection of diaries kept by the *jōdaigarō* (senior councillor left in charge of the domain in the absence of the daimyo) of Tōdō *han* in Tsu, Ise province.

In addition, there are numerous works of a historical, descriptive nature on prefectures, counties, cities, towns and villages, but space prevents a detailed listing. Finally, the *Mitamura Engyo zenshū* (Collected Works of Mitamura Engyo) [IV-30], should be mentioned, volumes two, six, seven, eight, ten, eleven, thirteen, fourteen and sixteen of which were published during the 1974–75 period.

文　　献

I-01　佐々木潤之介（編）Sasaki Junnosuke (ed.)『大系・日本国家史 3』（近世）
　　　 Studies in the History of the Japanese State, Vol. 3 (The Early Modern Period),
　　　 341 pp., 東京大学出版会, 1975.

　 02　原田伴彦 Harada Tomohiko『被差別部落の歴史』*The History of the Outcaste
　　　 Communities*, 395 pp., 朝日新聞社, 1975.

　 03　石尾芳久 Ishio Yoshihisa 『被差別部落起源論』*The Origin of the Buraku Com-
　　　 munities*, 144 pp., 大鐸社, 1975.

　 04　更池村文書研究会（編）Saraike Village Documents Research Association
　　　 (ed.)『河内国更池村文書』（第 3 巻）*Documents of Saraike Village, Kawachi
　　　 Province*, Vol. 3, 1158 pp., 部落解放研究所, 1975.

　 05　奥田家文書研究会 Okuda Family Documents Research Group『奥田家文
　　　 書』（第 12 巻, 第 13 巻）*Documents of the Okuda Family*, Vols. 12 and 13, 1128
　　　 pp.; 1181 pp., 大阪府同和事業促進協議会, 1975.

II-01　荒居英次（編）Arai Eiji (ed.)『日本近世史入門』*Introduction to Early Modern
　　　 Japanese History*, 567 pp., 小宮山出版, 1974.

　 02　西山松之助他（編）Nishiyama Matsunosuke, et al. (eds.)『歴史の視点』（中）
　　　 Perspectives on History, Vol. 2, 502 pp., 日本放送出版協会, 1975.

　 03　新保　博・速水　融他 Shimbo Hiroshi, Hayami Akira, et al.『数量経済史入
　　　 門』*Introduction to Quantitative Economic History*, 290 pp., 日本評論社, 1975.

　 04　井上光貞・永原慶二（編）Inoue Mitsusada and Nagahara Keiji (eds.)『日本
　　　 史研究入門』(IV) *Introduction to Research on Japanese History*, Vol. 4, 415 pp.,
　　　 東京大学出版会, 1975.

　 05　地方史研究協議会（編）Council for Research on Local History (ed.)『日本史
　　　 文献年鑑 75』*Annual Bibliography of Japanese History, 1975*, 574 pp., 柏書房,
　　　 1974.

　 06　井上鋭夫 Inoue Toshio『信長と秀吉』*Nobunaga and Hideyoshi* [日本の歴史文
　　　 庫 10] 333 pp., 講談社, 1975.
　　　 中田易直 Nakata Yasunao『江戸幕府』*The Edo Bakufu* [日本の歴史文庫 11]
　　　 365 pp., 講談社, 1975.
　　　 大石慎三郎 Ōishi Shinzaburō『庶民の抬頭』*Rise of the Commoners* [日本の歴
　　　 史文庫 12] 309 pp., 講談社, 1975.
　　　 沼田次郎 Numata Jirō『開国前後』*Opening the Doors* [日本の歴史文庫 13] 318
　　　 pp., 講談社, 1975.

　 07　今井林太郎（編）Imai Rintarō (ed.)『天下統一』*Unifying the Country* [図説日
　　　 本の歴史 9] 267 pp., 集英社, 1975.
　　　 岡田章雄（編）Okada Akio (ed.)『キリシタンの世紀』*The Christian Century*

[図説日本の歴史 10] 263 pp., 集英社, 1975.

箭内健次 (編) Yanai Kenji (ed.) 『江戸の開幕』 *Establishment of the Edo Bakufu* [図説日本の歴史 11] 263 pp., 集英社, 1975.

児玉幸多 (編) Kodama Kōta (ed.) 『変動する幕政』 *Change in the Tokugawa Government* [図説日本の歴史 12] 263 pp., 集英社, 1975.

08　藤木久志 Fujiki Hisashi 『織田・豊臣政権』 *The Regimes of Oda Nobunaga and Toyotomi Hideyoshi* [日本の歴史 15] 390 pp., 小学館, 1975.

09　北島正元 Kitajima Masamoto 『江戸幕府』 *The Tokugawa Bakufu* [日本の歴史 16] 406 pp., 小学館, 1975.

10　朝尾直弘 Asao Naohiro 『鎖国』 *National Seclusion* [日本の歴史 17] 406 pp., 小学館, 1975.

11　児玉幸多 Kodama Kōta 『大名』 *Regional Lords of the Tokugawa Period* [日本の歴史 18] 374 pp., 小学館, 1975.

12　尾藤正英 Bitō Masahide 『元禄時代』 *The Genroku Period* [日本の歴史 19] 358 pp., 小学館, 1975.

13　大石慎三郎 Ōishi Shinzaburō 『幕藩制の転換』 *Transformation of the Bakuhan System* [日本の歴史 20] 390 pp., 小学館, 1975.

14　中井信彦 Nakai Nobuhiko 『町人』 *The Townspeople of the Tokugawa Period* [日本の歴史 21] 390 pp., 小学館, 1975.

15　津田秀夫 Tsuda Hideo 『天保改革』 *The Tenpō Reforms* [日本の歴史 22] 422 pp., 小学館, 1975.

16　芝原拓自 Shibahara Takuji 『開国』 *Japan Opens Its Doors* [日本の歴史 23] 390 pp., 小学館, 1975.

17　日本アートセンター (編) The Japan Art Center (ed.) 『人物日本の歴史』 *Personalities in Japanese History*, 小学館, 1975.

『江戸の開府』 *Beginnings of the Edo Government* [人物日本の歴史 11] 281 pp.

『元禄の時代』 *The Age of Genroku* [人物日本の歴史 12] 265 pp.

『豪商と篤農』 *Wealthy Merchants and Industrious Farmers* [人物日本の歴史 14] 275 pp.

『封建の異端』 *Heresy of Feudalism* [人物日本の歴史 15] 267 pp.

『開国と攘夷』 *"Open the Country" vs. "Expel the Barbarians"* [人物日本の歴史 18] 277 pp.

『近世の芸道』 *The Arts in the Early Modern Period* [人物日本の歴史 17] 267 pp.

18　佐々木潤之介 (編) Sasaki Junnosuke (ed.) 『日本民衆の歴史』 *A History of Japanese People*, 三省堂, 1974.

『天下統一と民衆』 *National Consolidation and the Common People* [日本民衆の歴史 3] 355 pp.

『世直し』 *Reform* [日本民衆の歴史 5] 399 pp.

『百姓一揆と打ちこわし』 *Peasant Revolts and Uprisings* [日本民衆の歴史 4]

409 pp.

19 今井庄次ほか（編）Imai Shōji, et al. (eds.) 『書の日本史』 *Calligraphy in Japanese History*, 平凡社, 1975.
『安土桃山・江戸初期』*Azuchi-Momoyama and Early Edo Periods* [書の日本史 5] 275 pp.
『江戸』 *The Edo Period* [書の日本史 6] 305 pp.

20 『岩波講座 日本歴史 9』（近世 1）*Iwanami Lectures on Japanese History*, Vol. 9 (Early Modern Period 1), 341 pp., 岩波書店, 1975.
『岩波講座 日本歴史 10』（近世 2）*Iwanami Lectures on Japanese History*, Vol. 10 (Early Modern Period 2), 366 pp., 岩波書店, 1975.

21 芳賀　登 Haga Noboru 『民衆史の創造』 *Creating a Popular History*, 216 pp., 日本放送出版協会, 1974.

22 山川菊栄 Yamakawa Kikue 『覚書幕末の水戸藩』 *Reminiscences of Mito-han in the Bakumatsu Period*, 417 pp., 岩波書店, 1974.

23 外山幹夫 Toyama Mikio 『大友宗麟』 *Ōtomo Sōrin* [人物叢書 172] 344 pp., 吉川弘文館, 1975.

24 桑田忠親 Kuwata Tadachika 『徳川綱吉と元禄時代』 *Tokugawa Tsunayoshi and the Genroku Era*, 261 pp., 秋田書店, 1975.

25 宮崎道生 Miyazaki Michio 『新井白石の時代と世界』 *The World and Times of Arai Hakuseki*, 224 pp., 吉川弘文館, 1975.

26 大石慎三郎 Ōishi Shinzaburō 『大岡越前守忠相』 *Ōoka Tadasuke, Lord of Echizen* [岩波新書] 215 pp., 岩波書店, 1974.

27 岡本良一 Okamoto Ryōichi 『大塩平八郎』（改訂版）*Ōshio Heihachirō* (Revised), 282 pp., 創元社, 1975.

28 守田志郎 Morita Shirō 『二宮尊徳』 *Ninomiya Sontoku* [朝日評伝選 2] 268 pp., 朝日新聞社, 1975.

29 信夫清三郎 Shinobu Seizaburō 『象山と松陰――開国と攘夷の論理――』 *Sakuma Shozan and Yoshida Shōin, The Logic of the "Open the Country" and "Expel the Barbarians" Policies*, 322 pp., 河出書房新社, 1975.

30 石井　孝 Ishii Takashi 『勝海舟』 *Katsu Kaishū* [人物叢書 178] 284 pp., 吉川弘文館, 1974.

31 松浦　玲 Matsuura Rei 『徳川慶喜』 *Tokugawa Yoshinobu*, 203 pp., 中央公論社, 1975.

32 北島正元（編）Kitajima Masamoto (ed.) 『徳川将軍列伝』 *Biographies of the Tokugawa Shoguns*, 461 pp., 秋田書店, 1974.

33 大矢真一 Ōya Shin'ichi 『日本科学史散歩――江戸期の科学者たち――』 *The History of Science in Japan: A Study of Scientists of the Tokugawa Period* [自然選書] 254 pp., 中央公論社, 1974.

III-01 脇田　修 Wakita Osamu 『織田政権の基礎構造――織豊政権の分析 I――』

64

The Basic Structure of the Oda Regime: An Analysis of Nobunaga and Hideyoshi's Power (I), 327 pp., 東京大学出版会, 1975.

02 山口啓二 Yamaguchi Keiji『幕藩制成立史の研究』 *Historical Studies on the Establishment of the Bakuhan System*, 388 pp., 校倉書房, 1974.

03 藤野　保 Fujino Tamotsu『新訂幕藩体制史の研究——権力構造の確立と展開——』 *History of the Bakuhan System: The Establishment and Development of Power Structure* (Revised), 954 pp., 吉川弘文館, 1975.

04 金井　圓 Kanai Madoka『藩制成立期の研究』 *A Study of the Period of Han Establishment*, 548 pp., 吉川弘文館, 1975.

05 大石慎三郎 Ōishi Shinzaburō『日本近世社会の市場構造』 *The Market Structure of Early Modern Japanese Society*, 340 pp., 岩波書店, 1975.

06 飯沼二郎 Iinuma Jirō『石高制の研究——日本型絶対主義の基礎構造——』 *A Study of the Kokudaka System: The Fundamental Structure of Japanese Absolutism*, 214 pp., ミネルヴァ書房, 1974.

07 北島正元（編）Kitajima Masamoto (ed.)『土地制度史 II』 *History of the Land System*, Vol. 2 [体系日本史叢書 7] 405 pp., 山川出版社, 1975.

08 中部よし子 Nakabe Yoshiko『近世都市社会経済史研究』 *Studies of the Socio-economic History of Early Modern Cities*, 263 pp., 晃洋書房, 1974.

09 西山松之助（編）Nishiyama Matsunosuke (ed.)『江戸町人の研究』（第 4 巻） *Research on the Edo Townsmen*, Vol. 4, 533 pp., 吉川弘文館, 1579.

10 荒居英次 Arai Eiji『近世海産物貿易史の研究——中国向け輸出貿易と海産物——』 *The History of Trade in Marine Products in the Early Modern Period: Export Trade to China and Marine Products*, 599 pp., 吉川弘文館, 1975.

11 佐久高士 Saku Takashi『近世農村の数的研究——越前国宗門人別御改帳の分析綜合——』 *Quantitative Research on Early Modern Farm Villages: An Analysis of Temple Registration Records of Echizen Province*, 590 pp., 吉川弘文館, 1975.

12 土肥鑑高 Dohi Noritaka『近世米穀金融史の研究』 *History of Rice Finance in the Early Modern Period*, 280 pp., 柏書房, 1974.

13 丸山雍成 Maruyama Yasunari『近世宿駅の基礎的研究』（第 1, 第 2）*Basic Research on Post Towns of the Early Modern Period*, Vols. 1 and 2, 1188 pp.; 762 pp., 吉川弘文館, 1975.

14 五十嵐富夫 Igarashi Tomio『近世関所制度の研究』 *Studies of the Check Station System of the Early Modern Period*, 645 pp., 有峰書店, 1975.

15 高橋恭一 Takahashi Kyōichi 『浦賀奉行史』 *History of the Uraga Commissioners*, 1132 pp., 名著出版, 1974.

16 林屋辰三郎 Hayashiya Tatsusaburō『近世伝統文化論』 *Traditional Culture of the Early Modern Period*, 324 pp., 創元社, 1974.

17 片岡弥吉・圭室文雄・小栗純子 Kataoka Yakichi, Takamuro Fumio and Oguri Junko『近世の地下信仰』 *Underground Faiths of Early Modern Japan*, 328

pp., 評論社, 1974.

18 木村陽二郎 Kimura Yōjirō 『日本自然誌の成立──蘭学と本草学──』 *The Origins of Natural History Research in Japan: Dutch Learning and Botany* [自然選書] 386 pp., 中央公論社, 1974.

19 内山孝一 Uchiyama Kōichi 『和蘭事始──「蘭学事始」古写本の校訂と研究──』 *The Beginnings of Dutch Studies in Japan: Research and Text Critique of the "Rangaku Kotohajime" Codices* [自然選書] 194 pp., 中央公論社, 1974.

20 日本銀行調査局 Bank of Japan Research Bureau 『近世幣制の展開』 *The Evolution of Currency Systems in Early Modern Japan* [図録日本の貨幣 3] 354 pp., 東洋経済新報社, 1974.

21 日本銀行調査局 Bank of Japan Research Bureau 『近世信用貨幣の発達 1』 *Development of the Fiduciary Money System in the Early Modern Period*, Vol. 1 [図録日本の貨幣 5] 322 pp., 東洋経済新報社, 1974.

22 日本銀行調査局 Bank of Japan Research Bureau 『近世信用貨幣の発達 2』 *Development of the Fudiciary Money System in the Early Modern Period*, Vol. 2 [図録日本の貨幣 6] 324 pp., 東洋経済新報社, 1975.

23 林　董一 (編) Hayashi Tōichi (ed.) 『尾張藩家臣団の研究』 *Studies of the Retainers of Owari Han* [地方史研究叢書 6] 488 pp., 名著出版, 1975.

24 森田誠一 (編) Morita Seiichi (ed.) 『肥後細川藩の研究』 *A Study of Hosokawa Han, Province of Higo* [地方史研究叢書 2] 362 pp., 名著出版, 1974.

25 村上　直 (編) Murakami Tadashi (ed.) 『近世神奈川の研究』 *A Study of Early Modern Kanagawa* [地方史研究叢書 3] 374 pp., 名著出版, 1975.

26 坂井誠一 (編) Sakai Seiichi (ed.) 『近世越中の社会経済構造』 *Social Economic Structure of Etchū Province in the Early Modern Era* [地方史研究叢書 4] 374 pp., 名著出版, 1975.

27 三好昭一郎 (編) Miyoshi Shōichirō (ed.) 『徳島藩の史的構造』 *Historical Structure of Tokushima Han* [地方史研究叢書 5] 296 pp., 名著出版, 1975.

28 古島敏雄 Furushima Toshio 『徭役労働制の崩壊過程』 *The Dissolution of the Corvée Labor System* [古島敏雄著作集 第 1 巻] 294 pp., 東京大学出版会, 1974.

29 古島敏雄 Furushima Toshio 『日本封建農業史家族形態と農業の発達』 *History of Feudal Agriculture in Japan: Familial Patterns and the Development of Agriculture* [古島敏雄著作集 第 2 巻] 370 pp., 東京大学出版会, 1974.

30 古島敏雄 Furushima Toshio 『近世日本農業の構造』 *The Structure of Agriculture in Early Modern Japan* [古島敏雄著作集 第 3 巻] 576 pp., 東京大学出版会, 1974.

31 古島敏雄 Furushima Toshio 『信州中馬の研究』 *A Study of Transport Horses in Shinano Province* [古島敏雄著作集 第 4 巻] 416 pp., 東京大学出版会, 1974.

32 古島敏雄 Furushima Toshio 『日本農学史第 1 巻』 *History of Japanese Agricultural Science*, Vol. 1 [古島敏雄著作集 第 5 巻] 492 pp., 東京大学出版会, 1975.

33 古島敏雄 Furushima Toshio『日本農業技術史』*History of Agricultural Technology in Japan* [古島敏雄著作集 第6巻] 672 pp., 東京大学出版会, 1975.

IV–01 斎木一馬・岡山泰四・相良 亨 (校注) Saiki Kazuma, Okayama Yasushi and Sagara Tōru (eds.)『三河物語・葉隠』*The Tales of Mikawa; The Hagakure* [日本思想大系 26] 702 pp., 岩波書店, 1974.

02 山井 湧・山下竜二・加地伸行・尾藤正英 (校注) Yamanoi Yū, Yamashita Ryūji, Kaji Nobuyuki and Bitō Masahide (eds.)『中江藤樹』*Nakae Tōju* [日本思想大系 29] 501 pp., 岩波書店, 1974.

03 石井紫郎 Ishii Shirō『近世武家思想』*Warrior Class Ideology in the Early Modern Period* [日本思想大系 27] 542 pp., 岩波書店, 1974.

04 沼田次郎・松沢弘陽 Numata Jirō and Matsuzawa Hiroaki『西洋見聞集』*Accounts of Travel in the West* [日本思想大系 66] 684 pp., 岩波書店, 1974.

05 松村 明・尾藤正英・加藤周一 (校注) Matsumura Akira, Bitō Masahide and Katō Shūichi (eds.)『新井白石』*Arai Hakuseki* [日本思想大系 35] 617 pp., 岩波書店, 1975.

06 石田一良・金谷 治 (校注) Ishida Ichirō and Kanaya Osamu (eds.)『藤原惺窩・林羅山』*Fujiwara Seika, Hayashi Razan* [日本思想大系 28] 520 pp., 岩波書店, 1975.

07 中村幸彦 (校注) Nakamura Yukihiko (ed.)『近世町人思想』*Values and Ideals of the Townsmen of Tokugawa Japan* [日本思想大系 59] 445 pp., 岩波書店, 1975.

08 原田伴彦 (編) Harada Tomohiko (ed.)『日本都市生活史料集成 3』(城下町篇 I) *Collection of Historical Materials on Japanese Urban Life*, Vol. 3 (Castle Towns, Part 1), 664 pp., 学習研究社, 1975.

09 原田伴彦 (編) Harada Tomohiko (ed.)『日本都市生活史料集成 6』(港町篇 I) *Collection of Historical Materials on Japanese Urban Life*, Vol. 6 (Port Towns, Part I), 680 pp., 学習研究社, 1975.

10 大阪市立中央図書館市史編集室 Osaka City Central Library, City History Room (ed.)『大阪編年史』(第18巻) *The Chronicles of Osaka*, Vol. 18, 385 pp., 大阪市立中央図書館, 1974.

11 大阪市立中央図書館市史編集室 (編) Osaka City Central Library, City History Room (ed.)『大阪編年史』(第19巻) *The Chronicles of Osaka*, Vol. 19, 403 pp., 大阪市立中央図書館, 1975.

12 大阪市立中央図書館市史編集室 (編) Osaka City Central Library, City History Room (ed.)『大阪編年史』(第20巻) *The Chronicles of Osaka*, Vol. 20, 417 pp., 大阪市立中央図書館, 1975.

13 秀村選三 (校注) Hidemura Senzō (ed.)『博多津要録』(第1巻) *Records of Hakata Port*, Vol. 1, 646 pp., 西日本文化協会, 1975.

14 日本塩業大系編集委員会 Editorial Committee for the Series on Japanese Salt

Manufacture 『日本塩業大系 史料篇』(近世 1) *Series on Salt Manufacture in Japan: Historical Materials* (Early Modern Period 1), 1045 pp., 日本専売公社, 1975.

15 日本塩業大系編集委員会 Editorial Committee for the Series on Japanese Salt Manufacture 『日本塩業大系 史料篇』(近世 4) *Series on Salt Manufacture in Japan: Historical Materials* (Early Modern Period 4), 1249 pp., 日本専売公社, 1975.

16 木村 礎 (校訂) Kimura Motoi (ed.) 『旧高旧領取調帳 近畿編』 *Records of the Investigations of Tokugawa Period Stipends and Domains: The Kinki Region* [日本史料選書 11] 492 pp., 近藤出版社, 1975.

17 村上 直・荒川秀俊 (編) Murakami Tadashi and Arakawa Hidetoshi (eds.) 『江戸幕府代官史料 ——県令集覧——』 *Documents on the Bakufu Magistrates Appointed to the Provinces: Directory of Prefectural Governors*, 456 pp., 吉川弘文館, 1975.

18 大岡家文書刊行会 Ōoka Family Documents Publication Committee 『大岡越前守忠相日記』(下巻) *The Diary of Ōoka Tadasuke, Lord of Echizen*, Vol. 2, 752 pp., 三一書房, 1975.

19 箱根関所研究会 (編) Association for Research on the Hakone Sekisho, (ed.) 『東海道箱根宿関所史料集 3』 *Collection of Historical Sources on the Tōkaidō Hakone Border Check Station*, Vol. 3, 430 pp., 吉川弘文館, 1975.

20 国立公文書館内閣文庫 National Archives Cabinet Library (ed.) 『譜牒餘録』 (中) *Supplementary Genealogical Records*, Vol. 2, 911 pp., 国立公文書館, 1974.

21 国立公文書館内閣文庫 National Archives Cabinet Library (ed.) 『譜牒餘録』 (下) *Supplementary Genealogical Records*, Vol. 3, 955 pp., 国立公文書館, 1975.

22 東京大学史料編纂所 (編) Tokyo University Historiographical Research Institute (ed.) 『オランダ商館長日誌 訳文編之 2』(上) *Diaries of the Dutch Factors: Part II, Translation*, Vol. 1 [日本関係海外史料] 202 pp., 東京大学出版会, 1975.

23 東京大学史料編纂所 (編) Tokyo University Historiographical Research Institute (ed.) 『オランダ商館長日誌 訳文編之 2』(下) *Diaries of the Dutch Factors: Part II, Translation*, Vol. 2 [日本関係海外史料] 212 pp., 東京大学出版会, 1975.

24 平 重道 (編) Taira Shigemichi (ed.) 『伊達治家記録 4』 *Records of the House of Date*, Vol. 4, 500 pp., 宝文堂出版販売㈱会社, 1974.

25 平 重道 (編) Taira Shigemichi (ed.) 『伊達治家記録 5』 *Records of the House of Date*, Vol. 5, 679 pp., 宝文堂出版販売㈱会社, 1974.

26 平 重道 (編) Taira Shigemichi (ed.) 『伊達治家記録 6』 *Records of the House of Date*, Vol. 6, 644 pp., 宝文堂出版販売㈱会社, 1975.

27 豊田 武 (監修) Toyota Takeshi (gen. ed.) 『会津藩家世実紀』(第 1 巻)

Genealogy of Aizu Han, Vol. 1, 682 pp., 吉川弘文館, 1975.

28 児玉幸多 (校訂) Kodama Kōta (ed.)『阿部家史料集 1 公餘録』(上) *Collection of Historical Materials on the House of Abe*, Vol. 1 (*Kōyoroku*, Part 1), 529 pp., 吉川弘文館, 1975.

29 上野市古文献刊行会 (編) Ueno City Association for the Publication of Historical Documents (ed.)『永保記事略──藤堂藩城代家老日誌──』*Records for Posterity: Diaries of the Jōdaigarō of Tōdō-han*, 560 pp., 同朋舎出版部, 1974.

30 三田村鳶魚 Mitamura Engyo『三田村鳶魚全集』(2, 6, 7, 8, 10, 11, 13, 14, 16), *Collected Works of Mitamura Engyo*, Vols. 2, 6, 7, 8, 10, 11, 13, 14, 16, 398 pp.; 401 pp.; 390 pp.; 386 pp.; 387 pp.; 380pp.; 384 pp.; 385 pp.; 403 pp., 中央公論社, 1975.

JAPANESE HISTORY —MODERN PERIOD

Itō Takashi
University of Tokyo
Arima Manabu
University of Kyushu

Translated by Ronald P. Loftus

I. Introduction

During the past two years, there have been no striking new developments or significant new trends emerging in research on modern Japanese history. As usual, the Marxist perspective, whether in its narrowly dogmatic or more flexible revisionist form, continues to play an important role in shaping historical research. However, a survey of recent research in the field would show that positivist or empirical research, that is, research founded on a careful scrutinizing of all relevant documents and historical materials, is also well represented. In this connection, we should note the recently industrious efforts in uncovering new primary materials and preparing them for publication. Many of the studies appearing now are attempts to organize, classify and rationally interpret these newly discovered materials. Even so, in terms of quantity, the primary thrust of research is still the narrowly focused monograph treating in detail some specific problem. Consequently, there persists a dearth of broad and comprehensive analyses of the major issues in modern Japanese history.

Likewise, there have been few attempts to write synoptic histories of the modern period. A possible exception is a recent cooperative endeavor by American and Japanese scholars to present an overall structure of Japan's outlook toward the rest of the world during the modern period. Featuring a variety of approaches to numerous topics,

Satō Seizaburō and Roger Dingman, eds., *Kindai Nihon no taigai taido* (Japan Looks at the World) [I-01] analyzes Japanese perceptions of and attitudes toward other nations as the basic element of foreign policy formation and diplomatic negotiation.

An important event for the field of Japanese history as a whole was the appearance in 1975, under new editorship, of *Iwanami kōza Nihon rekishi* (Iwanami Lectures on Japanese History) [I-02], a multivolume series of essays by leading specialists. This new series replaces the earlier version published a decade ago which until now has been considered a definitive work in the field. Although all the essays in the recent volumes are new, the format is essentially the same: each of the twenty-six volumes contains a series of between five and eight thematic essays which together provide a comprehensive treatment of a particular period. During the period under review here, two volumes treating the modern period appeared. *Kindai, 1*, treats the early Meiji years while *Kindai, 5*, focuses on the Taishō period. On the whole, the essays in these volumes reflect the Marxist viewpoint. Let us now turn to a detailed examination of the major publications in 1974 and 1975 according to subject matter.

II. POLITICAL HISTORY—MEIJI

Although the class struggle approach is still the most widely used frame for analyzing political change in the bakumatsu and Meiji Restoration period, no novel interpretation or thoroughly convincing treatment has yet to be produced. Therefore, it is sufficient to note one representative work by Takagi Shunsuke, *Meiji ishin sōmō undōshi* (A History of Grass-roots Movements and the Meiji Restoration) (Keisō Shobō, 1974). In contrast to this treatment is Inoue Isao, "Bakumatsu ishinki ni okeru 'Kōgi-yoron' kannen no shosō" (The Various Dimensions of "Kōgi-yoron" [arriving at political decisions through consultation and debate] in Late Tokugawa and Early Meiji Japan), an essay which appears in *Shisō* magazine No. 609 (March 1975). In this article, Inoue proposes a new framework for understanding basic political developments during these crucial years.

Looking at the same period from a different angle is Satō Seizaburō's essay "Bakumatsu-Meiji shoki ni okeru taigai ishiki no shoruikei"

(Patterns in Japanese Attitudes toward Other Nations during Late Tokugawa and Early Meiji), in the above-mentioned *Kindai Nihon no taigai taido* [I-01], which classifies Japanese views of the world into several patterns by historical period and then analyzes the function of these attitudes in each period. Generally useful for early Meiji developments is the *Kindai, 1* volume of the *Iwanami kōza Nihon rekishi* series. Ōishi Kaichirō's introductory essay, "Kindaishi josetsu" (An Introduction to Modern Japanese History), and the six essays which follow all skillfully cover the main issues, though most seem unable to go beyond the prevailing Marxist formula for interpreting the events of the period.

For a general account of Meiji political history, the reader should consult Tōyama Shigeki, *Nihon kindaishi, I* (Modern Japanese History—I) [II-01]. Although Tōyama also takes a basically Marxist stance, he tries to incorporate into his research the fruits of recent positivist empirical research as well. The result is a kind of hybrid scholarship which owes much to Marxism but which also modifies many basic Marxist interpretations. Although examples of this kind of synthesis can be found in writing on the entire modern period, this does not mean that the positivist empirical approach can readily be grafted onto an abstract schema for interpreting history such as Marxism, with no visible signs of stress or awkward aftereffect. In this regard, Tōyama's work is no exception.

Another valuable approach to Meiji political history can be found in Haraguchi Kiyoshi, *Meiji zenki chihō seijishi kenkyū* (Studies in Local Political History of the Early Meiji Period) [II-02], an in-depth, highly empirical work focusing on a single prefecture, Shizuoka. Also noteworthy in the field of local history is *Kindai Nihon to Kumamoto* (Kumamoto and Modern Japan) [II-03] compiled by the Kumamoto Kindaishi Kenkyūkai (Kumamoto Modern Historical Research Society). In the form of a special issue of the magazine *Kindai Kumamoto* (Modern Kumamoto), which is put out by the same research organization, this study contains some excellent work by a dedicated group of specialists in local history. Two essays in particular can be singled out for bringing to light new information and materials on a previously unexplored topic. They are Uemura Kimio, "Kumamoto kokkentō no seiritsu" (The Formation of the Kumamoto National Rights Party) and Mizuno Kimihisa, "Kyū-Kyushu Kaishintō no saisoshiki katei" (The Reorganization of the Former Kyushu Progressive Party). Another interesting work dealing with the Kumamoto National Rights Party is Itō Takashi and Banno Junji, "Meiji hachinen zengo no Sasa Tomofusa to Kumamoto" (Sasa Tomofusa and Kumamoto in the mid-1870s) in *Nihon no rekishi* (no. 323), which is based on the letters of the political leader Sasa Tomofusa and presents a precise analysis of his activities during the early Meiji years.

In our previous essay for this bibliography series we identified Banno Junji's *Meiji kenpō taisei no kakuritsu* (The Establishment of the Meiji Constitutional System) (Tokyo Daigaku Shuppankai, 1971) as a decisively influential work, and today a number of studies written under the influence of Banno's book have begun to appear. Among such works, Ariizumi Sadao, "Minken undō hōkaigo no chihō seiji jōkyō" (Local Political Conditions after the Collapse of the Popular Rights Movement) [II-04], while basically retaining Banno's perspectives intact, focuses on Yamanashi prefecture between 1884 and 1890 and offers a persuasive interpretation of the state of local politics during that period. With this model work in mind, and recalling the contributions of Haraguchi and the Kumamoto Kindaishi Kenkyūkai, it is probably accurate to say that among the numerous works on local history in recent years, these represent the very best examples of a new brand of local history which is distinctive for its long-range national perspective.

Of course we should not overlook the source of this new variety of local history. Attempts by many prefectural governments, city, town and village administrations and prefectural assemblies throughout the nation to write their histories have led to rich discoveries of local historical materials and encouraged classification and examination of those documents. (For a thorough listing of these compilations, see the local history section of *Shigaku zasshi*, "Nihonshi bunken mokuroku" [A Catalogue of Japanese Historical Documents]). Also as a consequence of the widespread availability of material on local history, we should expect to see in the near future some solid research on local conditions during the Taishō and Shōwa periods as well.

Turning to another example of work which emerged under the influence of Banno's seminal study, there is Fukuchi Atsushi's essay,

"Daiichiji Matsukata naikaku no seifukei shinbun tōitsu mondai" (Efforts to Consolidate Pro-government Newspapers under the First Matsukata Cabinet), which appears in *Shigaku zasshi* (Vol. 83, No. 6). Focusing on the problem of government-supported newspapers, Fukuchi presents firmly grounded arguments on the nature of conflict among the *hanbatsu* leadership at this time.

An example of Banno's own work which offers fresh insights on a very interesting theme can be found in his chapter in Satō and Dingman, eds., *Kindai Nihon no taigai taido* [I-01], " 'Tōyō meishuron' to 'Datsu-A-nyū-Ō ron'—Meiji chūki Ajia shinshutsuron no ni ruikei" (The "Japan, the Leader of East Asia" Thesis and the "Dissociate from Asia, Join the Europeans" Thesis—Two Mid-Meiji Justifications for a Japanese Advance into Asia). With clear and convincing logic, Banno completely revises the accepted interpretations of leading spokesmen Fukuzawa Yukichi and Kuga Katsunan, and in the process, offers some fascinating new perspectives on the political history of the period.

Crucial to the further development of research along the lines of the above examples is the continued compilation and publication of key primary materials. One such publication is volume three of *Itō Hirobumi kankei monjo* (Documents Related to Itō Hirobumi) [II-05]. Another study in the field of political history is Yamamoto Shirō, *Shoki Seiyūkai no kenkyū* (Studies on the Early Seiyūkai) [II-06], which is an empirical work that makes ample use of relevant documents and primary materials. Its weakness, however, is that it does not go beyond the level of basic research, for it fails to provide a lucid presentation of facts and explanations regarding Seiyūkai activities.

During the period under review a great many useful historical materials pertaining to the Meiji period were published. On the years leading up to the Restoration there is *Ruisan no bu: Ii-ke shiryō, 9* (Collected Documents: Materials on the History of the Ii Family, Vol. 9) which is part of the *Dai Nippon ishin shiryō* (Materials on the Meiji Restoration) series compiled at the Tokyo Daigaku Shiryō Hensanjo (Tokyo University Historiographical Research Institute) [II-07]. Also, numerous volumes have been published growing out of the two sets of complete works of Katsu Kaishū which are presently being issued [II-08, 09]. Moreover, two useful catalogues of listings have recently appeared: *Dajō ruiten mokuroku, 1* (A Catalogue of Codes Pertaining to the Prime Minister's Office, 1867–71) prepared by the National Archives [II-10], and *Meiji ishin kankei monjo mokuroku* (Catalogue of Documents Relating to the Meiji Restoration) published by Waseda Daigaku Shakaikagaku Kenkyūjo (Waseda University Social Science Research Institute) in 1974 as an index of their own holdings.

There are numerous listings for the early Meiji years, one of the most significant being *Meiji shoki naimushō nisshi* (A Record of the Early Meiji Ministry of Home Affairs) compiled by the Home Affairs Ministry [II-11]. This account fills an important gap where information has long been scanty, so it is expected that research will now flourish in this area. Also, volumes six and seven of the Tokyo Daigaku Shiryō Hensanjo, ed., *Hogo Hiroi—Sasaki Takayuki nikki* (Diary of Sasaki Takayuki) [II-12] appeared, covering the years 1874–77. Another interesting compilation of materials is *Shiryō oyatoi gaikokujin* (Material on Teachers, Advisors and Other Experts Hired from Abroad) (Shōgakkan, 1975) prepared by the UNESCO East Asian Cultural Research Center. Also useful is Naikaku Kanpōkyoku (Cabinet Gazette Bureau), ed., *Hōrei zensho* (Complete Collection of Laws and Ordinances) [II-13] which has recently been reprinted in a readily available, easy to use edition.

On materials pertaining to the leading political figures, in addition to the above-mentioned *Itō Hirobumi kankei monjo*, an especially important contribution is *Inoue Kowashi den, shiryōhen dai 5* (Selected Materials on the Life of Inoue Kowashi, Vol. 5) [II-14], compiled and edited by Inoue Kowashi Denki Hensan Iinkai (Committee for Compiling the Biography of Inoue Kowashi). Two more useful sets of materials on individuals are Nihon Keieishi Kenkyūjo (Japanese Business History Research Institute), ed., *Godai Tomoatsu denki shiryō* (Documents on the Life of Godai Tomoatsu), Volume 4, (Tōyō Keizai Shinpōsha, 1974) and *Kataoka Kenkichi nikki* (The Diary of Kataoka Kenkichi) (Kōchi Shimin Toshokan, 1974) compiled by Risshisha Sōritsu Hyakunen Kinen Shuppan Iinkai (Publication Committee for the Hundred Year Anniversary of the Founding of Risshisha). "Arimatsu Hideyoshi kankei monjo 8–11" (Documents Relating to Arimatsu Hideyoshi, 8–11), prepared under the auspices of Tokyo

Daigaku Kindai Rippō Katei Kenkyūkai (Tokyo University Research Association for Modern Legislative Processes), was serialized in *Kokka gakkai zasshi* (Vol. 87, No. 9–10 through Vol. 88, No. 9–10).

Also very useful is Kokuritsu Kokkai Toshokan Sankōshoshibu (National Diet Library, Reference Department), ed., *Inoue Kaoru kankei monjo mokuroku* (Catalogue of Papers Relating to Inoue Kaoru) [II-15], a listing prepared from the Diet Library's special holdings on materials related to the Constitution. Likewise, Waseda University Library's *Ōkuma monjo mokuroku hoi* (Supplementary Catalogue of Documents Relating to Ōkuma Shigenobu), published in 1974, is based on the library's holdings of the Meiji statesman's papers.

Next, some extremely valuable political history documents have been published on a little-researched institution of the prewar period, the House of Peers (Kizokuin). Sakeda Masatoshi, ed., *Kizokuin kaiha ichiran* (House of Peers Members Classified According to Party and Factional Affiliation) [II-16] is an especially welcome contribution because it fills many of the gaps, particularly for the early years, which plagued the *Gikai seido nanajūnenshi, seitō kaiha hen* (A Seventy-year History of the Parliamentary System—Volume on Parties and Factions) (1963), a source researchers have frequently relied on up until now. Also quite useful for studying the House of Peers is *Kenkyūkai seiji nenpyō* (A Political Chronology of the *Kenkyūkai*) (Shōyū Kurabu, 1975), a record of the activities of a key faction in the prewar upper house.

Finally, in addition to the collections cited above, we should note the publication of three more volumes in the *Meiji Tennōki* (Annals of the Meiji Emperor) [II-17] series, a valuable source for the Meiji period as a whole. Likewise, the Meiji Bunken Shiryo Kankokai (Society for the Publication of Meiji Documents and Materials) began reprinting *Meiji zenki shomoku shūsei* (A Compilation of Early Meiji Books and Records) in 1974, and this has provided useful information about books published in the first half of the Meiji period.

III. POLITICAL HISTORY—TAISHŌ

Our previous essay in this bibliography series introduced a significant number of exciting new studies on the Taishō period. Four of these works have since been carefully discussed in a *Shigaku zasshi*

(Vol. 84, No. 3) review article by Itō Takashi and Arima Manabu: Matsuo Takayoshi, *Taishō demokurashii* (Taishō Democracy) (Iwanami Shoten, 1974); Kano Masanao, *Taishō demokurashii no teiryū* (Undercurrents of Taishō Democracy) (Nihon Hōsō Shuppankyōkai, 1973); Kinbara Samon, *Taishōki no seitō to kokumin* (Political Parties and the Populace in the Taishō Period) (Hanawa Shobō, 1974) and Mitani Taichirō, *Taishō demokurashii ron* (Essays on Taishō Democracy) (Chūō Kōronsha, 1974). This review essay gives special attention to the continuities between the Taishō and Shōwa periods, and points out the tendency of writers to neglect the impact of contemporary international relations. More fundamentally it probes diligently into the validity of the concept of "Taishō democracy." The essay is highly suggestive of future directions for research on the Taishō period.

A related book of interest is *Taishō demokurashii kenkyū* (Studies on Taishō Democracy) (Shinsensha, 1975) by Ōta Masao. Although there is probably no better account of the activities of intellectuals during this era available, in terms of its overall characterization of the Taishō period, unfortunately this study offers nothing fresh or original. The above-mentioned volume from the *Iwanami kōza Nihon rekishi* series, *Kindai, 5*, focuses on the Taishō period, and while it contains some excellent essays, by and large they are without startling new insights. Andō Minoru's essay, "Daiichiji sekai taisen to Nihon teikokushugi" (World War I and Japanese Imperialism) appears first and sets the tone for the volume. Of the nine essays included in the volume, two noteworthy contributions are Nimura Kazuo, "Rōdōsha kaikyū no jōtai to rōdō undō" (Working Class Conditions and Labor Movements), which raises some interesting questions, and Takamura Naosuke, "Dokusen shihonshugi no kakuritsu to chūshō kigyō" (The Establishment of Monopoly Capitalism and Small and Medium Enterprises), which offers a rigorous economic analysis.

An interesting essay on social movements in the Taishō period is Arima Manabu, "Takabatake Motoyuki to kokkashakaishugiha no dōkō" (Takabatake Motoyuki and the Activities of State Socialist Groups) [III-01] which is noteworthy for its stress on the links between the mid-Taishō period and the 1930s. Useful documentary materials for the study of Taishō social movements can be found in the published recollections of former Japan Communist party leader Nosaka Sanzō,

Fūsetsu no ayumi (Footsteps in a Snowstorm) *2, 3* (Shin Nihon Shuppan-sha, 1975).

IV. POLITICAL HISTORY—SHŌWA

Little substantial new research on the Shōwa period has made its appearance. However, since abundant new materials have been uncovered and published in recent years, studies based on these new documents should be available fairly soon. One very accomplished piece of research which utilizes a wide range of basic materials is Usui Katsumi, *Manshū jihen* (The Manchurian Incident) [IV-01]. Beginning with the incident itself, the author skillfully summarizes key internal political developments and relates them to the principal external repercussions arising from Japan's seizure of Manchuria.

In addition to Usui's work, numerous other studies dealing with the 1930s might be mentioned. Furuya Tetsuo's essay, "Minshū dōin seisaku no keisei to tenkai" (The Formation and Development of the Mass Mobilization Policy) in *Kikan gendaishi*, 6, is a historical examination of the wartime government's measures for organizing and mobilizing the Japanese masses. However, it is not the kind of study which brings together the results of several concrete research pieces, but is a general treatment of the question, sketching out the directions further research should take. Also, Itō Takashi, " 'Kyokoku-itchi' naikakuki no seikai saihensei mondai, III" (The Problem of Political Realignment during the Period of "National Unity" Cabinets, Part III) [IV-02] has appeared. This is the third section of a larger study of political history during the second decade of the Shōwa period, which examines the leadership and political organization of radical *"kaku-shinha"* or reformist groups such as Nakano Seigō and the Tōhōkai (Eastern Society), and Akamatsu Katsumaro and the Nihon Kaku-shintō (Japan Reform Party).

Matsuzawa Tetsunari and Suzuki Masasetsu, *Ni-ni-roku to seinen shōkō* (The Young Officers and the February 26 Incident) (San'ichi Shobō, 1974) offers a good overall account of the Young Officers Movement, coupled with an original analysis of one of the movement's key leaders, Nishida Mitsugi. Also, a unique intellectual movement which originated in Manchuria is examined in detail for the first time by Tanaka Takeo in *Tachibana Shiraki to Satō Daishirō* (Ryūkei Shosha, 1975). Volumes twenty-six through thirty of a very interesting historical work, *Shōwa-shi no tennō* (The Emperor and the Shōwa Period) [IV-03] have appeared, drawing extensively on contemporary accounts and personal recollections. Volumes twenty-six through twenty-nine deal with the second Nomonhan incident, while volume thirty covers negotiations between Japan and the U.S.

Gordon Berger's contribution to *Kindai Nihon no taigai taido* [I-01] is also noteworthy. Entitled "Ajia shin-chitsujo no yume—daitōa kyōeiken kōsō no shosō" (The Three-dimensional Empire: Japan's Vision of a New Order in Asia), this essay traces the historical development of Japan's perception of the world order throughout the modern period, and argues that Japan sought to integrate its own self-image with its conception of the world order through the "Plan for a Greater East Asian Co-Prosperity Sphere."

In terms of historical materials, as we saw above, a good many documents and new types of source materials have become available, and are now awaiting analysis by historians. Among the most important collections of primary materials is Imai Seiichi and Itō Takashi, eds., *Kokka sōdōin 2: seiji* (National Mobilization 2: Politics) [IV-04] which is a volume in the *Gendaishi shiryō* (Modern Historical Documents) series. Focusing primarily on the movement for a new party centered around Konoe Fumimaro, the sources in this volume reveal the thought and activities of the various political forces involved in this volatile period. This work opens many new avenues in research on the 1935–45 portion of Shōwa political history. Also valuable on this score is Ishikawa Junkichi, ed., *Kokka sōdōinshi-shiryōhen* (History of National Mobilization Efforts—Materials) [IV-05], a compilation of the prewar Planning Board materials, which pertain to all aspects of the wartime mobilization program from conception to implementation. Since the editor of the volume was himself a member of the Planning Board, the compilation includes an element of first-hand familiarity with the circumstances of the time.

Several interesting diaries have recently come to light. For example, the first volume of Yabe Teiji's diary, a political science professor at prewar Tokyo Imperial University, appeared not long ago as *Yabe Teiji nikki—ichō no maki* (The Diary of Yabe Teiji—the Ginkgo Volume)

[IV-06]. His diary is of special interest because of its numerous references to his involvements with Prince Konoe. Also to be noted is the appearance of volumes two through four of Ōkura Kinmochi nikki (The Dairy of Ōkura Kinmochi) [IV-07] making publication complete. Prepared jointly by the Naiseishi Kenkyūkai (Research Society for the History of Internal Affairs) and the Nihon Kindaishiryō Kenkyūkai (Modern Japanese Historical Materials Research Association), these three volumes provide very useful information on the activities of the Kokusaku Kenkyūkai (National Policy Research Association) and of War Minister Ugaki Kazushige and his faction. Finally, Kizaki Masaru's diary, Kizaki nikki, Volumes 2–4 (Gendaishi Shuppankai, 1975), is available, and it has the attraction of being a personal account of a journalist in Shōwa Society and of the key events of the era.

Another useful historical source for the Shōwa period is interviews with people present and active at the time. For example, the Naiseishi Kenkyūkai has continued to publish its extensive collection of interviews as Naiseishi kenkyū shiryō (Materials for Research on Internal Affairs) [IV-08]. These include interviews with Yokomizo Mitsuteru, Home Ministry official and chief of the Cabinet's Public Information Bureau; Suzuki Tadakatsu, Foreign Office official, secretary-general of the Central Liaison Office; Sakuma Toyozō, newspaper reporter; Matsukuma Hideo, vice minister, Ministry of Finance; Yoshizawa Seijirō, Foreign Office, head of the American Affairs Bureau; Katsura Takashi, labor management specialist, and a member of the postwar Central Labor Relations Board; and Murata Gorō, Home Ministry official, deputy director of the Cabinet's Public Information Bureau. Likewise, Nihon Kindai Shiryō Kenkyūkai, ed., Nihon kindai shiryō sōsho (A Collection of Modern Japanese Historical Materials) [IV-09] includes useful records of interviews with Hayashi Hidezumi of the military police, Tsukui Tatsuo, a rightwing leader and Suzuki Teiichi, former official in the War Ministry. Finally, of related interest is Makise Kikue, ed., Kutsumi Fusako no koyomi (The Chronicles of Kutsumi Fusako) (Shisō no Kagakusha, 1975), which makes extensive use of interviews with Kutsumi herself and others in order to reconstruct her career as an old-line socialist who recanted, taking the story up through her involvement in the Sorge affair.

Several interesting personal memoirs and autobiographies have also been published. Prewar Finance Minister Kaya Okinori, who was also active in postwar politics, published his *Senzen-sengo hachijūnen* (Eighty Years in Prewar and Postwar Japan) (Keizai Ōraisha, 1975). Matsumoto Shigeharu provides a journalist's account of his years in China during the Sino-Japanese war in his book *Shanhai jidai* (The Shanghai Years) [IV-10]. Another useful account is prewar Home Ministry official Yokomizo Mitsuteru's *Shōwashi henrin* (Glimpses of Shōwa History). Former Prime Minister Wakatsuki Reijirō's memoirs, *Kofūan kaikoroku* (Yomiuri Shinbunsha, 1975) include many valuable insights into prewar politics and society. As a long-time bureaucrat and twice prime minister, Wakatsuki's personal experiences were wide-ranging, making this reissue of his recollections, including commentary and an index to personal names, a very handy source.

Another recently republished volume of reminiscences that is worth noting is the highly regarded *Watakushi no Shōwashi* (A Personal History of the Shōwa Period) (Misuzu Shobō, 1974) by Suematsu Tahei, formerly a leader in the Young Officers Movement. Finally, an important new biography to appear is *Matsuoka Yōsuke* (Kōdansha, 1974) prepared by the Matsuoka Yōsuke Denki Kankōkai (Committee for the Publication of Matsuoka Yōsuke's Biography).

Another volume in the *Gendaishi shiryō* series of note is Uchikawa Yoshimi, ed., *Masu media tōsei* (The Control of Mass Media) [IV-11]. On the history of social movements, useful Ministry of Justice materials continue to be published under the auspices of the Shakai Mondai Shiryō Kenkyūkai (Research Association for Materials on Social Problems) as *Shakai mondai shiryō sōsho* (Materials for the Study of Social Problems) [IV-12]. On the military, the war history office of the Defense Agency has been publishing a multivolume *Senshi sōsho* (A History of War) among which *Daitōa sensō kaisen keii* (The Origin of the Pacific War), Vol. 4 [IV-13] and *Dai hon'ei rikugunbu* (Imperial Headquarters, Department of the Army) [IV-14] are especially valuable. Finally, on the Sino-Japanese War, Yoda Yoshiie, ed., *Nit-Chū sensōshi shiryō* (Materials on the History of the Sino-Japanese War) [IV-15], is in the process of being published.

V. Diplomatic History and Foreign Relations

Two recent essays on early Meiji diplomatic relations by Fujimura Michio demonstrate a sound grasp and astute interpretation of the complexities of early Meiji diplomacy. One is, "Taikun gaikō taisei no ronri" (The Logic of "Tycoon" Diplomacy) in *Nagoya daigaku Nihonshi ronshū* (Nagoya University: Collected Essays on Japanese History) (Yoshikawa Kōbunkan, 1975) and the other, "Yūshisensei no gaikō seisaku" (Official Despotism and Foreign Policy) in *Nihon rekishi* (No. 322). Nihon Kokusai Seiji Gakkai (Japan Association of International Relations) has prepared an interesting collection of essays, *Nihon gaikō no kokusai ninshiki* (International Awareness in Japanese Foreign Policy) [V-01] which examines the degree of understanding of international political conditions by foreign policy makers in Japan, and among the individuals and groups who so vociferously opposed certain foreign policy positions. Another useful collection of essays, Shinobu Seizaburō, ed., *Nihon gaikōshi* (Japanese Diplomatic History) I, II (Mainichi Shinbunsha, 1974), covers the growth and development of Japan's diplomatic relations throughout the modern period.

For more specialized monographic treatment, there is Miyake Masaki, *Nichi-Doku-I sangoku dōmei no kenkyū* (A Study of the Tripartite Alliance of Germany, Italy and Japan) (Nansōsha, 1975), a major undertaking which utilized all the key documents and source materials. Also of interest is Shiozaki Hiroaki, "'Nichi-Bei kaidan' zenshi" (The Quest for a "Roosevelt-Konoe" Summit) in *Shigaku zasshi* (84: 7) which draws on documents from both the American and Japanese sides in reconstructing the activities designed to effect high-level negotiations between the U.S. and Japan as an alternative to war, and follows closely the activities of Ikawa Tadao.

Nihon gaikō monjo (Japanese Diplomatic Documents) [V-02] is a set of basic documents made available by the Ministry of Foreign Affairs, of which the volume for 1921 (Taishō 10) was recently published. *Munakata Kotarō monjo* (Munakata Kotarō Papers) (Hara Shobō, 1975), compiled and edited by Kamiya Masao, contains some extremely useful insights into Japan's continental policy. Munakata was an agent sponsored by the Japanese navy in China and his reports on conditions on the continent in late Meiji and Taishō are included in this volume. Also concerned with Japan's policy toward the continent is Ichimata Masao, ed., *Yamaza Enjirōden* (The Biography of Yamaza Enjirō) (Hara Shobō, 1974), a reissue of the biography of Yamaza, a diplomat influential in China policy formation.

If we leave the narrow confines of diplomacy per se and enter the broader field of Japan's foreign relations in general, one of the first problems we come up against is Japan's colonial practices in overseas territories. For example, on Japan-Korea relations, Moriyama Shigenori, "Kindai Nik-Kan kankeishi kenkyū no dōkō to shiryō oyobi bunken" (Research Trends on the History of Modern Japan-Korea Relations: Sources and Documents) [V-03], does a thorough job of evaluating and organizing the available documents covering the period up through the first Sino-Japanese War (1894–95). Jo Teruhiko, *Nippon teikokushugika no Taiwan* (Taiwan under Japanese Imperialism) (Tokyo Daigaku Shuppankai, 1975), provides a very detailed and reliable treatment of Japan's colonial practices on Taiwan, coupled with a solid and meticulous analysis of the economic aspects of the relationship. On the subject of Japan's urge to "move southward," Yano Tōru presents a unique treatment in his '*Nanshin*' *no keifu* (Patterns and Development of the "Move Southward" Concept) (Chūō Kōronsha, 1975). His approach is unique in that he traces the lure of expansion south from the beginnings of Japan's modern history, and on through its postwar economic penetration into Southeast Asia.

A useful guide to research materials for this area is Ajia Keizai Kenkyūjo Toshoshiryōbu, ed., *Kyū-shokuminchi kankei kikan kankōbutsu sōgōmokuroku—Manshūkoku Kantōshū hen* (Complete Catalogue of Official Publications Concerned with Former Colonies—Section on Manchukuo and Kwantung) [V-04]. In addition, South Manchurian Railway Corporation, ed., *Minami Manshū Tetsudō Kabushiki Kaisha nijūnenshi* (A Twenty-year History of the South Manchurian Railway Corporation) (Hara Shobō, 1974) and *Minami Manshū Tetsudō Kabushiki Kaisha sanjūnen ryakushi* (An Abbreviated Thirty-year History of the SMR Corporation) (Hara Shobō, 1975) have both recently been reissued.

VI. Intellectual History

While there are numerous good studies on individual thinkers, covering their careers and their ideas, and many studies which examine in detail a single aspect of the intellectual trends of specific periods, there are still not many works which aim at presenting a comprehensive overview of the major intellectual landmarks of the modern period. One book which has attracted much attention recently is Yasumaru Yoshio, *Nihon kindaika to minshū shisō* (Japan's Modernization and Popular Thought) [VI-01], a study dealing with a currently fashionable topic, "popular thought." However, one has to be cautious about defining something as amorphous as "popular thought" in order to make it viable as a research concept. Attempts to do so inevitably raise questions of methodology and cast doubt on the effectiveness of such intellectual perspectives.

Another subject much in vogue is taken up by Miyamoto Seitarō, *Kita Ikki kenkyū* (Studies on Kita Ikki) (Yūhikaku, 1975). Although the author analyzes a wealth of material relating to this thinker and activist, ultimately he does little to place Kita in historical perspective, and does not succeed in relating him to his own times. Ienaga Saburō has produced an interesting study of an eminent philosopher of the prewar period, Tanabe Hajime. His book *Tanabe Hajime no shisōshiteki kenkyū* (Tanabe Hajime in Intellectual History) (Hōsei Daigaku Shuppankyoku, 1975) attempts to examine, through Tanabe's ideas, the qualities of an intellectual stance which could justify the Pacific War.

A very thorough treatment of a little-explored subject is Hatsuse Ryūhei, "Dentōteki uyoku—Uchida Ryōhei no shisō to kōdō" (Uchida Ryōhei: The Thought and Behavior of a Traditional Rightist), which goes far to illuminate this shadowy right-wing figure, and the activities of his Kokuryūkai (Amur River Society) organization. This study can be found in *Kita Kyūshū Daigaku hōsei ronshū* where it was serialized between March 1974 and March 1976.

In terms of material for intellectual history, the most important new item to appear is the diary of the leader of a unique and popular Buddhist movement, *Senoo Girō nikki* (The Diary of Senoo Girō) (Kokusho Kankōkai, 1974) in the process of being published.

VII. Economic History

In the field of economic history, the Marxist viewpoint prevails among researchers. However, even among the historians who share the Marxist framework, there are numerous differences in emphasis, which result in a wide range of opinions. Ōishi Kaichirō, ed., *Nihon sangyō kakumei no kenkyū* (Studies on Japan's Industrial Revolution) [VII-01] is a recent collection of essays by Marxist scholars on the general theme of the development of Japanese capitalism which clearly reveals the wide variety of perspectives and conclusions that can be embraced by Marxist scholars. Taken together, this collection of empirical studies represents the most recent statement of the Marxist position on some central issues in Japanese economic history, so it must be considered an important new work in the field. A very crucial part of the story of Japan's recent industrial growth is the textile industry and it is analyzed by Yamazaki Hiroaki in *Nihon kasen sangyō hattatsushi ron* (The Historical Development of Japan's Synthetic Fiber Industry) (Tokyo Daigaku Shuppankai, 1975).

In the area of quantitative studies, the most comprehensive work to date is Ohkawa Kazushi and Minami Ryōshin, eds., *Kindai Nihon no keizai hatten* (The Economic Development of Modern Japan) [VII-03], which relies upon *Chōki keizai tōkei* (Long-term Economic Statistics) [VII-02], a multivolume collection of basic economic statistics presently being published by Tōyō Keizai Shinpōsha.

Meiji zenki sangyō hattatsushi shiryō (Documentary Materials on Industrial Development in the early Meiji Period) [VII-04] is a voluminous collection of useful economic sources published in serial form by the Meiji Bunken Shiryō Kankōkai (Association for the Publication of Meiji Historical Materials). For the period after the beginning of the Sino-Japanese War, there is Tanaka Shin'ichi (revised by Hara Akira), *Nihon sensō keizai hishi* (Japan's War Economy, an Inside Story) [VII-05] which discusses the plan for mobilizing resources. Finally, corresponding to *Kindai Nihon seijishi hikkei* (A Handbook for Modern Japanese Political History) (1961) Andō Yoshio has edited *Kindai Nihon keizaishi yōran* (A Handbook for Modern Japanese Economic History) [VII-06] for the field of economic history. This contains most of the basic statistics on the Japanese economy throughout the modern period, and is a very useful reference tool.

VIII.   The Postwar Period

The postwar period, and the Occupation in particular, has only become an object of serious research in the last few years. However, interest in this era has begun to grow markedly and reflecting this, the annual supplement published by Shigaku-kai (The Historical Society of Japan) *Kaiko to tenbō* (Review and Prospects), began a special feature in 1975 entitled "Postwar History." What has stimulated this growing interest in postwar history is the release of important government documents by both the American and Japanese sides. Recently the U.S. made many documents from the Occupation period available to the public, and, beginning in 1976, Japanese diplomatic papers for the Occupation period were also released. Since we can now anticipate an increasing flow of declassified documents released to the public in the coming years, we may also expect that scholarly research based on these documents and materials will grow considerably.

Let us review briefly some of the earlier basic works on postwar history. A list of such works should include the following: Oka Yoshitake, ed., *Gendai Nihon no seiji katei* (The Modern Japanese Political Process) (Iwanami Shoten, 1958); Ishida Takeshi, *Hakyoku to heiwa* (Catastrophe and Peace), *Nihon Kindaishi taikei*, Vol. 8 (Tokyo Daigaku Shuppankai, 1968); Masumi Junnosuke, *Gendai Nihon no seiji taisei* (The Modern Japanese Political System) (Iwanami Shoten, 1969); Takemae Eiji, *Amerika tai-Nichi rōdōseisaku no kenkyū* (A Study of America's Labor Policy toward Japan) (Nihon Hyōronsha, 1970); Watanabe Akio, *Sengo Nihon no seiji to gaikō—Okinawa mondai o meguru seiji katei* (Postwar Japanese Politics and Diplomacy—the Okinawan Problem and the Political Process) (Fukumura Shuppan, 1970); and Shinobu Scizaburō, *Sengo seijishi* (Postwar Political History) Vols. I-IV (Keisō Shobō, 1965).

For a detailed and reliable catalogue of relevant documentary material, the reader should consult Nihon Gakujutsu Shinkōkai (Japan Society for the Promotion of Science), ed., *Nihon senryō bunken mokuroku* (A Catalogue of Documents Pertaining to the Occupation of Japan) which was published by the Society in 1972.

For the two-year period under review in this volume, a key work to mention is Tokyo Daigaku Shakaikagaku Kenkyūjo (Tokyo University Institute of Social Science), ed., *Sengo kaikaku* (The Postwar Reforms) [VIII-01], an eight-volume collection of essays on the Occupation period. The themes for the eight volumes are as follows: problems and perspectives, the international environment, the political process, judicial reform, labor rights, land reform, economic reform and the post-reform Japanese economy. Each volume is compiled under a different editor (though most of them share the Marxist viewpoint), so the quality varies somewhat. However, since most of the volumes deal rather broadly with some major issue in the Occupation reform program, their many excellent essays will undoubtedly stimulate further research on these problems.

Other useful books on the Occupation reforms are Amakawa Akira, *Sengo seiji kaikaku no zentei* (The Premises of Postwar Political Reform), Taniuchi Yuzuru, et al., eds., *Gendai gyōsei to kanryōsei* (Modern Public Administration and the Bureaucracy) Vol. II (Tokyo Daigaku Shuppankai, 1974), and Kaigo Tokiomi, ed. *Kyōiku kaikaku* (Educational Reform) (Tokyo Daigaku Shuppankai, 1975), which cover some of the most important questions in the field of postwar history. In addition, some useful studies of the Okinawa situation include Miyazato Seigen, ed., *Sengo Okinawa no seiji to hō* (Postwar Okinawan Law and Politics) (Tokyo Daigaku Shuppankai, 1975) and Kokusai Seiji Gakkai, ed., "Okinawa henkan kōshō no seiji katei" (The Political Process of the Okinawa Reversion Negotiations) in *Kokusai seiji*, No. 52 (Yūhikaku, 1975).

For materials on the postwar reforms there is Nōchi Kaikaku Shiryō Hensan Iinkai (Committee for Compiling Materials on Agricultural Land Reform), ed., *Nōchi kaikaku shiryō shūsei* (Collected Materials on Agricultural Land Reform) [VIII-02] now in the process of publication. Also, in the field of economic history, and important as an indicator of basic trends, is the recently republished *Keizai hakusho* (Economic White Papers) [VIII-03].

Finally, we should note that in early 1976, the Financial History Office of the Ministry of Finance's *Shōwa zaiseishi—shūsen kara kōwa made* (A Financial History of the Shōwa Period—From the End of the War until the Peace Treaty) began to appear. This twenty-volume study has been in preparation for the last several years.

文　　献

I–01　佐藤誠三郎・R. ディングマン(編) Satō Seizaburō and Roger Dingman(eds.) 『近代日本の対外態度』 *Japan Looks at the World*, 274 pp., 東京大学出版会, 1974.

02　『岩波講座　日本歴史』近代 1, 近代 5 *Iwanami Lectures on Japanese History*, Vol. 14 (The Modern Period 1); Vol. 18 (The Modern Period 5) [岩波講座日本歴史 14, 18] 364 pp.; 376 pp., 岩波書店, 1975.

II–01　遠山茂樹 Tōyama Shigeki 『日本近代史 I』 *Modern Japanese History*, Vol. 1 [岩波全書] 323 pp., 岩波書店, 1975.

02　原口　清 Haraguchi Kiyoshi 『明治前期地方政治史研究』(上・下) *Studies in Local Political History of the Early Meiji Period*, Vols. 1 and 2, 463 pp.; 589 pp., 塙書房, 1972, 1974.

03　熊本近代史研究会 Kumamoto Modern Historical Research Society 『近代日本と熊本』 *Kumamoto and Modern Japan* [近代熊本　第 17 号] 248 pp., 熊本近代史研究会 (葦書房), 1975.

04　有泉貞夫 Ariizumi Sadao 民権運動崩壊後の地方政治状況――明治 17–23 年――"Local Political Conditions after the Collapse of the Popular Rights Movement—1884–90—" 「史学雑誌」第 84 編第 4 号, pp. 1–34, 史学会 (山川出版社), 1975 年 4 月.

05　伊藤博文関係文書研究会(編) Association for the Study of Documents Related to Itō Hirobumi (ed.) 『伊藤博文関係文書 3』 *Documents Relating to Itō Hirobumi*, Vol. 3, 394 pp., 塙書房, 1975.

06　山本四郎 Yamamoto Shirō 『初期政友会の研究――伊藤総裁時代――』 *Studies on the Early Seiyūkai—The Period under Itō Hirobumi's Presidency*, 331 pp., 清文堂出版, 1975.

07　東京大学史料編纂所(編) Tokyo University Historiographical Research Institute (ed.) 『類纂之部　井伊家史料 9』 (自安政 5 年 8 月至同年 9 月) *Collected Documents: Materials on the History of the Ii Family*, Vol. 9 (From August through September 1858) [大日本維新史] 298 pp., 東京大学出版会, 1975.

08　勝　安芳 Katsu Yasuyoshi 『海軍歴史 3』 *History of the Navy*, Vol. 3; 『陸軍歴史 1, 2, 3, 4』 *History of the Army*, Vols. 1–4; 『開国起源 4, 5』 *Opening Japan*, Vols. 4 and 5 [勝海舟全集 10, 11, 12, 13, 14, 18, 19] 401 pp.; 414 pp.; 613 pp.; 574 pp.; 457 pp.; 773 pp.; 816 pp., 講談社, 1974–75.

09　勝　安芳 Katsu Yasuyoshi 『吹塵録』 *Writings on Bakufu Finance*; 『海舟座談

他』 *Conversations with Kaishū*; 『海軍歴史』 *History of the Navy*, Vol. 3, [勝海舟
全集 (勝部真長, 松本三之介, 大口勇次郎編) 7, 8, 11, 13] 546 pp.; 449 pp.;
538 pp.; 506 pp., 勁草書房, 1974–75.

10 国立公文書館(編) National Archives (ed.) 『太政類典目録』上 (慶応 3 年—
明治 4 年) *A Catalogue of Codes Pertaining to the Prime Minister's Office*, Vol. 1,
(1867–1871), 626 pp., 国立公文書館, 1974.

11 内務省(編) Ministry of Home Affairs (ed.) 『明治初期内務省日誌』(2 冊) *A
Record of the Early Meiji Ministry of Home Affairs* (2 vols.), 3946 pp., 国書刊行
会, 1975 (1875–1878 年刊の複製).

12 東京大学史料編纂所(編) Tokyo University Historiographical Research Institute (ed.) 『保古飛呂比・佐々木高行日記』6 巻 34–36 (明治 7 年 1 月〜同 8 年
12 月), 7 巻 37–40 (明治 9 年 1 月〜同 10 年 12 月) *Hogo Hiroi: The Diary of
Sasaki Takayuki*, Vols. 6 and 7, 344 pp.; 447 pp., 東京大学出版会, 1975.

13 内閣官報局(編) Cabinet Gazette Bureau (ed.) 『法令全書』第 1 巻 (慶応 3 年,
明治元年), 第 2 巻 (明治 2 年), 第 3 巻 (明治 3 年), 第 4 巻 (明治 4 年), 第
5 巻ノ 1 (明治 5 年ノ 1), 第 5 巻ノ 2 (明治 5 年ノ 2), 第 6 巻ノ 1 (明治 6 年
ノ 1), 第 6 巻ノ 2 (明治 6 年ノ 2), 第 7 巻ノ 1 (明治 7 年ノ 1), 第 7 巻ノ 2
(明治 7 年ノ 2), 第 8 巻ノ 1 (明治 8 年ノ 1), 第 8 巻ノ 2 (明治 8 年ノ 2), 第
9 巻ノ 1 (明治 9 年ノ 1), 第 9 巻ノ 2 (明治 9 年ノ 2), 第 10 巻 (明治 10 年),
第 11 巻 (明治 11 年), 第 12 巻ノ 1 (明治 12 年ノ 1), 第 12 巻ノ 2 (明治 12 年
ノ 2), *Complete Collection of Laws and Ordinances*, Vols. 1–12, 737 pp.; 636
pp.; 810 pp.; 1008 pp.; 815 pp.; 1349 pp.; 978 pp.; 1826 pp.; 686 pp.; 792
pp.; 880 pp.; 974 pp.; 684 pp.; 1474 pp.; 674 pp.; 518 pp.; 1190 pp., 原書
房, 1974–75 (1887–90 年刊の復刻).

14 井上毅伝記編纂委員会(編) Committee for Compiling the Biography of Inoue
Kowashi (ed.) 『井上毅伝 史料編』(第 5) *Selected Materials on the Life of Inoue
Kowashi*, Vol. 5, 765 pp., 国学院大学図書館, 1975.

15 国立国会図書館参考書誌部(編) National Diet Library, Reference Department (ed.) 『井上馨関係文書目録』*Catalogue of Papers Relating to Inoue Kaoru*
[憲政資料目録] 407 pp., 国立国会図書館, 1975.

16 酒田正敏(編) Sakeda Masatoshi (ed.) 『貴族院各派一覧 1890–1919』*House of
Peers Members Classified According to Party and Factional Affiliation: 1890–1919*,
[日本近代史料叢書 C–二] 285 pp., 日本近代史料研究会, 1974.

17 宮内省臨時編修局(編) Imperial Household Ministry Interim Compilation
Bureau (ed.) 『明治天皇紀』(第 10 巻, 第 11 巻, 第 12 巻) *Annals of the Meiji
Emperor*, Vols. 10–12, 958 pp.; 858 pp.; 847 pp., 吉川弘文館, 1974–75.

III–01 有馬 学 Arima Manabu 高畠素之と国家社会主義派の動向——大正中期社
会運動の一面 "Takabatake Motoyuki and the Activities of the State Socialist Group: A Focus on Mid-Taishō Social Movements" 「史学雑誌」第 83 編

第 10 号，pp. 1–28，山川出版社，1974 年 10 月．

IV-01 臼井勝美 Usui Katsumi『満州事変 ——戦争と外交と——』*The Manchurian Incident: War and Diplomacy* [中公新書] 214 pp., 中央公論社，1974.

02 伊藤　隆 Itō Takashi「挙国一致」内閣期の政界再編成問題 (三) "The Problem of Political Realignment during the Period of 'National Unity' Cabinets Part III"「社会科学研究」第 27 巻第 2 号，pp. 25–108，東京大学社会科学研究所，1975 年 12 月．

03 読売新聞社(編) Yomiuri Shinbunsha (ed.)『昭和史の天皇』(26, 27, 28, 29, 30), *The Emperor and the Shōwa Period*, Vols. 26–30, 341 pp.; 341 pp.; 351 pp.; 419 pp.; 406 pp., 読売新聞社，1974–76.

04 今井清一・伊藤　隆(編) Imai Seiichi and Itō Takashi (eds.)『国家総動員 2』(政治) *National Mobilization*, Vol. 2 (Politics) [現代史資料] 677 pp., みすず書房，1974.

05 石川準吉(編) Ishikawa Junkichi (ed.)『国家総動員史資料編』(第 1, 第 2, 第 3) *History of National Mobilization Efforts—Materials*, Vols. 1–3, 1283 pp.; 1189 pp.; 1261 pp., 国家総動員史刊行会 (通商産業研究社)，1975.

06 矢部貞治 Yabe Teiji『矢部貞治日記』銀杏の巻　自昭和 12 年 5 月 28 日至昭和 20 年 12 月 31 日，紅葉の巻　自昭和 30 年 1 月 1 日至昭和 35 年 12 月 31 日，躑躅の巻　自昭和 36 年 1 月 1 日至昭和 42 年 5 月 4 日，*The Yabe Teiji Diary*, 1937–1967, 876 pp.; 868 pp.; 772 pp., 読売新聞社，1974–75.

07 内政史研究会・日本近代史料研究会(編) Research Society for the History of Internal Affairs and Modern Japanese Historical Materials Research Association (eds.)『大蔵公望日記』第 2 巻　昭和 10〜12 年，第 3 巻　昭和 13〜16 年，第 4 巻　昭和 17〜20 年，*The Diary of Ōkura Kinmochi*, Vols. 2–4 [内政史研究資料別集 II-1，日本近代史料叢書 A-3] 396 pp.; 393 pp.; 371 pp., 内政史研究会，日本近代史料研究会，1974–75.

08 内政史研究会(編) Research Society for the History of Internal Affairs (eds.)『内政史研究資料』*Materials for Research on Internal Affairs*
松隈秀雄氏談話速記録 (上) [内政史研究資料 93–95] 163 pp., 1975.
古沢清次郎氏談話速記録 [内政史研究資料 165–169] 225 pp., 1975.
佐久間豊三氏談話速記録 [内政史研究資料 104–105] 101 pp., 1975.
鈴木九万氏談話速記録「内政史研究資料 171–175] 219 pp., 1975.
横溝光暉氏談話速記録 (上) [内政史研究資料 158–160] 192 pp., 1974.
　　　　　　　　　(下) [内政史研究資料 161–164] 200 pp., 1974.
桂皐氏談話速記録 (上) [内政史研究資料 146–148] 238 pp., 1974.
　　　　　　　(下) [内政史研究資料 149–152] 276 pp., 1975.
杜田五郎氏談話速記録 [内政史研究資料 123–128] 296 pp., 1975.

09 日本近代史料研究会(編) Modern Japanese Historical Materials Research Association (ed.)『日本近代史料叢書』*A Collection of Modern Japanese Historical*

90

Materials, 日本近代史料研究会, 1974.

『鈴木貞一氏談話速記録』(下) *A Record of Interviews with Suzuki Teiichi*, Vol. 2 [日本近代史料叢書 B-4] 395 pp.

日本近代史料研究会, 木戸日記研究会(編) Modern Japanese Historical Materials Research Association and Kido Diary Research Group (eds.) 『林秀澄氏談話速記録』(1), *A Record of Interviews with Hayashi Hidezumi*, Vol. 1 [日本近代史料叢書 B–5] 279 pp.

『津久井竜雄氏談話速記録』 *A Record of Interviews with Tsukui Tatsuo* [日本近代史料叢書 B-6] 238 pp.,

10　松本重治 Matsumoto Shigeharu『上海時代, ジャーナリストの回想』(上・中・下) *The Shanghai Years: A Journalist's Reminiscences* (3 vols.) [中公新書] 325 pp.; 325 pp.; 359 pp., 中央公論社, 1974–75.

11　内川芳実(編) Uchikawa Yoshimi (ed.) 『マス・メディア統制 2』 *The Control of Mass Media*, Vol. 2 [現代史資料] 569 pp., みすず書房, 1975.

12　社会問題資料研究会(編) Research Association for Materials on Social Problems (ed.) 『社会問題資料叢書』 *Materials for the Study of Social Problems*, 東洋文化社, 1974–75.

『治安維持法に関する議事速記録並委員会議録』 *Stenographic Minutes of Diet Proceedings and Committee Meetings on the Peace Preservation* Law (5 vols.), 441 pp.; 872 pp.; 431 pp.; 869 pp.; 1331 pp.

『思想事務家会同議事録』 *Proceedings of the Conference of Thought Problem Officials*, 190 pp.

『思想実務家会同議事録』 *Proceedings of the Conference of Thought Problem Officials*, 409 pp.

『思想情勢視察報告集』 *Collected Reports on Thought Conditions*, 397 pp.

『国家主義乃至国家社会主義団体輯』 *Directory of Nationalist and State Socialist Groups*, 556 pp.

『右翼思想犯罪事件の綜合的研究』 *Comprehensive Research on Rightwing Thought Crimes*, 441 pp.

『所謂「天皇機関説」を契機とする国体明徴運動』 *The So-called "Organ Theory" as a Pretext for the Movement to Clarify the National Polity*, 330 pp.

『帝国議会誌』 *A Record of the Imperial Diet* (3 vols.) 580 pp.; 596 pp.; 571 pp.

『所謂「日比谷焼打事件」の研究』 *Research on the So-called Hibiya Riots*, 212 pp.

13　防衛庁防衛研修所戦史室(編) Defense Agency, Defense College, Office of War History (ed.) 『大本営陸軍部大東亜戦争開戦経緯 4』 *The Origin of the Pacific War, Imperial Headquarters, Department of the Army*, Vol. 4 [戦史叢書] 593 pp., 朝雲新聞社, 1974.

14　防衛庁防衛研修所戦史室(編) Defense Agency, Defense College, Office of War History (ed.) 『大本営陸軍部』 (8–10), *Imperial Headquarters, Department of the Army*, Vols. 8–10 [戦史叢書] 552 pp.; 579 pp.; 537 pp., 朝雲新聞社, 1974, 1975, 1975.

15 依田憲家(編) Yoda Yoshiie (ed.)『日中戦争史資料』4. 占領区支配 1, *Materials on the History of the Sino-Japanese War*, Vol. 4 (Administration in Occupied Areas, Part 1) 729 pp., 河出書房新社, 1975.

16 洞 富雄(編) Hora Tomio (ed.)『日中戦争史資料』8. 南京事件 1, 9. 南京事件 2, *Materials on the History of the Sino-Japanese War*, Vol. 8 (The Nanking Incident, Part 1); Vol. 9 (The Nanking Incident, Part 2), 411 pp.; 346 pp., 河出書房新社, 1973.

V–01 日本国際政治学会(編) Japan Association of International Relations (ed.)『日本外交の国際認識, その史的展開』*International Awareness in Japanese Foreign Policy: Its Historical Development* [国際政治 51 号] 172 pp., 日本国際政治学会 (有斐閣), 1974.

02 外務省 Ministry of Foreign Affairs『日本外交文書大正期』大正 10 年第 1 冊下巻, 大正 10 年 第 2 冊, 大正 10 年 第 3 冊 上巻, 大正 10 年 第 3 冊 下巻, *Japanese Diplomatic Documents: The Taishō Period*, 1921 (4 vols.), 597 pp.; 722 pp.; 579 pp.; 719 pp., 外務省, 1974–75.

03 森山茂徳 Moriyama Shigenori 近代日韓関係史研究の動向と史料及び文献 ——甲午改革研究を中心として—— "Research Trends on the History of Modern Japan-Korea Relations: Sources and Documents, with Special Reference to the 1894 Reforms"「国家学会雑誌」第 88 巻第 11・12 号, pp. 694–726 (66–98), 国家学会 (有斐閣), 1975 年 12 月.

04 アジア経済研究所図書資料部(編) Institute of Developing Economies, Books and Materials Division (ed.)『旧植民地関係機関刊行物総合目録, 満州国関東州編』*Complete Catalogue of Official Publications Concerned with Former Colonies— Sections on Manchukuo and Kwantung*, 192 pp., アジア経済出版会, 1975.

VI–01 安丸良夫 Yasumaru Yoshio『日本の近代化と民衆思想』*Japan's Modernization and Popular Thought*, 298 pp., 青木書店, 1974.

VII–01 大石嘉一郎(編) Ōishi Kaichirō (ed.)『日本産業革命の研究 ——確立期日本資本主義の再生産構造——』(上, 下) *Studies on Japan's Industrial Revolution: The Structure of Capitalist Reproduction in the Age of Consolidation* (2 vols.), 384 pp.; 314 pp., 東京大学出版会, 1975.

02 大川一司・篠原三代平・梅村又次(編) Ohkawa Kazushi, Shinohara Miyohei and Umemura Mataji (eds.)『長期経済統計, 推計と分析』(全 13 巻) *Long-term Economic Statistics, Estimates and Analysis* (13 vols.), 東洋経済新報社, 1965–74.

03 大川一司・南 亮進(編) Ohkawa Kazushi and Minami Ryōshin (eds.)『近代日本の経済発展——「長期経済統計」による分析』*The Economic Development of Modern Japan: An Analysis Based on Long-term Economic Statistics*, 699 pp., 東

洋経済新報社，1975.

04 明治文献資料刊行会(編) Association for the Publication of Meiji Historical Materials (ed.)『勧業博覧会資料』(121–180) *Materials on Industrial Expositions*, 121–180 [明治前期産業発達史資料] 50 冊，明治文献資料刊行会，1974–75.

05 田中申一 (原朗校訂) Tanaka Shin'ichi (edited by Hara Akira)『日本戦争経済秘史──十五年戦争下における物資動員計画の概要』*Japan's War Economy, an Inside Story—An Outline of the Wartime Plan to Mobilize Resources*, 665 pp., 日本戦争経済秘史刊行会，1974.

06 安藤良雄(編) Andō Yoshio (ed.) 『近代日本経済史要覧』 *A Handbook for Modern Japanese Economic History*, 225 pp., 東京大学出版会，1975.

VIII–01 東京大学社会科学研究所(編) Tokyo University Institute of Social Science (ed.)『戦後改革』1. 課題と視角，2. 国際環境，3. 政治過程，4. 司法改革，5. 労働改革，6. 農地改革，7. 経済改革，8. 改革後の日本経済，*The Postwar Reforms*, Vols. 1–8, 317 pp.; 407 pp.; 441 pp.; 496 pp.; 395 pp.; 459 pp.; 395 pp.; 320 pp., 東京大学出版会，1974–75.

02 農地改革資料編纂委員会(編) Committee for Compiling Materials on Agricultural Land Reform (ed.)『農地改革資料集成』第 1 巻 第一次農地改革篇，第 2 巻 第二次農地改革立法経過篇，*Collected Materials on Agricultural Land Reform*, Vol. 1 (The First Agricultural Land Reform Program); Vol. 2 (Legislative Processes in the Second Agricultural Land Reform Program), 1068 pp., 1210 pp., 御茶の水書房，1974–75.

03 経済安定本部(編) Economic Stabilization Board (ed.)『復刻経済白書』第 1 巻 昭和 22〜25 年，第 2 巻 昭和 26 年, *Republished Economic White Papers*, Vols. 1 and 2, 294 pp.; 206 pp., 日本経済評論社，1975.

ARCHAEOLOGY

MIKAMI Tsugio, YOSHIDA Shōichirō
and TAMURA Kōichi
Aoyama Gakuin University

Translated by Patricia Murray

I. INTRODUCTION—GENERAL WORKS

For a long period until 1974, fieldwork and excavation flourished with an unprecedented wealth of new discoveries resulting mainly from the new sites laid bare by construction and development accompanying Japan's period of rapid economic growth. Research and excavation continued during 1974–75, but not with the vigor of previous years. The comparative lull in activity that followed gave scholars a chance to review and digest the achievements and findings of the past decade, and to tackle some new issues in archaeology which emerged from the previous period of sustained fieldwork. This summary, in outlining the nature of the considerable quantity of reports and monographs that appeared during 1974–75, aims at helping the archaeology student in identifying the currently controversial issues of the field, and presenting an overview of the approaches being used as scholars try to resolve some unanswered questions.

Very few general works with important new contributions to the field appeared during this period, and no publisher planned any major new series on Japanese archaeology. However, a series inaugurated in 1975, *Iwanami kōza Nihon rekishi* (Iwanami Lectures on Japanese History), offers some studies of a comprehensive nature. *Genshi oyobi kodai I* (The Prehistoric and Ancient Periods, Part I) and *Kodai II* (The Ancient Period, Part II) [1-01, 02], together cover the important themes in the respective periods. Specific topics are brought together in each volume to portray a systematic overview of the aspects basic to understanding Japan's prehistoric and ancient periods. The authors of volume one include documentary historians as well as archaeologists, among them Kamaki Yoshimasa, Okamoto Isamu, Sahara Makoto, and Amakasu Ken; and volume two, Mori Kōichi. The essays have been coordinated in such a way as to present a broad perspective on the development of Japanese society from the Palaeolithic to the Nara period, from the point of view of archaeology based on the latest findings. These two works incorporate both the archaeological and historical approaches, in an attempt to promote a better understanding of ancient Japan by synthesizing the two disciplines. Both represent advanced academic treatises.

Another series is the five-volume *Nihon no kyūsekki bunka* (Japan's Palaeolithic Culture) edited by Asō Yutaka, Katō Shinpei, and Fujimoto Tsuyoshi. Volume one [I-03] and volume two [I-04] are already in print. The former contains essays by nine scholars, which provide a general survey of the epoch and deal with questions of research methodology on Palaeolithic culture. In the same volume is a symposium on aspects of the Palaeolithic in Japan and the degree to which Japan's Palaeolithic shared universal characteristics, or conversely, was a unique culture. It is a handy source of information on the nature of Palaeolithic culture as well as a good account of recent research on the Palaeolithic age. In level of information and analysis, this volume is aimed at relatively knowlegeable readers. Volume two contains essays by nineteen scholars who focus on detailed observations of excavations and artifacts in specific sites in Hokkaido, Tōhoku, Kantō, and Chūbu.

Of the ten volumes planned for the *Kodaishi hakkutsu* (Discovery of Ancient History) series (see Vol. I, Part 2 of this bibliography, pp. 72, 85), those published in 1974–75 are volume four, *Inasaku no hajimari* (The Beginnings of Rice Cultivation), edited by Sahara Makoto and Kanazeki Hiroshi [I-05], and volume six, *Kofun to kokka no naritachi* (The Tumuli and the Emergence of the State), edited by Onoyama Setsu [I-06]. Altogether twelve scholars contributed to volume four, a very readable account of the Early Yayoi as reconstructed through archaeological excavation and research. Volume six, the work of ten authors, provides, as in volume four, a thorough and well-illustrated portrayal of the Early Kofun (Tumulus) period. It focuses on archaeological evidence regarding the rise of the Japanese state with emphasis on the development of society.

The first volume of a series of six called the *Shintō kōkogaku kōza* (Lectures on Shinto Archaeology) appeared in 1972. So-called Shinto archaeology is that branch of the field which pursues the history of the Shinto religion, and volume four, *Rekishi Shintōki* (Historical Shinto Period) [I-07], is written with a perspective on the historical relationship between Shinto and Buddhism.

Archaeologia Japonica, the annual report appearing since 1948 of the field's leading organization, the Japanese Archaeologists Association, provides an itemized description of the important finds unearthed in excavations over each given year, as well as a handy guide to trends in Japanese archaeology, and is a valuable title for any specialist. The 1972 issue of that journal, Volume 25 [I-08], and Volume 26 (1973) [I-09] appeared in 1974 and 1975 respectively .

Finally, it is appropriate here to mention the reprinting of the collected works of Torii Ryūzō (1870–1965), the foremost archaeologist in the history of the field in Japan, and a pioneer scholar in East Asian archaeology as a whole. The reprinting aims at a twelve-volume set, two of which have now been published. The set will include all the work of this prolific scholar, who engaged in ground-breaking work from the late nineteenth century until his death. Torii worked not only on Japan, his vision ranged widely to Korea, Manchuria, Mongolia, Eastern Siberia, North and West China, the Kurile Islands, Taiwan and other parts of Asia as well.

The first two volumes contain his research on Japan. Among the chapters in volume one [I-10], are "Jinruigakujō yori mitaru waga jōdai no bunka" (Archaeological View of Japan's Ancient Culture) (1925) and "Yūshi izen no Nihon" (Prehistoric Japan) (1925). Volume two [I-11] includes "Musashino oyobi sono shūi" (Musashino and Its Environs) (1924), "Musashino oyobi sono yūshi izen" (Musashino and Its Prehistory) (1925), and "Jōdai no Tōkyō to sono shūi" (Ancient Tokyo and Its Surroundings) (1927). Those are the most noteworthy titles, but suffice it to say that the work of Torii is of lasting value as a milestone in the field.

II. PREPOTTERY PERIOD

The most important work done recently on the Prepottery period is the five-volume series entitled *Nihon no kyūsekki bunka*. Volume one [I-03] and volume two [I-04] appeared by 1975, the first containing general commentary, the second, articles on sites and artifacts. When all five volumes are in print, the series will merit further, more careful appraisal.

Noteworthy reports on excavation and study of Prepottery period sites include one on Tokyo's Nishinodai [II-01] and another on the Suzuki site in Kodaira, Tokyo [II-02]. The authors have confirmed in the former that the Tachikawa loam contains fourteen culture layers, and in the latter, that the Suzuki site contains twelve. The very bottom layer of the Nishinodai site yielded drill-shaped stone implements, scrapers and pebble tools, and others, all predating the appearance of the backed blade. The Suzuki site also yielded a group of stone implements from layer nine, quite close to the bottom, that predate the backed blade. Partially ground stone axes and chipped stone axes were also found in the same place, bunched together. These finds have been instrumental in helping to reconstruct the form-progression of stone implement groups that date from before the backed blade in the south Kantō region. Interestingly, representative artifacts from all stages of that progression have been found in the Tachikawa loam. But it is worth questioning whether, as Oda and Keally have posited, these are indeed Japan's oldest stone implement groups.

Included in a general survey of the work done on the many sites at the foot of Mt. Futagami in western Japan [II-03], is a study of the manufacturing techniques of a backed blade unique to western Japan, known as the Kokufu-type knife. One scholar who claims that there was a clearly definable Lower Palaeolithic in Japan is Kamaki Yoshimasa in "Kyūsekki jidairon" (The Case for a Palaeolithic in Japan) [II-04]. His work on implement production covers the entire Prepottery period, and in the process his stand for a Lower Palaeolithic is made very clear. The chronology of stone implements is determined according to the layer they are found in as well as C-14 dating, but he feels that attention to development of style is inadequate. Kamaki

believes that evidence from work on the last Prepottery phase reveals
a parallel relationship between the microblades which persisted in
Kyushu and the stemmed points of Hokkaido and Honshu.

III.   Jōmon Period

The most conspicuous trend in recent studies and excavation of
Jōmon sites and artifacts is the use of new methods to analyze the sub-
sistence economy. By using water flotation at the Nakayamadani site in
Tokyo, researchers flushed out of a Middle Jōmon dwelling the remains
of fruit of the madder, Chinese cork, polygonum, wild rocambole, and
many kinds of walnuts [III-01]. The same technique used at the
Kuwakaishita site in Kyoto also produced plant remains [III-02].
This method has not yet been widely applied in Japan, and is still in
an experimental stage. Scholars anticipate that it will produce increasingly helpful information.

Other scholars are employing plant opal detection, in the attempt
to prove that rice was indeed cultivated as early as the Final Jōmon.
Fujiwara Hiroshi seeks in a recent work [III-03] to establish the possibility of slash-and-burn rice cultivation in the early phase of the Final
Jōmon. But as Fujiwara himself recognizes, there is still insufficient
accumulation of evidence to support such a view. Scholars will have to
lay much more groundwork in continued research.

Emerging from flourishing excavation and research are many
reports and essays dealing with Jōmon settlements and pit-dwelling
sites. The Sengo site at the foot of Mt. Fuji is important as a settlement
accompanied by a large-scale remains of a Middle Jōmon stone structure. There, adjacent to a cluster of dwellings, a twenty-meter-square
area marked off by rows of stones was discovered. Apparently nothing
like pits or holes has been found beneath the stone square, but though
it is difficult to identify them for certain, it is expected that they will
prove quite different in nature from the stone circles discovered up
until this point [III-04].

Stone-paved dwellings did not appear until the Middle or Late
Jōmon and even then they were unusual. Another unique form was
shaped like a handled mirror. According to Murata Fumio, a specialist
on the subject, this particular form had a very limited lifetime, appear-

ing for a brief period between the end of Middle and the first half of Late Jōmon. They also seem to be confined to the area between western Kantō and the Chūbu mountain range. Sometimes one, sometimes two or three of these sites are found in a single settlement, and Murata believes that they date from the later stage in the formation of the settlements [III-05]. Murata's thesis may be premature, but in view of the scarcity of work on this subject so far, the function of these uniquely shaped dwellings merit continued study.

Jōmon burials are of many types. One, found in southern Kantō, consists of an arrangement of stones placed upon the ground. A typical example of this has been found at Ishigamidai site in Kanagawa prefecture [III-06]. The human skeletal remains discovered there all faced south, from which evidence Takayama Jun has deduced that the inhabitants of the area very possibly had some conception of another land beyond the sea. There is almost no evidence to support the existence of a concept of another world among the Jōmon people, and so it is difficult to accept Takayama's thesis until more proof is found.

A related and significant article [III-07], by Kamimura Tōru, dealing with *umegame* (burial jars) and the *fusegame* (inverted jar) found to date between the Chūbu mountain range and the Kantō region, describes the distinguishing marks of these two types of jars. Kamimura believes that the latter type were intended to capture and hold the spirits of a particular dwelling. Nonetheless, the peculiar kind of jar called *fusegame* is not found in all dwelling sites, and if we follow his logic, some dwellings had spirits and others did not. But the fact remains that there is no evidence to back up his theory.

A volume by Okamoto Isamu [III-08] focuses on the Jōmon period as a whole. He attempts to reformulate the periodization based on overall cultural tendencies rather than on chronologies formulated on the basis of pottery periodization, as has been the general rule. Despite his efforts, nonetheless, his hypotheses do not escape the influence of pottery dating and chronology. Okamoto asserts that it cannot be proved that cultivation had begun by Middle Jōmon in his discussion of Jōmon production, but claims that sooner or later proof of cultivation during Final Jōmon will emerge.

IV. YAYOI PERIOD

A truly astonishing discovery has been made concerning the most unique product of the Yayoi, the *dōtaku*, or bronze bell. In the city of Ibaraki, Higashi Nara, Osaka, the top (outer) half of a *dōtaku* mold made of tuffic-sandstone was found [IV-01] in near-perfect condition. Beside this complete specimen, more than five different types of mold fragments were found in the same site, each one reported to belong to five different molds. One of these fragments has been identified as the mold from which two *dōtaku*, discovered in Toyonaka, Osaka and Zentsūji in Kagawa prefecture, were cast, and still another is believed to be part of the mold from which a *dōtaku* found in Toyooka city, Hyōgo prefecture, was made.

Archaeologists have for some time been able to predict the geographic distribution of given types of *dōtaku*, based on the location of production centers and the general area over which particular *dōtaku* were found, but this recent discovery has added an exciting new dimension to our understanding of Yayoi artifacts. It proves beyond doubt that more than one, in fact several, types of *dōtaku* were cast in one production center, and that they were scattered over a very extensive area.

The find is made even more significant by the discovery at the same site of molds for casting bronze ceremonial halberds and glass *magatama* (crescent-shaped jewels), providing scholars with definitive proof of communities of skilled craftsmen who specialized in the casting techniques of these various types of implements and ornaments. We are thus presented with tantalizing new questions: what was the social position or rank of these groups? What role did they play in the Yayoi society as a whole?

Burials, another major aspect of the Yayoi period is the subject of two or three important reports. One concerns a square-ditched burial (*hōkei shūkōbo*) discovered at Saikachido site in Kanagawa prefecture [IV-02]. The wide dispersion of the relatively common square-ditched style of burial in the Yayoi has been noted in Vol. I, Part 2 of this bibliography (pp. 77–78). In the southern Kantō region, as the Saikachido site shows, the type seems to have first emerged in the latter half of Middle Yayoi. The early half of Middle Yayoi still carried on the Jōmon tradition of reburial (*saisōbo*), or interring the remains in another place, sometimes after bonewashing. An archetypal example of *saisōbo* is found in Chiba prefecture, at the Tenjinmae site [IV-03]. Inside one pit were found several pottery jars in which human bones had been placed. At the very tip of Kyushu, at Narikawa site in Kagoshima prefecture, a unique system of standing stone burials is reported [IV-04]. This burial system consists of a large stone erected upright, standing central in a ring of several dozen burials. Traces of fires have also been found. Large quantities of various types of ceremonial weaponry were found buried with the bodies, but almost no personal ornaments or accessories. Yayoi burials apparently took several forms, but this discovery adds still another to those already known.

It has long been known that the cultural influence of the Korean peninsula was strong during the Yayoi, bringing many new objects and techniques to Japan. The question of exactly how that influence reached Japan has been focused until recently mostly on metal artifacts, making it difficult to know with any certainty the genesis and meaning of the Korean cultural influx. At the Morooka site in Fukuoka prefecture, however, pottery vessels identical in shape to pottery from the southern part of the Korean peninsula have been found which may open a new door to learning about the connection between Korea and Japan [IV-05]. This discovery constitutes further evidence supporting the belief that some degree of migration from the Korean peninsula to Japan took place.

Sahara Makoto's essay, "Nōgyō no kaishi to kaikyū shakai no keisei" (The Rise of Agriculture and Formation of a Class Society) [IV-06] is among several comprehensive studies of the entire Yayoi. Sahara has long been an authority on the subject of *dōtaku* and Yayoi pottery, but has recently expanded his research to stone implements. On the basis of changes in stone spears and arrowheads, he infers that considerable development occurred in the society of the Yayoi period. According to Sahara, by the Middle Yayoi, military power was pushing unification toward completion in the Yamato region, and during Late Yayoi, central authority was exercising military power in order to expand outward from the Kinai. What must be examined now is the relation between that expansion and the spread of what is considered symbolic of the Yamato court, the local custom of building tumuli.

V. TUMULUS (*Kofun*) PERIOD

Study of the Tumulus period during 1974–75 did not move in any significantly new directions but was essentially a continuation of previous trends. The field has been enriched by the appearance of several findings that add to and build upon issues already under study, thereby bringing closer a resolution of some long-standing questions relating to the Tumulus period. As noted above, the recent downswing in the economy has meant a slacking-off in land development and construction, and this has had a marked effect upon excavating and fieldwork in general. Excavating has continued in all areas of Japan, however, on perhaps a relatively larger scale, allowing for more minute examination and study of the sites and finds, and consequently encouraging new ideas on given subjects.

New general studies on tomb culture include articles in the volume published by Shūeisha, *Zusetsu Nihon no rekishi* (Pictorial Study of Japanese History). One of them, an article by Amakasu Ken, "Kofun no shutsugen to tōitsu kokka no keisei" (The Emergence of Tumuli and the Formation of a Unified State), focuses on the development of Kofun period tumuli out of those of the Yayoi [V-01]. Another by Kurihara Akinobu and Takeuchi Rizō entitled "San-go seiki no higashi Ajia no keisei" (East Asia in the Third-Fifth Centuries) [V-02] places Japanese tomb culture in the context of the cultural and social milieu of Asia as a whole during those centuries. On the theme of the transition of this period from, and its relationship to, the Yayoi, an article entitled "Kofun no shutsugen" (Rise of the Tumuli) by Izumori Kō and Sugaya Fuminori [V-03] in Volume 4 of the series *Nihon kodaishi no tabi* (Journeys into the Ancient History of Japan) argues the tenuous possibility of establishing a definite, continuous lineage between the Late Yayoi mounded graves of Yamato and those that marked the beginning of the Tumulus period.

For a comprehensive and graphically detailed account of the mounded tombs of the period and the archaeological work that has helped to illuminate them, *Kofun no kōkū taikan* (Aerial Views of the Old Tumuli) [V-04] by Suenaga Masao is excellent. The inclusion of abundant aerial and ground-level photographs as well as description by graph and diagram of actual surveys and excavations, especially of the royal tombs, gives this volume the breadth and depth of a first-class work in the field. It should exert considerable influence and will probably become a guide for further study of the Tumulus period.

In studying the origins of mounded tombs, the connection between the tumuli and the regional characteristics of the respective areas where they are found cannot be overlooked. Oda Fujio has published an article in *Kōkogaku zasshi* (Journal of Archaeology) entitled "Buzen-Usa chihō ni okeru koshiki kofun no chōsa" (Study of Old Form Mounded Tombs in the Buzen-Usa Region) [V-05]. Here Oda reports the presence of mounded tombs in Kyushu that predate the Kinai-style, formerly thought to be the earliest of the old-type tombs. In a paper reporting another divergence from commonly accepted theories on the Kinai tumuli, Makabe Tadahiko, et al., "Okayama-ken Ōbosan isekigun" (Artifact Group at Ōbosan, Okayama Prefecture) [V-06], suggest on the basis of discoveries at Ōbosan the possibility of a tradition of religious ceremonies associated with mounded tombs distinct from traditions revealed by the Kinai tombs. This paper was published in a regional periodical journal, *Kurashiki Kōkokan kenkyū shūhō*, No. 10.

Other general works on the origins and development of tumuli coming out during 1974–75 include *Iwanami kōza Nihon rekishi* [I-01, 02] and Kōdansha's *Kodaishi hakkutsu* [I-06]. Works on regional characteristics of mounded tombs in a given area include Shiraishi Taiichirō, "Kofun jidai no nishi Nihon" (Western Japan in the Tumulus Period) [V-07], and "Kofun jidai no higashi Nihon" (Eastern Japan in the Tumulus Period) [V-08], both published in *Nihon rekishi chiri sōsetsu* (Surveys on Japanese History and Geography). A third is Nishikawa Hiroshi, *Kibi no kuni* (The Province of Kibi) [V-09] on the area of Okayama, among the other regional reports on this period.

A large number of noteworthy reports on the mounded tombs themselves have recently been published, dealing with the significance of certain uniquely shaped tumuli: *hōfun* (square tumuli), *zenpō kōhōfun* (square-front, square-back tumuli), and *zenpō kōenfun* (keyhole-shaped or square-front, round-back tumuli), for example. A book by Mogi Masahiro, *Zenpō kōhōfun* (Square-Front, Square-Back Tumuli) [V-10], and an article by Okita Masaaki, "Yamato no zenpō kōhōfun" (The Square-Front, Square-Back Tumuli of Yamato) [V-11] published in *Kōkogaku zasshi* 59-4, are two such studies. Another published by the Kumamoto Prefectural Board of Education, *Tsukahara kofungun chōsa* (Investigation of the Tsukahara Tumulus Group) [V-12] and another regional report from Shimane prefecture, *Miyayama kofun* (The Miyayama Tumulus) would also fit this category.

On the technical side, the study by Ueda Kōhan, "Zenpō kōenfun ni okeru chikuzō kikaku no tenkai" (The Structural Maturation of the Keyhole-Shaped Tumulus) [V-14], published by the Kashiwara Archaeological Institute, and that by Kunugi Kunio, "Kofun no sekkei" (Design of Tumuli) [V-15] published by Tsukiji Shokan, deal with the construction of mounded tombs. The stone and other materials used in the construction of tumuli often tell us rather precisely where the materials were produced. Another work by Makabe Tadahiko, et al. focuses on the transport of stone destined for tumulus construction and on the movement of builders and craftsmen in an article entitled "Sekkan, sekizai no dōtei to Okayama-ken no sekkan o meguru mondai" (The Sources of Materials in Sarcophagi and the Sarcophagi of Okayama Prefecture) [V-16], published as *Kurashiki Kōkokan kenkyū shūhō*, No. 9.

On the Late Tumulus period, the article "Shiseki Nakaoyama kofun kankyō seibi jigyō hōkokusho" (Report on the Maintenance of the Environment of the Historical Site of Nakaoyama Tumulus) by Aboshi Yoshinori, reports an unusual eight-sided tumulus. On the same Late Tumulus period tombs Ōtsuka Hatsushige reports the discovery of wall-paintings inside a horizontal corridor-style stone burial chamber (*yokoana-shiki sekishitsu*) rare in Kantō. His article, "Ibaraki-ken Torazuka kofun to sono hekiga" (The Torazuka Tumulus and Its Wall Paintings) [V-17], describes a type of burial that suggests a possible relationship with the wall-paintings in the corridor-type tombs of Kyushu. A further work on decorated tumuli is that by Otomasu Shigetaka, "Sōshoku kofun no bunpu to sono haikei" (The Distribution of Decorated Tumuli and Their Background) [V-18].

On the subject of corridor-style (*yokoana*) tombs, Kanaizuka Yoshikazu has produced a work that has been highly commended for the monumental achievement of the scholar in assembling and analyzing the materials on the Yoshimi Hyakuana ("thousand tombs" of Yoshimi), which are so important in the history of Meiji period archaeology. His book, *Yoshimi hyakuana yokoanabogun no kenkyū* (Studies on the Excavation of the Corridor Tombs of Yoshimi) [V-19], is only one of a number of works on specific types of tumuli. Another reports the existence of an enormous group of corridor tombs, over one thousand in all, in "Takenami iseki, Fukuoka-ken, Yukuhashi-shi, Takenami shozai iseki no chōsa gaihō" (Report on the Investigation of the Takenami Site, Fukuoka Prefecture, Yukuhashi City). Also meriting attention is an article on the tunnel tombs unique to the area centered on Miyazaki prefecture, in which an underground chamber forms part of the structure of the tumulus itself: Ishikawa Tsunetarō, "Chika-shiki kofun" (Underground-type Tumuli) [V-20].

Work on artifacts is somewhat spare, but there have appeared a few commendable studies on *haniwa*. One of these is Ōtsuka Hatsushige, *Haniwa seisaku to kōjin shūdan* (Haniwa Production and Craftsmen's Groups) [V-21], which is volume seven of Kōdansha's *Kodaishi hakkutsu* series. While Ōtsuka focuses on the manufacture and system of supply of *haniwa*, Ōwaku Shinpei, in "Tochigi-ken Nanamawari Kagamizuka kofun" (Nanamawari Kagamizuka Tumulus in Tochigi Prefecture) [V-22], reports the rare instance of finding organic matter well preserved inside the tumulus.

Another category of studies is directed toward subject matter falling within the same time period as the Tumulus but does not involve tumuli per se. Most in this category deal with communities and villages, but since the scale of the sites is so huge, any attempt to carry out a comprehensive survey faces insurmountable difficulties. Reports on individual sites are abundant, but there is no major study that seeks a common thread to tie them all together.

VI. Historic Period

Not many years ago archaeological study of the Historic period was comparatively unusual, but having once begun to grow, it has quickly become an actively developing branch in the field. Research today on certain topics is steadily gaining depth and precision. Artifacts from the Historic period offer huge variety, and of course they far outnumber those of earlier periods, so the scope of subject matter is much wider. It is virtually impossible to cover all Historic sites and artifacts related to a given topic in a short-term investigation, as a result. Study of this period is passing through what is perhaps a transition stage characterized by information and fact-collecting, excavation and fieldwork, all carried on concurrently on a wide range of subjects in order to build up a body of material for slow, careful analysis later.

Archaeologists now believe that artifacts from the Historic period are abundant beyond reckoning, judging from what has already been found. They include many different types in the edifice category: castles and palaces, official buildings and residences, temples and shrines, and settlements. They also include graves, tombs, and sutra mounds (*kyōzuka*, which are underground or buried, sealed repositories for sutras, written prayers, etc.). Workshop sites and centers of production, tiles, pottery, wooden tallies (*mokkan*, or wooden flute-shaped pipes with sutras carved into the sides), and a long list of other items also join the ranks of Historic period subjects. Since this branch of archaeology is so wide open right now, there is no established basis from which to single out representative publications in any category of studies, and this summary will therefore cover only a few of the recent ones.

To a certain extent, historical archaeology today is rooted in the investigation and study of the ancient capital in present-day Nara, Heijōkyō, which served as the seat of imperial rule from 710–87. Central to it was the so-called Great Enclosure (*daidairi*) in which government offices and the Royal Palace (*heijōkyū*) were located. Among the outstanding works that attempt to combine and analyze the results of research and excavation on the Heijōkyō capital and palace remains are "Heijōkyū-ato to sono shūhen no hakkutsu chōsa" (Excavation of the Remains of Heijō Palace and Its Surroundings) [VI-01] (*Nara Kokuritsu Bunkazai Kenkyūsho nenpō*, 1973); *Heijōkyū hakkutsu chōsa hōkoku IV* (Report on the Excavation of Heijō Palace) [VI-02]; Abe Gihei, "Heijōkyū no dairi, chugu, saigū-kō" (Enclosure,

Central Court and Western Court of Heijō Palace) [VI-03]. An interesting report entitled *Heijōkyō sakyō sanjō nibō* (literally, "Third Avenue, Second Street, Left Quarter, Heijō Capital) describes a new discovery in the history of gardens. The excavation of a *mokkan* (wooden tally) at the site which is dated "Wadō Five" (Wadō is the era name for the rule of Empress Genmei, r. 708–15) seems to indicate that a certain type of poetry-writing party was held there. Such a gathering was known as *kyokusui no en*, and was always held near a flowing river or stream, sometimes between January and March when the plum trees were in bloom.

Investigation of the site of the Asuka capital has yielded what are thought to be the remains of the court at Asuka Palace (Asuka Itabuki-no-Miya). This find is reported in *Asukakyō-ato* (Site of the Asuka Capital) [VI-04], put out by the Nara Prefectural Board of Education. Also, research on the Naniwa, Kuni and Nagaoka palace remains is progressing steadily. The excavation and study of the Taga castle remains have proven fruitful as well, and some of the results appear in "Tagajō-ato: Shōwa 48 nendo hakkutsu chōsa gaihō" (Summary Report on the 1973 Excavation of the Taga Castle Remains) [VI-05], published in the *Annual Report on Research on the Taga Castle Remains*, 1973. Noteworthy in the report is the description of fragmentary documents that are unearthed there. They are thought to be parts of the account books of the province of Mutsu. In the same annual report from the following year, 1974, the excavation of a wooden tally is reported, as well as some potentially important finds assumed to be related to the practice of yin-yang divination. Another local report from Hamamatsu city, "Iba iseki, dai-roku, dai-shichiji hakkutsu chōsa gaihō" (Summary Report on the Sixth and Seventh Excavations of the Iba Site) [VI-06] includes description of items that appear to be wooden *tankō*, or fitted armor, as well as wooden tallies, many of which bear inscriptions.

On temples and shrines, *Shinpan Bukkyō kōkogaku kōza* (Revised Lectures on Buddhist Archaeology) by Ishida Mosaku presents the latest results of excavations and fieldwork done all over Japan, and is an accurate representation of the present status of research.

Kokubunji (provincial state temples) were temples established in each province by Emperor Shōmu in 741, in an attempt to strengthen the religious underpinnings of a unified state and to assert the single identity of the institutional church and political administration. Tsuboi Kiyotari, in "Saikin hakkutsu chōsa sareta shokoku kokubunji (II)" (Study of Recently Excavated Provincial Temples, II) [VI-07], has compiled and summarized the results of excavations and research to date on these Buddhist temples. Studies on individual *kokubunji* include "Bungo kokubunji-ato: Shōwa 49 nendo hakkutsu chōsa gaihō" (Remains of the Bungo Provincial Temple: Survey of the 1974 Excavation) [VI-08], and "Wakasa kokubunji-ato" (II) (Remains of the Wakasa Provincial Temple II) [VI-09], a report published by Obama City Board of Education on the cultural properties of the city. Some of the *kokubunji* were convents or held convents within them. In many cases it is still not clear whether a given temple was a convent or not, but concerning those that are certain, we have the following reports: "Izumo kokubunji dainiji chōsa gaihō" (Summary of the Second Research Project on Izumo Provincial Temple Convent), and "Minami Mukōhara Kazusa kokubunjidai iseki chōsa hōkoku II" (The Minami Mukōhara Kazusa Kokubunjidai Site: Report of Investigation II) [VI-10].

Kyōzuka have been the focus of considerable interest recently, especially as more and more are discovered. These underground, mounded repositories often contained wooden tallies, stone tablets and other items inscribed with sutras, and sometimes had markers that are themselves the subject of study. One report that focuses on a written petition of the year 1114 to certain deities, discovered buried in a *kyōzuka*, is entitled "Kōyasan okunoin no chihō" (The Underground Repository of the Inner Temple at Mt. Kōya) [VI-11].

Other recent finds from the Historic period fall into the category of communities and settlements. Related to these is another report on the excavation and study of Kusado Sengenchō site in Fukuyama City (see also Vol. I, Part 2 of this bibliography, pp. 82, 88). Apparently an ancient trading center, the site has recently yielded examples of writing on wooden tablets, Sue pottery, lacquerware and other pottery finds that date from the late Nara period or the early Heian. The report is entitled *Kusado Sengenchō iseki hakkutsu chōsa gaiyō dai-ku, jū* (Outline of Excavations 9 and 10 of the Kusado Sengenchō Remains) [VI-12]. Two good reference works for the study of communities and settlements in the Early Historic period are *Igashira, Tochigi-ken maizō bunkazai hōkoku 14* (Report No. 14 on the Underground Cultural Properties of Igashira, Tochigi Prefecture) [VI-13], and *Yachiyoshi Murakami iseki* (Murakami, Yachiyo City Remains) [VI-14].

Finally, dealing with production, two works are of particular interest to those studying tiles, tile-manufacture and kilns. One of these is *Nara Kokuritsu Bunkazai Kenkyūsho gaihō 1973* (1973 Report of Nara National Cultural Properties Research Institute), which describes finds from areas believed to hold the kiln that produced tiles for the Heijō Palace. The other is entitled *Tagajō sōken kawara no seisaku gihō* (Production Techniques of Tiles Used in the Construction of Taga Castle) by Shindō Akiteru and others.

文　　献

I-01　『岩波講座　日本歴史 1』（原始および古代 1）*Iwanami Lectures on Japanese History*, Vol. 1 (The Prehistoric and Ancient Periods, Part 1) 401 pp., 岩波書店, 1975.

02　『岩波講座　日本歴史 2』（古代 2）*Iwanami Lectures on Japanese History*, Vol. 2 (The Ancient Period, Part 2) 377 pp., 岩波書店, 1975.

03　麻生　優・加藤晋平・藤本　強（編）Asō Yutaka, Katō Shinpei and Fujimoto Tsuyoshi (eds.)『日本の旧石器文化』（第 1 巻　総論篇）*Japan's Palaeolithic Culture*, Vol. 1 (General Survey) [日本の旧石器文化 1] 255 pp.; illustrations, 8 pp., 雄山閣, 1975.

04　麻生　優・加藤晋平・藤本　強（編）Asō Yutaka, Katō Shinpei and Fujimoto Tsuyoshi (eds.)『日本の旧石器文化』（第 2 巻　遺跡と遺物 上）*Japan's Palaeolithic Culture*, Vol. 2 (Sites and Artifacts, Part 1) [日本の旧石器文化 2] 282 pp.; illustrations, 8 pp., 雄山閣, 1975.

05　佐原　真・金関　恕（編）Sahara Makoto and Kanazeki Hiroshi (eds.)『稲作の始まり』*The Beginnings of Rice Cultivation* [古代史発掘 Vol. 4] 164 pp.; illustrations, 16 pp., 講談社, 1975.

06　小野山節（編）Onoyama Setsu (ed.)『古墳と国家の成立ち』*The Tumuli and the Emergence of the State* [古代史発掘 Vol. 6] 164 pp.; illustrations, 16 pp., 講談社, 1975.

07　大場磐雄（編）Ōba Iwao (ed.)『歴史神道期』*Historical Shinto Period* [神道考古学講座 Vol. 4] 276 pp.; illustrations, 4 pp., 雄山閣, 1974.

08　日本考古学協会（編）The Japanese Archaeologists Association (ed.)『日本考古学年報』(Vol. 25) *Archaeologia Japonica*, Vol. 25, 262 pp.; illustrations, 12 pp.; English summary, 2 pp., 日本考古学協会, 1974.

09 日本考古学協会(編) The Japanese Archaeologists Association (ed.) 『日本考古学年報』 (Vol. 26) *Archaeologia Japonica*, Vol. 26, 262 pp.; illustrations, 12 pp.; English summary, 2 pp., 日本考古学協会, 1975.

10 鳥居龍蔵 Torii Ryūzō 『鳥居龍蔵全集』 (第 1 巻) *Complete Works of Torii Ryūzō*, Vol. 1, 643 pp., 朝日新聞社, 1975.

11 鳥居龍蔵 Torii Ryūzō 『鳥居龍蔵全集』 (第 2 巻) *Complete Works of Torii Ryūzō*, Vol. 2, 616 pp., 朝日新聞社, 1975.

II–01 小田静夫・C. T. キーリー Oda Shizuo and C. T. Keally 立川ローム最古の文化 "The Oldest Culture in the Tachikawa Loam" 「貝塚」 13 号, pp. 5–10, 物質文化研究会, 1974.

02 小平市鈴木遺跡調査会 Investigation Committee for the Suzuki Site, Kodaira City 『鈴木遺跡』 *The Suzuki Site*, 29 pp., 小平市鈴木遺跡調査会, 1975.

03 同志社大学旧石器文化談話会(編) Dōshisha University Discussion Group on Palaeolithic Culture (ed.) 『ふたがみ』 *Mt. Futagami*, 200 pp.; illustrations, 77 pp., 学生社, 1974.

04 鎌木義昌 Kamaki Yoshimasa 旧石器時代論 "The Case for a Palaeolithic in Japan" 『岩波講座　日本歴史』 (第 1 巻), pp. 35–74, 岩波書店, 1975.

III-01 J. E. キダー・小田静夫他 J. E. Kidder, Oda Shizuo, et al. 『中山谷遺跡』 *Nakayamadani Site*, 231 pp.; illustrations, 55 pp., 日本信託銀行, 1975.

02 渡辺　誠他 Watanabe Makoto, et al. 『桑飼下遺跡発掘調査報告書』 *Report on Excavation of Kuwakaishita Site*, 327 pp.; illustrations 72 pp., 舞鶴市教育委員会, 1975.

03 藤原宏志 Fujiwara Hiroshi 野方中原遺跡の Plant Opal 分析 *Plant Opal Analysis at Nogata Nakahara Site* 『福岡市埋蔵文化財調査報告書』 (30 巻), 1974.

04 小野真一他 Ono Shin'ichi, et al. 『千居』 *Sengo*, 438 pp.; illustrations, 118 pp., 加藤学園考古学研究所, 1975.

05 村田文夫 Murata Fumio 柄鏡形住居址考 "Handled-Mirror-Type Dwellings" 「古代文化」 27 巻 11 号, pp. 1–33, 古代学協会, 1975.

06 宮本延人・高山　純 Miyamoto Nobuto and Takayama Jun 『大磯石神台配石遺構発掘報告書』 *Report on Stone Structures at Ōiso-Ishigamidai Site*, 76 pp.; illustrations, 59 pp., 大磯町教育委員会, 1974.

07 神村　透 Kamimura Tōru 埋甕と伏甕 "Burial Jars and Inverted Jars" 「長野県考古学会誌」 19–20 合併号, pp. 17–33, 長野県考古学会, 1974.

08 岡本　勇 Okamoto Isamu 原始社会の生産と呪術 "Production and Sorcery in Primitive Society" 『岩波講座　日本歴史 1』 pp. 75–112, 岩波書店, 1975.

IV-01 田代克己他 Tashiro Katsumi et al., 東奈良遺跡出土の銅鐸鋳笵について "On the Dōtaku Mold Excavated at Higashi Nara Site" 「考古学雑誌」 61 巻 1 号, pp. 2–10, 日本考古学会, 1975.

110

02 岡本　勇他 Okamoto Isamu, et al. 『歳勝土遺跡』 *Saikachido Site* [港北ニュータウン埋蔵文化財調査報告 V] 227 pp.; illustrations, 71 pp., 横浜市埋蔵文化財調査委員会, 1975.

03 杉原荘介・大塚初重 Sugihara Sōsuke and Ōtsuka Hatsushige 『千葉県天神前における弥生時代中期の墓址群』 *Middle Yayoi Grave Cluster at Tenjinmae, Chiba* [明治大学文学部研究報告考古学　第 4 冊] 48 pp.; illustrations, 40 pp., 明治大学文学部考古学研究室, 1974.

04 斎藤　忠 Saitō Tadashi 『成川遺跡』 *Narikawa Site* [埋蔵文化財発掘調査報告 第 7] 157 pp.; illustrations, 28 pp., 文化庁, 1974.

05 後藤　直他 Gotō Tadashi, et al. 『板付周辺遺跡調査報告書 (2)』 *Report No. 2 on Investigation of Sites near Itazuke* [福岡市埋蔵文化財調査報告書　第 31 集] 120 pp.; illustrations, 10 pp., 福岡市教育委員会, 1975.

06 佐原　真 Sahara Makoto 農業の開始と階級社会の形成 "The Rise of Agriculture and Formation of a Class Society" 『岩波講座　日本歴史 1』 pp. 113–82, 岩波書店, 1975.

V–01 甘粕　健 Amakasu Ken 古墳の出現と統一国家 "The Emergence of the Tumuli and the Formation of a Unified State" 『図説日本の歴史』第 1 巻, pp. 194–264, 集英社, 1975.

02 栗原明信 Kurihara Akinobu 3–5 世紀の東アジアの形成 "East Asia in the Third-Fifth Centuries" 『図説日本の歴史』第 2 巻, pp. 68–89, 集英社, 1975.

03 泉森　皎・管野文則 Izumori Kō and Sugaya Fuminori 古墳の出現 "Rise of the Tumuli" 『古墳と王墓』 [日本古代史の旅 第 4 巻] pp. 17–40, 小学館, 1974.

04 末永雅雄 Suenaga Masao 『古墳の航空大観』 *Aerial Views of the Old Tumuli*, 455 pp., 学生社, 1975.

05 小田富士雄 Oda Fujio 豊前宇佐地方における古式古墳の調査 "Study of Old Form Mounded Tombs in the Buzen Usa Region" 「考古学雑誌」 60–2, 日本考古学会, 1974.

06 間壁忠彦ほか Makabe Tadahiko, et al. 『岡山県王墓山遺跡群』 *Artifact Group at Ōbosan, Okayama Prefecture* [倉敷考古館研究集報 10] 210 pp., 倉敷考古館, 1974.

07 白石太一郎 Shiraishi Taichirō 古墳時代の西日本 "Western Japan in the Tumulus Period" 『日本歴史地理総説』 (先史・歴史編) pp. 173–191, 吉川弘文館, 1975.

08 白石太一郎 Shiraishi Taichirō 古墳時代の東日本 "Eastern Japan in the Tumulus Period" 『日本歴史地理総説』 (先史・歴史編) pp. 193–207, 吉川弘文館, 1975.

09 西川　宏 Nishikawa Hiroshi 『吉備の国』 *The Province of Kibi*, 260 pp., 学生社, 1975.

10　茂木雅博 Mogi Masahiro 『前方後方墳』 *Square-Front, Square-Back Tumuli*, 287 pp., 雄山閣, 1974.

11　置田雅昭 Okita Masaaki 大和の前方後方墳 "The Square-Front, Square-Back Tumuli of Yamato"「考古学雑誌」59-4, 日本考古学会, 1973.

12　『熊本県城南町塚原古墳群の調査』 *Investigation of the Tsukahara Tumulus Group*, 379 pp., 熊本県教育委員会, 1975.

13　『出雲国分尼寺第2次調査概報』 *Summary Report of the Second Research Project on Izumo Kokubun Convent*, 10 pp., 島根県教育委員会, 1974.

14　上田宏範 Ueda Kōhan 前方後円墳における築造企画の展開 "The Structural Maturation of the Keyhole-Shaped Tumulus"「橿原考古学研究所論集」pp. 119-38, 橿原考古学研究所, 1974.

15　椚　国男 Kunugi Kunio 『古墳の設計』 *Design of Tumuli*, 188 pp., 筑地書館, 1975.

16　間壁忠彦 Makabe Tadahiko 『石棺石材の同定と岡山県の石棺をめぐる問題』 *The Sources of Materials in Sarcophagi and the Sarcophagi of Okayama Prefecture* [倉敷考古館研究集報 9] 28 pp., 倉敷考古館, 1974.

17　大塚初重 Ōtsuka Hatsushige 茨城県虎塚古墳とその壁画 "The Torazuka Tumulus and Its Wall Paintings"「月刊文化財」pp. 13-22, 第一法規出版 K. K., 1974 年 2 月.

18　乙益重隆 Utomasu Shigetaka 『装飾古墳の分布とその背景』 *The Distribution of Decorated Tumuli and Their Background* [古代史発掘 8] 163 pp., 講談社, 1974.

19　金井塚良一 Kanaizuka Yoshikazu 『吉見百穴横穴墓群の研究』 *Studies on the Excavation of the Corridor Tombs of Yoshimi*, 611 pp., 校倉書房, 1975.

20　石川恒太郎 Ishikawa Tsunetarō 地下式古墳 "Underground-type Tumuli"「考古学ジャーナル」103, pp. 24-26, サイエンス社, 1974.

21　大塚初重 Ōtsuka Hatsushige 『埴輪製作と工人集団』 *Haniwa Production and Craftmen's Groups* [古代史発掘 7] 163 pp., 講談社, 1974.

22　大和久震平　Ōwaku Shinpei 『七廻り鏡塚古墳』（栃木県下都賀郡大平町）*Nanamawari Kagamizuka Tumulus in Tochigi Prefecture*, 131 pp., 帝国地方行政学会, 1974.

VI-01　奈良国立文化財研究所 Nara National Cultural Properties Research Institute 平城宮跡とその周辺の発掘調査 "Excavation of the Remains of Heijō Palace and Its Surroundings"『奈良国立文化財研究所年報 1973』pp. 18-35, 奈良国立文化財研究所, 1974.

02　奈良国立文化財研究所 Nara National Cultural Properties Research Institute 『平城京発掘調査報告 IV』 *Report on the Excavation of Heijō Palace*, 71 pp., 奈良国立文化財研究所, 1974.

03　阿部義平 Abe Gihei 平城宮の内裏・中宮・西宮考 "Enclosure, Central Court

and Western Court of Heijō Palace"『奈良国立文化財研究所学報 22』pp. 69–91, 奈良国立文化財研究所, 1974.

04 『飛鳥京跡』*Site of the Asuka Capital*, 386 pp., 奈良県教育委員会, 1974.

05 『多賀城跡』(昭和 48 年度発掘調査概報) "*Summary Report on the 1973 Excavation of the Taga Castle Remains*" [宮城県多賀城研究報告] 94 pp., 宮城県多賀城跡調査研究所, 1974.

06 『伊場遺跡第 6, 第 7 次調査概報』*Summary Report on the Sixth and Seventh Excavations of the Iba Site*, 68 pp., 浜松市教育委員会, 1975.

07 坪井清足 Tsuboi Kiyotari 最近発掘調査された諸国国分寺 II "*Study of Recently Excavated Provincial Temples, II*"「仏教芸術」No. 103, 毎日新聞社, 1974.

08 『豊後国分寺跡, 昭和 49 年発掘概報』*The Remains of the Bungo Provincial Temples: Survey of the 1974 Excavation*, 14 pp., 大分県教育委員会, 1975.

09 『若狭国分寺跡 [II] 第 3 次調査概報』*Remains of the Wakasa Provincial Temples II*, 7 pp., 小浜市教育委員会, 1975.

10 『南向原・上総国分寺台遺跡調査報告 (II)』*The Minami Mukōhara Kazusa Kokubunjidai Site: Report of Investigation II*, 168 pp., 市原市教育委員会 (千葉県), 1975.

11 『高野山奥之院の地宝』*The Underground Repository of the Inner Temple at Mt. Kōya*, 168 pp., 和歌山県教育委員会, 1975.

12 『草戸千軒第 9・第 10 次調査概要』*Outline of Excavations 9 and 10 of the Kusado Sengenchō Remains*, 42 pp., 広島県教育委員会, 1975.

13 『井頭・栃木県埋蔵文化財報告 14』*Report No. 14 on the Underground Cultural Properties of Igashira, Tochigi Prefecture*, 360 pp., 下野古代文化研究会, 1975.

14 『八千代村上遺跡』*Murakami, Yachiyo City Remains*, 608 pp., 千葉県都市開発公社, 1975.

RELIGION

Tamaru Noriyoshi
University of Tokyo

Edited by Lynne E. Riggs

I. New Developments

The annotations of Volume I, Part 2 of this series indicated several factors which, since the sixties, have promoted renewed interest in formal research on Japanese religion. Studies by individual scholars, while being quite different in focus and approach, exhibited several common concerns. Most of the listed works addressed themselves to either or both of two themes: Japanese religiosity and cross-cultural comparative study. Accordingly, research in that period revolved around questions such as how to determine the source or prototype for Japan's unique religiosity or how to define the relationship between the indigenous and the foreign and the traditional and modern in Japanese religion.

For the period of 1974 and 1975, the above-mentioned trends of writing on Japanese religion have not faded; but rather, have continued to stimulate valuable scholarly activity. In addition, however, several new developments have emerged. First is the increasing preoccupation among specialists with the problem of methodology in the study of Japanese religion. The upshot of this has been the thoughtful reappraisal of the work of earlier generations. Anesaki Masaharu (1873–1949) and Yanagita Kunio (1875–1962), two pioneers in religious scholarship, would both have been centarians in this period, the perfect occasion for a rethinking of trends in the field. A small symposium was arranged to commemorate the hundredth birthday of Anesaki, the founder of modern scientific study of religion in this country, who first held the Chair of Religious Studies at the University of Tokyo (beginning in 1905) and whose *History of Japanese Religion* (first edition, 1930, Kegan Paul, London) still ranks among standard reference works on the subject. The lectures of this symposium were published as *Anesaki Masaharu sensei no gyōseki* (The Works of Professor Anesaki Masaharu, Anesaki Masaharu Sensei Seitan Hyakunen Kinenkai, 1974, 170 pp.) along with an extensive bibliography of his works. Reprinting of his more important publications was begun in 1976.

Perhaps more remarkable is the sustained and widespread interest in Yanagita Kunio's work among students of religion, as well as of folklore and anthropology. This was illustrated in an international symposium held in the summer of 1975, sponsored jointly by the Japan Folklore Society and the Committee for the Commemoration of Yanagita's Hundredth Birthday, and by the ever growing number of books and articles analyzing his work and theory [e.g., I-04, 06, 12]. A series of valuable studies was published in a special journal devoted to interpreting his work and related subjects, *Yanagita Kunio kenkyū* (Studies on Yanagita Kunio) by Hakugeisha beginning in 1973. Some scholars, such as Itō Mikiharu [I-04], attempted to carry the latent cross-cultural comparative approach only hinted at by Yanagita one step further; others analyzed the treatment of subjects central to his approach, such as ancestor worship [I-12]. Both critical and appreciative, there seems among the critics a firm consensus that his work provided an excellent beginning point and a challenge to further elaboration and revision. In much the same vein is the focus on Orikuchi Shinobu (1887–1953), scholar and poet and one of Yanagita's senior disciples, distinguished by his unique views on the religion of the ancient Japanese. Tanikawa Ken'ichi, ed., *Hito to shisō: Orikuchi Shinobu* (Orikuchi Shinobu: The Man and His Thought) [I-05] is a collection of essays together with a convenient bibliography. *Nihonteki shikō no genkei: minzokugaku no shikaku* (Prototypes of Japanese Thought: A Folklore Approach) [I-07] contains a comparative analysis of the theories of both these scholars. As with other disciplines the study of Japanese religion will continue to grow out of the work of past generations, and this sort of critical reappraisal is indispensable.

The popularity of Yanagita and Orikuchi (Anesaki, as Yanagawa

Keiichi has shown [I-06], may be less popular because of his academic orientation) has additional implications, for research on religion has ceased to be the preserve of specialists alone, but is now shared by a much wider reading public. This growing interaction of academic and nonacademic worlds is another conspicuous trend of recent years and is supported by a growing list of publications on religious topics, including the emergence of new periodical literature. For instance, the bimonthly journal *Dentō to gendai* (Tradition and Modern Times), begun early in the 1970s, steadily featured topics such as myth, ritual, taboo, attitudes on life and death, on life after death, on the fundamental nature of religion and so on, which stimulated heightened public interest. Again, early in 1975, a new quarterly called *Gendai shūkyō* (Contemporary Religion) published by Enu Esu Shuppankai, was created under the editorial supervision of Furuno Kiyoto with the cooperation of many younger scholars. Its aim is basically to be a channel of communication between specialists and a general readership, and it has dealt with the religious aspect of the Japanese emperor system, shamanism, and the new religious movements of the modern era, among other topics.

Also conspicuous during this period is the appearance of comparative studies of a new brand (see list in Section V below). Actually, since several religious traditions have always existed side by side in Japan, the comparative approach is not new. But developments in recent years have been much influenced by the ecumenical movement as a whole, and are typified by serious efforts in "dialogue" and "encounter." At first, such dialogue took place primarily on a practical level, with leaders of different denominations meeting in the hope of establishing better mutual understanding. Such endeavors were initiated in the 1960s by the International Institute for the Study of Religions in Tokyo and by the NCC Center for the Study of Japanese Religions in Kyoto. Now, the concern has been transferred to a theoretical level and attempts are being made at a systematic comparison of the fundamental motifs of different religions. Iwamoto Yasunami [V-01] and Ishida Mitsuyuki, et al., [V-03] (a collection of essays by fourteen scholars) deal mainly with Pure Land Buddhism and Christianity; while Kadowaki Kakichi [V-04] and Morimoto Kazuo [V-05] compare Zen and Western thought. Naturally comparative exposition of this sort is often highly philosophical, even apologetic, and really can only be undertaken between the so-called world religions. Incidentally, the Hikaku Shisō Gakkai (Japanese Association for Comparative Philosophy) was also founded early in 1974, and publishes annually an official journal entitled *Hikaku shisō kenkyū* (Studies in Comparative Philosophy).

In Volume I, Part 2 we noted the complexity, both in subject matter and methodology, of research in this field; for example the philosophical or speculative approach, fading at times into an apologetic one. There are also philological studies of religious documents, historical research on major events, personalities or ideas, field surveys or statistical analyses of contemporary religious phenomena. In addition, we have witnessed the perceptible influence on scholars of phenomenology, Freudian or neo-Freudian psychoanalysis, of existentialism, structuralism and so on. These and other new trends in the study of religion in the West have been introduced to Japan and are reflected in research going on here as well. This is not surprising since Japan has always been quite susceptible to foreign influence and the discipline itself is now considerably internationalized.

II. General Research

Rather than tackling the monumental task of comprehensive study of Japanese religion, most of the works published over the period 1974–75 are more specific, focussing on particular periods, personalities or other aspects of religious life. At the same time, many scholars remain deeply concerned with broad perspectives in their continuing search for the qualities of Japan's religiosity. Among the ambitious efforts in this area (supplementing those already mentioned in Volume I, Part 2) is the work of Hori Ichirō [I-01], which was intended as a continuation of his *Nihon shūkyōshi kenkyū* (Studies in the History of Japanese Religion, three volumes, Miraisha, 1963–71). Published after the author's death in 1974, it seeks to clarify the fundamental elements of Japan's religious mentality by an examination of specific topics including shamanistic practices, the priestly function of the emperor and initiation ceremonies.

While Hori's perspective is primarily that of history and folklore,

Toda Yoshio takes a somewhat different approach. His attempt to illuminate the peculiar religious feeling of the Japanese [I-02, 03] employs the concepts of ethnolinguistics and the methodology of language analysis. He posits two major types of religious language: one type having a systematic interpretative framework, the other relying more on the immediate aesthetic experiences of everyday life. Toda proposes that, as the Japanese language is of the latter type, it would potentially reveal much concerning the nature of Japanese religiosity.

In a paper concerning "paternal" and "maternal" forms of religion [I-14], Matsumoto Shigeru presents still another theory. He adopts the insights of the "climate and culture" theory, so popular in comparative cultural studies, and combines it with Freud's stages of personality development to produce a hypothetical framework upon which he believes the religious mentality of a given nation may be drawn. He advocates that Japanese religion, deep down, should be regarded as maternal for its profound dependence on nature, and illustrates its contrast to the more conscious orientation to norms of a "paternal" religion.

These valuable studies will undoubtedly serve to stimulate future research. At present they represent rather tentative answers to a question which will continue to concern many in the field.

III.   SHINTO

For the sake of convenience, let us introduce a provisional classification of the several contexts in which the term "Shinto" is used. On the one hand it is a term designating institutionalized religion based on indigenous tradition. This includes first, Shrine Shinto, which refers to the religious activities centering on local or national shrines, and second, the so-called Shinto sects such as Tenrikyō and Konkōkyō, most of which emerged before the Meiji Restoration. The latter have grown independent of mainstream Shrine Shinto to the extent that they are often grouped together with other "new religions." On the other hand, it is, thirdly, applied rather loosely to the diverse beliefs and religious practices of the general populace, namely Folk Shinto.

The above are contemporary applications of Shinto. The long history and prehistory of the religion entails a number of additional distinc-

tions beginning with Ancient Shinto—the Shinto of Japan's rich
mythology. Naturally, this aspect is of vital interest to scholars seeking
to clarify the origins of the Japanese and their culture [II-1–16] as well
as being the foundation of all other aspects of religious and cultural
life. As pointed out in Volume I, research falls in two general categories,
that of historians and of anthropologists or mythologists. The focus of
the former is naturally to clarify the place of myths in recorded history
and to learn more of the circumstances of their formation. The latter
is more concerned with identifying structural traits and lineage, often
from a cross-cultural point of view. The work of the historians is represented by Matsumae Takeshi [II-01, 02] and that of the mythologists
and anthropologists by Ōbayashi Taryō [II-04, 05, 07] and Yoshida
Atsuhiko [II-08]. On the other hand, these various perspectives have
been joined in such works as the series entitled *Nihon no shinwa* (Myths
of Japan [II-06, 09] growing out of a symposium (see Literature),
and the essays in *Nihon no kamigami* (Deities of Japan) [II-16].

As a religion without the elaborate doctrinal structure of Buddhism
or Christianity, the role and significance of ritual, especially the
community-oriented *matsuri* (festival), is much more the center of scholarly attention. In this regard, Kurabayashi Shōji [II-19] has analyzed
the character of religious feasts and other rituals, concluding that these
types of *matsuri* were the prototypes of many other aspects of Japanese
culture. Since festivals go on every year in rural and urban areas, they
are not only objects of historical research but of contemporary study as
well. Yoneyama Toshinao [II-24] conducted a careful survey of the
Yasaka Shrine Gion festival in Kyoto, showing how it relates to the
supporting organizational structure of society. Yoneyama's work
represents a trend gaining popularity among younger scholars to
approach festivals from a sociological-anthropological point-of-view.
A very different approach is Sonoda Minoru's *Shukusai to seihan*
(Festivity and Sacrilege) [II-22], which is more concerned with the
structure and symbolic function of *matsuri*. His discussion is an excellent
example of the phenomenological approach and is based on a case
study of *matsuri* in the Hida district of Gifu prefecture. He observes
two antithetical elements of *matsuri*, the formal ritual itself and the
celebration among the populace, which is often accompanied by
sacrilegious behavior.

A useful reference is the detailed glossary of basic terminology of Shinto ritual, originally published in the *Transactions* of the Institute for Japanese Culture and Classics of Kokugakuin University, with the cooperation of many specialists in the field and now published anew [II-25]. Finally there is a work which focuses particularly on the still little explored subjects of Shinto's legal status and shrine organization [II-17] by Umeda Yoshihiko, a specialist in the history of religious policy and administration.

IV. FOLK RELIGION

The concept of folk religion, first introduced by Anesaki Masaharu and firmly established in usage by Hori Ichirō, is usually applied to the broad range of belief and ritual practiced by the common people. A folk religion is amorphous, lacking a founder, a recorded scripture or any specific organization and overlapping largely with the above-mentioned Folk Shinto. However, a quick look at history indicates that not a few religious movements have emerged directly from this folk background by adopting some degree of organization and certain rituals or ideas from institutionalized religions. Shugendō, for example, is an indigenous form of mountain worship which adopted many elements from Buddhism. Movements like this lie somewhere between the diffuse, unstructured religious beliefs of ordinary people and the highly institutionalized religions. Here, then, I will treat folk religion as a multilayered matrix, into which elements of institutionalized religion constantly permeate and out of which new movements have recurrently appeared.

The recent popularity of this "little tradition" has stimulated scholars to direct their efforts to aspects hitherto little studied in Japan's religious history. Among the efforts to illuminate some obscure corners of religious and mystical practice is Yoshino Hiroko's [III-01, 02] study of magic among the ancient Japanese, which, except for festival and sexual customs, she believes was the major focus of their daily lives. She traces the process of absorption and transformation of China's yin-yang doctrine and believes that its influence was powerful enough to bring about a major revision of the Shinto pantheon. Many events of early history such as the shifting of the imperial residence, the reburial of imperial tombs or the construction of tumuli like the Taka-matsuzuka tomb, can be attributed to the impact of the doctrine.

In a similar vein, Shimode Sekiyo [III-03] has stressed the in-fluence of Taoism in popular religious belief. Arriving in Japan coincidentally with Buddhism, Taoism was prevented from growing institutionally by the official preference of the court for Buddhism; but it struck firm roots among the general populace by offering concrete means to attain worldly happiness and success.

The partially organized folk religion, Shugendō, mentioned above, took shape by the end of the medieval period and is still active today. It assimilated many ideas from Esoteric Buddhism (*mikkyō*) while at the same time maintaining a strong attachment to worship of certain sacred mountains, such as the Dewa peaks in northeastern Japan. Several studies have appeared on this unique movement [III-11–16], one of the best of which is the collection of essays entitled *Sangaku shūkyōshi kenkyū sōsho* (Studies in the History of Mountain Worship) [III-13–15].

The early modern period saw other religious movements standing between established religion and common folk belief, among them the underground faiths of the *kakure kirishitan* (hidden Christians) and of Pure Land and Nichiren Buddhism. Kept alive among the people during the suppression of the Tokugawa regime, these increasingly took on the traits of folk religion [III-07, cf. IV-32].

A contemporary as well as historic phenomenon, folk religion has also become the subject of fieldwork, as in the extensive research on shamanistic practices surviving in rural districts conducted by Sakurai Tokutarō [III-09]. His book, a continuation of an earlier publication on Okinawan shamanism (*Okinawa no shamanizumu* [Shamanism in Okinawa] Kōbundō, 1973, 432 pp.), contains much valuable material on female shamans, called *itako*, still active in northeastern Japan. Another useful volume is Inokuchi Shōji's [III-06] succinct summary of belief in omens and ghosts and the practice of divination in the daily lives of ordinary people.

V. BUDDHISM

In the study of Buddhism, perhaps the most significant achievement over the 1974–75 period has been the publication of several dictionaries. Of great service to students of religion as well as Japanese culture in general is the voluminous work of Nakamura Hajime [IV-01]. He has compiled detailed etymological and bibliographical information on nearly 45,000 specialized Buddhist terms appearing in the Sanskrit and Chinese scriptures and has also indicated their equivalents and interpretations in Japanese. Samples of Japanese usage are also taken from such classics as *The Tale of Genji* and the *Tale of the Heike*. Also, specialized dictionaries devoted to the terminology of particular Buddhist sects have been published, including a dictionary of Esoteric Buddhism [IV-03], of Pure Land (Jōdo-shū) Buddhism [IV-04, 05] and another encompassing all the sects or schools of Buddhism [IV-02]. The publication of the two Pure Land dictionaries mentioned was occasioned by the celebration in 1975 of the 800th anniversary of the sect's founding by Hōnen. These and all the others are, in fact, a useful mixture of dictionary and encyclopedic information, including details on temples and religious personalities in addition to terminology and explanatory information on doctrine.

Turning now to more specific aspects of Buddhism, we have a large group of period studies, from those on pre-Nara religion [IV-07] and the Heian period [IV-08, 09, 12, etc.] to those on contemporary religion. The very breadth of material makes it difficult to pinpoint any definite trends or pervasive tendencies of style. Generally speaking, however, we may observe among research on earlier periods a relatively strict historiographical objectivity. By contrast, discussion on Buddhism after the medieval period seems to be influenced by a desire to reinterpret and reappraise their teachings in view of the modern condition [e.g., see IV-30, 31].

This reapplication has made especial use of the teachings of Hōnen [IV-19], Shinran, Dōgen, Nichiren [IV-26], Ippen and others. Matsuno Junkō [IV-20] and Takeuchi Yoshinori [IV-21], for instance, have reevaluated Shinran's thought by testing it on modern problems and by comparison with existentialism. This difference in approach derives in part from a growing recognition, not only by followers of the respective sects but by intellectuals in general, that the above-mentioned leaders of Kamakura Buddhism are in fact among the greatest thinkers in Japan's history. The Buddhist tradition deriving from the

Kamakura sects is still very much alive, as proven by themes of widely read philosophical journals such as *Risō* (Risōsha) and *Jitsuzonshugi* (edited by Jitsuzonshungi Kyōkai, Ibunsha): Zen and modern times, Dōgen, Shinran, etc., with contributions by leading scholars of religion.

The following are only a few selected studies among the vast amounts of material rapidly appearing. Concerning the early stages of Buddhist thought is Tamaki Kōshirō's interesting work *Nihon Bukkyō shisōron* (The Philosophy of Japanese Buddhism) [IV-06], notable for its comparative analysis of Japanese and Chinese Buddhism, an approach previously not much explored. Modern Buddhism has been relatively neglected until recently, but we now have several valuable studies including Miyamoto Shōson's essay on Inoue Enryō (1858–1919), a Meiji Buddhist who sought to apply Buddhism's way of coping with the problems posed by modernity [IV-34] and two works on Senoo Girō (1889–1961) [IV-35, 36], who initiated a Buddhist socialist movement and remained a conscientious objector throughout World War II and whose thought represented a response unique among Buddhists to modern life.

VI. CHRISTIANITY

Research on Christianity in Japan seems to have been carried out chiefly in terms of the "indigenization problem"—an issue of major concern to scholars since the late sixties (see comments in Volume I, Part 2, p. 98). This trend still prevails, especially in the works of Ebisawa Arimichi [VI-01] who deals with the conditions under which Japan accepted or rejected Christianity, and Ōuchi Saburō on the encounter between Christianity and *bushidō*, the traditional value system of the samurai class [VI-02]. All these studies grapple with the historical, social and intellectual milieu into which Christianity was introduced, in order to determine the degree of its acceptance, the transformations it underwent in confronting the traditional values of Japanese society and, conversely, what significant or lasting impact it exercised on the Japanese mind.

The "indigenization" theme has been approached in two different ways. One, typical of intellectual history, traces the formation and transformation of the thought of selected personalities, as in Suyama

Tsutomu, *Chi to shin no ningenzō: Ōnishi Hajime to Uchimura Kanzō* (Men of Wisdom and Faith: Ōnishi Hajime and Uchimura Kanzō) [VI-06]. This can be further elaborated by adding biographical data and information on their social environment, as in Suzuki Norihisa's book on Uchimura Kanzō (1861–1930) *Uchimura Kanzō to sono jidai: Shiga Shigetaka to no hikaku* (Uchimura Kanzō and His Age: A Comparison with Shiga Shigetaka) [VI-07]. Adopting an approach similar to Erikson's psychohistorical analysis of religious personalities, Suzuki demonstrates how this central figure of modern Japanese intellectual history arrived at one peculiar version of Christianity while his contemporary and friend, Shiga Shigetaka (or Jūkō, 1863–1927), though growing up in quite similar circumstances, showed little interest in this alien faith but became a typically ardent nationalist. The comparison of these two unique figures vividly reflects the meeting of Christianity with the traditional value system of Japan.

The other approach is that of field surveys conducted in existing Christian communities, as with Suzuki's slim volume on Ryūjin village in Wakayama prefecture and Suga village in Kyoto [VI-08] both areas of central Japan which experienced mass conversions to Catholicism following World War II. Another similar study is Izumi Ryūji's article, "Sanson ni okeru Kirisutokyō no juyō" (The Acceptance of Christianity in a Mountain Village) [VI-09], which overlaps Suzuki's study in its focus on Ryūjin. Together, the two represent a clear picture of the manner and degree of acceptance of Christianity in rural communities.

Also, a number of essays [VI-10–16] concentrate on the problem of Christianity's relationship to the Japanese state and value system during the 1930s and the war years. This period saw the emergence of many Christians who argued for a synthesis of Christian teachings with Japanese nationalism under the motto *Nihonteki Kirisutokyō* (Japanese Christianity). In fact, only a small minority clung faithfully to the pacifist principle despite the risk of government reprisal. These studies are characterized by serious reconsideration of these generations of Japan's recent past and go hand-in-hand with works such as that on Buddhist socialism mentioned earlier. They are also typical of the appeal of the indigenization issue, particularly on a political, ethical plane.

One additional article, a review in *Shingaku nenpō* (Annals of

Theology) by Ōuchi Saburō deserves note, as it offers an overview of recent research on the history of Japanese Christianity.

VII. STUDIES ON THE MODERN AND CONTEMPORARY PERIOD

Among the various approaches of the literature in this category is the comparative. A helpful volume in this vein is *Meiji shisōka no shū-kyōkan* (Meiji Intellectuals' Views of Religion) [VII-01], written jointly by five scholars who have surveyed and analyzed the opinions vis-à-vis religious issues of leading popular authors, Buddhists, Christians, philosophers and educators. In contrast to this study, largely of the intellectual community, Murakami Shigeyoshi portrays the lives of the *kyōso* (founders of new religious movements) seeing them as the leaders of a kind of reformation [VII-06].

Murakami has also written on the Ḧonmichi movement of the late 1920s, a basically sympathetic treatment of this group which dared to face government persecution by opposing the emperor system in 1928 [VII-08]. He has also examined, in *Irei to shōkon: Yasukuni no shisō* (Memorial and Shrine to War Dead: What Yasukuni Shrine Embodies) [VII-07], the circumstances, including the rise of State Shinto, which led to the establishment of Yasukuni Shrine in 1888.

The relationship between religious bodies and the state is an ongoing issue, but religious policy after 1945 has received little attention, except from Abe Yoshiya, who has published an article in *Shūkyō kenkyū* [VII-11] and two in *Tenbō* (May and June 1975) [VII-12, 13] on this too long neglected topic. Abe has researched the policy-making process on both the Japanese and American sides, showing how the issuance of *Shintō shirei* (Shinto Directives, 1945) and *Shūkyō hōjin-hō* (Religious Juridical Persons Law, 1951) set the stage for all religious activities in the postwar period.

Contemporary religion is a popular area of current research and Ikado Fujio's studies, *Kami goroshi no jidai* (The Age of Deicide) [VII-02] and *Shūkyō to shakai hendō: sezoku-ka no imi o motomete* (Religion and Social Change: The Meaning of Secularization) [VII-03] are valuable contributions to the field. Partly in response to the "secularization debate" and the "civil religion debate" going on among Western scholars of religion, he undertakes a discussion of secularization in

Japan. He argues that though religion is seemingly secularized in Japan, this does not represent decline, so much as a fundamental change in its form, having grown increasingly personal and internalized, in place of its previous institutional form. He observes that this amounts to a shift in religion's very function, a phenomenon to be found not only in Japan, but in many other modern societies.

A more empirical study on the devitalizing of established religion is by sociologist Morioka Kiyomi, who analyzes three trends of contemporary society, the growth of individualism, the nuclear family and urbanization, and discusses the implications of these upon religious belief and practice.

Fujii Masao's *Gendaijin no shinkō kōzō: shūkyō fudō jinkō no kōdō to shisō* (The Structure of Belief among Modern Japanese: The Thought and Practice of a Religiously Uprooted Population) [VII-04] is a contemporary study of an increasingly urbanized population. He follows the migration after 1955 of large numbers to urban areas and the process of reestablishing religious ties in the city. He observes that death in the families which have thus moved, often serves as the occasion for forming new affiliation with temples, illustrating how traditional patterns of religious behavior persist throughout periods of change.

Another study on this theme is *Gendai seishōnen no shūkyō ishiki* (Religious Consciousness among Contemporary Japanese Youth) [VII-14]. Edited by the Committee on Religion and Education of the Japanese Association for Religious Studies, it grew out of surveys conducted on over 12,000 school and university students in 1970–71 after twenty-five years of background research. Eminently fulfilling its goal of determining concrete information on religious attitudes among youth, specialists will find its data and analysis very helpful. The information there may be supplemented with relevant sections of the survey by the Office of the Prime Minister, Commission on Youth, *Sekai no seinen Nihon no seinen* (Youth in Japan and the World, Ōkurashō, 1973).

VIII. Periodical References

As a supplement to the perhaps sketchy and uneven selections introduced above, the following is a review of periodical literature in the field, some of which has already been mentioned (see also *K.B.S.*

Bibliography of Standard Reference Books for Japanese Studies, Vol. 4, Religion, 1963, Part VII).

Periodical literature in the field is published in three categories: 1) commercially; 2) by academic societies or associations; and 3) by universities and/or their various faculties and institutes. *Shisō* and *Bungaku*, published by Iwanami Shoten, and *Risō*, *Dentō to gendai* and *Gendai shūkyō*, all mentioned earlier, belong to the first category, mirroring perhaps most sensitively the general trends of society.

In the second category are *Shūkyō kenkyū* of the Japanese Association for Religious Studies (*K.B.S. Bibliography*, no. 315); for Shinto, *Shinto shūkyō* of the Society of Shinto Studies (*K.B.S.* no. 319); for Buddhism, *Indogaku Bukkyōgaku kenkyū* of the Japanese Association of Indian and Buddhist Studies (*K.B.S.* no. 320), *Nippon Bukkyōgakkai nenpō* (*K.B.S.* no. 322) of the Nippon Buddhist Research Association and *Bukkyōshigaku* (*K.B.S.* no. 321), edited by the Society for the Study of the History of Buddhism and published by Heirakuji Shoten; for Christianity, *Kirisutokyōshigaku* of the Society of Historical Study of Christianity (*K.B.S.* no. 323), *Nihon no shingaku* of the Japan Association of Research on Christianity, published by Kyōbunkan (*K.B.S.* no. 325) and others.

The number of university publications is immense, the following being only a selection of the more important among them: *Nihonbunka kenkyūjo kiyō* (Transactions of the Institute for Japanese Culture and Classics of Kokugakuin University) (*K.B.S.* no. 318), *Kokugakuin zasshi* (The Journal of Kokugakuin University) (*K.B.S.* no. 317), or *Kirisutokyō shakaimondai kenkyū* (Studies of Christianity and Society), edited by the Committee of Christianity and Social Problems of Dōshisha University and published by Kyōbunkan (*K.B.S.* no. 324). Periodicals in this group are usually less well-known and not as readily available. Nonetheless, they offer important material of great potential value to students and scholars alike.

These academic periodicals are partially indexed in *Current Contents of Academic Journals in Japan*, compiled annually by the Center for Academic Publications in Japan (published until 1976 by the Japan Foundation). In addition, the *Annotated Catalogue of 270 Books Published in Japan 1973–75* by the Publishers Association for Cultural Exchange, Tokyo, includes about twenty titles on philosophy and religion.

文　　献

I-01 堀　一郎 Hori Ichirō 『聖と俗の葛藤』 *Conflct between the Sacred and the Profane*, 291 pp., 平凡社, 1975.

02 戸田義雄 Toda Yoshio 『宗教の世界』 *The World of Religion*, 169 pp., 大明堂, 1975.

03 戸田義雄 Toda Yoshio 『宗教と言語』 *Religion and Language*, 193 pp., 大明堂, 1975.

04 伊藤幹治 Itō Mikiharu 『柳田国男——学問と視点』 *Yanagita Kunio: His Scholarship and Perspective*, 〔潮選書〕193 pp., 潮出版社, 1975.

05 谷川健一(編) Tanikawa Ken'ichi (ed.) 『人と思想——折口信夫』 *Orikuchi Shinobu: the Man and His Thought*, 326 pp., 三一書房, 1974.

06 柳川啓一 Yanagawa Keiichi 官の科学・野の科学——姉崎正治と柳田国男 "Official and Private Academism: Anesaki Masaharu and Yanagita Kunio," 「展望」第188号, pp. 68–83, 筑摩書房, 1974年8月.

07 高取正男 Takatori Masao 『日本的思考の原型——民俗学の視角』 *Prototypes of Japanese Thought: A Folklore Approach* 〔講談社現代新書 406〕197 pp., 講談社, 1975.

08 和歌森太郎 Wakamori Tarō 『神と仏の間——日本人の宗教意識』 *Between God and the Buddha—Religious Attitudes of the Japanese People*, 244 pp., 弘文堂, 1975.

09 宮家　準 Miyake Hitoshi 『日本宗教の構造』 *The Structure of Japanese Religions*, 337 pp., 慶応通信, 1974.

10 笠原一男(編) Kasahara Kazuo (ed.) 『日本における政治と宗教』 *Religion and Politics in Japan*, 380 pp., 吉川弘文館, 1974.

11 竹田聴洲 Takeda Chōshū 祖先崇拝シンポジウム——第9回国際人類学民族学会議から "A Symposium on Ancestral Worship—Impressions of the 9th Congress of the International Union of Anthropological and Ethnological Sciences" 「季刊人類学」5–1, pp. 184–218, 京都大学人類学研究会(社会思想社), 1974.

12 綱沢満昭 Tsunazawa Mitsuaki 柳田国男の祖先崇拝観 "Yanagita Kunio's Views on Ancestral Worship" 「教養部研究紀要」6–1, pp. 1–12, 近畿大学, 1974.

13 田中　元 Tanaka Gen 『古代日本人の時間意識——その構造と展開』 *The Structure and Development of the Concept of Time among the Ancient Japanese*, 233 pp., 吉川弘文館, 1975.

14 松本　滋 Matsumoto Shigeru 父性的宗教と母性的宗教——日本文化伝統への一視点——(上・下) "Patriarchal and Matriarchal Religions—A Perspective on Japan's Cultural Traditions" 「UP」Nos. 22, 23. pp. 1–10; 1–10, 東京大

学出版会，1974 年 8 月，9 月.

II–01 松前　健 Matsumae Takeshi『日本の神々』 Deities of Japan 〔中公新書 372〕 217 pp., 中央公論社，1974.

02 松前　健 Matsumae Takeshi『古代伝承と宮廷祭祀』 Ancient Folklore and Court Rituals, 410 pp., 塙書房，1974.

03 三谷栄一 Mitani Eiichi『日本神話の基盤』 The Foundations of Japanese Mythology, 630 pp., 塙書房，1974.

04 大林太良 Ōbayashi Taryō『日本神話の構造』 The Structure of Japanese Mythology, 307 pp., 弘文堂，1975.

05 大林太良(編) Ōbayashi Taryō (ed.)『日本神話の比較研究』 Japanese Mythology: A Comparative Study, 433 pp., 法政大学出版局，1974.

06 大林太良(編) Ōbayashi Taryō (ed.)『日向神話』 Myths of Hyūga 〔シンポジウム日本の神話 4〕294 pp., 学生社，1974.

07 大林太良 Ōbayashi Taryō 日本神話の構造 "The Structure of Japanese Myths"「日本文化研究所紀要」No. 34, pp 162–81, 国学院大学，1974.

08 吉田敦彦 Yoshida Atsuhiko『日本神話と印欧神話――構造論的分析の試み』 Japanese and Indo-European Myths: An Effort at Structural Analysis, 270 pp., 弘文堂，1974.

09 伊藤清司(編) Itō Seiji (ed.)『日本神話の原形』 Prototypes of Japanese Myths 〔シンポジウム　日本の神話 5〕268 pp., 学生社，1975.

10 佐藤四信 Satō Shinobu『出雲国風土記の神話』 Myths in the "Izumo fudoki" 〔笠間叢書〕538 pp., 笠間書院，1974.

11 川副武胤 Kawazoe Taketane 古事記における神の不死と死――神々の物語 (上) "Mortality and Immortality of the Gods in the Kojiki," Part 1「神道学」No. 81, pp. 1–21, 神道学会，1974 年 5 月.

12 川副武胤 Kawazoe Taketane 神話と平均的日本人の宗教意識 "Myths and the Religious Mentality of the Average Japanese"「金沢文庫研究」20–5, pp. 1–14, 神奈川県立金沢文庫，1974 年 5 月.

13 溝口睦子 Mizoguchi Mutsuko 記紀神話解釈の一つのこころみ　―中の 2― 「神」を再検討する "Reinterpreting the Kojiki and Nihonshoki —Part 2–2: 'Kami' Reconsidered"「文学」42–2, pp. 170–187 (56–73), 岩波書店，1974年 2 月.

14 溝口睦子 Mizoguchi Mutsuko 記紀神話解釈の一つのこころみ ―下―「神」概念を疑う立場から "Reinterpreting the Kojiki and Nihonshoki――Part 3: Skepticism about 'Kami' "「文学」42–4, pp. 484–502 (82–100), 岩波書店，1974.

15 吉野　裕 Yoshino Yutaka スサノヲ神話外伝――常陸型 ＜大蛇退治＞ の話 "A Variation of the Susanoo Myth—The Hitachi Version of the Eight-headed Dragon,"「文学」42–6, pp. 669–83 (1–15), 岩波書店，1974 年 6 月.

16 山口昌男・渡辺守章他 Yamaguchi Masao, Watanabe Moriaki, et al. 対談・神々の根他 "The Roots of Japanese Deities: A Discussion" and other essays「国文学」20–1, 〔特集, 日本の神々〕pp. 6–155, 学燈社, 1975 年 1 月.

17 梅田義彦 Umeda Yoshihiko『神道の思想』全 3 巻 1. 神道思想篇, 2. 神祇制度篇, 3. 神社研究篇 *Shintoism* (3 vols.: 1. Ideas; 2. Cermonies and Institutions; 3. Shrines), 327, 398, 392 pp., 雄山閣出版, 1974.

18 原田敏明 Harada Toshiaki『村の祭祀』*Village Rituals and Festivals*, 333 pp., 中央公論社, 1975.

19 倉林正次 Kurabayashi Shōji『祭りの構造──饗宴と神事』*The Structure of Festivals: Banquets and Rites* 〔NHK ブックス 238〕228 pp., 日本放送出版協会, 1975.

20 伊藤幹治 Itō Mikiharu『稲作儀礼の研究』*Studies in Rice Cultivation Rites*, 294 pp., 而立書房, 1974.

21 村武精一 Muratake Seiichi『神・共同体・豊穣──沖縄民俗論』*Kami, Community and Fertility—the Folklore of Okinawa*, 368 pp., 未来社, 1975.

22 薗田 稔 Sonoda Minoru 祝祭と聖犯 "Festivity and Sacrilege"「思想」No. 617, pp. 1548–68 (62–82), 岩波書店, 1975 年 11 月.

23 鈴木満男 Suzuki Mitsuo『マレビトの構造──東アジア比較民族学研究』*Guests—A Study in East Asian Comparative Ethnology*, 342 pp., 三一書房, 1974.

24 米山俊直 Yoneyama Toshinao『祇園祭』*Gion Festival*〔中公新書〕216 pp., 中央公論社, 1974.

25 国学院大学日本文化研究所(編) Kokugakuin University, Institute for Japanese Culture and Classics (ed.)『神道要語集 祭祀篇 I』*Shinto Vocabularies: Ceremonies I*, 410 pp., 神道文化会, 1974.

III-01 吉野裕子 Yoshino Hiroko『日本古代呪術』*Magic in Ancient Japan*, 236 pp., 人和書房, 1974.

02 吉野裕子 Yoshino Hiroko『隠された神々──古代信仰と陰陽五行』*Hidden Gods: Religious Faith in Ancient Times and the Principles of Yin, Yang and the Five Elements*〔講談社現代新書 405〕216 pp., 講談社, 1975.

03 下出積与 Shimode Sekiyo『道教と日本人』*The Japanese and Taoism*〔講談社現代新書 411〕202 pp., 講談社, 1975.

04 志田諄一 Shida Jun'ichi『日本霊異記とその社会』*Society as Depicted in the Nihon Ryōiki*, 218 pp., 雄山閣出版, 1975.

05 服部幸雄 Hattori Yukio 宿神論──芸能神信仰の根源に在るもの ─上・中・下─"*Shukujin*: the Origins of Belief in Deities of the Performing Arts"「文学」, 42–10, 43–1, 43–2, pp. 64–79; 54–63; 76–97, 岩波書店, 1974–5.

06 井之口章次 Inokuchi Shōji『日本の俗信』*Folk Belief in Japan*, 283 pp., 弘文堂, 1975.

07 片吉弥吉・圭室文雄・小栗純子 Katayoshi Yakichi, Tamamuro Fumio and

Oguri Junko 『近世の地下信仰——かくれキリシタン・かくれ題目・かくれ念仏』 *Underground Religions in the Early Modern Period: Pure Land and Nichiren Buddhism and Christianity* 〔日本人の行動と思想 30〕 328 pp., 評論社, 1974.

08 宮田 登 Miyata Noboru 『原初的思想——白のフォークロア』 *Primitive Thought: the Folklore of "White"*, 261 pp., 大和書房, 1974.

09 桜井徳太郎 Sakurai Tokutarō 『日本のシャマニズム——民間巫女の伝承と生態——』上巻 *Shamanism in Japan: Rural Shamans and Their Role*, 628 pp., 吉川弘文館, 1974.

10 波平恵美子 Namihira Emiko 日本民間信仰とその構造 "The Structure of Japanese Folk Religions" 「民族学研究」38-3～4, pp. 230-56, 日本民族学会, 1974 年 3 月.

11 花見 恭 Hanami Takashi 民間信仰と神仏習合——修験道をめぐって "Folk Religion and Shinto-Buddhist Syncretism: the Case of *Shugendo*" 「思想」 No. 607, pp. 54-77, 岩波書店, 1975 年 1 月.

12 月光善弘 Tsukimitsu Yoshihiro——山寺院の研究——東北地方を中心として "A Study of Mountain Temples in the Tōhoku Region" 「宗教研究」第 47 巻 4 輯 219 号, pp. 475-96, (27-48) 日本宗教学会, 1974 年 6 月.

13 和歌森太郎(編) Wakamori Tarō (ed.)『山岳宗教の成立と展開』 *The Emergence and Development of the Mountain Sects* 〔山岳宗教史研究叢書 1〕 388 pp., 名著出版, 1975.

14 村山修一(編) Murayama Shūichi (ed.) 『比叡山と天台仏教の研究』 *Mount Hiei and Tendai Buddhism* 〔山岳宗教研究叢書 2〕 437 pp., 名著出版, 1975.

15 戸川安章(編) Togawa Anshō (ed)『出羽三山と東北修験の研究』 *The Dewa Peaks and Shugendō in Tōhoku* 〔山岳宗教史研究叢書 5〕 444 pp., 名著出版, 1975.

16 戸川安章 Togawa Anshō 『出羽三山のミイラ仏』 *The Embalmed Buddhas in the Dewa Mountains*, 262 pp., 中央書院, 1974.

IV-01 中村 元 Nakamura Hajime 『仏教語大辞典』(上・中・下巻) *Comprehensive Dictionary of Buddhist Terms* (3 vols.), 805; 669; 370 pp., 東京書籍, 1975.

02 金岡秀友(編) Kanaoka Shūyū (ed.) 『仏教宗派辞典』 *A Dictionary of Buddhist Sects*, 346 pp., 東京堂出版, 1974.

03 佐和隆研(編) Sawa Ryūken (ed.) 『密教辞典』 *A Dictionary of Esoteric Buddhism*, 906 pp., 法蔵館, 1975.

04 恵谷隆戒 (監修)・仏教大学仏教文化研究所 (編) Etani Ryūkai (gen. ed.), Bukkyō University Institute of Buddhist Culture (ed.)『新浄土宗辞典』 *A New Dictionary of Pure Land Buddhism*, 943 pp., 隆文館, 1974.

05 浄土宗大辞典編纂委員会(編) Dictionary of Pure Land Buddhism Editorial Committee (ed.)『浄土宗大辞典』(第 1 巻 あ-こ) *A Dictionary of Pure Land Buddhism* (Vol. 1), 480 pp., 浄土宗大辞典刊行会(山喜房仏書林), 1974.

06 玉城康四郎 Tamaki Kōshirō 『日本仏教思想論』（上巻）*The Philosophy of Japanese Buddhism* (Vol. 1), 376 pp., 平楽寺書店, 1974.

07 田村圓澄 Tamura Enchō 『飛鳥・白鳳仏教論』 *Asuka and Hakuhō Period Buddhism* 〔古代史選書 2〕335 pp., 雄山閣出版, 1975.

08 速水 侑 Hayami Tasuku『平安貴族社会と仏教』*Buddhism and the Aristocratic Society of Heian* 〔日本宗教史研究叢書〕271 pp., 吉川弘文館, 1975.

09 景山春樹 Kageyama Haruki『比叡山』*Mt. Hiei* 〔角川選書〕252 pp., 角川書店, 1975.

10 村山修一 Murayama Shūichi 『本地垂迹』 *Honji Suijaku: the Union of the Shinto and Buddhist Pantheons* 〔日本歴史叢書〕406 pp., 吉川弘文館, 1974.

11 小沢富夫 Ozawa Tomio『末法と末世の思想』*The Latter Day of the Law and the Concept of Masse*, 246 pp., 雄山閣出版, 1974.

12 伊藤真徹 Itō Shintetsu『平安浄土教信仰史の研究』 *Studies in the Religious History of the Pure Land Sect in the Heian Period*, 524 pp., 平楽寺書店, 1974.

13 伊藤真徹 Itō Shintetsu 『日本浄土教文化の研究』 *A Cultural Study of Pure Land Buddhism in Japan*. 530 pp., 隆文館, 1975.

14 服部英淳 Hattori Eijun 『浄土教思想論』*Pure Land Buddhist Thought*, 452 pp., 山喜房仏書林, 1974.

15 仏教大学法然上人研究会（編）Bukkyō University Study Group on the Priest Hōnen (ed.)『法然上人研究』*A Study of the Priest Hōnen*, 562 pp., 隆文館, 1975.

16 恵谷隆戒（編）Etani Ryūkai (ed.) 『法然上人の伝記と思想』 *The Life and Thought of Hōnen*, 443 pp., 隆文館, 1974.

17 香月乗光 Kazuki Jōkō『法然浄土教の思想と歴史』*The Philosophy and History of Hōnen's Pure Land Buddhism*, 502 pp., 山喜房仏書林, 1974.

18 藤古慈海 Fujiyoshi Jikai『浄土教の諸問題』*Issues of Pure Land Buddhism*, 257 pp., 山喜房仏書林, 1974.

19 大橋俊雄 Ōhashi Shunnō『法然——その行動と思想』*The Thought and Work of Hōnen* 〔日本人の行動と思想 1〕240 pp., 評論社, 1975.

20 松野純孝 Matsuno Junkō『親鸞——その行動と思想』*The Thought and Work of Shinran* 〔日本人の行動と思想 2〕334 pp., 評論社, 1974.

21 武内義範 Takeuchi Yoshinori『親鸞と現代』*Shinran Today* 〔中公新書 367〕208 pp., 中央公論社, 1974.

22 大橋俊雄 Ōhashi Shunnō『一遍——その行動と思想』*The Thought and Work of Ippen* 〔日本人の行動の思想 14〕248 pp., 評論社, 1975.

23 金井清光 Kanai Kiyomitsu『一遍と時衆教団』*Ippen and the Jishū Order*, 557 pp., 角川書店, 1975.

24 橘 俊道 Tachibana Shundō『時宗史論考』*A Historical Study of the Jishū Order*, 366 pp., 法蔵館, 1975.

25 大橋俊雄 Ōhashi Shunnō『踊り念仏』*Nembutsu Dancing*〔大蔵選書〕293 pp., 大蔵出版, 1974.

26 田村芳朗 Tamura Yoshirō『日蓮――殉教の如来使』*Nichiren: Martyrdom and Buddhahood*〔NHK ブックス 240〕221 pp., 日本放送出版協会, 1975.

27 影山堯雄 Kageyama Gyōō『日蓮宗布教の研究』*Research on the Propagation of Nichiren Buddhism*, 570 pp., 平楽寺書店, 1975.

28 影山堯雄(編) Kageyama Gyōō (ed.)『中世法華仏教の展開』*The Evolution of Medieval Hokke Buddhism*, 610 pp., 平楽寺書店, 1974.

29 笠原一男 Kasahara Kazuo『女人往生思想の系譜』*The Concept of Enlighten-ment for Women: A Historical Study*〔日本宗教史研究叢書〕427 pp., 吉川弘文館, 1975.

30 笠原一男 Kasahara Kazuo『現代人と仏教――親鸞, 蓮如, 新興宗教の七人の教祖たち』*Buddhism and Modern Man: Shinran, Rennyo and Seven Founders of New Religions.*〔日本人の行動と思想 21〕346 pp., 評論社, 1975.

31 笠原一男 Kasahara Kazuo『仏教にみる中世と現代』*The Medieval and Modern Age of Buddhism*〔日本人の行動と思想 25〕306 pp., 評論社, 1974.

32 小栗純子 Oguri Junko『妙好人とかくれ念仏――民衆信仰の正統と異端』*Eminent and Hidden Practitioners of Nenbutsu: Orthodoxy and Heresy in Popular Belief*〔講談社現代新書 419〕186 pp., 講談社, 1975.

33 速水 侑 Hayami Tasuku『地蔵信仰』*Worship of Jizō*〔塙新書〕174 pp., 塙書房, 1975.

34 宮本正尊 Miyamoto Shōson『明治仏教の思潮――井上円了の事績』*Philo-sophical Trends of Meiji Buddhism: the Achievements of Inoue Enryō*, 297 pp., 佼成出版社, 1975.

35 松根 鷹(編) Matsune Yō (ed.)『妹尾義郎と「新興仏教青年同盟」』*Senoo Girō and the New Buddhist Youth League*, 285 pp., 三一書房, 1975.

36 稲垣真美 Inagaki Masami『仏陀を背負いて街頭へ――妹尾義郎と新興仏教青年同盟』*Taking the Buddha to the People: Senoo Girō and the New Buddhist Youth League*〔岩波新書 892〕230 pp., 岩波書店, 1974.

37 由木義文 Yuki Yoshifumi 日本における仏陀観――特に仏(ぶつ)とホトケの問題に関連して "Japanese Concepts of the Buddha, with Special Reference to the Terms 'Butsu' and 'Hotoke'"「哲学」No. 63, pp. 107–122, 三田哲学会, 1975 年 2 月.

V–01 岩本泰波 Iwamoto Yasunami『キリスト教と仏教の対比』*A Comparison of Christianity and Buddhism*, 471 pp., 創文社, 1974.

02 八木誠一 Yagi Seiichi『仏教とキリスト教の接点』*Convergence of Buddhism and Christianity*, 419 pp., 法蔵館, 1975.

03 石田充之・滝沢克己(編) Ishida Mitsuyuki and Takizawa Katsumi (eds.)『浄土真宗とキリスト教』*Pure Land Buddhism and Christianity*, 446 pp., 法蔵

館, 1974.

04 門脇佳吉(編) Kadowaki Kakichi (ed.) 『禅とキリスト教 瞑想＝自由への道』 *Zen and Christianity : Meditation and a Way to Freedom*, 227 pp., 創元社, 1975.

05 森本和夫 Morimoto Kazuo 『道元とサルトル──「存在」と「無」の哲学』 *Dōgen and Sartre : Philosophy of "Existence" and "Nothingness"* [講談社現代新書 374] 237 pp., 講談社, 1974.

VI-01 海老沢有道 Ebisawa Arimichi 日本におけるキリスト教受容の前提的研究視点 "Basic Research Perspectives on the Acceptance of Christianity in Japan" 「キリスト教史学」 No. 28, pp. 1–15, キリスト教史学会, 1974 年 9 月.

02 大内三郎 Ōuchi Saburō 日本人のキリスト教受容──武士道との接触 "Japanese Acceptance of Christianity—Contact with *Bushidō*" 「日本文化研究所研究報告」 No. 10, pp. 1–33, 東北大学文学部, 1974 年 3 月.

03 大内三郎 Ōuchi Saburō 最近の日本基督教史関係著作の概観 "Recent Writings on the History of Christianity in Japan : A Survey" 「神学年報」(日本の神学) 1974 年, pp. 94–103, 日本基督教学会編(教文館).

04 助野健太郎・村田安穂 Sukeno Kentarō and Murata Yasuo 『キリシタンと鎖国』 *Christianity and National Seclusion*, 220 pp., 桜楓社, 1974.

05 土肥昭夫 Tohi Akio 『日本プロテスタント教会の成立と展開』 *The Establishment and Development of the Protestant Church in Japan*, 335 pp., 日本基督教団出版局, 1975.

06 陶山 務 Suyama Tsutomu 『知と信の人間像 大西祝と内村鑑三』 *Men of Wisdom and Faith : Ōnishi Hajime and Uchimura Kanzō* [笠間選書] 260pp., 笠間書院, 1975.

07 鈴木範久 Suzuki Norihisa 『内村鑑三とその時代──志賀重昂との比較』 *Uchimura Kanzō and His Age : A Comparison with Shiga Shigetaka*, 269 pp., 日本基督教団出版局, 1975.

08 鈴木範久 Suzuki Norihisa 『日本のカトリック村』 *The Catholic Village in Japan*, 90 pp., 新栄社, 1974.

09 泉 琉二 Izumi Ryūji 山村におけるキリスト教の受容 ─2─ 和歌山県日高郡龍神村下柳瀬地区におけるカトリックへの集団改宗とイットウ組織 "The Acceptance of Christianity in a Mountain Village" (2) 「教育学部研究紀要」 25-3, pp. 1–25, 三重大学, 1974 年 3 月.

10 森岡 巌・笠原芳光 Morioka Iwao and Kasahara Yoshimitsu 『キリスト教の戦争責任──日本の戦前・戦中・戦後』 *Christian Responsibilities for the War —Japan before, during and after World War II*, 321 pp., 教文館, 1974.

11 嶋田啓一郎 Shimada Keiichirō 軍部ファッシズムと抵抗の 1930 年代──弾圧・転向とキリスト者の苦悩 "Military Fascism and Resistance in the 1930s—the Oppression, Ideological Conversion and the Christians' Agony"

134

「キリスト教社会問題研究」第22号, pp. 1–21, 同志社大学人文科学研究所キリスト教社会問題研究会, 1974年3月.

12 笠原芳光 Kasahara Yoshimitsu「日本的キリスト教」批判 "A Critique of Japanese Christianity"「キリスト教社会問題研究」第22号, pp. 114–39, 同志社大学人文科学研究所キリスト教社会問題研究会, 1974年3月.

13 土肥昭夫 Tohi Akio 1930年代における日本基督教会の活動 (1), (2) "The Activities of the Japanese Protestant Church in the 1930s" (1 and 2)「キリスト教社会問題研究」第22号, 第23号, pp. 140–60: 146–75, 同志社大学人文科学研究所キリスト教社会問題研究会, 1974年3月; 1975年3月.

14 武 邦保 Take Kuniyasu 海老名弾正の戦争論 "Ebina Danjō's View of War"「キリスト教社会問題研究」第23号, pp. 44–82, 同志社大学人文科学研究所キリスト教社会問題研究会, 1975年3月.

15 竹中正夫 Takenaka Masao 海老名をとらえる視点——海老名の神学思想についての一考察 "A Perspective on Ebina Danjō—A Consideration of His Theology"「キリスト教社会問題研究」第23号, pp. 28–43, 同志社大学人文科学研究所キリスト教社会問題研究会, 1975年3月.

16 今中寛司 Imanaka Kanshi 海老名弾正のキリスト教信仰とその思想——その楽天的積極主義神学 "Ebina Danjō: His Thought and Christian Faith"「キリスト教社会問題研究」第23号, pp. 1–27, 同志社大学人文科学研究所キリスト教社会問題研究会, 1975年3月.

VII-01 比較宗教思想史研究会（編）（小島・峰島・小山・伊藤・中里） Society for Comparative History of Religious Thought (ed.)『明治思想家の宗教観』 *Meiji Intellectuals' Views of Religion* [大蔵選書] 366 pp., 大蔵出版, 1975.

02 井門富二夫 Ikado Fujio『神殺しの時代』*The Age of Deicide*, 238 pp., 日本経済新聞社, 1974.

03 井門富二夫 Ikado Fujio 宗教と社会変動——世俗化の意味を求めて "Religion and Social Change: the Meaning of Secularization"「思想」No. 603, pp. 1227–253 (45–71), 岩波書店, 1974年9月.

04 藤井正雄 Fujii Masao『現代人の信仰構造——宗教浮動人口の行動と思想』 *Structure of Belief Among Modern Japanese: the Thought and Behavior of a Religiously Uprooted Population* [日本人の行動と思想 32] 256 pp., 評論社, 1974.

05 森岡清美 Morioka Kiyomi『現代社会の民衆と宗教』*The People and Religion of Modern Society* [日本人の行動と思想 49] 215 pp., 評論社, 1975.

06 村上重良 Murakami Shigeyoshi『教祖—近代日本の宗教改革者たち』*Religious Reformers in Modern Japan: the Founders*, 270 pp., 読売新聞社, 1975.

07 村上重良 Murakami Shigeyoshi『慰霊と招魂——靖国の思想』*Memorial and Shrine to War Dead: What Yasukuni Shrine Embodies* [岩波新書 904] 222 pp., 岩波書店, 1974.

08 村上重良 Murakami Shigeyoshi『ほんみち不敬事件——天皇制と対決した民

衆宗教』 *The Honmichi Lesé Majesté Incident—A Popular Religion that Rebelled against the Emperor System*, 293 pp., 講談社, 1974.

09 梅原正紀 Umehara Masanori 『ほんみち——民衆宗教の原像』 *Honmichi— the Archetype of Popular Religions*, 262 pp., 白川書院, 1975.

10 市川白弦 Ichikawa Hakugen 『日本ファシズム下の宗教』 *Religion under Japanese Fascism*, 322 pp., エヌエス出版会, 1975.

11 阿部美哉 Abe Yoshiya 占領軍の対日宗教政策 "The Occupation's Policy toward Religions in Japan"「宗教研究」第48巻 第1輯 220号, pp. 1-23 (1-23), 日本宗教学会, 1974年9月.

12 阿部美哉 Abe Yoshiya GHQ の宗教政策——宗教学的政教分離論の試み (上)——"SCAP's Religious Policy—A Preliminary Thesis on Separation of Politics and Religion (1)"「展望」第197号, pp. 51-65, 筑摩書房, 1975年5月.

13 阿部美哉 Abe Yoshiya 組合派宣教師と天台僧——宗教学的政教分離論の試み (下)——"Congregational Missionaries and Tendai Sect Priests—A Preliminary Thesis on Separation of Politics and Religion (2)"「展望」第198号, pp. 91-104, 筑摩書房, 1975年6月.

14 日本宗教学会「宗教と教育に関する委員会」(編) The Japanese Association for Religious Studies, Committee on Religion and Education (ed.)『現代青少年の宗教意識』 *Religious Consciousness among Contemporary Japanese Youth*, 375 pp., 鈴木出版社, 1975.

15 島尻勝太郎 Shimajiri Katsutarō 沖縄念仏の伝統 "The Nenbutsu Tradition in Okinawa"「人類科学」No. 27, pp. 67-84, 九学会連会会, 1975年3月.

INTELLECTUAL HISTORY

Yamamoto Takeo and Imaizumi Toshio
University of Tokyo

Translated by Ronald P. Loftus

I. General Works and Collections of Materials

The following pages are a review of some of the more recent contributions to the field of intellectual history. Although intellectual history is an independent field of research, it is a mistake to consider it as divorced from the larger realm of Japanese history. The history of ideas is not something which can be arbitrarily examined in isolation from the mainstream of history. On the contrary, intellectual history must be firmly rooted in the more general field of history which serves as the foundation from which ideas develop.

Since it is necessary to keep abreast of the major activities and developments in the numerous subfields of Japanese history, the Historical Association (Shigakkai) journal, *Shigaku zasshi*, should be consulted. Especially useful is the annual special supplement "Kaiko to tenbō" (Retrospects and Prospects).

A book which provides a solid introduction to the major themes and basic issues in the field is Tamura, Kuroda, Minamoto, et al. (eds.), *Nihon shisōshi no kiso chishiki* (The Fundamentals of Japanese Intellectual History) [I-01]. In this volume, major figures and topics are conveniently arranged in chronological order, and brief summaries of relevant facts and events are provided. A selection of key documents are included or summarized and the overall result is a very compact, yet detailed overview of Japanese intellectual history, quite useful as a basic reference.

As in all fields of history, the question of methodology is an important one for intellectual historians. Wakamori Tarō's essay, "Bunkashigaku no kadai to hōhō" (Problems and Methodology in Cultural Historiography) in the volume [I-02] he edited, *Nihon bunkashigaku e no teigen* (Towards the Development of Japanese Cultural Historiography) (Kōbundō, 1975), is a significant contribution on this topic. In this essay, Professor Wakamori draws on his long years of experience in synthesizing the research techniques of history and folklore studies in order to achieve a new "religious studies" approach to history. In presenting his ideas, he argues the case for a reevaluation of current methodology for research on cultural history. Included in the same volume is Kumakura Isao's essay "Dentōgeijutsu kenkyū no hōhō" (Methodology for Research on the Traditional Art Forms).

Another work on methodology, Morimoto Jun'ichirō's *Nihon shisōshi no kadai to hōhō* (Themes and Methodology in Japanese Intellectual History) [I-03] takes the problem of man and nature as its central theme. It deals with such topics as, a) the Japanese concept of the approach to nature; b) the establishment of Asiatic ideology (Shintoism) in Japan; c) Buddhism as an ancient ideology; d) the establishment of ancient ideology in Japan; e) the Asiatic aspects of Japanese feudalism; and f) the interplay of ideas in early modern Confucianism. This book is an implicit criticism of the work of Maruyama Masao from a Marxist point of view.

In terms of basic introductory materials, a well organized survey of the major issues is presented by Inoue and Nagahara, (eds.) in their *Nihonshi kenkyū nyūmon* (An Introduction to Japanese Historical Research, Vol. IV) [I-04]. Endō Motoo has edited a useful guide to reference works and research materials, *Nihonshi kenkyūsho sōran* (A Guide to Research Works in Japanese History) [I-05], while the group of bibliographic essays by Akamatsu Toshihide and others, "Shiseki kaidai" (An Introduction to Japanese Historical Documents) [I-06] contains the essential data on the classic documents of Japanese history. Also among the books aimed at the general reading public are those which accurately reflect the depth and scope of major issues, and at the same time touch on the kinds of themes and topics that are often overlooked in more narrowly focused research monographs. Tanaka Hajime's *Kodai Nihonjin no jikan ishiki—sono kōzō to hatten* (The Structure and Development of the Concept of Time among the

Ancient Japanese) [I-07] is a perfect example of this variety of book, similar to another book he compiled with several other scholars, *Shisō toshite no Nihon Bukkyō* (Japanese Buddhism as Philosophy) [I-08]. Likewise, Takashima Yūzaburō's *Matsu* (The Pine Tree in Japanese Culture) [I-09] fits in this category as well.

Another valuable source for basic materials are various series the separate volumes of which are continually being published, such as *Nihon shisō taikei* (Iwanami Library of Japanese Thought) [I-11] and *Kindai Nihon shisō taikei* (Chikuma Collection of Modern Japanese Thought) [I-21]. Each volume in these series is individually edited, providing the reader with excellent commentary and annotations accompanying the primary sources of that volume. These primary sources are an essential tool of the intellectual historian, for they represent the fundamental groundwork which is the prerequisite of any work in this field. It is the compilation of primary source materials which allows progress in textual criticism and analysis of material.

Finally, another major trend of recent historical research is the search for new documents concerning local history. Since this work goes on chiefly in local areas themselves, the results are often published only in small local journals. As a result, the alert researcher will make a special effort to familiarize himself with these valuable materials and learn where to find them, since it is often hard to locate copies of these smaller journals.

Let us now turn to a description of the principal new contributions to the field. The books and essays will be introduced according to the standard periodization: the Ancient, Medieval, Early Modern and Modern periods.

II.   Studies on the Premodern Era

A.   The Ancient Period

The most important contribution to be made recently in the field of ancient intellectual history is the publication by Iwanami Press of a series of thoroughly-researched and documented volumes on leading individual thinkers. This *Nihon shisō taikei* (Iwanami Library of Japanese Thought) [I-11] series is noted for presenting accurate and readable texts of major figures like Shōtoku Taishi, Kūkai and Saichō, as well as important records such as *jisha engi* (records of temples and shrines). Since these volumes all contain the latest research on the subject by specialists who have edited and annotated the volumes, they represent a strong foundation upon which subsequent progress in the field can be based.

The new *Iwanami kōza Nihon rekishi* (Iwanami Lectures on Japanese History) series is still in the process of being published (26 volumes are projected), and there are a number of interesting essays in the volumes on the ancient period. Ueda Masaaki's "Kodai no saishi to girei" (Ancient Religious Rituals and Ceremonies) [II-02] and Saeki Arikiyo's "Kizoku bunka no hassei" (The Birth of Aristocratic Culture) [II-03] are both good cases in point. When used together with existing compilations of primary materials, this new group of essays provides a tremendous challenge for further research in this area.

Related to the above-mentioned articles are two very interesting studies on mythology in ancient Japan. One is Saigō Nobutsuna's "Sumeramikoto-kō" (On 'Sumeramikoto,' the Earliest Imperial Title) (*Bungaku*, Vol. 43, No. 1) and Masuda Katsumi's "Monogami shūrai —tatarigami shinkō to sono henshitsu" (Visitation by Evil Spirits: the Growth and Development of the Ancient Japanese Belief in Vengeful Gods) (*Hōsei Daigaku bungakubu kiyō*, No. 20).

Turning to investigations of the documents of the ancient period, we have Iida Mizuho's essay, " '*Hifuryaku*' no sakubyū ni tsuite," (Concerning Errata in the *Hifuryaku*, an Early Heian Encyclopedia of Chinese Classics) [II-24]. Also by Iida are the related articles "Sonkeikaku Bunko kazō *Hifuryaku* no shihaimon ni tsuite" (Writings on the Reverse Side of Pages in the *Hifuryaku* from the Sonkeikaku Library Volumes), which appears in *Shigaku ronshū: taigai kankei to seiji bunka*, No. 2, and "*Hifuryaku* ni kansuru kōsatsu" (Studies on the *Hifuryaku*) in *Chūō Daigaku Kyūjūshūnen ronbunshū, Bungakubu*. Also to be noted here are Ōta Shōjirō, "*Kagaku Eireishū* ni tsuite" (On the *Kagaku Eireishū*) in *Kokugo-kokubun*, Vol. 43, No. 8, and Mikame Yoshio, "Takashina Moriyoshi sen *Honchō reisō* kenkyū" (A Study of *Honchō Reisō* Edited by Takashina Moriyoshi) in *Namiki no sato*, Nos. 8 and 9.

In recent years, there has been intensified interest in *Nihon ryōiki*, a collection of miraculous tales from Japanese Buddhism. Shida Jun'ichi's

Nihon ryōiki to sono shakai (Society as Depicted in the *Nihon Ryōiki*) [I-10] reflects the current interest in this eighth century work. Behind this research interest and the renewed attention to methodology noted above is a desire to penetrate beyond the level of religious dogma to observe the interplay between these doctrines or beliefs and the society of a given period, as well as the implications these beliefs have for that society.

Research on historical legends and tales (*rekishi monogatari*) has continued steadily over the years. Taga Sōshun's "Imakagami shiron" (A Study of the *Imakagami*) (*Shigaku zasshi*, Vol. 83, No. 2) and Matsumura Hiroshi's "*Eiga monogatari* ni okeru sakidori-kiji ni tsuite" (On the Prophetic Aspects of *The Tales of Glory*) (*Kodai bunka*, Vol. 26, No. 7) are two recent examples. Yamanaka Yutaka's *Heianchō bungaku no shiteki kenkyū* (A Historical Study of Heian Literature) (Yoshikawa Kōbunkan, 1974) represents the most recent compilation of this kind of literature by a leading specialist.

An exciting new development in intellectual history is the initiation of joint research being undertaken by Japanese and Korean scholars. Perhaps the most important work to be produced to date through such international cooperative efforts, is a study by Tamura Enchō and Hong Sun-ch'ang (eds.), *Shiragi to Asuka-Hakuhō no Bukkyō bunka* (Silla and Asuka-Hakuhō Buddhist Culture) [II-01]. Likewise, Momo Hiroyuki's article, "Sukuyōdō to sukuyō kanmon" (Astrology and Documents Pertaining to Astrological and Other Forms of Divination) [II-23] is a serious analysis of a subject frequently overlooked, the belief in magic and the role of superstitions and mystical beliefs in political and social life. After scrupulously analyzing the *sukuyo-kanmon*, or documents containing the recommendations and prognoses of specialists in astronomy, astrology and other divination techniques, the author concludes that, "*Rekidō* (the study of calendar making) and *tenmondō* (astronomy) represent a 'scientific' approach. When combined with the philosophic dimensions of *on-yōdō* (yin-yang cosmology), the three constitute a single unified system. *Sukuyōdō* by contrast is a more compact system which encompasses both scientific and philosophic modes." (p. 16) This important observation about the structure of the intellectual realm in ancient Japan is a significant and valuable guide for future research in this area.

Also of similar interest are Kimura Susumu, "Kamakura jidai no on-yōdō matsuri" (Yin-Yang Rituals in the Kamakura Period) (*Risshō shigaku*, No. 38) and Gotō Munetoshi's study of magical healing techniques, "Sō Hōren" (The Priest Hōren) (*Ōitaken chihōshi*, No. 76).

In addition, the major works of Itō Shintetsu, long a leading scholar in the field of Buddhist studies, are currently available, including *Heian Jōdokyō shinkōshi no kenkyū* (Studies in the Religious History of the Pure Land Sect in the Heian Period) (Heirakuji Shoten) and his *Nihon Jōdokyō bunkashi kenkyū* (Studies in the Cultural History of Japanese Pure Land Buddhism) (Ryūbunkan). Also important is Kageyama Gyōō, *Nichirenshū fukyō no kenkyū* (Research on the Propagation of Nichiren Buddhism) (Heirakuji Shoten). Furthermore, focussing on lifestyles in ancient times is Sekine Masataka, *Narachō shokuseikatsu no kenkyū* (Research on Diet and Eating Habits in the Nara Period) (Yoshikawa Kōbunkan), now supplemented by *Narachō fukushoku no kenkyū* (Research on Dress and Ornamentation in the Nara Period) (Yoshikawa Kōbunkan).

B. The Medieval Period

The most conspicuous feature of recent publications on medieval history is the steady stream of essay collections by established scholars. Unfortunately, there is not sufficient space here to provide a detailed description of these many excellent studies, but Kuroda Toshio's *Nihon chūsei no kokka to shūkyō* (State and Religion in Medieval Japan) [II-13] may be taken as an example.

The book is divided into three parts. Part one deals with the formation and structure of state authority in medieval Japan. Part two is comprised of five essays dealing with the following topics: 1) "Ikkō-senju" (exclusive reliance on Nenbutsu prayer) and "honji-suijaku" (Japanese Shinto gods as reincarnations of Buddhas and bodhisattvas) in Kamakura Buddhism; 2) medieval views of history: the Priest Jien's *Gukansho* and Kitabatake Chikafusa's *Jinnō shōtōki*; 3) the medieval state and the idea of Japan as the "Land of the Gods"; 4) the concept of "Buppōryō" (Buddhist Land)—the political ideals of *ikkō-ikki*; 5) hierarchy in medieval society and the concept of the "lowly" (*hisen*). All of these essays were initially published and widely read as monographs, making a strong impact upon the academic world. They have stimulated considerable debate and discussion, and have influenced scholarship in the field a great deal.

Kuroda's third section is a previously unpublished essay, "Chūsei ni okeru kenmitsu taisei no tenkai" (The Development of Exoteric and Esoteric Buddhism in the Medieval Period). This essay should be read in conjunction with his essay in the new *Iwanami kōza Nihon rekishi* series, "Chūsei jisha seiryokuron" (Secular Power of Medieval Temples and Shrines) [II-06].

In an earlier essay, "Shisōshi no hōhō ni tsuite no oboegaki—Chūsei no shūkyō shisō o chūshin ni" (Notes on Methodology in Intellectual History with Special Reference to Medieval Religious Thought) (*Rekishigaku kenkyū*, No. 239), Kuroda criticized the tendency of researchers to study religious groups in isolation, adhering to the rigid denominational lines which separate them. All that can emerge from this kind of approach, he contends, is a series of solitary studies on "the history of the Pure Land sect, the history of Zen or Nichiren Buddhism, the history of Shinto or Confucianism, and so on." Rather, Kuroda proposes, the common characteristics of religious movements should be stressed in the context of the given period. For medieval religion he summarizes four common characteristics, 1) magical qualities; 2) deification; 3) stress on "the other shore;" and 4) reliance on precepts.

According to Kuroda, these four characteristics typify so-called "medieval religion" (*chūseiteki shūkyō*), and religious history of the period should be approached with those qualities in mind. His own essays proceed from this perspective, combining a cultural-religious history approach with a broad view of political history. In this way, he sets the chronicles of the state as the backdrop for a stimulating interpretative analysis of the ebb and flow of human involvement with spiritual pursuits. The end product is a richer form of historical writing which achieves a skillful combination of orthodox techniques for interpreting documentary references with a highly creative and imaginative approach appropriate to popular religious attitudes of the medieval period.

This trend for a historian's concern to center around the people—their mindset, feelings and aspirations—is currently of major importance in Japanese scholarship. Illustrating this is Yokoi Kiyoshi's book

Chūsei minshū no seikatsu bunka (Popular Culture and Daily Life in Medieval Japan) [II-17] which the author describes as an attempt "to incorporate the fruit of historical research on the dominant thought patterns of Buddhism, yin-yang cosmology, Shugendō and Shinto" into a new variety of popular history. By drawing fully from sources in social and economic history, this study depicts the attitudes of the medieval populace towards the various religions which prevailed. Yokoi's work is deeply thought-provoking, particularly Chapter Three, entitled "Sabetsu to shokue shisō" (Discrimination and the Concept of the 'Untouchable'). The essays contained in this chapter have had a considerable impact and have been the cause of much self-reflection among scholars in the field.

Also of related interest are the following three collections of essays: Sakurai Yoshirō's *Chūsei Nihon no seishinshiteki keikan* (Medieval Japan's Spiritual Landscape) [II-14]; Mizuno Kyōichirō's *Buke jidai no seiji to bunka* (Politics and Culture in Japan under Warrior Rule) [II-18]; and Shingyō Norikazu's *Ikkō-ikki no kiso kōzō* (The Structure of the Ikkō Peasant Uprisings) [II-20].

The new *Iwanami kōza Nihon rekishi* series offers a number of excellent essays in its volumes on the medieval period. With essays by authors such as Ōsumi Kazuo [II-04], Sakurai Yoshirō [II-05], Kuroda Toshio [II-06] and Ishida Yoshihito [II-07], there is a good mixture of interpretive and informative analysis of leading academic theories, in addition to a number of articles presenting new and original theses. The Iwanami series is especially important because it contains the most up-to-date findings on the topics covered and sets the standard for further research. This series has distinguished itself as producing essays which become the point of departure for subsequent work in the field.

Above we noted that historical works for a general readership are often useful and stimulating because they are less restricted in scope than more narrowly focused research monographs. Their range is potentially much greater and their vision more comprehensive. By the same token, such histories can remain outside the fierce debates of specialists on the subtleties of historical detail, and create a smoothly flowing narrative of broad perspective. Amino Yoshihiko's *Mōko shūrai* (The Mongol Invasions) [II-09] and Ishii Susumu's *Chūsei bushidan* (Medieval Warrior Bands) [II-10] are two good examples of this kind of work. The authors draw upon a substantial fund of research and experience to portray the subject with boldness and accuracy.

Another important direction of medieval intellectual history is reflected in studies attempting to reconstruct the actual living conditions of specific local communities during the medieval period. Ogasawara Nagakazu's "Chūsei no tenjin shinkō to chihō bunka" (The Tenjin Faith and Local Culture in the Medieval Period) (*Jinbun kenkyū*, Chiba Daigaku, No. 4), the articles noted above by Mizuno Kyōichirō [II-18] and Suda Etsuo's "Muromachi kōki ni okeru chihō bunka keisei no danmen" (Aspects of the Formation of Local Culture in Late Muromachi) [II-26] are all examples of this methodological approach.

Of course, medieval intellectual currents do not all present obvious doctrines or clear systems of thought. Rather, they are also to be found in the form of literature and in other contemporary arts. Consequently the intellectual historian should be familiar with the numerous studies in art and literary history as well. For example, Nakamura Yasuo's "Shinzō kara kamen e" (From Shinto Images to Nō Masks) [II-22] is a thorough and interesting study based on the author's exhaustive search throughout Japan for antique Nō masks. Nakamura's pioneering study is a great stride in the systematic treatment of this unique type of historical material.

Nishino Haruo's "Nobumitsu no Nō" (The Nō Plays of Nobumitsu) [II-25] is a detailed and sophisticated analysis of the works of the Nō playwright Kanze Kojirō Nobumitsu; Wada Yoshiaki's "Chūsei Nara no furyū ni tsuite no ichi kōsatsu" (An Analysis of *Furyū* Dances in Medieval Nara) [II-29] is an examination of how medieval dance troupes were operated in the context of a volatile political milieu. I believe that these studies represent a vanguard of research which will become the model for future efforts in this field.

A particularly unique study along these same lines is Shimada Isao's fascinating work on the important medieval art of falconry. The essay, entitled "Hōyō shoryū to takakotoba no kankei ni tsuite no shiron" (A Preliminary Study of the Schools of Falconry and Their Relationship to Falconers' Jargon) [II-27] introduces much fresh material on a central dimension of medieval cultural life. This is yet another study which clearly breaks new ground and will undoubtedly inspire further research on a relatively unexplored topic. In an earlier essay which should be consulted along with this essay on falconry, Shimada included a study of the special language of falconers (*takakotoba*) with work on other "special social dialects and vocabularies" such as the language of medicinal herbology, Buddhist terminology, and other specialized speech forms (See *Kōza kokugoshi* 3, *Goi shi*, Chapter 5, published by Taishūkan, 1971).

A different, and important study that thoroughly scrutinizes historical facts or analyzes the detail of historical texts and records, is exemplified by the meticulous research of Tamamura Takeji, "Ōmi Katada Gyokusen-Shōzui nian no sōshō to Kengan Genchū" (A study of Kengan Genchū and His Inheritance of the Katada and Shōzui Temples at Ōmi) [II-28]. Tamamura earlier wrote two valuable articles, "Muromachi jidai kōki no gakusō Hōshuku Shusen den ni tsuite no shinsetsu" (A New Hypothesis on the Life of the Late Muromachi Scholar and Zen Priest, Hōshuku Shusen) (*Nihon rekishi*, No. 328) and "Ikkyū Sōjun kōin setsu no saikakunin" (A Reconfirmation of the Thesis that Ikkyū Sōjun Was of Imperial Blood) (*Zen bunka*, No. 79).

With the publication of Murayama Shūichi, ed., *Hieizan to Tendai Bukkyō no kenkyū* (Studies on Tendai Buddhism and the Temples of Mt. Hiei) (Meicho Shuppan) and other volumes in the series *Sangaku shūkyōshi kenkyū sōsho* (Studies on the History of the Mountain-Worship Sects) many older essays have been made more accessible. Hagiwara Tatsuo's *Chūsei saishi-soshiki no kenkyū zōhoban* (Studies on Organization and Ritual in Medieval Religion, Revised Edition) [II-19] and Kawase Kazuma's *Zōho shintei Ashikaga gakkō no kenkyū* (Studies on the Ashikaga School, Revised and Enlarged Edition) [II-21] are two additional examples of such reissues.

Unfortunately, space limitations prohibit a further listing of the many sources of related interest in the field of medieval intellectual history, but the other essays in this volume will be helpful guides to further references on history, as well as language, literature and art, for books and articles of this perspective. Indeed, it behooves all those interested in intellectual history to avoid restricting themselves only to those books and articles which can be clearly linked to the field by title, for such works merely scratch the surface of the subject. It is important that scholars penetrate beyond the superficialities and into the deeper strata of history from which "ideas" and "culture" spring.

III. The Early Modern Period

There are many useful books and articles in early modern intellectual history, but temporarily putting aside the subject of studies focused on single individual thinkers, we can identify two general categories of research in this field. First are studies which are mainly concerned with the ideology of control under the *bakuhan* system. Second are those which focus on thought and belief systems and on the day-to-day life of commoners during the Tokugawa period. Although this interest in the beliefs and values of ordinary people in the Edo period has been evident for several years, only recently has it become particularly pronounced. One can see evidence of this in research of great range in subject matter.

A major problem with the subfield of popular thought (*minshū no shisō*) is that no consistent methodology has been developed which might lend coherence or unity to the approach. Since no definitive work has made its appearance as yet, studies tend to be devoted to debates on the available evidence or existing interpretations, rather than on formulating an overall theoretical construct. Studies attempting to reconstruct popular thought focus not only on social and political phenomena, but on the religious and cultural dimensions of life as well. The result has been the appearance of numerous case studies illustrating the popular thought of the early modern period.

A very helpful work on the major issues and latest research developments in early modern history is Bitō Masahide, "Kinseishi josetsu" (An Introduction to the Early Modern History of Japan) (*Iwanami kōza Nihon rekishi*, Vol. 9). Another valuable discussion can be found in Inoue and Nagahara, eds., *Nihonshi kenkyū nyūmon* IV (An Introduction to Japanese Historical Research, Vol. IV) [I-04]. The comments in the latter on intellectual history are especially helpful and interesting.

Fujii Manabu's essay, "Kinsei shoki no seiji shisō to kokka-ishiki" (Political Thought and National Consciousness at the Beginning of the Early Modern Period) [III-03] juxtaposes late medieval and early modern political ideas and attitudes towards the nation. His main intent is to clarify the character of ideological control in the early modern period. Fujii asserts that secular authority in this period was essentially realistic, relying more and more as time went on, on the growing power of the military class, the *bushi*. With this new arrangement, religion was replaced as a source of legitimacy for political authority by the sharp division of society into the rulers and the ruled as the *bushi* class set itself apart from the rest of society. This hierarchical division of society grew out of the medieval *ōdo-ōmin* concept according to which the land and the people who inhabited it were the property of the lord.

An interesting contrast with this approach is Ishida Ichirō's "Zenki bakuhantaisei no ideorogii to Shushigaku-ha no shisō" (Neo-Confucian Thought and the Ideology of the Early *Bakuhan* System) [I-11(8)]. In this essay, Ishida argues that the Neo-Confucianist concept of *Tendō* (Way of Heaven) and the cult of Tokugawa Ieyasu constituted a single ideasystem, which provided the essential source of ideological control in the early *bakuhan* system. A third approach of interest may be found in Fukaya Katsumi, "Bakuhan taisei shihai to murayakuninsō no kokugaku juyō" (Control under the Bakuhan System and the Acceptance of National Learning by the Village Leadership) [III-33] in which the problem of political control is treated in the framework of state power. Yasumaru Yoshio, on the other hand, focuses on the conflict between popular values and the controlling ideology of the *bakuhan* system from late Tokugawa to the early Meiji period. His essay, "Nihon nashonarizumu no zen'ya" (The Eve of Japanese Nationalism) which appeared in the journal *Rekishigaku kenkyū* [III-10] concludes that emperor-centered nationalism, with its roots in Mitogaku and late Kokugaku thought, ultimately became the dominant ideological force underlying the modernization of Japan.

Studies of Tokugawa Confucianism are also quite plentiful. Perhaps because 1975 was the 250th anniversary of the death of the eighteenth century Confucianist Arai Hakuseki, numerous studies of this Tokugawa intellectual began to appear in that year. A survey of the results of research on Hakuseki to date indicate that while appraisals of his contributions to the *bakufu* and its policies have been adequate, work still needs to be done on how his philosophy of history and his brand of rationalism stand in the context of Japanese intellectual history as a whole and the evolution of early modern thought in particular.

In another essay on a Tokugawa Confucian, Miyake Masahiko has taken the thought of Itō Jinsai (1627–1705) as a framework for analyzing the ideas underlying the *sō*, or autonomous communal groups within the city of Kyoto [III-18] and tries to account for their survival from the medieval period. Miyake traces the process whereby Kyoto's autonomous communities were integrated into the lower echelons of the *bakufu* administrative structure, and analyzes this development against the background of intellectual history.

Another important branch of Tokugawa Confucian studies is Mitogaku. Tsuyuguchi Takuya's essay on the Late Mito school, singles out its notion of practical ethics (*jissen rinri*) as especially significant [III-29]. According to Tsuyuguchi, this notion was rooted in two important tendencies, on the one hand, by focusing attention on the common ancestry of the Japanese people as embodied in the unbroken line of emperors, the Mito school succeeded in making a fetish out of the concept that loyalty and filial piety could be rendered identical in the Japanese context. On the other hand, the Mito school also emphasized that the practice of these integrated ethical concepts could be interpreted as the embodiment of the Confucian ideal of sincerity (*sei*). Since Mitogaku and the [Ogyū] Sorai School of Ancient Learning (*Kogaku*) have both been rather popular subjects over the years, the reader is advised to consult the volumes on individual thinkers in the *Nihon shisō taikei* series [I-11]. Here again, the editor's explanatory notes and commentary on each personality and his times are very helpful.

Popular culture as expressed diversely in the daily lives of ordinary people has become the focus of a current trend towards analyzing its various forms of expression in search of popular thought. For a discussion of some of the basic materials for research of this kind, see Hayashi Motoi, "Kinsei minshū no shakai-seiji shisō kenkyū no shiryō-teki kiso" (Documentary Basis for Research on Early Modern Popular Social and Political Thought) [III-11]. This article discusses "underground" political documents and materials relating to peasant uprisings (*hyakushō-ikki*).

Of a similar nature is Haga Noboru, *Minshūshi no sōzō* (Creating a Popular History) [III-38], who examines written as well as other sources such as folklore and popular entertainment forms. This venture into the realm of folklore represents a new departure for intellectual historians and there is a need to combine basic historical groundwork with a fundamental study of methodology appropriate to the field.

The drive to "discover the masses" in history has also had an impact on the study of religion, for example in the growing interest in determining Buddhism's actual role in daily life and its relationship to popular thought and belief. Takeda Chōshū's essay, "Kinsei shakai to Bukkyō" (Society and Buddhism in the Early Modern Period) [III-05], examines the role of Buddhist temples in the activities of a local community and in the daily lives of ordinary people. A related essay, Akai Tatsurō, "Genrokuki no toshi seikatsu to minshū bunka" (Urban life and Popular Culture during the Genroku Period, 1688–1704) [III-04], deals with the thought and culture of the townspeople (chōnin) and is an attempt to link urban culture to popular faiths of that period. Akai focuses, for example, on how certain religious rituals such as the public display of Buddhist icons and the pacification of the souls of the deceased at Shinto shrines, influenced Kabuki theater. Unfortunately the whole notion of "chōnin shisō," the attempt to identify the mindset of city-dwellers, is fraught with both conceptual and methodological complications and inevitably many problems remain with this type of research.

Another popular approach to the study of early modern intellectual history is in educational history. The emphasis has been on the analysis of the roots of education at the local level and on case studies of local scholars. A study by Takahashi Satoshi, "Edo jidai no minshū kyōiku to sono shisō" (The Philosophy and Practice of Popular Education in the Tokugawa Period) [III-09], specifically treats the relationship between education and the development of ideas. Haga Noboru's "Tokugawa jidai chishikijin no gakumonron to sono shisō" (The Educational Philosophy and Approach to Learning of the Tokugawa Intelligentsia) [III-02] attempts to reconstruct the lives and philosophies of scholars in the Tokugawa period. The popularity of such studies is not the result of stagnation in research on well-known scholars. That work continues apace, supplemented with the growing interest in unknown figures at the lower levels of the academic hierarchy.

A number of case studies on local culture have also appeared, examining the development of thought and values among the various social strata in a specific locality. In addition to work on well-known figures such as Takano Chōei and Andō Shōeki, progress has also been made in making available new information on less well-known figures of the age. Unfortunately, limitations of space prohibit itemization of these studies. Nevertheless, their impact, which is to say, the impact of this new approach concentrating on local culture and village life, has been considerable. Yet work in this field is just beginning and scholars have yet to determine just what historical contribution such local culture made to intellectual history.

Two subjects which have yet to be adequately explored in terms of intellectual history are Western studies (*Yōgaku*) and the development of natural science in Japan. What has been done is mainly in the form of individual or specific case studies, as the entries below testify. *Inō Tadataka no kagakuteki gyōseki* (The Scientific Contributions of Inō Tadataka) [III-37] dealing with the work of a pioneer geographer, is written by Hoyanagi Mutsumi, himself a geographer. The intellectual historian must often rely on such specialists in other fields for access to information for figures like Inō. Satō Shōsuke's article, "Rangaku ni okeru jitsuri to jitsuyō—Sugita Genpaku no igaku shisō o chūshin ni shite" (Scientific Principles and Utility in Dutch Studies: Sugita Genpaku's Approach to the Study of Medicine) [III-36] does double duty, not only as an accurate portrayal of Sugita's medical knowledge, but also as a useful study of the overall nature of *Rangaku*.

IV. THE MODERN PERIOD

In scholarship dealing with the modern period, as with early modern, the idea of research on popular thought has been influential in each of its various subfields. The results are by no means complete at this stage, but remarkable progress has been made in numerous empirical case studies, discovery of new materials and critical evaluation of documents. There is likewise an increasing number of works on popular scholarship and the nature of local culture in various parts of Japan. Often, the results of this kind of research are published in local historical journals of limited circulation. Space here does not allow a full accounting of this research, but scholars in this area should be aware of these local historical journals.

Turning now to general accounts of intellectual developments in the modern period, we have Matsumoto Sannosuke's study of intellectual currents focused on the period from Tokugawa through the first half of Meiji, *Nihon seiji shisō gairon* (An Outline of Japanese Political Thought) [IV-01]. While Matsumoto stresses the political content of Japanese thought in this period, a study by Uete Michiari takes the "modernization" approach, focusing on key individual intellectuals in *Kindai Nihon shisō no keisei* (The Formation of Modern Japanese Thought) [IV-03]. An interesting counter-approach may be found in Minamoto Ryōen's two-part essay in the journal *Kokoro*, "Nihon no kindaika to jitsugaku—Nihon ni okeru jitsugaku undō no tenkai" (Japanese Modernization and Practical Learning—the Development of the School of Practical Learning in Japan) [IV-07].

In studies on the Meiji Restoration the trend is towards a strong emphasis on grassroots ideology (*sōmō shisō*) in the late Tokugawa period, along with its relationship to the *sonnō-jōi* (revere the emperor, expel the barbarians) movement. Momose Sōji's essay in the journal *Shinano* [IV-09] is a case study demonstrating how members of wealthy farmer (*gōnō*) class turned to the nationalist teachings of Kokugaku, and to the ideas of Hirata Atsutane in particular, in response to the popularity of *yonaoshi* (lit. "rectify the world") millenial movements among the peasants. By contrast, Numata Akira's article "Henkakuki ni okeru gōnō no shisō to kōdō" (Thought and Behavior among Wealthy Farmers in a Time of Change) [IV-10] seeks to explain why *gōnō* Kokugaku adherents adopted positions other than cooperation with official policies or contribution to the industrial and economic development of the local area.

Another interesting article on the late Tokugawa period is Inoue Isao's "Bakumatsu-ishinki ni okeru 'Kōgiyoron' kannen no shosō" (The Various Dimensions of the "Public Consultation and Public Opinion" Concept in the Bakumatsu-Restoration Period) which appeared in the journal *Shisō* [IV-11]. Inoue stresses how the concepts of *tennō* (the emperor) and *ten* (heaven) developed under pressure of Western encroachment, and how the notion of *kōgi*, or "public consultation," derived directly from the concept of *ten*.

However, with the collapse of the existing structure, i.e., the *bakuhan* system, which had made *kōgi* possible, there emerged at least two different conceptions of *kōgi*. One interpreted *kōgi* as a new basis for political morality, conceiving it as a mechanism for sharing power among a select few, when interpreted optimistically, or alternatively as an arbitrary and despotic approach to government featuring strong leadership. On the other hand, there was also a competing view stressing *yoron* or "public opinion"/"popular consensus." In this way, Inoue illustrates the conflicting attitudes which prevailed towards political leadership, that of a genuine consensus-seeking leadership versus a more authoritarian image where an oligarchic leadership controls from above.

In the field of Meiji thought, Hirota Masaki's essay in *Iwanami kōza Nihon rekishi* (Kindai 1), "Keimō shisō to bunmei kaika" [IV-12] describes the concept of "civilization and enlightenment" (*bunmei kaika*) envisioned by the intellectual leaders of the restoration period, and its relationship to popular consciousness and traditional thought. In other words, Hirota focuses not on the aspects of the *bunmei-kaika* which derived from abroad, but on what it drew from indigenous ideas and thought systems. Of course, studies on leading individuals from this era tend to focus on the immensely influential Fukuzawa Yukichi (1835–1901). There are also works on figures like Inoue Kowashi (1843–1895) and Nakae Chōmin (1847–1901), but on the whole, studies of leading Meiji thinkers tend to focus on the ranks of the opposition rather than on those who were a part of the establishment.

Evaluations of Fukuzawa Yukichi differ from author to author, for the progressive and authoritarian dimensions of his thought allow a wide range of criticism. Kageyama Noboru [IV-15], citing Fukuzawa's strong reaction to moralistic Confucian education, stresses his progressive side, while Hayashi Kiyomi [IV-16] emphasizes Fukuzawa's support for national as opposed to popular rights. Hō Takushū (Peng Tse-chou), focusing on Fukuzawa's economic thought, makes a very interesting comparison with Fukuzawa's Chinese contemporary K'ang Yu-wei in his essay "Keizai shisō kara mita Fukuzawa Yukichi to Kō Yūi," (The Economic Thought of Fukuzawa Yukichi and K'ang Yu-wei) [VI-17]. A useful biography of Fukuzawa can be found in the *Jinbutsu sōsho* (Yoshikawa Kōbunkan) series by Aida Kurakichi

[IV-14]; another source of commentary with biographical sketch is available in the *Kindai Nihon shisōshi taikei* [I-20] volume devoted to Fukuzawa.

Writing on Nakae Chōmin, Matsunaga Shōzō singles out Chōmin's grasp of the "people" as the main axis of his thought in " 'Nakaeni-zumu' no rekishiteki ichi" (The Historical Position of 'Nakae-ism') [IV-20]. Working through Nakae's numerous critical essays, Matsunaga has formulated a picture of his ideas on freedom, socialism and philosophy in general. What comes through most vividly is Chōmin's originality and staunch individualism which combined, made him one of the truly fertile minds of the period. Other studies on Chōmin vary in their methodology and emphasis but the overall trend is as with Matsunaga, to formulate a clear characterization of the nature of Nakae "Chōmin-ism."

An interesting two-part article on the mid-Meiji period by Watanabe Kazuyasu, "Meiji chūki no shisōteki kadai—Inoue Tetsujirō to Ōnishi Hajime" (Intellectual Currents of the Mid-Meiji Period: Inoue Tetsujirō and Ōnishi Hajime) [IV-27] focuses on the effort to devise a genuinely indigenous philosophic base in the wake of the dissolution of the Japanese "enlightenment," as represented in the thought of two leading intellectuals, Inoue Tetsujirō and Ōnishi Hajime. Recent case studies of the Meiji opinion leaders include studies of Tokutomi Sohō, Kuga Katsunan and Miyake Setsurei. Wada Mamoru, "Jiyū-minken undō to Sohō" (Sohō and the Popular Rights Movement) [IV-28] examines the thought and behavior of Tokutomi Sohō during the era of the popular rights movement. The *Kindai Nihon shisō taikei* [I-21] volume on Miyake Setsurei, edited by Motoyama Yukihiko, underlines the fact that Miyake's nationalism (*kokusuishugi*) was very different from the variety advocated by the authorities (*kokutaishugi*).

Among studies on the latter half of the Meiji period, many deal with socialism and the High Treason Incident. A conspicuous trend in these studies is the attention accorded to Kōtoku Shūsui and the links between his brand of socialism and traditional thought [IV-30]. Also, prompted by an interest in the prewar land reform movement, we find several studies of such personalities as Miyazaki Tamizō [IV-32].

Recent work on the Taishō period is remarkable for its diversity. The concept of "Taishō Democracy" is no longer associated exclusively with political thought, but has been extended to include folklore studies, currents of reaction against modern civilization and other aspects of Taishō culture and thought. One author who has made a conscious effort to develop a fresh perspective in this area is Kano Masanao. His essay "Taishō demokurashii no shisō to bunka" (The Culture and Thought of Taishō Democracy) [IV-35] features the people and their lifestyles, the trend towards breaking out of the framework of the emperor system and the drive to recover tradition and local distinctiveness. While Yoshino Sakuzō, the leading intellectual figure of the Taishō period, is still a favorite subject of intellectual biographies, it should be noted that there has been a surge of interest in the leading anarchist of the period, Ōsugi Sakae (1885–1925) [IV-37–39].

Also very prominent among works on key individuals are studies of the famous folklorist, Yanagita Kunio (1875–1962). Most of these works focus on the development of the so-called "folklore studies," but Yanagita's interests ranged very widely to include agricultural, national studies [IV-43], and so forth. As a consequence of the growing interest in Yanagita's work, attention has been drawn to figures such as Orikuchi Shinobu, Minakata Kumagusu and Yanagi Sōetsu. At the same time, there has also been an interest in the type of intellectuals who were known as *bunmei hihyōka* (critics of contemporary culture and society) such as Hasegawa Nyozekan, Watsuji Tetsurō and Tanabe Hajime.

Research on Japanese fascism has entered upon a reflective stage in which the major theoretical works of the 1950s are being reevaluated. However, research on a key contributor to the theory of Shōwa fascism, Kita Ikki, has been flourishing as new materials on him continue to be unearthed. For example, Miyamoto Seitarō, *Kita Ikki kenkyū* (A Study of Kita Ikki) [IV-44] focuses on Kita's principal writings and attempts to clarify their underlying logic.

In conclusion, we must add a few remarks concerning research on the religious aspect of intellectual history during the Meiji period. Perhaps the most important event which has attracted the attention of scholars in this area is the government order which resulted in the separation of Buddhism from Shinto, the ultimate impact of which was the widespread destruction of Buddhist images and artifacts. Most other research on religion in the Meiji period is concerned with Christianity, especially key figures such as Uchimura Kanzō and Uemura Masahisa [IV-47, 49]. The Hikaku Shisōshi Kenkyūkai (Comparative Intellectual History Research Group) has edited a comprehensive volume dealing with Meiji intellectuals and religion entitled *Meiji shisōka no shūkyōkan* (Meiji Intellectuals' Views of Religion) [IV-46]. This volume focuses mainly on the conflicts and tensions between traditional Japanese thought and modern Western ideas as expressed in the religious views of Meiji scholars and intellectuals.

文　献

I-01　田村圓澄・黒田俊雄・相良　亨・源　了圓(編) Tamura Enchō, Kuroda Toshio, Sagara Tōru, Minamoto Ryōen (eds.) 『日本思想史の基礎知識』 *The Fundamentals of Japanese Intellectual History*, 511 pp.＋15 pp. of index, 有斐閣, 1974.

　　02　和歌森太郎 Wakamori Tarō 文化史学の課題と方法 "Problems and Methodology in Cultural Historiography" 『日本文化史学への提言』 (和歌森太郎編), pp. 1–22, 弘文堂, 1975.

　　03　守本順一郎 Morimoto Jun'ichirō 『日本思想史の課題と方法』 *Themes and Methodology in Japanese Intellectual History*, 366 pp., 新日本出版社, 1974.

　　04　井上光貞・永原慶二(編) Inoue Mitsusada and Nagahara Keiji (eds.) 『日本史研究入門 IV』 *An Introduction to Japanese Historical Research*, Vol. 4, 415 pp., 東京大学出版会, 1975.

　　05　遠藤元男(編) Endō Motoo (ed.) 『日本史研究書総覧』 *A Guide to Research Works in Japanese History*, 402 pp.＋48 pp. of index, 名著出版. 1975.

　　06　赤松俊秀他 Akamatsu Toshihide, et al. 史籍解題 "An Introduction to Japanese Historical Documents" 「歴史読本」(臨時増刊号「特集日本歴史の名著100」) 315 pp., 新人物往来社, 1975 年 7 月.

　　07　田中　元 Tanaka Hajime 『古代日本人の時間意識──その構造と展開──』 *The Structure and Development of the Concept of Time among the Ancient Japanese*, 233 pp., 吉川弘文館, 1975.

　　08　田中　元・佐和隆研・笠原一男・寺田　透・高木　豊・真継伸彦・田村芳朗 (講述) Tanaka Hajime, Sawa Ryūken, Kasahara Kazuo, Terada Tōru, Takagi Yutaka, Matsugi Nobuhiko and Tamura Yoshirō 『思想としての日本仏教』 *Japanese Buddhism as Philosophy*, 248 pp., 大東急記念文庫, 1975.

　　09　高嶋雄三郎 Takashima Yūzaburō 『松』 *The Pine Tree in Japanese Culture* [ものと人間の文化史] 328 pp., 法政大学出版局, 1975.

10　志田諄一　Shida Jun'ichi 『日本霊異記とその社会』*Society as Depicted in the "Nihon Ryōiki"*, 227 pp., 雄山閣, 1975.

11　『日本思想大系』*Iwanami Library of Japanese Thought*, 岩波書店, 1974–75.

(1) 家永三郎・藤枝　晃・早島鏡正・築島　裕(校注) Ienaga Saburō, Fujieda Akira, Hayashima Kyōshō and Tsukishima Hiroshi (eds.)『聖徳太子集』*The Complete Works of Shōtoku Taishi* [日本思想大系 2] 592 pp.

(2) 安藤俊雄・薗田香融(校注) Andō Toshio and Sonoda Kōyū (eds.)『最澄』*Saichō* [日本思想大系 4] 514 pp.

(3) 川崎庸之(校注) Kawasaki Tsuneyuki (ed.)『空海』*Kūkai* [日本思想大系 5] 448 pp.

(4) 桜井徳太郎・萩原龍夫・宮田　登 (校注) Sakurai Tokutarō, Hagiwara Tatsuo and Miyata Noboru (eds.)『寺社縁起』*Accounts of the Origins of Temples and Shrines* [日本思想大系 20] 519 pp.

(5) 表　章・加藤周一(校注) Omote Akira and Katō Shūichi (eds.)『世阿弥・禅竹』*Zeami and Zenchiku* [日本思想大系 24] 582 pp.

(6) 斎木一馬・岡山泰四(校注) Saiki Kazuma and Okayama Yasushi (eds.)『三河物語・葉隠』*"Mikawa Monogatari" and "Hagakure"* [日本思想大系 26] 702 pp.

(7) 石井紫郎(校注) Ishii Shirō (ed.)『近世武家思想』*Warrior Ideology in the Early Modern Era* [日本思想大系 27] 542 pp.

(8) 石田一良・金谷　治(校注) Ishida Ichirō and Kanaya Osamu (eds.)『藤原惺窩・林羅山』*Fujiwara Seika and Hayashi Razan* [日本思想大系 28] 520 pp.

(9) 山井　湧・山下龍二・加地伸行・尾藤正英(校注) Yamanoi Yū, Yamashita Ryūji, Kaji Nobuyuki and Bitō Masahide (eds.)『中江藤樹』*Nakae Tōju* [日本思想大系 29] 501 pp.

(10) 松村　明・尾藤正英・加藤周一(校注) Matsumura Akira, Bitō Masahide and Katō Shūichi (eds.)『新井白石』*Arai Hakuseki* [日本思想大系 35] 617 pp.

(11) 中村幸彦(校注) Nakamura Yukihiko (ed.)『近世町人思想』*Values and Ideals of the Townsmen of Tokugawa Japan* [日本思想大系 59] 445 pp.

(12) 沼田次郎・松沢弘陽(校注) Numata Jirō and Matsuzawa Hiroaki (eds.)『西洋見聞集』*Accounts of Travel in the West* [日本思想大系 66] 684 pp.

12　目崎徳衛 Mezaki Tokue『漂泊　日本思想史の底流』*The Wanderer: Undercurrents in Japanese Intellectual History* [角川選書 78] 320 pp., 角川書店, 1975.

13　『日本の名著』*Great Books of Japan*, 中央公論社, 1974.

(1) 玉城康四郎(編) Tamaki Kōshirō (ed.)『道元』*Dōgen* [日本の名著 7] 476 pp.

(2) 尾藤正英・前野直彬・中野三敏(編) Bitō Masahide, Maeno Naoaki and Nakano Mitsutoshi (eds.)『荻生徂徠』*Ogyū Sorai* [日本の名著 16] 537 pp.

(3) 橋川文三(編)　Hashikawa Bunsō (ed.)　『藤田東湖・会沢正志斎・藤田幽谷』*Fujita Tōko, Aizawa Seishisai and Fujita Yūkoku* [日本の名著 29] 526 pp.

(4) 神島二郎・伊藤幹治(編)　Kamishima Jirō and Itō Mikiharu『柳田国男』*Yanagita Kunio* [日本の名著 50] 473 pp.

14　大隅和雄(編)　Ōsumi Kazuo (ed.)　『太平記人名索引』*Index of Names in the Taiheiki*'', 279 pp., 札幌，北海道大学図書刊行会，1974.

15　石田充之・千葉乗隆(編)　Ishida Mitsuyuki and Chiba Jōryū (eds.)　『真宗史料集成』(第一巻) *Collected Materials on Pure Land Buddhism*, Vol. 1, 同朋舎，1974.

16　河村孝道(編著) Kawamura Kōdō (ed.)『諸本対校　永平開山道元禅師行状建撕記』*"A Record of the Works of Dōgen" : A Comparative Study of Available Texts*, 229 pp., 大修館書店，1975.

17　山口県教育会(編)　Yamaguchi Prefecture Educational Association (ed.)『吉田松陰全集』(別巻) *Complete Works of Yoshida Shōin*, supplement, 550 pp., 大和書房，1974.

18　諸橋轍次・安岡正篤(監修) Morohashi Tetsuji and Yasuoka Masahiro (eds.)『日本の朱子学』(下) *Japanese Neo-Confucianism*, Vol. 2 [朱子学大系第 13 巻] 625 pp., 明徳出版社，1975.

19　西田太一郎・植手通有(編) Nishida Taichirō and Uete Michiari (eds.)『陸羯南全集』(第 9 巻) *The Complete Works of Kuga Katsunan*, Vol. 9, 683 pp., みすず書房，1975.

20　大杉栄研究会(編)　Ōsugi Sakae Research Association (ed.)　『大杉栄書簡集』*The Letters of Ōsugi Sakae*, 310 pp., 海燕書房，1974.

21　『近代日本思想大系』*Chikuma Collection of Modern Japanese Thought* (36 vols.), 筑摩書房，1974–75.

(1) 松永昌三(編・解説)　Matsunaga Shōzō (ed.)　『中江兆民集』Selected Writings of Nakae Chōmin [近代日本思想大系 3] 459 pp.

(2) 筑波常治(編・解説) Tsukuba Hisaharu (ed.)『丘浅次郎集』*Selected Writings of Oka Asajirō* [近代日本思想大系 9] 463 pp.

(3) 古田紹欽(編・解説)　Furuta Shōkin (ed.)『鈴木大拙集』*Selected Writings of Suzuki Daisetsu* [近代日本思想大系 12] 400 pp.

(4) 大沢正道(編・解説)　Ōsawa Masamichi (ed.)『大杉栄集』*Selected Writings of Ōsugi Sakae* [近代日本思想大系 20] 442 pp.

(5) 梅原　猛(編・解説)　Umehara Takeshi (ed.)『和辻哲郎集』*Selected Writings of Watsuji Tetsurō* [近代日本思想大系 25] 450 pp.

(6) 松田道雄(編・解説)　Matsuda Michio (ed.)　『昭和思想集 1』*Selections from Shōwa Thought*, Vol. 1 [近代日本思想大系 35] 450 pp.

(7) 石田　雄(編・解説)　Ishida Takeshi (ed.)『福沢諭吉集』*Selected Writings of Fukuzawa Yukichi* [近代日本思想大系 2] 614 pp.

(8) 本山幸彦(編・解説) Motoyama Yukihiko (ed.) 『三宅雪嶺集』 *Selected Writings of Miyake Setsurei* [近代日本思想大系 5] 416 pp.

(9) 内田芳明(編・解説) Uchida Yoshiaki (ed.) 『内村鑑三集』 *Selected Writings of Uchimura Kanzō* [近代日本思想大系 6] 602 pp.

(10) 武田清子(編・解説) Takeda Kiyoko (ed.) 『木下尚江集』 *Selected Writings of Kinoshita Naoe* [近代日本思想大系 10] 547 pp.

(11) 飛鳥井雅道(編・解説) Asukai Masamichi (ed.) 『幸徳秋水集』 *Selected Writings of Kōtoku Shūsui* [近代日本思想大系 13] 420 pp.

(12) 鶴見和子(編・解説) Tsurumi Kazuko (ed.) 『柳田国男集』 *Selected Writings of Yanagita Kunio* [近代日本思想大系 14] 472 pp.

(13) 橋川文三(編・解説) Hashikawa Bunsō (ed.) 『大川周明集』 *Selected Writings of Ōkawa Shūmei* [近代日本思想大系 21] 451 pp.

(14) 広末 保(編・解説) Hirosue Tamotsu (ed.) 『折口信夫集』 *Selected Writings of Orikuchi Shinobu* [近代日本思想大系 22] 413 pp.

(15) 鶴見俊輔(編・解説) Tsurumi Shunsuke (ed.) 『柳宗悦集』 *Selected Writings of Yanagi Sōetsu* [近代日本思想大系 24] 444 pp.

(16) 山口昌男(編・解説) Yamaguchi Masao (ed.) 『林達夫集』 *Selected Writings of Hayashi Tatsuo* [近代日本思想大系 26] 413 pp.

(17) 住谷一彦(編・解説) Sumiya Kazuhiko (ed.) 『三木清集』 *Selected Writings of Miki Kiyoshi* [近代日本思想大系 27] 527 pp.

II-01 田村圓澄・洪 淳昶(編) Tamura Enchō and Hong Sun-ch'ang (eds.) 『新羅と飛鳥・白鳳の仏教文化』 *Silla and Asaku-Hakuhō Buddhist Culture*, 376 pp., 吉川弘文館, 1975.

02 上田正昭 Ueda Masaaki 古代の祭祀と儀礼 "Ancient Religious Rituals and Ceremonies" 『岩波講座 日本歴史 1』 (原始および古代 1), pp. 323-48, 岩波書店, 1975.

03 佐伯有清 Saeki Arikiyo 貴族文化の発生 "The Birth of Aristocratic Culture" 『岩波講座 日本歴史 2』 (古代 2), pp. 175-206, 岩波書店, 1975.

04 大隅和雄 Ōsumi Kazuo 鎌倉仏教とその革新運動 "Kamakura Buddhism and Its Revolutionary Movements" 『岩波講座 日本歴史 5』 (中世 1), pp. 211-46, 岩波書店, 1975.

05 桜井好朗 Sakurai Yoshirō 中世における漂泊と遊芸 "Wanderers and Entertainers in the Medieval Period" 『岩波講座 日本歴史 5』 (中世 1), pp. 299-336, 岩波書店, 1975.

06 黒田俊雄 Kuroda Toshio 中世寺社勢力論 "Secular Power of Medieval Temples and Shrines" 『岩波講座 日本歴史 6』 (中世 2), pp. 245-89, 岩波書店, 1975.

07 石田善人 Ishida Yoshihito 都鄙民衆の生活と宗教 Religion and Daily Life of City and Country Folk" 『岩波講座 日本歴史 6』 (中世 2), pp. 297-337,

岩波書店，1975.

08 速水　侑 Hayami Tasuku『平安貴族社会と仏教』 *Buddhism and Heian Aristocratic Society* [日本宗教史研究叢書] 271 pp., 吉川弘文館，1975.

09 網野善彦 Amino Yoshihiko『蒙古襲来』 *The Mongol Invasions* [日本の歴史6]
   454 pp., 小学館，1974.

10 石井　進 Ishii Susumu『中世武士団』 *Medieval Warrior Bands* [日本の歴史
   12] 390 pp., 小学館，1974.

11 林屋辰三郎 Hayashiya Tatsusaburō『内乱のなかの貴族』 *The Aristocracy in
   the Civil Wars* [季刊論叢 日本文化1] 180 pp., 角川書店，1975.

12 岡部周三 Okabe Shūzō『南北朝の虚像と実像――太平記の歴史学的考
   察――』 *Images and Realities in the North-South Courts: A Historical Analysis of
   the "Taiheiki,"* 326 pp., 雄山閣，1974.

13 黒田俊雄 Kuroda Toshio『日本中世の国家と宗教』 *State and Religion in
   Medieval Japan,* 559 pp., 岩波書店，1975.

14 桜井好朗 Sakurai Yoshirō『中世日本の精神史的景観』 *Medieval Japan's Spiritual Landscape,* 380 pp., 塙書房，1974.

15 西尾　実 Nishio Minoru『世阿弥の能芸論』 *Zeami's Theory of Nō,* 504 pp.,
   岩波書店，1974.

16 後藤　淑 Gotō Hajime『能楽の起源』 *The Origins of Nō Drama,* 586 pp., 木
   耳社，1975.

17 横井　清 Yokoi Kiyoshi『中世民衆の生活文化』 *Popular Culture and Daily Life
   in Medieval Japan,* 376 pp., 東京大学出版会，1975.

18 水野恭一郎 Mizuno Kyōichirō『武家時代の政治文化』 *Politics and Culture in
   Japan under Warrior Rule,* 320 pp., 創元社，1975.

19 萩原龍夫 Hagiwara Tatsuo『中世祭祀組織の研究』（増補版） *Studies on
   Organization and Ritual in Medieval Religion* (rev. ed.), 842 pp., 吉川弘文館.

20 新行紀一 Shingyō Norikazu『一向一揆の基礎構造――三河一揆と松平
   氏――』 *The Structure of the Ikkō Peasant Uprisings* [日本宗教史研究叢書] 350
   pp., 吉川弘文館，1975.

21 川瀬一馬 Kawase Kazuma『増補新訂 足利学校の研究』 *Studies on the Ashikaga Academy* (Revised and Enlarged Edition) 295 pp., 講談社，1974.

22 中村保雄 Nakamura Yasuo 神像から仮面へ――翁面と男女の面を中心
   に―― "From Shinto Images to Nō Masks: a Focus on Masks of Old Men,
   Men and Women"「芸能史研究」No. 51, pp. 1-16, 芸能史研究会，1975年
   10月.

23 桃　裕行 Momo Hiroyuki 宿曜道と宿曜勘文 "Astrology and Documents
   Pertaining to Astrological and Other Forms of Divination"「立正史学」No.
   39, pp. 1-20, 立正大学史学会，1975.

24 飯田瑞穂 Iida Mizuho『秘府略』の錯謬について "Concerning Errata in

the *Hifuryaku*, an Early Heian Encyclopedia of the Chinese Classics" 「中央大学文学部紀要」(史学科) No. 20, pp. 75–115, 中央大学文学部, 1975 年3月.

25 西野春雄 Nishino Haruo 信光の能 (上・下) "The Nō Plays of Nobumitsu," (Parts One and Two) 「芸能史研究」No. 48, No. 51, pp. 33–47; pp. 41–52, 芸能史研究会, 1975 年 1 月, 10 月.

26 須田悦生 Suda Etsuo 室町後期における地方文化形成の断面 "Aspects of the Formation of Local Culture in Late Muromachi" 「芸能史研究」No. 46, pp. 12–31, 芸能史研究会, 1974 年 7 月.

27 島田勇雄 Shimada Isao 放鷹諸流と鷹詞との関係についての試論——武家礼式における小笠原流諸派の放鷹書の基礎的研究—— "A Preliminary Study of the Schools of Falconry and Their Relationship to Falconers' Jargon: Basic Research on Manuals Governing Falconry Practices Found in the Rules of Conduct for Samurai of the Various Ogasawara Schools" 「紀要」No. 4, pp. 79–112, 神戸大学文学部, 1974.

28 玉村竹二 Tamamura Takeji 近江堅田玉泉・聖瑞二庵の相承と謙巌原沖 "Kengan Genchū and His Inheritance of Katada and Shōzui Temples in Ōmi Province" 「仏教史研究」No. 8, pp. 1–24, 日本仏教史学会, 1974 年 10 月.

29 和田義昭 Wada Yoshiaki 中世奈良の風流についての一考察 "An Analysis of *Furyū* Dances in Medieval Nara" 「芸能史研究」No. 51, pp. 17–40, 芸能史研究会, 1975 年 10 月.

30 筧 泰彦 Kakei Yasuhiko 戦国武将の思想と上杉定正状 "A Military Commander in the Sengoku Period and his Thought: the Letters of Uesugi Sadamasa" 「研究年報」第 21 輯, pp. 1–25, 学習院大学文学部, 1974.

III–1 源 了圓 Minamoto Ryōen 徳川前半期における実学と経験的合理主義 "'Practical Learning' and Empirical Rationalism in the First Half of the Tokugawa Period" 「史艸」No. 16, pp. 61–111, 日本女子大学史学研究会, 1975 年 11 月.

02 芳賀 登 Haga Noboru 徳川時代知識人の学問論とその思想——とくに儒者を中心として——, "The Educational Philosophy and Approach to Learning of the Tokugawa Intelligentsia: Focus on Confucian Scholars" 「大阪教育大学紀要 社会科学・生活科学」22 の 2, pp. 1–9, 大阪教育大学, 1974.

03 藤井 学 Fujii Manabu 近世初期の政治思想と国家意識 "Political Thought and National Consciousness at the Beginning of the Early Modern Period" 『岩波講座 日本歴史 10』(近世 2) pp. 135–72, 岩波書店, 1975.

04 赤井達郎 Akai Tatsurō 元禄期の都市生活と民衆文化 "Urban Life and Popular Culture During the Genroku Period, 1688–1704" 『岩波講座 日本歴史 10』(近世 2) pp. 333–66, 岩波書店, 1975.

05 竹田聴洲 Takeda Chōshū 近世社会と仏教 "Society and Budddhism in the Early Modern Period" 『岩波講座 日本歴史 9』(近世 1) pp. 263–302, 岩波

書店，1975.

06　倉地克直 Kurachi Katsunao 鈴木正三の思想――幕藩制成立期の支配思想に
ついての一つの試み―― "The Thought of Suzuki Shōsan: An Examination
of the Thought of the Ruling Authorities During the Establishment of the
Bakuhan System"「日本史研究」No. 155, pp. 24–49, 日本史研究会，1975
年7月.

07　深谷克己 Fukaya Katsumi 前近代のイデオロギー研究――近世思想史研究を
中心に―― "A Study of Premodern Ideology: With an Emphasis on Research in Early Modern Intellectual History"『共同体奴隷制封建制』〔現代
歴史学の成果と課題〕pp. 167–83, 青木書店，1974年9月.

08　堀江宗生 Horie Muneo 日本思想史における市民権意識の系譜 (2)――教育
権を中心として―― "A Record of Civil Rights Awareness in Japanese Intellectual History," Part 2 (Focus on Educational Rights)「東海大学紀要 教
養学部」No. 6, pp. 81–93, 東海大学，1975年7月.

09　高橋　敏 Takahashi Satoshi 江戸時代の民衆教育とその思想――「余力学文」
の教育思想をめぐって―― "The Philosophy and Practice of Popular Education in the Edo Period"「史潮」No. 113, pp. 8–37, 大塚史学会，1974.

10　安丸良夫 Yasumaru Yoshio 日本ナショナリズムの前夜 "The Eve of Japanese Nationalism"「歴史学研究」別冊 pp. 2–12, 青木書店，1975年11月.

11　林　　基 Hayashi Motoi 近世民衆の社会・政治思想研究の史料的基礎 (二)
"Documentary Basis for Research on Early Modern Popular Social and
Political Thought, Part 2"「専修史学」No. 6, pp. 32–54 専修大学歴史学会，
1974年4月.

12　和島芳男 Wajima Yoshio 寛文異学の禁――その林門興隆との関係―― "The
Ban on Heterodoxy in the Kanbun Era (1661–73): The Rise of the Hayashi
School"「大手前女子大学論集」8号 pp. 137–50, 大手前女子大学，1974.

13　小沢栄一 Ozawa Eiichi『近世史学思想史研究』*Studies in Early Modern Concepts
of History*, 529 pp. 吉川弘文館，1974.

14　岡田武彦　Okada Takehiko 貝原益軒の儒学と実学 "The Confucianism and
Practical Learning of Kaibara Ekken"「文理論集」15巻1号 pp. 53–87, 西
南学院大学，1974年10月.

15　辻　哲夫 Tsuji Tetsuo 貝原益軒の学問と方法――大和本草における儒学と
科学―― "The Scholarship and Methodology of Kaibara Ekken: Confucianism and Science in *Yamato-honsō*"「思想」605号 pp. 57–70, 岩波書店，
1974年11月.

16　安川　実 Yasukawa Minoru 鵞峰史学と白石 "Hakuseki and the Historiography of Gahō [Hayashi Shunsai]"「神道学」85号 pp. 31–55, 神道学会，
1975年5月.

17　宮崎道生 Miyazaki Michio 新井白石と文治政治 "Arai Hakuseki's Rule of

Law Approach to Administration"「日本歴史」320 号 pp. 1–19, 吉川弘文館, 1975 年 1 月.

18　三宅正彦 Miyake Masahiko 仁斎学の原像——京都町衆における惣町結合の思想形態——"The Basis of Itō Jinsai's Teachings: the Formation and Development of the Idea of *Sō* among the Townspeople of Kyōto"「史林」57 巻 4 号 pp. 1–56, 京都大学史学研究会, 1974 年 7 月.

19　日野竜夫 Hino Tatsuo 『徂徠学派——儒学から文学へ——』 *The Sorai School: From Confucianism to Literature*, 230 pp., 筑摩書房, 1975.

20　吉川幸次郎 Yoshikawa Kōjirō 『仁斎・徂徠・宣長』 *Jinsai, Sorai and Norinaga*, 392 pp., 岩波書店, 1975.

21　尾藤正英 Bitō Masahide 『大平策』の著者について "On the Authorship of the *Taiheisaku*",『名古屋大学日本史論集』(下), pp. 261–84, 吉川弘文館, 1975.

22　高橋博巳 Takahashi Hiromi 太宰春台論 "Dazai Shundai"「文化」38 巻 3・4 合併号 pp. 97–121, 東北大学文学部, 1975 年 3 月.

23　野口武彦 Noguchi Takehiko 徂徠学派における老子受容 (上・下) "The Incorporation of Lao-Tzu's Thought by the Sorai School" (Parts I and II)「文学」42 巻 10 号, 42 巻 11 号 pp. 32–47; pp. 75–85, 岩波書店, 1974 年 10 月, 11 月

24　加地伸行 Kaji Nobuyuki 真祐本「孝経啓蒙」と安井真祐 "Shinyū's Version of *Kōkyō Keimō* and Yasui Shinyū"「密教文化」109 号 pp. 11, 高野山大学, 1975 年 1 月.

25　杉本　勲 Sugimoto Isao 広瀬旭荘の海外認識と海防思想 "Hirose Kyokusō's Perception of the Outer World and His Ideas on Coastal Defense"『森克己博士古稀記念会史学論集　三』(政治文化　近世・近代篇), pp. 415–46, 吉川弘文館, 1974.

26　三宅正彦 Miyake Masahiko 安藤昌益と大館・八戸の風土 "Andō Shōeki and the Climate of Ōdate and Hachinohe"「民族芸術研究所紀要」2 号 pp. 95–111, 民族芸術研究所, 1975 年 7 月.

27　新谷正道 Shintani Masamichi 安藤昌益の農本的国家論——ユートピア思想を通してみたその萌芽性—— "Andō Shōeki's Conception of an Agrarian State: The Outgrowth of His Utopian Thought"「史学研究」121・122, pp. 2–17, 広島史学研究会, 1974 年 6 月.

28　八戸市立図書館(編) Hachinohe Municipal Library (ed.)『安藤昌益』*Andō Shōeki*, 501 pp., 伊吉書院 (八戸), 1974.

29　露口卓也 Tsuyuguchi Takuya 幕末における国家的理念の創出——後期水戸学の国体論について——"The Development of the Doctrine of the State in the Bakumatsu Period: the Last Mito Theory of National Polity"「文化史学」31 号 pp. 44–50, 同志社大学文学部内文化史学会, 1975 年 12 月.

164

30　草間俊一 Kusama Shun'ichi 高野長英 "Takano Chōei"「岩手史学研究」60号 pp. 87–106, 岩手大学学芸学部岩手史学会, 1975 年 5 月.

31　岡田千昭 Okada Chiaki 宣長学の性格についての一考察――その日本至上主義思想を中心として―― "An Examination of the Character of Motoori Norinaga's Theories: The Notion of Japan's Superiority"「九州史学」57 号 pp. 34–54, 九州史学研究会, 1975 年 7 月.

32　渡辺　浩 Watanabe Hiroshi「道」と「雅び」――宣長学と「歌学」派国学の政治思想史的研究 (1–4), "*Michi* and *Miyabi*: The Political Thought of the 'Kagaku' School of National Learning after Norinaga's Death"「国家学会雑誌」87 巻 9・10 号, 11・12 号, 88 巻 3・4 号, 5・6 号 pp. 1–85, pp. 1–75; pp. 114–44; pp. 1–72; 東京大学法学部国家学会, 1974 年 9 月, 11 月, 1975 年 3 月 5 月.

33　深谷克己 Fukaya Katsumi 幕藩体制支配と村役人層の国学受容 "Control Under the Bakuhan System and the Acceptance of National Learning by the Village Leadership"「史観」91 号 pp. 13–23, 早稲田大学史学会, 1975 年 3 月.

34　柴田　実 Shibata Minoru 石門心学と「徒然草」――近世町人哲学の一源流――"Ishida Baigan's Shingaku and *Tsurezuregusa*: An Origin of Folk Philosophy among Early Modern Townspeople"「日本歴史」323 号 pp. 1–10, 吉川弘文館, 1975 年 4 月.

35　村田　全 Murata Tamotsu 和算の伝統と性格――西欧数学との思想的対比―― "The Formation and Character of Japanese Mathematics: An Intellectual Contrast with Western Mathematics"「思想」No. 604, pp. 45–63 (pp. 1373–91), 岩波書店, 1974 年 10 月.

36　佐藤昌介 Satō Shōsuke「蘭学における実理と実用――杉田玄白の医学思想を中心にして――」"Scientific Principles and Utility in Dutch Studies: Sugita Genpaku's Approach to the Study of Medicine"「科学史研究」No. 110, pp. 74-85, 岩波書店, 1974.

37　保柳睦美 Hoyanagi Mutsumi『伊能忠敬の科学的業績』*The Scientific Contributions of Inō Tadataka*, 510 pp., 古今書院, 1974.

38　芳賀　登 Haga Noboru 民衆史の方法的模索―史料との対話 "Toward a Methodology for Popular History: A Dialogue with Historical Documents"『民衆史の創造』*Creating a Popular History*, 224 pp., [NHK ブックス] 日本放送出版協会, 1974.

IV-01　松本三之介 Matsumoto Sannosuke『日本政治思想史概論』*A History of Japanese Political Thought*, 200 pp., 勁草書房, 1975.

02　田口富久治・田中　浩(共編) Taguchi Fukuji and Tanaka Hiroshi (eds.)『国家思想史』(下・現代) *A History of Statist Thought*, Vol. 2 (Contemporary Times) 282 pp., 青木書店, 1974.

03 植手通有 Uete Michiari 『近代日本思想の形成』 *The Formation of Modern Japanese Thought*, 344 pp., 岩波書店, 1974.

04 松本健一 Matsumoto Ken'ichi 『歴史という闇 近代日本思想史覚書』 *History's Dark Unknowns: Notes on Modern Japanese Intellectual History*, 265 pp., 第三文明社, 1975.

05 安丸良夫 Yasumaru Yoshio 『日本の近代化と民衆思想』 *Popular Thought in Japanese Modernization*, 298 pp., 青木書店, 1974.

06 色川大吉・布川清司 Irokawa Daikichi and Fukawa Kiyoshi 民衆思想史の方法と課題 "Problems and Methodology in Popular Intellectual History" 「思想の科学」 No. 31, pp. 121–36, 思想の科学社, 1974 年 5 月.

07 源 了圓 Minamoto Ryōen 日本の近代化と実学──日本における実学運動の展開 (一)── "Japanese Modernization and Practical Learning: The Development of the School of Practical Learning in Japan" 「心」 27 巻 9 号, pp. 91–102, 生成会, 1974 年 9 月.

08 高木俊輔 Takagi Shunsuke 『明治維新草莽運動史』 *A History of Grass-Roots Movements During the Meiji Restoration*, 441 pp., 勁草書房, 1974.

09 百瀬宗治 Momose Sōji 「信州木曾贄川宿における平田篤胤没後門人について──草莽層形成の問題──」 "The Problem of the Formation of Grass-roots Strata: An Examination of Students of Hirata Atsutane's in Kiso Niekawajuku" 「信濃」 26–11, 12, pp. 1–12; pp. 36–58, 信濃史学会, 1974.

10 沼田 哲 Numata Akira 「変革期における一豪農の思想と行動──木曾馬籠・島崎正樹の場合──」 "Thought and Behavior of a Wealthy Farmer in a Time of Change; the Case of Shimazaki Masaki in Kiso Magome" 「文経論叢」 9–2, pp. 1–32, 弘前大学, 1974.

11 井上 勲 Inoue Isao 「幕末・維新期における「公議輿論」観念の諸相──近代日本における公権力形成の前史としての試論──」 "The Various Dimensions of the 'Public Consultation and Public Opinion' Concept in the Bakumatsu-Restoration Period" 「思想」 609 号, pp. 66–79, 岩波書店, 1975 年 3 月.

12 ひろたまさき Hirota Masaki 啓蒙思想と文明開化 "Enlightenment Thought and Civilization" 『岩波講座日本歴史 14』 (近代 1) pp. 311–64, 岩波書店, 1975.

13 堀尾輝久 Horio Teruhisa 明治「啓蒙」の学問・教育思想 "The Academic and Educational Philosophy of the Meiji 'Enlightenment'" 「科学と思想」 14 号, pp. 54–76, 新日本出版社, 1974 年 10 月

14 会田倉吉 Aida Kurakichi 『福沢諭吉』 *Fukuzawa Yukichi* 〔人物叢書〕 280 pp., 吉川弘文館, 1974.

15 影山 昇 Kageyama Noboru 明治十年代前半期の徳育施策と福沢諭吉の徳育論 "Policies of Moral Education in the Late 1870s and Early 1880s and

Fukuzawa Yukichi's Views on Moral Education"「愛媛大学教育学部紀要」
I 部 21 号, pp. 1–16, 愛媛大学, 1975.

16　林喜代美 Hayashi Kiyomi 福沢諭吉における国権論と民権論 "State Rights and Popular Rights in the Thought of Fukuzawa Yukichi"「教養部紀要」10 号 pp. 29–45, 徳島大学, 1975 年 2 月.

17　彭　沢周 Hō Takushū (Peng Tse-chou) 経済思想から見た福沢諭吉と康有為 "The Economic Thought of Fukuzawa Yukichi and Kang Yu-wei"「史林」58 巻 6 号, pp. 35–60, 京都大学史学研究会, 1975 年 11 月.

18　佐志　伝 Sashi Tsutae「文明論之概略」研究 (上) "A Study of *Bunmeiron no Gairyaku* [An Outline of a Theory of Civilization]," Part 1「史学」47 巻, 1・2, pp. 35-64, 三田史学会, 1975 年 12 月.

19　田中　明 Tanaka Akira『文明論之概略』にいたる「風俗」の思想について ――丸山思想史学の批判的再検討―― "A Critical Reexamination of Maruyama Masao's Approach to Intellectual History: The Importance of *fūzoku* [custom] in the Early Writings of Fukuzawa"「三田学会雑誌」67 巻 6 号, pp. 127–42, 慶応義塾経済学会, 1974 年 6 月.

20　松永昌三 Matsunaga Shōzō「ナカエニズム」の歴史的位置 "The Historical Position of Nakaeism"「史潮」No. 113, pp. 38–62, 大塚史学会, 1974 年 4 月.

21　宮城公子 Miyagi Kimiko 一つの兆民像――日本における近代的世界観の形成 "One Portrait of Nakae Chōmin: The Formation of a Modern World-View in Japan"「日本史研究」No. 143, pp. 1–23, 日本史研究会, 1974 年 6 月.

22　井田進也 Ida Shin'ya 兆民研究における『政理叢談』の意義について "The Significance of *Seiri Sōdan* in Research on Nakae Chōmin"「文学」43 巻 9 号 pp. 43–75, 岩波書店, 1975 年 9 月.

23　中島三千男　Nakajima Michio 明治国家と宗教――井上毅の宗教観・宗教政策の分析――"Religion and the Meiji State: An Analysis of Inoue Kowashi's Views on Religion and Religious Policy"「歴史学研究」No. 413, pp. 29–43, 青木書店, 1974 年 10 月.

24　渡辺和靖 Watanabe Kazuyasu 西周に於ける儒学と洋学――明治啓蒙思想の構造分析―― Confucianism and Western Learning in Nishi Amane: the Structure of Meiji Enlightenment Thought"「哲学と教育」22 号, pp. 13–25, 愛知教育大学哲学会, 1974 年 12 月.

25　吉田曠二　Yoshida Kōji 加藤弘之のコンミュニズム論 "Katō Hiroyuki's Views on Communism"「史朋」No. 9, pp. 31–41, 史朋同人, 1974 年 4 月.

26　園田英弘 Sonoda Hidehiro 森有礼の思想体系における国家主義教育の成立過程――忠誠心の射程―― "The Development of the Idea of Nationalistic Education in the Framework of Mori Arinori's Thought: the Limits of Loyalty"「人文学報」No. 39, pp. 1–73, 京都大学人文科学研究所, 1975 年 3 月.

27　渡辺和靖 Watanabe Kazuyasu 明治中期の思想的課題――井上哲次郎と大西

祝——(一，二) "Intellectual Themes of the Mid-Meiji Period" (2 parts)
「日本文化研究所研究報告」No. 10, pp. 95–112, 東北大学日本文化研究所,
1974 年 12 月.

28　和田　守　Wada Mamoru　自由民権運動と蘇峰 "Sohō and the Popular
Rights Movement,"「山形大学紀要 社会科学」5 巻 2 号, pp. 21–45, 山形
大学, 1975 年 2 月.

29　小寺正　・ Kodera Shōichi　陸羯南の「国民旨義」——明治期のナショナリズ
ム研究 (1)——"Kuga Katsuan's 'Kokuninshigi' [Nationalism]: A Study of
Meiji Nationalism," Prat 1「紀要」A:46, pp. 63–72, 京都教育大学, 1975 年
3 月.

30　狭間直樹　Hazama Naoki　幸徳秋水の第一回社会主義講習会における演説に
ついて "Kōtoku Shūsui's Lecture at the First Seminar on Socialism"「鷹陵
史学」No. 1, pp. 63–84, 仏教大学, 1975 年 3 月.

31　上条宏之　Kamijō Hiroyuki　今村真幸小論——国学者から日本社会党員への
道—— "Imamura Masayuki: From National Learning Scholar to Socialist
Party Member"『明治国家の展開と民衆生活』〔和歌森太郎先生還暦記念論
文集〕pp. 191–219, 弘文館, 1975.

32　牧原憲夫　Makihara Norio　宮崎民蔵の思想と行動 "The Thought and Work
of Miyazaki Tamizō"「歴史学研究」426 号, pp. 16–30, 青木書店, 1975 年
11 月.

33　大島英介　Ōshima Eisuke　山崎為徳の思想——『天地大原因論』の世界——
"The Thought of Yamazaki Tamenori: The World of Tenchi Daigen'inron"
「岩手史学研究」No. 60, pp. 293–312, 岩手大学学芸学部岩手史学会, 1975
年 5 月.

34　三木民夫　Miki Tamio　宮崎滔天における「支那革命主義」の確立——「暹羅
殖民」活動を中心に——"The Formulation of Miyazaki Tōten's Idea of a
Revolution in China"「民衆史研究」No. 12, pp. 195–215, 早稲田大学文学
部民衆史研究会, 1974 年 5 月.

35　鹿野政直　Kano Masanao　大正デモクラシーの思想と文化 "The Thought
and Culture of Taishō Democracy"『岩波講座日本歴史 18』(近代 5), pp.
333–76, 岩波書店, 1975.

36　太田雅夫　Ōta Masao『大正デモクラシー研究——知識人の思想と行動——』
Studies in Taishō Democracy: The Thought and Behavior of the Intelligentsia, 350
pp., 新泉社, 1975.

37　森山重雄　Moriyama Shigeo　大杉栄——エロス的アナキズム—— "The
Erotic Anarchism of Ōsugi Sakae"「文学」42 巻 6 号, pp. 63–77, 岩波書
店, 1974 年 6 月.

38　高木近明　Takagi Chikaaki「冬の時代」への反撃——大杉栄と『近代思想』
—— "Challenging the Era of Oppression Following the Kōtoku Incident:

Ōsugi Sakae and *Kindai Shisō* [Modern Thought]" 「社会運動史」 No. 4, pp. 93–124, 社会運動史研究会, 1974 年 9 月

39 森山重雄 Moriyama Shigeo 大杉栄年譜 "The Chronology of Ōsugi Sakae's Life," 「人文学報」104 号, pp. 23–51, 東京都立大学, 1975 年 1 月.

40 有馬 学 Arima Manabu 高畠素之と国家社会主義派の動向——大正中期社会運動の一面—— "Takabatake Motoyuki and the Activities of the State Socialist Group—A Focus on the Mid-Taishō Social Movement" 「史学雑誌」83 編 10 号, pp. 1–28, 山川出版社, 1974 年 10 月.

41 飯田泰三 Iida Taizō 長谷川如是閑における「文明批評家」の成立 (一)——大正政治思想史論のためのノート その一—— "The Emergence of Hasegawa Nyozekan as a Critic of Modern Civilization (Notes for a History of Taishō Political Thought)," Part 1 「法学志林」72 巻 2 号, pp. 1–18, 法政大学, 1975 年 3 月.

42 中村 哲 Nakamura Akira 『柳田国男の思想』(新版) *The Ideas of Yanagita Kunio* (rev. edition), 315 pp., 法政大学出版局, 1974.

43 大久保正 Ōkubo Tadashi 柳田国男における国学の伝統 "The *Kokugaku* Tradition in the Work of Yanagita Kunio" 「国語と国文学」52 巻 7 号, pp. 1–15, 東京大学国語国文学会, 1975 年 7 月.

44 宮本盛太郎 Miyamoto Seitarō 『北一輝研究』 *A Study of Kita Ikki*, 321 pp., 有斐閣, 1975.

45 岩瀬昌登 Iwase Masato 『北一輝と超国家主義』 *Kita Ikki and Ultranationalism*, 203 pp., 雄山閣, 1974.

46 比較思想史研究会 (編) Comparative Intellectual History Research Group (ed.) 『明治思想家の宗教観』 *Meiji Intellectuals' Views of Religion*, 365 pp., 大蔵出版, 1975.

47 大内三郎 Ōuchi Saburō 日本人のキリスト教受容——武士道との接触—— "Japanese Acceptance of Christianity —Contact with *Bushido*" 「日本文化研究所研究報告」No. 10, pp. 1–33, 東北大学日本文化研究所, 1974 年 12 月.

48 大内三郎 Ōuchi Saburō 植村正久の思想基礎論——その多岐性と統一性について "The Fundamentals of Uemura Masahisa's Thought: Its Unity and Diversity" 「日本文化研究所研究報告」Vol. 11, pp.–124, 東北大学日本文化研究所, 1975 年 3 月.

49 田代和久 Tashiro Kazuhisa 植村正久における神学思想 "The Theological Thought of Uemura Masahisa" 「日本思想史研究」Vol. 7, pp. 1–10, 東北大学, 1975 年 3 月.

50 河原 宏 Kawahara Hiroshi 戦時科学・技術政策の思想的背景 "The Ideological Background of Wartime Government Policies on Science and Technology" 「社会科学討究」21 巻 1 号, pp. 1–36, 早稲田大学社会科学研究所, 1975 年 5 月.

THE JAPANESE LANGUAGE

Nomoto Kikuo
National Language Research Institute

Translated by David O. Mills

In recent years the general public in Japan has shown an enthusiastic and unflagging interest in reading about various aspects of their language. Wide curiosity and the concomitant flood of publications are referred to as the *kotoba būmu* (language boom), which has continued unabated from the period covered in Vol. I, Part 2 of this series. As the word "boom" indicates, the content is limited to popular topics. In addition there is widespread general interest in matters pertaining to the origin of the Japanese language. Conferences and talks which deal with these questions draw large numbers of people.

Due to the oil crisis, however, this has also been a time of economic slowdown. In spite of the increase in popular works, fewer scholarly studies were published during this period than in the previous one. Nevertheless, while the pages of books are fewer the prices have risen so much that scholars are hard pressed to find the money to purchase them. This may very well act as a brake on the book publishing industry. One category apparently unaffected by this trend is indexes, as I will show in Section VIII. Works of this type have continued to appear at a prodigious rate.

I. JAPANESE LINGUISTICS

First, in the area of methodology, Murayama Shichirō's use of modern linguistic techniques in his study of the Japanese language is destined to receive considerable attention. *Nihongo no kenkyū hōhō*

(Japanese Language Research Methods) [I-01] uses Murayama's research on ancient Japanese phonology (his speciality) and the origins of the Japanese language as illustrations of his methods, and on that basis this work could just as well have been included in Section II. It goes together with [I-02], however, in asserting that linguists cannot uncover the origin of the Japanese language through philological studies alone, but must rely on the comparative method. Thus, the relationship between linguistics and Japanese language studies is under increasing discussion.

Minami Fujio's *Gendai Nihongo no kōzō* (The Structure of Modern Japanese) [I-03] was published in March of 1974, so it should have been included in the review of the previous period. Since it was not, and is too important a work to ignore, I have listed it here. Minami is trying various new approaches to the analysis of the Japanese language, particularly at the level of the sentence. The reason for discussing this work here rather than in Section VI is that in terms of methodology it is not simply a grammar but incorporates the sociolinguistic approach as well—an increasingly important part of Japanese language studies. Actually, this book is a superb introduction to sociolinguistics.

Noji Jun'ya's *Yōjiki no gengo seikatsu no jittai* (Actual Record of Language Use in Childhood) [I-04] is part of a multivolume set which presents a detailed record of his own son's early language development. This work, the third in the series, covers the year when the child was three years old. It is valuable also for the raw data it provides.

Turning to works on the history of the Japanese language, I-05 is the first volume of *Shinpojiumu Nihongo* (Symposia on the Japanese Language). I considered listing this entire set in Section VIII, with the other series, but decided instead to mention each volume separately at the beginning of the relevant section. It follows the format of a *zadankai* (discussion), and includes information useful not only to younger scholars but to more established ones as well. In this volume Sakakura Atsuyoshi reports on how to deal with change, Satō Kiyoji on historical change in the Japanese language, Tsukishima Hiroshi on source materials, and Shibata Takeshi on linguistic geography, and their reports form the basis for this symposium.

I-06 and I-07 stand out among the studies being done on their respective historical periods. I-08 is also on the ancient period, but contains more essays on literature than on linguistics. Numerous collections of this type were published, but I will let this one stand as representative.

In *Kokugogaku itsutsu no hakken saihakken* (Japanese Language Studies, Five Discoveries or Rediscoveries) [I-09], Mizutani Shizuo reexamines some long-standing conclusions of Japanese language research through the application of mathematical principles. Actually the last of the five items describes the process by which the author discovered his own lexico-statistical formula. Methodologically this work poses an important question.

Perhaps I should also mention that among the eight recorded conversations which comprise IV-14 there are several which could be included in this section.

II.   Genetic Relationships and Contrastive Studies

There has been a great deal of research into the origin and genetic relationships of Japanese as well as the language of the ancient period, and interest among the general public is also quite high. The number of books which have appeared on these topics is so large that I am able to mention only a few.

As I pointed out in Section I, items I-01 and I-02 by Murayama are also related to this area. In January 1974 Murayama published *Nihongo no gogen* (Etymologies of the Japanese Language) (Kōbundō) in which he discussed fifty-four words pertaining to body parts and kinship terms by means of the comparative method he likes so well. This earlier work forms the basis of the two cited above, and underlying all three is a sense of the presence of Ōno Susumu. One source of motivation for Murayama is Ōno's *Nihongo o sakanoboru* (Tracing Back the Japanese Language) [II-01]. Using essentially the same approach as the work introduced in the previous bibliography, the author of II-01 states that the meanings of words grow and change, and so do the forms of words. He then makes what seem to those who do not share his viewpoint to be quite daring assumptions. And this is the point of criticism Murayama wants to make. Ōno discusses the worldview of the ancient Japanese, i.e., their beliefs and way of thinking about time and space, based on his semantic studies. This II-01, however, is not a scholarly treatise but is for general consumption.

There are two works worthy of mention concerning ancient Japanese phonology. They are both journal articles, not books, but I will include them here. The appearance of scholarship which boldly questions existing theories is certainly never harmful.

Matsumoto Katsumi's work [II-02], which is based on his study of patterns of vowel alternation in the ancient period, refutes the phenomenon of vowel harmony, and replaces the traditional eight vowel analysis with his own theory that there are six vowels—five which correspond to those of the modern period plus *otsu-rui* (type B) [i].

In II-03 Morishige Satoshi concludes that the ancient Japanese vowel system contained only five vowels after all, and the *otsu-rui* vowels were nothing more than the *kō-rui* (Type A) vowels with the addition of an [i] on-glide. Thus, the orthographical systems which appeared in the *Man'yōshū* and elsewhere are not phonemic but phonetic transcriptions. Given the fact that the so-called *otsu-rui* vowels do not exist as independent vowels, this analysis does appear to deserve serious consideration.

II-04 and II-05 are interesting in that while their titles are similar, they are in reverse order. Kim Sa-hwa's II-04 is written with the idea that one major reason a genetic relationship between Korean and Japanese has not been scientifically proven is the lack of research on the history of the Korean language. II-05, edited by Ōno, is a record of the proceedings from the ninth meeting of the Society to Consider Ancient Cultures of East Asia held June 15–16, 1974. It contains transcripts of five lectures, and a discussion by nine people on "The Languages of Ancient Japan and Korea." In Japan there has not been much interest in Korean, despite the fact that it is the language of our closest neighbor, but in the last few years there has been a sharp increase in those who want to study Korean. If the study of Korean gains popularity among the general public, it is expected that scholarly linguistic studies will also increase, with considerable long-range effects on the study of the genetic affiliations of Japanese.

Next I should like to turn to contrastive linguistic studies. In 1975 Suzuki Takao published two works—II-06 and II-07. These two follow his earlier work *Kotoba to bunka* (Language and Culture) which was discussed as II-05 in the previous volume of this bibliography, to form what may be called Suzuki's trilogy of the mid-1970s. The three do overlap somewhat in content. II-06 consists of previously published articles and essays which deal with what in the broad sense are socio-linguistic questions. In that regard, this work could have been introduced in Section I, but the author seems to have a particular interest in the relationship between Japanese and other languages, so I decided to discuss it here. Of course, his interest also shows up in II-07 in the form of studies of the culture from the standpoint of language. He says that Japanese people tend not to take very good care of their language. I agree with this viewpoint, but when discussing the nature of the Japanese people through language there is a tendency to select only those examples which prove his point, whereas a careful observer will realize that opposing examples are equally possible. In fact, there are instances of others quoting absolutely contradictory examples. I have discussed this point in Nomoto Kikuo, "Kotoba kara mita Nihonjin-ron" (Studies of Japanese from the Standpoint of Language) (*Nihonjin kenkyū 1*, 1974, Shiseidō).

Toyama Shigehiko's *Nihongo no kankaku* (The Sensibilities of the Japanese Language) [II-08] is also a collection of previously published writings which is a sequel to a work introduced in the preceding volume of this bibliography as II-06. Toyama is known for his unusual ways of thinking, and this work is typical in that respect.

Watanabe Shōichi's II-09 discusses the relationship between the so-called *yamato-kotoba* (words of Japanese origin) and foreign borrowings, particularly the way words are borrowed by Japanese in contrast to what happens in English, German and French. Watanabe writes prolifically not only on language and culture but on politics and other subjects. This study of the Japanese language is also distinguished by a broad perspective.

In II-10 Kindaichi Haruhiko explains with specific examples the characteristics of the modes of linguistic expression in the Japanese language, and compares them with those of other languages. As mentioned above in connection with another work, the examples he cites substantiate his point of view, but one can easily find as many which prove the opposite point of view.

Nihongo yokochō (Byways of the Japanese Language) [II-11], written by Itasaka Gen, who is best known for the Japanese language textbook he co-authored with Howard Hibbett, is a collection of essays on Japanese language. As the title suggests it is not a purely scholarly work, but rather an interesting view from outside aimed at the general reader.

Among the works which contrast Japanese with other languages there are as usual a large number which choose English. The ones I have chosen from that group are listed as II-12 through II-16. All except II-13 are by English language specialists, and that one is by Umegaki, who has lectured on English at the university level. II-08 and II-09 are also written by scholars of the English language. I think that more Japanese language specialists should do work in the area of contrasting Japanese and other languages.

Hasegawa Kiyoshi's II-12 takes up common Japanese phrases, and by comparing them with their English equivalents, attempts to clarify differences in the ways the two languages express things and structure perceptions.

Umegaki Minoru's II-13 is a piece of solid scholarship which deals head-on with a number of issues. Published in April 1975, this would appear to be the last scholarly work of Umegaki, who died on February 29, 1976, since the other work of his published in July 1975, *Gairaigo* (Foreign Borrowings) (Kōdansha), is more in the *zuihitsu* (miscellany) vein.

II-14 by Ōe Saburō is a very interesting work which compares Japanese and English in terms of verbs of motion and direction, such as *kuru, yuku, yaru, kureru, morau,* etc.

Suzuki Tōzō's II-17 deals with tongue twisters, puns, riddles and other word games, and I have added it here with the idea that it is possible to observe certain unique aspects of the Japanese language through these quintessentially Japanese tidbits.

Finally, II-18 concerns the teaching of Japanese as a foreign language, but since it is not pure pedagogy but involves also general studies of the language, I have included it here for the sake of convenience. This is a collection of articles written by eight scholars based on the papers they presented at the 1973 Institute for Teaching Japanese as a Second Language sponsored by the Agency for Cultural Affairs. Umegaki Minoru's "Nichi-Ei hikaku hyōgenron" (A Comparative Study of Japanese and English Expression) is also included.

III. PHONETICS AND PHONEMICS

There have not been very many outstanding works in this category during the period under review. There are probably a number of reasons for this, but the principal one is perhaps that most of the research in this field is being done by means of the most up-to-date acoustical techniques and apparatus. This involves such things as abstracting parameters through phonetic analysis, synthesizing speech sounds determined through such analysis, and experiments into the perception of those sounds. Those who graduate from the usual linguistics department probably feel that research using this kind of electronic equipment is beyond their capabilities. On top of that, the study of physiology as it relates to speech pathology has been growing rapidly, as have detailed examinations of the correlation between the movements of the speech organs in continuous speech and phonemes as a sequence in time. This too is beyond the training of the traditional phoneticist, and so he is gradually being squeezed out of concrete phonetic analysis. I do not see this as inevitable, however. There are still areas in which his services are needed. For example, in the field of computational linguistics, those who are working on machine translation need the cooperation of specialists trained in linguistics.

For those reasons, most likely, there has not been much noteworthy activity over the last two years. And the chief contributions have appeared in the area of the history of accent, which is beyond the scope of the new breed of "phoneticians."

The date of publication of III-01 is March 1974, so strictly speaking it is outside the time period covered here, but I include it because it occasioned several other contributions in this area. It is essential reading for those interested in the history of accent, as it contains copious explanations about the source materials in that field. It is a reworking of articles published in *Kokugo akusento no hanashi* (Discussions of Japanese Accent), and gives some prominence to the methods of comparative linguistics.

III-02 is a collection of previously published papers, including the celebrated "*Tōzai ryō-akusento no chigai ga dekiru made*" (Until the East-West Accentual Difference Arose). The methodology is the same as that of III-01. Some have criticized this approach, saying that one should treat the accent patterns not only of individual words but of utterances found in actual speech. III-03 contains nine essays on the forms of accent from the Nara period through the Insei period, all of which have appeared elsewhere.

There is also a volume commemorating the 77th birthday of Dr. Ōnishi Masao entitled *Onseigaku sekai ronbun-shū* (Worldwide Collection of Essays on Phonetics) (1974), but the content is not limited to Japanese and most of the papers are in a Western language, so it is not appropriate for inclusion here.

IV. ORTHOGRAPHY CONTROVERSY

One work which presents the basic thinking about orthographical symbols is IV-01. In this book it is abundantly clear that participants in a symposium do not necessarily agree with each other. The problem is whether the writing system should be considered a direct structural constituent of language. This view of characters is also related to Suzuki Takao's ideas on Chinese characters as expressed in II-07. In particular, there is the notion that the *on* and *kun* readings for the characters in Japanese are not just allomorphs of that character but are two completely separate entities, and this notion relates directly to one's approach to orthographical and other problems of the Japanese language.

Itaiji kenkyū shiryō shūsei (A Compendium of Materials for the Study of Variant Forms of Kanji), volume one of which was introduced in the previous volume of this bibliography, is now complete. It consists of ten volumes plus two supplements, and is listed here as IV-02 through IV-12. Volume 6 was actually published in February 1974, but was inadvertently omitted from the earlier listing. With the completion of this series we now have photographic reproductions of 32 different volumes of materials related to variant forms of *kanji* ranging from the first year of *Kōō* (1389) to 1910. In addition, the supplementary volumes present eight of materials from China.

IV-13 is somewhat different, but is a basic study in the field of orthography. It is good to see books like this coming out in greater numbers, but the prices are just astounding. This one is ¥9800 (about $35), and the above series runs ¥5500 (nearly $20) per volume!

IV-14 through IV-17 are concerned with aspects of problems on orthography. The participants in the controversy fall into two large groups—the progressives and the conservatives, often referred to as the phonetic school and the ideographic school. All the works discussed here come from the latter group, an indication of how much they have grown in strength. IV-14 is not purely a problem-oriented book. It includes, among other things, a discussion of the origin of the Japanese language, but I decided to include it here because I believe it presents the editor's basic ideas. IV-15 is Maruya Saiichi's criticisms of Japanese language education in Japan from the point of view of a creative writer.

The Council on Japanese Language Problems responsible for IV-16 and VI-17 is considered to be a bastion of the ideographic school, and those works are typical expressions of that viewpoint. However, looking at works such as IV-16, I must confess I cannot help wondering why all linguistic change must be labelled *kuzure* (decay). After pondering the problem I have come to the conclusion that one's attitude toward this is tied to one's view of orthography, of the language, and even one's view of life, the world and the universe, so it is not the sort of thing one can convince others of through argument. Words will not do it. For a person to change his viewpoint would mean denying everything he stands for—something very few people can do. Thus, the reason I avoid this whole area is precisely because I realize the futility of such a debate.

Nihongo no genba (Japanese at Work) (IV-18) is not written from one particular point of view, but is rather a collection of short pieces from the *Yomiuri* Newspaper which were run with the idea of presenting information as objectively as possible and giving the readers something to think about. Material was gathered from school teachers and language specialists, with special attention to introducing a variety of problems encountered in the classroom. This first volume deals with the subject of *kanji*, covering such interesting topics as proper form, stroke order, radicals, simplified characters, etc.

V.   VOCABULARY

There seem to be three general areas of interest within this category.

The first is the structure of compound lexical items. This includes studies of the rules for forming three- and four-character Chinese-derived compound nouns. One reason for the widespread interest in this area derives, I believe, from the need to make decisions in linguistic data processing concerning the disposition of such long compounds.

A second area of interest is semantic analysis, and in this regard V-01 discusses a number of interesting questions. One of the contributors, Kunihiro Tetsuya, considers "sememe" to be an abstract unit distinct from the concrete utterance, while Suzuki Takao on the other hand is of the opinion that semantic constants do not exist, and that meaning is not something to be described but rather to be defined. V-02 is representative of works which have been both the cause and the result of a general interest in semantics, although they are not necessarily limited to the Japanese language. The third area is etymology, which has seen a dramatic rise in public interest.

V-03 is a compilation of writings done over the years, and released on the occasion of the fortieth anniversary of the founding of NHK's Committee on Broadcast Language Usage, and comprises a general introduction to that subject.

In the field of premodern Japanese dictionaries there are two works, V-04 and V-05. These should be useful along with the indexes which are given in Section VIII. In this period there are also some important dictionaries of the classical language. The first is V-06, which has the unique features of listing all verb entries in the *ren'yōkei* (conjunctive form) instead of the *shūshikei* (conclusive form), and marking the ancient *kō-otsu* vowel distinctions found in the Nara period materials (see discussion in Section III). The use of verbal *ren'yōkei* as the base form can be seen in studies done by the National Language Research Institute and others, but it is rare in a dictionary intended to be sold commercially. The Ōno Susumu style of definitions is somewhat daring in places, but it gives this work a distinctive flavor, and the use of examples shows ingenuity. There are over 40,000 words included.

V-07 includes modern as well as premodern entries, but has more of the characteristics of a historical dictionary. Compilation was begun in honor of the fiftieth anniversary of the founding of the Shōgakkan Publishing Company, and the entire set of twenty volumes was completed between 1972 and 1976. I include it here even though its dates are prior to the time period covered by this volume. There are a few problems because the editorial work was done on a commercial basis, but it is still the best dictionary of the Japanese language. The choice of examples is somewhat disjointed, but they are indentified as to source and so are more reliable than constructed examples. It contains about 300,000 words. The next task should be a government sponsored project to compile a large dictionary containing an exhaustive listing of examples from selected materials.

This period also produced a number of dictionaries which specialize in a particular area, and of those V-08 through V-16 represent the more notable ones. V-08 is an explanation of about 5000 lexical items related to clothing and accessories worn in the Heian court and is aimed principally at providing a comprehensive list of examples. V-09 brings together the color terms used in the chief works of the medieval period, along with quotations from identified sources. *Bukkyō-go daijiten* (Comprehensive Dictionary of Buddhist Terms) [V-10] probably will also be useful in the study of the history of the Japanese language. It contains about 30,000 words, and has several useful indexes, including one by pronunication and one by stroke count, and one each for Tibetan, Pali and Sanskrit terms.

V-12 has about 30,000 words, most of which are believed to have been in daily use among the Edo townspeople. Drawing on about 1000 works which date as far back as 1750, this dictionary gives meanings and examples for each entry. This impressive work turned out to be the final effort of the editor, Maeda Isamu.

V-13 deals with the language of the imperial court. It is not restricted to vocabulary, but because of its last section entitled "Lexicon of the Court Language" and its close relationship to V-14, I have listed it here. V-14 contains about 2000 items from the language of the court (i.e., of the women of the court), and various occupation groups, as well as from the general speech of Kyoto. For each item it gives accent, examples in context, meaning and usage, etc. It is related also to works in Section VII (and see also VII-01 in Vol. I, Part 2).

The *meisū* (number words) in the title of V-15 refers to collections of like items which have special names that include a number as part of the name. For example, there are *gozan* (five Zen monasteries), *shitennō* (the four devas), etc. The number one also occurs, as in *ichi no hito* (regent). This work explains about 2000 such items of both Japanese and Chinese origin taken from classical materials.

V-16 presents various kinds of onomatopoeia in common use in Japanese society today, gives the meaning with a commentary, and provides examples of how they are used. Most of the examples are taken from newspapers, with the source clearly identified. The work opens with a general introduction to onomatopoetic expressions.

Next are works concerned with etymology. Murayama's *Nihongo no gogen* has already been discussed in Section II. The works discussed here are different from Murayama's, however, in that they are in a more popular vein. They are said to have sold well, and can be considered products of the increasing interest in etymology mentioned in connection with the third area of interest at the beginning of this section.

V-17 presents seventy-four items, such as *akanuke* (urbane) and *oiraku no koi* (love in old age), tracing each one's etymology and explaining the semantic change. Included also is a brief "excursion" into the twelve signs of the zodiac. V-18, also by Iwabuchi, is not pure etymology. It consists of a series which the author did for the Japanese edition of the *Reader's Digest* called "Kokugo no chikara o mashimashō" (Ways to Increase Your Word Power). Each installment deals with twenty words, and the "etymology" is in the explanation which is added by the author.

V-19 discusses the etymology of the animal names in the zodiac, and in addition includes the *ahiru* (duck), *u* (cormorant), *ugui* (dace), *ottosei* (seal), and other bird and animal names for a total of forty-three. V-20 traces the origins of personal names, both family and given, and includes studies of place names as well. This work is clear evidence of the extensive knowledge of its author. And in connection with geographical place names V-21 should not be overlooked.

VI. GRAMMAR

VI-01 provides a handy summary of Japanese grammar, and is built out of four papers—"Bunpō to imi" (Meaning and Grammar) by Ikegami Yoshihiko, "Bunpō no tan'i" (Units of Grammar) by Minami

Fujio, "Chinjutsu-ron" (Predication) by Watanabe Minoru, and "Yondai bunpō-ron" (The Four Great Theories of Grammar) by Miyaji Yutaka.

Items VI-02 through VI-04 are all works in which the author presents his view on the way to systematize Japanese grammar. VI-05 is an extensive work by Okutsu Keiichirō, who is a well-known generative-transformationalist and is particularly important for the research it presents on the structure of attributive expressions. From a standpoint that approaches that of case grammar Okutsu classifies attributive clauses in terms of the way they are related to attributive nouns.

There are also grammatical studies focussing on particular periods of history, such as VI-06 on the ancient period, and what might be called its supplementary volume VI-07. The former is not limited to grammar, but includes sections on characters and ways of writing, as well. I include it here because it is particularly informative on the syntax and style of ancient Japanese folktales.

Iwai Yoshio's study of the Edo period [VI-08] is a sequel to his earlier studies (see Vol. I, Part 2, VI-01 and VI-02), and like them discusses the inflected forms, auxiliaries and particles. VI-09 also deals specifically with the Edo period, chiefly with the first- and second-person expressions, but includes other aspects of the grammar as well.

Saeki Tetsuo's VI-10 is work of very high quality which stands as a pinnacle in the research on Japanese word order. VI-11 presents a morphological analysis of verbs, adjectives and predicative nouns found in the speech of children between the ages of three and six. This work uses the same materials as Ōkubo Ai's study cited in Vol. I, Part 2, [VIII-07].

Books on style and stylistics also appeared in large numbers. One is written from a more literary standpoint [VI-12], while the rest [VI-13 through VI-15] have a linguistic frame of reference. VI-13 is a collection of nineteen previously published essays, and is divided into four general topics—analysis of special terms used in literary works, discourse analysis of sentence types, discussion of style, and analysis of speech acts found in works of literature. VI-14 is also a collection of articles which have already been published, seventeen in all. In both this work and VI-13, there are certain aspects of the discussion of speech acts which are quite unique and interesting. In VI-14 Hayashi

Shirō takes the position that the speech acts of ordinary people who do not produce works of literature should be called "stylistics of people," and analyzed using empirical data gathered from actual situations.

Sakakura Atsuyoshi in VI-15, on the other hand, draws chiefly on classical literature for his material, and tries to ascertain a classical stylistics. The twenty-three selections in this work are divided into four areas: the style of *monogatari* (tales), the function of style, changes in expression, and characters and the meaning of words.

VII. DIALECTS

Minami Fujio has some unique things to say in his section of VII-01 on the structural description of dialects. He points out, for example, that when discussing the structure of a particular dialect, everything, from the choice of speech-act types through discourse, sentence, word and even phoneme levels, ought to be analyzed from one consistent standpoint. This still has a long way to go before it becomes reality.

Research in the field of linguistic geography has continued to increase in this period. First of all, the National Language Research Institute published volume six of *Nihon gengo chizu* (Linguistic Atlas of Japan) [VII-02] in 1975, completing this collection of 300 maps. The number of investigation sites ran to 2400, and in each location an elderly person was used as informant. I hope they will be widely used as basic source material in future linguistic geography studies.

The size of the *Nihon gengo chizu* volumes is certainly large, but the dimensions of the two volumes in VII-03 (21.7 inches by 22.8 inches) will also present problems in storing and shelving. Volume one has 115 items and volume two has 121 for a total of 236 items covered in this investigation. Each map is divided into two parts, with the top half representing the elderly and the bottom half the young. This makes it easy to see differences which are due to age. The investigation covered all of the 701 villages on 126 islands in the Inland Sea, plus 141 strategic locations surrounding the Inland Sea, thus making a total of 842 sites.

VII-04 has a total of 157 maps, including twenty-eight on accent, ninety-nine on single morphemes, twenty-seven on compounds, and three showing the overall breakdown into regions. The investigation included 277 sites covering all of the Kanto area including the various Izu islands.

VII-05 is a general introduction to dialectology. Within this work there are certain problems as to what exactly constitutes the standard language, but the fundamental approach is to define it in terms of its differences from the dialects. Each dialect is outlined in part three, and a corpus for each is in part four. Each dialect is handled by a scholar who comes originally from that area, so the descriptions are quite reliable.

VII-06 presents the results of an investigation which attempted to combine synchronic and diachronic dialect research, e.g., to synthesize studies of language structure with studies of linguistic geography. The dialect chosen for this study was that spoken in the river basin of Yōrō-gawa in Chiba prefecture. Using 178 sites in that area, the phonology, accent, grammar and lexicon were systematically described, and 86 distribution maps, including such nonlinguistic things as school districts and shopping areas, were drawn up, in an attempt to achieve a comprehensive interpretation. It cannot be said to have been successful in every respect, but it certainly is leading the way in the field of structural linguistic geography.

VII-07 deals with the problems of methodology in the instruction of the standard language as opposed to the local dialect in the schools. The work is permeated with the author's philosophy that more emphasis should be given to the dialect students use in daily life.

VII-08 is a piece of geographical research done under the guidance of Nobayashi Masamichi. Treating linguistics broadly as one approach to the study of symbols, he brings a freshness to the field by relating it to nonlinguistic matters such as burial rites.

Fujiwara Yoichi is in the process of setting up several series as a forum for the presentation of dialect descriptions and research in the field of dialectology. VII-09 represents one such series—the second of a twenty-one volume series which will report on investigations at fifty key sites spread across the entire country. The description of each dialect consists of a general outline, followed by a discussion of the pronunciation, grammar, lexicon, and a conclusion, all based on primary source material. The first volume appeared in 1973 and dealt with the dialect of Kushio, Nagahama-chō, Kita-gun, Ehime prefecture.

The next three items, VII-10 through VII-12, are collections of essays on dialects. VII-10 has no subtitle to specify its contents, but it contains four selections which deal principally with accent. VII-11 consists of three articles, and VII-12 has four which focus on sentence-final expressions.

VIII. OTHER

In Japan there are many series with *kōza* [course in] as part of the title, and the linguistics field is no exception. There are two which were completed during the period under review, so I will mention them first. Series called *kōza* are usually geared to a nonspecialist audience, but they are useful in providing an overview of a subject, and so are quite helpful to the specialist as well. Moreover, many authors seize the opportunity to present new ideas, and they are worth a quick perusal.

The series which was completed in 1974 is *Keigo kōza* [Lectures on Honorifics] and is given in order as VIII-01 through VIII-10. The other one is listed as VIII-11 through VIII-20, and its arrangement is somewhat unorthodox. The title of VIII-12, *Nihon bunpō no miete kuru hon* (For an Understanding of Japanese Grammar) is intriguing, and the series as a whole appears to emphasize the relationship of language to daily life and society. And it is rare to have a volume like VIII-19 included in a *kōza* series: *Gendai Nihongo no kensetsu ni kurō shita hitobito* (Those Who Labored in the Formulation of Modern Japanese).

There continues to be a proliferation of index-type publications, some of which are listed from VIII-21 through VIII-33, in no particular order. There are also a number of photostatic reproductions, which are given as VIII-34 and VIII-35.

Volume seven in the continuing National Language Research Institute series *Denshi keisanki ni yoru kokugo kenkyū* (Japanese Language Studies Done by Computer) has come out [VIII-36]. It contains nine essays.

Quite a few out-of-print books have been reissued, so I have listed some [VIII-37 to VIII-39]. All three are grammatical studies, and it is nice to have them available once more.

Some notes of university lectures from the Meiji period have been published. They are extremely valuable as a key to understanding the situation in linguistics and Japanese language studies at that time. VIII-40 and VIII-41 are said to represent lectures given in 1891 and 1904, respectively.

The last two volumes listed here contain bibliographies of works on Japanese language and linguistics from the period under review. These are handy volumes which also include a general review of the trends of that year, and a list of scholars in the field with their address, specialty, and much other useful information.

文　　献

I–01　村山七郎 Murayama Shichirō 『日本語の研究方法』 *Japanese Language Research Methods*, 301 pp., 弘文堂, 1974.

02　村山七郎 Murayama Shichirō 『国語学の限界——日本語学における』 *Limitations of National Language Research—The Case of Japanese*, 324 pp., 弘文堂, 1975.

03　南不二男 Minami Fujio 『現代日本語の構造』 *The Structure of Modern Japanese*, 332 pp., 大修館書店, 1974.

04　野地潤家 Noji Jun'ya 『幼児期の言語生活の実態 3』 *Actual Record of Language Use in Childhood*, Vol. 3, 828 pp., 文化評論出版, 1974.

05　松村明 (司会) Matsumura Akira (moderator) 『日本語の歴史』 *History of the Japanese Language* [シンポジウム日本語 1] 276 pp., 学生社, 1975.

06　津之地直一 Tsunochi Naoichi 『万葉集の国語学的研究』 *The Language of the "Man'yōshū,"* 399 pp., 桜楓社, 1975.

07　森野宗明 Morino Muneaki 『王朝貴族社会の女性と言語』 *Women's Speech in the World of Heian Court Aristocracy*, 236 pp., 有精堂, 1975.

08　境田教授喜寿記念論文集刊行会 (編) Committee for the Publication of Essay Collection Commemorating Professor Sakaida Shirō's Seventy-seventh Birthday (ed.) 『上代の文学と言語』 *Language and Literature in the Ancient Period*, 654 pp., (前田書店), 1974.

09　水谷静夫 Mizutani Shizuo 『国語学五つの発見再発見』 *Japanese Language Studies, Five Discoveries or Rediscoveries*, 159 pp., 東京女子大学会, 1974.

II–01　大野晋 Ōno Susumu 『日本語をさかのぼる』 *Tracing Back the Japanese Language*, 219 pp., 岩波書店, 1974.

02　松本克己 Matsumoto Katsumi 古代日本語母音組織考——内的再建の試み "Vowel Formation in Ancient Japanese: An Internal Reconstruction" 「金

沢大学法文学部論集・文学」22, pp. 83–152, 金沢大学法文学部, 1975.

03 森重　敏 Morishige Satoshi 上代特殊仮名遣とは何か "Special *Kana* Usages of Ancient Times"「万葉」89, pp. 1–51, 万葉学会, 1975.

04 金　思燁 Kim Sa-hwa『古代朝鮮語と日本語』*Ancient Korean and Japanese*, 484 pp., 講談社, 1974.

05 大野　晋 (編) Ōno Susumu (ed.)『日本古代語と朝鮮語』*Ancient Japanese and Korean*, 191 pp., 毎日新聞社, 1975.

06 鈴木孝夫 Suzuki Takao『ことばと社会』*Language and Society*, 264 pp., 中央公論社, 1975.

07 鈴木孝夫 Suzuki Takao『閉された言語・日本語の世界』*The Closed World of the Japanese Language*, 239 pp., 新潮社, 1975.

08 外山滋比古 Toyama Shigehiko『日本語の感覚』*The Sensibilities of the Japanese Language*, 277 pp., 中央公論社, 1975.

09 渡辺昇一 Watanabe Shōichi『日本語のこころ』*The Spirit of the Japanese Language*, 213 pp., 講談社, 1974.

10 金田一春彦 Kindaichi Haruhiko『日本人の言語表現』*How Japanese Use Their Language*, 241 pp., 講談社, 1975.

11 板坂　元 Itasaka Gen『日本語横丁』*Byways of the Japanese Language*, 184 pp., 至文堂, 1974.

12 長谷川潔 Hasegawa Kiyoshi『日本語と英語——その発想と表現』*Patterns of Thought and Expression of Japanese and English*, 261 pp., サイマル出版会, 1974.

13 楳垣　実 Umegaki Minoru『日英比較表現論』*A Comparative Study of Expression in Japanese and English*, 301 pp., 大修館書店, 1975.

14 大江三郎 Ōe Saburō『日英語の比較研究——主観性をめぐって』*A Comparative Study of the English and Japanese Languages, with Special Reference to the Subjective*, 294 pp., 南雲堂, 1975.

15 最所フミ Saisho Fumi『英語と日本語——発想と表現の比較』*English and Japanese: A Comparative Study of Logic and Usage*, 261 pp., 研究社出版, 1975.

16 岩倉国浩 Iwakura Kunihiro『日英語の否定の研究』*A Study of Negatives in Japanese and English*, 321 pp., 研究社出版, 1974.

17 鈴木棠三 Suzuki Tōzō『ことば遊び』*Word Play*, 219 pp., 中央公論社, 1975.

18 文化庁・国立国語研究所 (編) Agency for Cultural Affairs, National Language Research Institute (eds.)『日本語と日本語教育——発音・表現編』*Japanese and Japanese Language Teaching: Pronunciation and Usage* [国語シリーズ別冊 3] 199 pp., 大蔵省印刷局, 1975.

III-01 金田一春彦 Kindaichi Haruhiko『国語アクセントの史的研究——原理と方法』*A Historical Study of Japanese Accent: Principles and Methods*, 306 pp., 塙書房, 1974.

02 金田一春彦 Kindaichi Haruhiko『日本の方言——アクセントの変遷とその

実相』*Japanese Dialects: Accent Changes and Their Current Status*, 277 pp., 教育出版, 1975.

03　桜井茂治　Sakurai Shigeharu　『古代国語アクセント史論考』 *A History of Japanese Accents in Ancient Times*, 241 pp., 桜楓社, 1975.

IV-01　森岡健二・柴田武 (司会) Morioka Kenji and Shibata Takeshi (moderators) 『日本語の文字』*Japanese Orthography* [シンポジウム日本語 4] 298 pp., 学生社, 1975.

02　杉本つとむ (編) Sugimoto Tsutomu (ed.) 『異体字研究資料集成 2』(異体字辨) *A Compendium of Materials for the Study of Variant Forms of Kanji*, Vol. 2, 383 pp., 雄山閣, 1974.

03　杉本つとむ (編) Sugimoto Tsutomu (ed.) 『異体字研究資料集成 3』(異字篇・正俗字例・刊繆正俗字辨) *A Compendium of Materials for the Study of Variant Forms of Kanji*, Vol. 3, 412 pp., 雄山閣, 1974.

04　杉本つとむ (編) Sugimoto Tsutomu (ed.) 『異体字研究資料集成 4』(倭楷正訛・道斎随筆・楷林) *A Compendium of Materials for the Study of Varint Forms of Kanji*, Vol. 4, 399 pp., 雄山閣, 1974.

05　杉本つとむ (編) Sugimoto Tsutomu (ed.) 『異体字研究資料集成 5』(俗書正譌・省文纂攷・正楷字覧・古今字様考・疑字貫奴) *A Compendium of Materials for the Study of Variant Forms of Kanji*, Vol. 5, 404 pp., 雄山閣, 1974.

06　杉本つとむ (編) Sugimoto Tsutomu (ed.) 『異休字研究資料集成 6』(別體字類・楷法辨體・古今異字叢) *A Compendium of Materials for the Study of Variant Forms of Kanji*, Vol. 6, 479 pp., 雄山閣, 1974.

07　杉本つとむ (編) Sugimoto Tsutomu (ed.) 『異体字研究資料集成 7』(異体字彙・正楷録) *A Compendium of Materials for the Study of Variant Forms of Kanji*, Vol. 7, 415 pp., 雄山閣, 1974.

08　杉本つとむ (編) Sugimoto Tsutomu (ed.)『異体字研究資料集成 8』(抜萃正俗字辨・古今文字・古今字様・古字便覧・別躰字考) *A Compendium of Materials for the Study of Variant Forms of Kanji*, Vol. 8, 399 pp., 雄山閣, 1975.

09　杉本つとむ (編) Sugimoto Tsutomu (ed.) 『異体字研究資料集成 9』(和字正俗通・国字考・倭字攷・瑣工集・小野篁可字盡・廓憲費字盡・小野憲謐字盡) *A Compendium of Materials for the Study of Variant Forms of Kanji*, Vol. 9, 427 pp., 雄山閣, 1975.

10　杉本つとむ (編) Sugimoto Tsutomu (ed.) 『異休字研究資料集成 10』(異休同字編・和名類聚抄箋註異体字辨・俗字略字・玉篇・字彙・止字通・康熙字典・下学集・節用集) *A Compendium of Materials for the Study of Variant Forms of Kanji*, Vol. 10, 390 pp., 雄山閣, 1975.

11　杉本つとむ (編) Sugimoto Tsutomu (ed.) 『異体字研究資料集成別巻 1』(千禄字書・五経文字・九経字様・字考・字学七種・字学挙隅・碑別字) *A Compendium of Materials for the Study of Variant Forms of Kanji*, supplementary vol-

188

ume 1, 418 pp., 雄山閣, 1975.

12 杉本つとむ（編）Sugimoto Tsutomu (ed.)『異体字研究資料集成別巻 2』（龍龕手鑑）*A Compendium of Materials for the Study of Variant Forms of Kanji*, supplementary volume 2, 370 pp., 雄山閣, 1975.

13 竹尾正子 Takeo Masako『人麻呂用字考』*A Study of Kakinomoto no Hitomaro's Orthography*, 330 pp., 桜楓社, 1974.

14 大野 晋（編）Ōno Susumu (ed.) 『対談日本語を考える』*Considering the Japanese Language: A Dialogue*, 261 pp., 中央公論社, 1975.

15 丸谷才一 Maruya Saiichi『日本語のために』*To Preserve Our Language*, 213 pp., 新潮社, 1974.

16 国語問題協議会（監修）福田恆存・宇野精一・土屋道雄他（編）Council on Japanese Language Problems: Fukuda Tsuneari, Uno Seiichi, Tsuchiya Michio, et al. (eds.)『崩れゆく日本語——あなたの日本語はこんなに乱れている』*The Degenerate State of the Japanese Language*, 216 pp., 英潮社, 1975.

17 国語問題協議会（編著）岩下保・土屋道雄・萩野貞樹（編）Council on Japanese Language Problems; Iwashita Tamotsu, Tsuchiya Michio, and Hagino Sadaki (eds.)『国語問題協議会十五年史』*A Fifteen-year History of the Council on Japanese Language Problems*, 356 pp., 国語問題協議会, 1975.

18 読売新聞社会部（編）Yomiuri Newspapers, City News Department (ed.)『日本語の現場 1』*Japanese at Work*, Vol. 1, 210 pp., 読売新聞社, 1975.

V-01 阪倉篤義（司会）Sakakura Atsuyoshi (moderator)『日本語の意味・語彙』*Meaning and Vacabulary in Japanese* [シンポジウム日本語 3] 260 pp., 学生社, 1975.

02 池上嘉彦 Ikegami Yoshihiko『意味論——意味構造の分析と記述』*Semantics: A Description and Analysis of the Structure of Meaning*, 517, pp., 大修館書店, 1975.

03 NHK 総合放送文化研究所編 NHK National Broadcasting Cultural Research Center『放送用語論』*Standard Broadcast Language Usage*, 562 pp., 日本放送出版協会, 1975.

04 亀井孝（案並閲）・高羽五郎（校並刻）Kamei Takashi (sup. ed.) and Takaha Gorō (ed.)『五本対照 改編節用集』（上・下）*Revised "Setsuyōshū": A Comparison of Five Texts* (2 vols.), 2 冊, 勉誠社, 1974.

05 杉本つとむ（編著）Sugimoto Tsutomu (ed.)『早大本節用集』（本文・研究・索引|）*The Waseda University Text of the "Setsuyōshū"* (Text, Analyses, Index), 510 pp., 雄山閣, 1975.

06 大野 晋・佐竹昭広・前田金五郎（編）Ōno Susumu, Satake Akihiro and Maeda Kingorō (eds.)『岩波古語辞典』*Iwanami's Classical Japanese Dictionary*, 1504 pp., 岩波書店, 1974.

07 日本大辞典刊行会（編）Committee for Publication of the Compendium Japanese Dictionary (ed.)『日本国語大辞典』(1–20) *Compendium Dictionary of*

the Japanese Language (20 vols.), 小学館, 1972–1976.

08 あかね会 (編) Akane Society (ed.) 『平安朝服飾百科辞典』 Encyclopedia of Attire and Accessories at the Heian Court, 906 pp., 講談社, 1975.

09 伊原　昭 Ihara Aki 『日本文学色彩用語集成 中世』 A Catalogue of Color Words in Japanese Literature: The Medieval Period, 419 pp., 笠間書店, 1975.

10 中村　元 Nakamura Hajime 『仏教語大辞典』(上・下・別巻──索引) Comprehensive Dictionary of Buddhist Terms (2 vols., plus supplementary index volume), 805, 668, 392, pp., 東京書籍, 1975.

11 田辺尚雄 Tanabe Hisao 『邦楽用語辞典』 Dictionary of Traditional Japanese Musical Terminology, 199 pp., 東京堂出版, 1975.

12 前田　勇 (編) Maeda Isamu (ed.) 『江戸語大辞典』 A Dictionary of Edo Speech, 1085 pp., 講談社, 1974.

13 井之口有一・堀井令以知 Inokuchi Yūichi and Horii Reiichi 『御所ことば』 The Language of the Imperial Palace [風俗文化史選書12] 261 pp., 雄山閣, 1974.

14 井之口有一・堀井令以知 (編) Inokuchi Yūichi and Horii Reiichi (eds.) 『京都語辞典』 A Dictionary of Kyoto Speech, 157 pp., 東京堂出版, 1975.

15 朝倉治彦・井門　寛・森　睦彦 (編) Asakura Haruhiko, Ikado Hiroshi, and Mori Mutsuhiko (eds.) 『日本名数辞典』 A Dictionary of Number Words in Japanese, 234 pp., 東京堂出版, 1974.

16 天沼　寧 (編) Amanuma Yasushi (ed.) 『擬音語・擬態語辞典』 A Dictionary of Japanese Onomatopoeia, 462 pp., 東京堂出版, 1974.

17 岩淵悦太郎 Iwabuchi Etsutarō 『語源散策』 Reflections on Etymology, 243 pp., 毎日新聞社, 1974.

18 岩淵悦太郎 Iwabuchi Etsutarō 『語源のたのしみ 1』 The Pleasures of Etymology, Vol. 1, 245 pp., 毎日新聞社, 1975.

19 山中襄太 Yamanaka Jōta 『語源十二支物語 付・鳥獣名語源物語』 The Derivations of the Twelve Signs of the Zodiac: Tales Connected with the Names of Birds and Animals, 263 pp., 大修館, 1974.

20 山中襄太 Yamanaka Jōta 『人名地名の語源』 The Etymology of Personal and Place Names, 284 pp., 大修館書店, 1975.

21 山口恵一郎 (編著) Yamaguchi Keiichirō (ed.) 『地図と地名』 Maps and Place Names, 286 pp., 古今書院, 1974.

VI-01 森岡健二 (司会) Morioka Kenji (moderator) 『日本語の文法』 Japanese Grammar [シンポジウム日本語 2] 273 pp., 学生社, 1974.

02 三浦つとむ Miura Tsutomu 『日本語の文法』 Japanese Grammar, 316 pp., 勁草書房, 1975.

03 本位田重美 Hon'iden Shigeyoshi 『国語文法論への道』 The Way to a Japanese Grammar, 196 pp., 笠間書院, 1975.

01 大久保忠利 Ōkubo Tadatoshi 『日本文法と言語の理論』 Japanese Grammar

and Language Theory, 477 pp., 春秋社, 1975.

05 奥津敬一郎 Okutsu Keiichirō 『生成日本文法論——名詞句の構造』 *Generative Theory in Japanese Grammar: The Structure of the Noun Phrase*, 383 pp., 大修館書店, 1974.

06 春日和男 Kasuga Kazuo 『説話の語文——古代説話文の研究』 *Writing Style of Japan's Legends: A Study of the Texts of Ancient Legends*, 248 pp., 桜楓社, 1975.

07 春日和男・原 栄一 (編) Kasuga Kazuo and Hara Eiichi (eds.) 『説話の語文 別冊』(日本霊異記漢字索引) *The Writing Style of Japan's Legends: Supplementary Volume* (Index to the Kanji of *Nihon Ryōiki*), 185 pp., 桜楓社, 1975.

08 岩井良雄 Iwai Yoshio 『日本語法史——江戸時代編』 *The History of Japanese Grammar: The Edo Period*, 367 pp., 笠間書院, 1974.

09 小島俊夫 Kojima Toshio 『後期江戸ことばの敬語体系』 *The Pattern of Honorific Speech in the Late Edo Period*, 315 pp., 笠間書院, 1974.

10 佐伯哲夫 Saeki Tetsuo 『現代日本語の語順』 *Modern Japanese Syntax*, 322 pp., 笠間書院, 1975.

11 高橋太郎 Takahashi Tarō 『幼児語の形態論的な分析——動詞・形容詞・述語名詞』 *A Morphological Analysis of Verbs, Adjectives and Predicative Nouns in Children's Speech from 3 to 6* [国立国語研究所報告 55] 242 pp., 秀英出版, 1975.

12 原 子朗 Hara Shirō 『文体論考』 *Writing Style*, 245 pp., 冬樹社, 1975.

13 林 四郎 Hayashi Shirō 『文学探求の言語学』 *Linguistics for Literary Appreciation*, 437 pp., 明治書院, 1975.

14 林 四郎 Hayashi Shirō 『言語表現の構造』 *The Structure of Language Usage*, 414 pp., 明治書院, 1974.

15 阪倉篤義 Sakakura Atsuyoshi 『文章と表現』 *Sentence and Expression*, 381 pp., 角川書店, 1975.

VII-01 柴田 武 (司会) Shibata Takeshi (moderator) 『日本語の方言』 *Japanese Dialects* [シンポジウム日本語 5] 290 pp., 学生社, 1975.

02 国立国語研究所 National Language Research Institute 『日本言語地図 6』 *Linguistic Atlas of Japan*, Vol. 6 [国立国語研究所報告 30-6] 50 図, 参考図 1, 解説 147 pp., 大蔵省印刷局, 1975.

03 藤原与一・広島方言研究所 Fujiwara Yoichi, Hiroshima Dialect Research Center 『瀬戸内海言語図巻』(上・下) *Linguistic Atlas of the Inland Sea Region* (2 vols.) 東京大学出版会, 1974.

04 大橋勝男 Ōhashi Katsuo 『関東地方域方言事象分布地図 1』(音声篇) *A Distribution Chart of Dialects in the Kantō Region*, Vol. 1 (Phonemes), 19 pp., 157 図, 大橋勝男, 1974.

05 大石初太郎・上村幸雄 (編) Ōishi Hatsutarō and Uemura Yukio (eds.) 『方言と標準語——日本語方言学概説』 *Dialects and Standard Language: An Outline*

of Japanese Dialectology, 457 pp., 筑摩書房, 1975.

06 平山輝男（編）Hirayama Teruo (ed.)『方言体系変化の通時論的研究』*A Diachronic Study of Changes in Dialect Systems*, 269 pp., 地図 44 枚, 明治書院, 1974.

07 藤原与一 Fujiwara Yoichi 『方言生活指導論──方言・共通語・標準語』*Guidance for the Use of Dialects in Everyday Life: Dialects, Common Parlance, Standard Language*, 263 pp., 三省堂, 1975.

08 法政大学言語社会学講座（編）Hōsei University Chair of Socio-Linguistics (ed.) 『言語・文化・社会の構造──房総南端地域における記号学的研究』*The Structure of Language, Culture and Society: A Study in Symbols in the Bōsō Peninsula*, 179 pp., 法政大学人文科学研究室, 1975.

09 藤原与一 Fujiwara Yoichi『四国三要地方言対照記述 高知県浦の内方言・徳島県平谷方言・香川県滝の宮方言』*A Comparative Analysis of Three Major Dialects of Shikoku: Uranouchi Dialect in Kōchi, Hiratani Dialect of Tokushima, and Takinomiya Dialect of Kagawa*, [昭和日本語の方言 2] 364 pp., 三弥井書店, 1974.

10 藤原与一（編修）Fujiwara Yoichi (ed.)『方言研究叢書 3』*Series on Dialect Research*, Vol. 3 [広島方言研究所紀要] 209 pp., 三弥井書店, 1974.

11 藤原与一（編修）Fujiwara Yoichi (ed.)『方言研究叢書 4』（方言生活語彙）*A Library of Dialect Research*, Vol. 4, (A Vocabulary of Everyday Dialect) [広島方言研究所紀要] 217 pp., 三弥井書店, 1975.

12 藤原与一（編修）Fujiwara Yoichi (ed.)『方言研究叢書 5』（方言文表現法）*A Library of Dialect Research*, Vol. 5 (Usage in Dialect Writing) [広島方言研究所紀要] 248 pp., 三弥井書店, 1975.

VIII-01 林 四郎・南不二男（編）Hayashi Shirō and Minami Fujio (eds.)『敬語の体系』*An Outline of Honorific Speech* [敬語講座 1] 240 pp., 明治書院, 1974.

02 林 四郎・南不二男（編）Hayashi Shirō and Minami Fujio (eds.) 『上代・中古の敬語』*Honorific Speech in Ancient and Early Medieval Times* [敬語講座 2] 216 pp., 明治書院, 1973.

03 林 四郎・南不二男（編）Hayashi Shirō and Minami Fujio (eds.) 『中世の敬語』*Honorific Speech in Medieval Times* [敬語講座 3] 286 pp., 明治書院, 1974.

04 林 四郎・南不二男（編）Hayashi Shirō and Minami Fujio (eds.) 『近世の敬語』*Early Modern Honorific Speech* [敬語講座 4] 288 pp., 明治書院, 1973.

05 林 四郎・南不二男（編）Hayashi Shirō and Minami Fujio (eds.)『明治大正時代の敬語』*Honorific Speech in Meiji and Taishō Times* [敬語講座 5] 258 pp., 明治書院, 1974.

06 林 四郎・南不二男（編）Hayashi Shirō and Minami Fujio (eds.)『現代の敬語』*Contemporary Honorific Speech* [敬語講座 6] 243 pp., 明治書院, 1973.

07 林 四郎・南不二男（編）Hayashi Shiro and Minami Fujio (eds.) 『行動の

192

中の敬語』*Honorific Speech in Practice* [敬語講座 7] 253 pp., 明治書院, 1973.

08 林　四郎・南不二男 (編) Hayashi Shirō and Minami Fujio (eds.)『世界の敬語』*Honorific Speech Around the World* [敬語講座 8] 275 pp., 明治書院, 1974.

09 林　四郎・南不二男 (編) Hayashi Shirō and Minami Fujio (eds.)『敬語用法辞典』*Dictionary of Honorific Usage* [敬語講座 9] 229 pp., 明治書院, 1974.

10 林　四郎・南不二男 (編) Hayashi Shirō and Minami Fujio (eds.)『敬語研究の方法』*Methods of Research on Honorific Speech* [敬語講座 10] 242 pp., 明治書院, 1974.

11 岩淵悦太郎・西尾寅弥 (編) Iwabuchi Etsutarō and Nishio Toraya (eds.)『現代日本語の単語と文字』*Words and Orthography in Modern Japanese* [新・日本語講座 1] 242 pp., 汐文社, 1975.

12 大久保忠利・奥津敬一郎 (編) Ōkubo Tadatoshi and Okutsu Keiichirō (eds.)『日本文法の見えてくる本』*For an Understanding of Japanese Grammar* [新・日本語講座 2] 274 pp., 汐文社, 1975.

13 平山輝男・大島一郎 (編) Hirayama Teruo and Ōshima Ichirō (eds.)『現代日本語の音声と方言』*Dialects and the Sound of Modern Japanese* [新・日本語講座 3] 326 pp., 汐文社, 1975.

14 岩淵悦太郎・飛田良文 (編) Iwabuchi Etsutarō and Hida Yoshifumi (eds.)『日本語の歴史』*A History of the Japanese Language* [新・日本語講座 4] 263 pp., 汐文社, 1975.

15 高橋太郎・井上尚美 (編) Takahashi Tarō and Inoue Naomi (eds.)『日本人の言語生活』*The Daily Use of Language among the Japanese* [新・日本語講座 5] 238 pp., 汐文社, 1975.

16 林　進治・大久保忠利 (編) Hayashi Shinji and Ōkubo Tadatoshi (eds.)『国語教育の過去現在そして未来』*The Past, Pre. ent and Future of Japanese Language Teaching* [新・日本語講座 6] 289 pp., 汐文社, 1974.

17 倉持保男・鈴木敬司 (編) Kuramochi Yasuo and Suzuki Keiji (eds.)『作家と文体』*Writers and Writing Style* [新・日本語講座 7] 253 pp., 汐文社, 1975.

18 芳賀　綏・田中　積 (編) Haga Yasushi and Tanaka Seki (eds.)『現代人の話しことば』*The Spoken Language of Modern Man* [新・日本語講座 8] 268 pp., 汐文社, 1975.

19 武藤辰男・渡辺　武 (編) Mutō Tatsuo and Watanabe Takeshi (eds.)『現代日本語の建設に苦労した人々』*Those Who Labored in the Formation of Modern Japanese* [新・日本語講座 9] 266 pp., 汐文社, 1975.

20 波多野完治・野林正路 (編) Hatano Kanji and Nobayashi Masamichi (eds.)『ことばと文化・社会』*Language, Culture and Society* [新・日本語講座 10] 292 pp., 汐文社, 1975.

21 阪倉篤義・高村元継・志水富夫 (編) Sakakura Atsuyoshi, Takamura Mototsugu and Shimizu Tomio (eds.)『夜の寝覚総索引』*Complete Index to "Yoru no*

Nezame," 286 pp., 明治書院，1974.

22　増田繁夫・長野照子・居安稔恵・柴崎陽子・寺内統子（編）Masuda Shigeo, Nagano Teruko, Iyasu Toshie, Shibasaki Yōko, and Terauchi Noriko (eds.) 『宇治拾遺物語総索引』 *Complete Index to the "Ujishūi Monogatari,*" 389 pp., 清文堂，1975.

23　小林芳規（編）Kobayashi Yoshinori (ed.)『法華百座聞書抄総索引』*Index to the "Hokke Hyakuza Kikigakishō,*" 712 pp., 武蔵野書院，1975.

24　宇津保物語研究会（編）Committee for Research on the *Utsubo Monogatari* (ed.)『宇津保物語本文と索引』（索引編）*"Utsubo Monogatari": Text and Index* (Index Volume), 512 pp., 笠間書院，1975.

25　大友信一・木村　晟（編）Ōtomo Shin'ichi and Kimura Akira (eds.)『日本一鑑 本文と索引』*"Nihon'ichi no Kagami": Text and Index* [笠間索引叢刊 41] 496 pp., 笠間書院，1974.

26　峰岸　明・王朝文学研究会（編）Minegishi Akira and Heian Literature Study Group (eds.)『閑居友 本文及び総索引』*"Kankyo no Tomo": Text with Index* [笠間索引叢刊 45] 196 pp., 笠間書院，1974.

27　駒沢大学国文学研究室（編）渡辺三男・大友信一・木村　晟 Komazawa University Japanese Literature Department, Watanabe Mitsuo, Ōtomo Shin'ichi and Kimura Akira (eds.)『游歴日本図経 本文と索引』*"Yūreki Nihon Zukyō": Text and Index* [笠間索引叢刊 49] 177 pp., 笠間書院，1975.

28　坂詰力治（編）Sakazume Rikiji (ed.)『無名草子総索引』*Index to "Mumyōzōshi*" [笠間索引叢刊 47] 138 pp., 笠間書院，1975.

29　池田利夫（編）Ikeda Toshio (ed.)『唐物語 校本及び総索引』*Text of "Karamonogatari" with Index* [笠間索引叢刊 48] 254 pp., 笠間書院，1975.

30　塚原鉄雄・秋本守英・神尾暢子（編）Tsukahara Tetsuo, Akimoto Morihide and Kamio Nobuko (eds.)『狭衣物語語彙索引』*Glossary to "Sagoromo Monogatari*" [笠間索引叢刊 50] 412 pp., 笠間書院，1975.

31　杉本つとむ（編）Sugimoto Tsutomu (ed.)『邇言便蒙抄の研究並びに索引』*Studies of "Jigen Benmōshō" with Index*, 288 pp., 文化書房博文社，1975.

32　鈴木　博 Suzuki Hiroshi『妙本寺蔵永禄二年 いろは字 影印・解説・索引』*"Iroha" Alphabet Letters of 1559 at the Myōhonji Temple: Photo Reproduction, Commentary and Index*, 394 pp., 清文堂出版，1974

33　斎賀秀夫・飛田良文・梶原滉太郎 Saiga Hideo, Hida Yoshifumi, and Kajihara Kōtarō『牛店雑談 安愚楽鍋 用語索引』*Index of Vocabulary in "Ushiyazōzan Aguranabe*" [国立国語研究所資料集 9] 208 pp., 秀英出版，1974.

34　林田　明 Hayashida Akira『スピリツアル修行の研究 影印・翻字篇』*A Study of "Spiritual Xuguio": Photo Reproduction and Transliteration*, 1660 pp., 風間書房，1975.

35　柳出征司 Yanagida Seiji『詩学大成抄の国語学的研究』（影印篇上・下 研究

194

篇) *A Japanese Language Study of* "*Shigaku Taisei-shō*" (Photo Reproduction, 2 vols.; Research, 1 vol.), 718, 604, 687 pp., 清文堂, 1975.

36 国立国語研究所 National Language Research Institute 『電子計算機による国語研究 VII』 *Japanese Language Study Done by Computer*, Vol. VII [国立国語研究所報告 54] 198 pp., 秀英出版, 1975.

37 時枝誠記 Tokieda Motoki 『時枝誠記博士論文集 2』(文法・文章論) *Collected Essays by Tokieda Motoki*, Vol. 2 (Grammar and Syntax), 327 pp., 岩波書店, 1975.

38 小林英夫 Kobayashi Hideo 『小林英夫著作集 7』(文体論の建設) *Collection of the Works of Kobayashi Hideo*, Vol. 7 (Toward a Theory of Style), 344 pp., みすず書房, 1975.

39 三上 章 Mikami Akira 『三上章論文集』 *A Collection of Essays by Mikami Akira*, 478 pp., くろしお出版, 1975.

40 新村出 (筆録)・柴田武 (校訂)・信光社 (編) Shinmura Izuru (transcriber), Shibata Takeshi (editor) and Shinkōsha (compiler) 『上田万年 言語学』 *Lecture on Linguistics by Ueda Mannen* [シリーズ名講義ノート] 350 pp., 教育出版, 1975.

41 金田一京助 (筆録), 金田一春彦 (校訂), 信光社 (編) Kindaichi Kyōsuke (transciber), Kindaichi Haruhiko (editor) and Shinkōsha (compiler) 『新村出国語学概説』 *An Introduction to the Study of the Japanese Language: Lectures by Shinmma Izuru* [シリーズ名講義ノート] 365 pp., 教育出版, 1974.

42 国立国語研究所 (編) National Language Reseearch Institute (ed.) 『国語年鑑 昭和 49 年版 (1974)』 *The Japanese Language Yearbook, 1974*, 441 pp., 秀英出版, 1974.

43 国立国語研究所 (編) National Language Research Institute 『国語年鑑 昭和 50 年版 (1975)』 *The Japanese Language Yearbook, 1975*, 422 pp., 秀英出版, 1975.

JAPANESE LITERATURE

KUBOTA Jun and SHIRAISHI Yoshihiko
University of Tokyo

KANAI Seiichi
Ancient Literature Research Society

Translated by Lynne E. Riggs

I. GENERAL

The period under review saw continued interest in producing a comprehensive history of Japanese literature. Two prominent literary critics, Katō Shūichi and Muramatsu Takeshi, published *Nihon bungakushi josetsu* (Introduction to the History of Japanese Literature), Vol. I and *Shi no Nihon bungakushi* (Death in Japan's Literary Traditions), respectively. First serialized in *Asahi jānaru*, the volume by Katō [I-01] begins with an introductory chapter on the unique qualities of Japanese literature and continues on to a discussion of the *Kojiki*, the *Man'yōshū*, *Genji monogatari*, *Konjaku monogatari*, *Heike monogatari*, and *Shasekishū*. It goes on to discuss works of *Nō* and *Kyōgen*, making it a very broad study and a bold treatment of major Japanese classics. Muramatsu's work [I-02] is also a collection of essays first serialized in *Shinchō* and dealing with the concept of death in the major works of classical Japanese literature, including the poems of Kakinomoto no Hitomaro and those of Fujiwara no Shunzei's daughter, *Genji monogatari* (The Tale of Genji), *Heike monogatari* (The Tale of the Heike), *Towazugatari* (Confessions of Lady Nijō), *Taiheiki* and others.

Akiyama Ken, et al., *Nihon koten bungakushi no kisochishiki* (The Fundamentals of the History of Classical Japanese Literature) [I-03] is the joint work of many scholars, each contributing short essays on topics of their specialty. Entries include material heretofore overlooked in literary history, making a useful volume even for specialists.

Recent developments in research on *kanbun* literature are reflected in the publication of Yamagishi Tokuhei, ed., *Nihon kanbungakushi ronkō* (Essays on the History of Japan's *Kanbun* Literature) [I-04]. Eighteen scholars have contributed to the volume's twenty articles relating to *kanbun* literature from the ancient to the early modern period. Another useful book is *Nihon kikō bungaku benran: kikō bungaku kara mita Nihonjin no tabi no sokuseki* (Handbook of Japan's Literary Travelogues: Footprints of the Traveler in Diary Literature) [I-05] edited by Fukuda Hideichi and P. Herbert. This work serves as a kind of annotated bibliography with maps of the journeys recorded in Heian and medieval period travel literature. It concludes with two essays by the editors.

A work that straddles the fields of literature and painting is Katano Tatsurō's *Nihon bungei to kaiga no sōkansei no kenkyū* (The Correlation between Literature and Painting in Japan) [I-06], a truly valuable contribution to the field. It analyzes the relationship between the illustration and the narrative in picture scrolls such as "Genji monogatari emaki," the pictures and poems on folding screens and *shōji* doors, and the paintings and *tanka* poetry of Saitō Mokichi. A work in the same vein is Ihara Aki, *Nihon bungaku shikisai yōgo shūsei—chūsei* (A Catalogue of Color Words in Japanese Literature: the Medieval Period) [I-07], which is an analysis of the relationship between colors and literature.

Another study from the field of cultural history relevant to Japanese literature is Ōmori Shirō's *Nihon bunkashi ronkō* (Studies in Japanese Cultural History) [I-08]. Essays like "Makibi nittō densetsu to Yabadai no shi no shinkō" (Legend of Kibi no Makibi's Entry into T'ang China and the Related Belief in a Chinese Poem on Yamatai) were originally published quite some time ago, but along with others such as "Chūsei massekan toshite no hyakuō shisō" (The Medieval View of the Latter Days as Revealed in the Belief in the Fall of the Kingdom after One Hundred Generations) today have a renewed relevance.

Among collections of documents is the publication of *Yōmei sōsho* (Yōmei Library Series) [I-09], which presents photocopies of the treasured documents of the Konoe family's Yōmei Library.

II. ANCIENT LITERATURE

During the period 1974–75 there was no particularly significant work encompassing the whole range of literature in the ancient period. Therefore, we shall introduce individual works of a more specialized nature.

First, in the field of mythology, the publication of volume four, *Hyūga shinwa* (The Myths of Hyūga Province) [II-05] and volume five, *Nihon shinwa no genkei* (The Original Form of Japanese Myths) [II-06], of *Shinpojiumu Nihon no shinwa* (Symposium on Japanese Mythology) now makes the series complete. Recently, research on mythology has become very popular, stimulated by developments in comparative mythology and cultural anthropology, as well as by contributions from historians and folklorists. This series is a direct reflection of such a trend; while most of the participants in the symposium were scholars from the above fields, there were only one or two in literary research. Volume 20, No. 1 of *Kokubungaku: kaishaku to kyōzai no kenkyū* (Japanese Literature: Research on Interpretation and Teaching Materials) [II-39], devoted to Japanese myths, evidences the same diversity of perspective. Mythology is not only an important aspect of the study of the *Kojiki* and *Nihon shoki* but offers a rich body of material for research on the origins of literature in general and oral literature in particular. Still scholars of Japanese literature do not yet seem to have found in mythology a major source of information for literary research.

Turning to the *Kojiki*, we are struck with the predominance of works of commentary and annotation. Volume one [II-11] and volume three [II-12] of *Kojiki zenchūshaku* (A Complete Commentary on the *Kojiki*) have been published, indicating that the laborious work of Kurano Kenji, who has devoted his whole career to *Kojiki* research, is making steady progress towards completion. These volumes contain many revisions of his earlier renditions, and his detailed commentaries make the work extremely valuable. This will surely become a basic reference work for subsequent research on the "Record of Ancient Matters." Saigō Nobutsuna's *Kojiki chūshaku* (Commentary on the *Kojiki*) [II-13] has also come out in print, and is filled with the kind of original interpretations for which the author is so well known. Among the early commentaries,

Saigō attaches the greatest value to Motoori Norinaga's *Kojikiden* and, in applying the methods of recent anthropological research, he attempts to understand the ancient masterpiece as one deeply and intimately absorbed in it. He includes, however, very little philological criticism of the text. Other works of merit are the essays by Nishimiya Kazutami [II-1, 2, 37] who codified and published an excellent text of the *Kojiki* in 1972.

These works indicate that research on the *Kojiki* has finally reached the level of mature, reliable commentary. Definitive character renditions, semantic interpretation and contextual understanding are undoubtedly of tremendous benefit to the research on mythology going on in the various other fields mentioned above. For scholars of Japanese literature as well, these developments should encourage further research on mythology in general, and the *Kojiki* in particular.

Unlike in the case of the *Kojiki*, annotative research on the *Man'yōshū* has more or less reached its final stage. Following the four volumes in the Iwanami series on classical Japanese literature (*Nihon koten bungaku taikei*) and Chūō Kōronsha's twenty-volume commentary by the late Professor Omodaka Hisataka (*Man'yōshū chūshaku*), we now have another set on the *Man'yōshū* published as part of Shōgakkan's *Nihon koten bungaku zenshū* (A Complete Collection of Classical Japanese Literature). The final, fourth volume [II-19] came out in 1975. A definitive edition of the famous Edo period commentary, *Man'yōdaishōki* has also been completed by Iwanami Shoten as the first seven volumes of *Keichū zenshū* (Complete Works of Shimokawa Keichū) [II-14—18]. A basic document for research, *Man'yōshū sōsakuin* (General Index to the *Man'yōshū*) which was, until recently, very difficult to obtain, has now been reprinted [II-20, 21] and made much easier to use by the addition of *Kokka taikan* numbers to epigraphs and footnotes. Research on the *Man'yōshū* from here on, with this groundwork in fundamental research and documentation, should see all manner of developments. As a matter of fact, important works building on such a heritage have already appeared. Among those not to be overlooked is the extremely valuable *Kodai wakashi kenkyū* (Studies in the History of Ancient Japanese Poetry) [II-23—27], in six volumes by Itō Hiroshi. Presently this set has been published as far as volume five but the first two volumes on "The Structure and Formation of the *Man'yōshū*" alone, represent epoch-making research which examines the internal structure of all twenty volumes of that classic, treating it as a single organic unit, and clarifying greatly the process by which it was formed. Hashimoto Tatsuo's *Man'yō kyūtei kajin no kenkyū* (The Man'yō Court Poets) [II-28] too, is an outstanding study, especially of Kakinomoto no Hitomaro, and a major contribution to the field of literary history. Work on the formative process of the *Man'yōshū* has noticeably advanced in recent years and research on the poets themselves is as popular as ever (although there has been a shift in the particular authors under study). While research has developed in various directions, one that should be particularly emphasized from now on will be studies with a literary history approach.

Especially since the work of Doi Kōchi, Okazaki Yoshie and others, little has been done in crosscultural comparative research seeking to determine whether the phenomena observable in historical literary developments elsewhere in the world can be applied to Japanese classical literature on a comprehensive scale. We hope that new efforts in this area will be forthcoming.

It is unfortunate that there has been almost no scholarly debate during the period under review, which might provide some incentive or stimulus to research. The only event along these lines was the dialogue between Umehara Takeshi and Masuda Katsumi on Hitomaro [I-49–51], but it did little to inspire further research.

The death of Takagi Ichinosuke at eighty-six in December 1974, whose excellent work was distinguished by a particularly keen insight into the literary qualities of all genres of ancient literature, and who was the mentor of many scholars, was a sad loss to all in the field. Volume 36 of *Jōdai bungaku* [II-42] and Volume 19 of *Mifukushi* [II-43], are in memorium to this much respected scholar.

III. HEIAN LITERATURE

Several works spanning the various fields of medieval literature have been published, among them Yamanaka Yutaka's *Heianchō bungaku no shiteki kenkyū* (A Historical Study of Heian Literature) [III-01], Uemura Etsuko's *Heian joryū sakka no kenkyū* (The Women Authors of the Heian Period) [III-02] and Kawaguchi Hisao, *Sei-iki no tora—Heianchō hikaku bungaku ronshū* (Tiger of Western Asia: Comparative Studies of Heian Literature) [III-03]. Yamanaka's book centers around the *Eiga monogatari* (The Tales of Glory) and the *Ōkagami*; his historical methods provide valuable insights to specialists in Japanese literature. The women authors Uemura discusses are Izumi Shikibu, Murasaki Shikibu, Sei Shōnagon and Suōnonaishi. Beginning with a basic biographical sketch, she touches on the respective works of each author. On the subject of *waka*, Ozawa Masao has rearranged the *Kokinwakashū* selections in sequence according to the historical development of *waka* poetry. Entitled *Sakushabetsu/nendaijun Kokinwakashū* (*Kokinwakashū* Rearranged by Author and Chronological Sequence) [III-04], this is a basic reference work supplemented with detailed research on the time and circumstances of writing for each poem. The August 1975 issue of the journal *Bungaku* is also devoted to the *Kokinshū*. Research on authors and poetry focuses on *shikashū*, or collections of the work of individual poets. Publications of this nature include Sasaki Kōji, *Sarumaru-shū to Sarumarudayū setsuwa* (The *Sarumarushū* and Sarumarudayū Legends) [III-05]; Yokota Yukiya, *Ono no Komachi denki kenkyū* (Biographical Studies of Ono no Komachi) [III-06]; Kansaku Kōichi, *Sone no Yoshitada-shū no kenkyū* (A Study of the *Sone no Yoshitada-shū*) [III-07]; Kansaku Kōichi and Shimada Ryōji, *Sone no Yoshitada-shū zenshaku* (A Complete Commentary on the *Sone no Yoshitada-shū*) [III-08]. Yasuda Ayao's *Ōchō no kajin* (Poets of the Heian Court) [III-10], based on an earlier radio program, is unique among other works of its kind for simplicity and attention to the *waka* poets of the later Heian period.

On the *monogatari* genre, there are several general works among which is Mitani Eiichi, *Monogatari bungaku no sekai* (The World of *Monogatari* Literature) [III-11]. This opens with a discussion of the beginnings of the *monogatari* form, and goes on to describe the major works, including the *Taketori monogatari* (Tale of the Bamboo Cutter), *Utsubo monogatari* (A Tale of Utsubo), *Ochikubo monogatari* (The Tale of Lady Ochikubo), *Genji monogatari* (The Tale of Genji), *Sagoromo monogatari* (The Tale of Sagoromo), as well as several of the *giko* (pseudo-classical) tales of the medieval period. Research on *monogatari* literature concentrates, as one might expect, on the *Genji monogatari*, and a few of the works growing out of this are Ikeda Tsutomu, *Genji monogatari shiron* (An Essay on *The Tale of Genji*) [III-12]; Abe Akio, ed., *Genji monogatari no kenkyū* (A Study of *The Tale of Genji*) [III-13]; Mekata Sakuo, *Genji monogatari-ron* (On *The Tale of Genji*) [III-14]; Koyama Atsuko, *Genji monogatari no kenkyū* (Research on *The Tale of Genji*) [III-15] and Ōasa Yūji, *Genji monogatari seihen no kenkyū* (A Study on the Principal Portions of *The Tale of Genji*) [III-16]. Ikeda's work is mainly an analysis of the structure of its successive volumes, Abe includes the essays of authors and Mekata's monograph aims at an analysis of the *Genji*'s organization. Koyama's work consists of two parts, the first of which analyzes the pattern of naming characters in The *Genji* and the process of the novel's creation. The second part investigates its historical background. Also, the classic commentary on the *Genji*, the *Sairyūshō*, has been reprinted under Ii Haruki's editorship [III-17]. Suzuki Hiromichi, *Heian makki monogatari kenkyūshi— Nezame Hamamatsu hen* (A History of Research on Late Heian *Monogatari*: The *Yoru no nezame* and *Hamamatsu Chūnagon monogatari*) [III-18]; Isobe Sadako, *Bishū Tokugawake bon Sumiyoshi monogatari to sono kenkyū* (Research on the Owari Tokugawa Family Text of *The Tale of Sumiyoshi*) [III-19]; Kudō Shinjirō, et al., *Yume no kayoiji monogatari* (Tale of the Dream Trail) [III-20] are all works concerning the late Heian tales and the "pseudo-classics" mentioned earlier.

Besides these, straddling the genres of *waka* and *monogatari* in Heian literature, is a volume commemorating Professor Sekine Yoshiko's retirement, *Nezame monogatari taikō, Heian bungaku ronshū* (A Textual Critique of *Nezame monogatari*: Essays on Heian Literature) [III-21]. This publication consists of twelve essays and a comparison of different *Nezame monogatari* texts.

On *setsuwa* [legends], the first presentation in published form is the work of Takahashi Mitsugu, *Chūko setsuwa bungaku kenkyū josetsu* (Introductory Studies in Early Medieval *Setsuwa* Literature) [III-22], as well as Moriya Toshihiko's *Nihon ryōiki no kenkyū* (Research on *The Tales of Wonder*) [III-23]. Takahashi's study deals mainly with *Nihon ryōiki* and *Konjaku monogatari*, but also touches on the *Kohon setsuwashū* and the *Uchigikishū*. Moriya considers the world of the *Nihon ryōiki* through its editor Kyōkai, and discusses eight stories to examine its methodology.

On diaries, there is Moriya Shōgo's *Kagerō nikki keiseiron* (On the

Formation of *The Gossamer Years*, a Diary by Fujiwara no Michitsuna's Mother) [III-24], a volume-by-volume analysis of the process by which this diary came into being. Also we have Mekata Sakuo's *Makura no sōshi-ron* (On *The Pillow Book*) [III-25], which discusses the artistic qualities of Sei Shōnagon's work, as well as a four-volume series, *Makura no sōshi kōza* (Lectures on *The Pillow Book*) [III-26], which illuminates the work from a variety of angles.

IV. MEDIEVAL LITERATURE

Through the literature of Saigyō, Kamo no Chōmei and Yoshida Kenkō, Itō Hiroyuki has explored the spirit of what might be called "hermit" literature, or that written in ascetic, reflective solitude. His *Inton no bungaku: mōnen to kakusei* (The Writings of the Recluses: Delusion and Enlightenment) [IV-01] has been the subject of much interest. Kobayashi Tomoaki's final work, *Zoku chūsei bungaku no shisō* (Thoughts on Medieval Literature) [IV-02] is a systematic discourse displaying the author's special expertise in the fields of Buddhist and scriptural literature. He also deals with the major works of the medieval period such as the *Hōjōki* (An Account of My Hut) by Kamo no Chōmei, *Tsurezuregusa* (Essays in Idleness) by Yoshida Kenkō, and *Heike monogatari*. Chapters such as the one entitled "*Kaidōki* o meguru mondai" (The Significance of the *Kaidōki*) drew attention when first published as particularly helpful essays on the philosophical aspects of this work, so long treated as no more than travelogue literature.

Chūsei bungaku ronkō (Studies of Medieval Literature) [IV-03] by Fukuda Hideichi is a collection of material distinguished by its systematic organization of the results of prior research, and covers diary (*nikki*) or pensée (*zuihitsu*) literature such as *Towazugatari* (The Confessions of Lady Nijō), *Tsurezuregusa* and the *Takemukigaki*, as well as military tales such as the *Taiheiki*.

Presently it is popular for scholars in the field of *waka* to work very closely with primary source materials. In "Hyakunin isshu e no michi" (The Evolution of the *Hyakunin Isshu*) (*Bungaku*, May 1975) Higuchi Yoshimaro introduces a new perpective into the long-debated subject of the process of how the hundred poems were eventually selected. The collection of essays published as *Teika karon to sono shūhen* (Fujiwara

no Teika's Prosody and Related Questions) [IV-04] by Fukuda
Yūsaku, is the late author's final work, and includes studies of the
Maigetsushō and the *Shinchokusen wakashū*. Morimoto Motoko's *Shikashū
to Shinkokinshū* [IV-05] reveals the degree of the *Shinkokinshū*'s debt
to court poetry; it also includes a study concerning the tenth century
woman court poet, Saigū no Nyōgo. There are many other works
of this nature including Handa Kōhei, *Jakuren Hōshi zenkashū to sono
kenkyū* (Research on the Poetry of the Priest Jakuren) [IV-06]; Manaka
Fujiko, *Jichin Kashō oyobi Shūgyokushū no kenkyū* (Studies of the Priest
Jichin and the *Shūgyokushū*) [IV-07]; Kamata Gorō, *Minamoto no Sanetomo no sakkaronteki kenkyū* (A Study of Minamoto no Sanetomo as a
Poet) [IV-08] and Iwasa Miyoko, *Kyōgokuha kajin no kenkyū* (A Study
of the Poets of the Kyōgoku School) [IV-09]. Among these the Iwasa
study is especially valuable as a work striking out into unexplored
territory. Among several outstanding essays in *Waka renga no kenkyū*
(Waka and Renga Poetry) [IV-10] by Ishimura Yasuko is a portrait
of the patron of poets Kujō Kanezane, through his *kanbun* diary
Gyokuyō. It also includes studies on Ninagawa Chiun and Ikenobō
Senjun.

Okuno Jun'ichi's *Ise jingū shinkan renga no kenkyū* [IV-11] focuses on
a prominent regional style of *renga*, incorporating the results of a basic
survey of Ise *renga*. His work includes reprints of Arakida family papers
and documents.

Kadokawa Gen'yoshi died suddenly soon after publication of his
Katarimono bungei no hassei (The Emergence of the Genre of Narrative
Tales) [IV-12], making this his final work. His book is an attempt to
deal with the *Heike monogatari*, the *Soga monogatari*, *Gikeiki*, *Taiheiki*
and other *gunki monogatari* (military tales) as narrative literature. It
is a monumental work which cannot be overlooked in considering
the formative and developmental process of these tales.

The two-volume *Heike mabushi* [IV-13], edited by the Committee
for Publication of the *Heike mabushi*, is a photostated version of the
original scores edited in the Edo period by Ogino Kengyō. These
scores for the *Heike monogatari* are intended for *biwa* accompaniment.
In addition, the set includes an essay on music and bibliographical
sources by Atsumi Kaoru. Another work in this area is the recently
completed English translation, *The Tale of the Heike* by Kitagawa

Hiroshi and B. T. Tsuchida [IV-14]. A study in primary materials is Yamanouchi Junzō, *Hiramatsukebon Heike monogatari no kenkyū* (The Hiramatsu Family Version of the *Tale of the Heike*) [IV-15] and the *Heike* as literature is Sasaki Hachirō, *Heike monogatari no tassei* (The Completion of the *Tale of the Heike*) [IV-16].

The December 1974 issue of *Bungaku* featured five separate studies on *gunki monogatari*, with "an index of research on the military romances." Ōsumi Kazuo's *Taiheiki jinmei sakuin* (Index of Names in the *Taiheiki*) [IV-17], provides a preliminary foothold for finding our way into the world of the *Taiheiki*.

Two works have appeared successively on the *setsuwa*: Shimura Kunihiro, *Chūsei setsuwa bungaku kenkyū josetsu* (Introductory Studies of *Setsuwa* Literature of the Medieval Period) [IV-18] and Haruta Akira, *Chūsei setsuwa bungakuron josetsu* (An Introductory Analysis of *Setsuwa* as a Literary Genre) [IV-19]. Shimura's work is mainly a bibliographical study of representative works of medieval *setsuwa* such as the *Ujishūi monogatari* and the *Kokonchomonjū*. Haruta's work contains essays which attempt to apply the customary approach to *setsuwa* to the *Heike monogatari* and essays on the *Konjaku monogatari* and the *Ujishūi monogatari*. J. Piggot's "Otogi-zōshi ni okeru michi-yukibun" (The *Michiyuki* Style in Popular Short Stories of the Muromachi Period) (*Bungaku*, June 1975) does not limit itself to the *otogi-zōshi* genre, but includes reference to the style of military romances and *jōruri* ballads.

On the *Tsurezuregusa*, the four-volume series *Tsurezuregusa kōza* (Lectures on the *Tsurezuregusa*) [IV-20] has been completed. The critique and commentary on each passage of Kenkō's work is uneven in quality, but volume one, entitled *Kenkō to sono jidai* (Yoshida Kenkō and His Age) and volume four, *Gengo, gensen, eikyō* (Language, Sources and Influences), are outstanding essays. Nakagawa Tokuno-suke has published *Kenkō no hito to shisō* (Yoshida Kenkō: The Man and His Thought) [IV-21], which examines passages of the *Tsurezure-gusa* and Kenkō's collected poems for an image of the famed recluse, and goes on to investigate his outlook on life and humanity itself as well as his sense of the impermanence of things.

"Shukujinron: geinōshin shinkō no kongen ni aru mono" (*Shukujin*: The Origin of Belief in Dieties of the Performing Arts) in *Bungaku*,

October 1974, January, February, June 1975, is a study by Hattori Yukio of the gods worshipped by performing artists, and the author traces the origin of *shukujin* to *Okina* and other plays of *sarugaku noh*. Kobayashi Mitsugu, *Kyōgenshi kenkyū* (A History of *Kyōgen*) [IV-22], is a discussion of the various schools of *kyōgen*, their beginnings and their master performers.

V. EARLY MODERN LITERATURE

Nakamura Yukihiko, a highly respected scholar in the field of early modern literature, has put together fourteen of his essays in *Kinsei bungei shichōkō* (Early Modern Trends in Literary Thought) [V-01]. They deal with the work of Confucian scholars, men of letters, *kokugaku* scholars, and *waka* poets. These essays include a discussion of the methodology of literary research which offers researchers much food for thought and reflection.

Kinsei bungei no kenkyū—shiryōhen (Research on Early Modern Literature: Basic Documents) [V-02], edited by Shuzui Kenji, is a collection of reprints and photocopies of four jōruri-related documents such as "Jōruri-michi no shiori" (Guide to the *Jōruri* Art).

On *haikai* is the eagerly awaited work of Miyamoto Saburō, *Shōfū haikai ronkō* (A Study of Bashō-style Haiku) [V-03] whose fourteen analytical essays crown twenty years of diligent research. The volume includes many important essays, a few of which are, "Haikai bungeiron: Bashō to Bashō izen" (A Study of the Art of Haiku: Bashō and His Predecessors), "Kyojitsuron josetsu" (Preliminary Study on the Fiction vs. Realism Debate), "Shōfū renku no tsuki to hana" (The Moon and Flowers in Bashō-style Linked Verse) and "*Oi no kobumi* e no gimon*" (Questions Concerning *Manuscript in My Knapsack*). Akabane Manabu's *Bashō no Sarashina kikō no kenkyū* (A Study of Bashō's *Sarashina Journey*) [V-04] is made up of two parts: one of documents and one of research papers. Abe Masami's *Bashō renkushō* (Selected Linked Verse by Bashō) [V-05] is coming out. Miyawaki Shōzō, et al., eds., *Kaya Shirao zenshū* [V-06] is a basic reference source for the primary documents of the prominent mid-Edo period haiku poet. The volume includes Shirao's *hokku*, *renku*, as well as his letters and essays on haiku.

Ishida Yoshisada in *Ryokan—sono zenbō to genzō* (Ryōkan: The Man and His Image) [V-07] presses close upon the inner qualities of the reticent Edo period poet (1758–1831).

Hino Tatsuo's work in *Sorai gakuha* (The Ogyū Sorai School) [V-08] is a collection of essays on early modern poets and Confucian scholars which he has energetically produced in recent years.

In the area of fiction, several works on *kanazōshi* have appeared, including Tanaka Shin, *Kanazōshi no kenkyū* (A Study of *Kanazōshi*) [V-09], Tanaka Shin, et al., eds., *Kashōki taisei: ei'in, kōi, kenkyū* (The Complete *Kashōki*: Photocopies of Original Editions, Textual Critique, and Analysis) [V-10], and Kishi Tokuzō's final work, *Kanazōshi to Saikaku* (Ihara Saikaku and *Kanazōshi*) [V-11]. Tanaka's work on *kanazōshi* focuses mainly on a critique of *Uraminosuke*, the *Kashōki*, *Ninin bikuni*, *Ukigumo monogatari* and others, and is supplemented with reprints of the original manuscripts. On *ukiyozōshi*, Noma Kōshin, ed., *Saikaku ronsō* (Essays on Saikaku) [V-12] is a compilation of thirty studies by twenty-nine authors, and attempts an internal approach to the work of Saikaku both as novelist and haiku poet. Mizuno Minoru, *Edo shōsetsu ronsō* (Essays on the Fiction of the Edo Period) [V-13] contains articles focusing on late Edo period works, particularly of Kyōden (Santō Kyōden, 1769–1816) and Bakin (Kyokutei Bakin, 1767–1848), is a long-awaited work among scholars in the field.

Introducing a reprint of an original document handed down in the Chiyokura family of Nagoya, Morikawa Akira, *Enpō yonen Saikaku saitanchō* (Saikaku's Annual Anthology of *Haiku*, 1676) is an important element of biographical research on that versatile author. In addition, Yokoyama Kuniharu, *Yomihon no kenkyū: Edo to Kamigata to* (Tokugawa Period Novelettes of Edo and Osaka) [V-14] has been published, and the first eight volumes of *Hanashi-bon taikei* (Series on the Light Fiction of the Edo Period) [V-15], edited by Mutō Sadao and Oka Masahiko, has begun publication. The series consists of reprints of some *karukuchi-bon* (light, satiric novels), a genre which emerged in the period 1764–1771; and should be useful in various ways. Mutō has also written *Edo kobanashi no hikaku kenkyū* [V-16], which attempts a comparative study of the humorous stories of the Edo period, the *kobanashi*, with China's literature of humor and with *kyōgen*.

There is also much of note in the field of drama and the theatre arts. First are Yūda Yoshio's final works, *Jōrurishi ronkō* (Essays on the History of *Jōruri*) [V-17] and *Zenkō Shinjū ten no Amijima* (A Comprehensive Commentary on "The Love Suicides at Amijima") [V-18]. The latter volume contains many pictures of Bunraku performances of the play which should add much to the appreciation of playgoers as well.

Two works by Suwa Haruo have been published, *Chikamatsu sewa jōruri no kenkyū* (A Study of Chikamatsu's *Jōruri*) [V-19] and *Kabukishi no gashōteki kenkyū* (A Pictorial Study of Kabuki History) [V-20]. The first is a discussion of the world and methods of *sewa jōruri*, including a study of Chikamatsu Monzaemon as a playwright. *Hengeron— kabuki no seishinshi* (Ghost Plays: A History of the Kabuki Spirit) [V-21] is a persuasive work by Hattori Yukio exploring the ethos behind the popularity of the mystery plays. A work seeking to clarify the true qualities of kabuki from the point of view of the actors themselves is Imao Tetsuya's *Hokahibito no matsuei* (Descendants of Beggars) [V-22].

Kokugo to kokubungaku has produced two important special editions featuring early modern literature, October 1974, and Japan's dramatic literature, October 1975, which provide helpful information.

VI. MODERN/CONTEMPORARY LITERATURE

For the sake of convenience we shall take up individual authors or their works in a more or less chronological order.

One section is still extant of the diary of Narushima Ryūhoku (1837– 84), most of which was destroyed in the bombings of 1945. Maeda Ai acquired this manuscript and published "Narushima Ryūhoku no nikki" (Dairy of Narushima Ryūhoku) in *Bungaku* (February, March 1975) [VI-01]. Maeda portrays the process by which Ryūhoku, then a young *bakufu* tutor, came to write *Ryūkyō shinshi* and regard himself as a "superfluous man." The discovery of new material is highly significant in considering the emergence of Ryūhoku as an important writer. Hiraoka Toshio has cast new light on Kōda Rohan's work, using newly uncovered documents for an article for *Bungaku* (November 1975) entitled "Satsuriku suru Rohan" (Rohan, the Hunter) [VI-02]. Hiraoka makes clear that Rohan relied on descriptions of whaling scenes in the *Isanatori ekotoba*, an illustrated story written in the bakumatsu period, for his *Isanatori* (The Whalers) and investigates the extent to which Rohan elaborated on or abridged the original narrative.

He discusses Rohan's concept of human existence as something ominously dark—a sentiment which runs through the entire length of *Isanatori*. Hiraoka's essay provides a fresh perspective on Rohan's little touched long novel.

Although skipping to another period, we would like to take up Gamō Yoshirō's *"Abe ichizoku-ron"* which appeared in *Bungaku* (November 1975) [VI-03] focusing on the use of historical materials in Mori Ōgai's work. Much has been written on this historical novel since the discovery of *Abe saijidan*, the document Ōgai used as a basis for his novel, but Gamō's essay counters the general tendency to overemphasize the gap between the mediums of historical documents and fiction, and thereby to criticize Ōgai's arbitrary addition of other material. The point of this essay is that, by creating anew the world of the *Abe saijidan*, Ōgai expressed his sympathy with the traditional, and, in turn, discarded his "modern" sense of criticism. Gamō's work deserves note as an effort to formulate a pattern of "modern" Japanese intellectuals who have turned their backs on "modernity."

Another writer who refused to recognize Japan's modernity was Nagai Kafū, the subject of Oketani Hideaki's essay in *"Danchōtei Nichijō oboegaki"* (Notes on Kafū's "Dyspepsia House Days") (*Umi*, April 1974) [VI-04]. Oketani identifies the time when Kafū began to keep this diary "Danchōtei Nichijō" with his decision to turn away from the world around him, and quotes abundantly from this to show how Kafū endeavored to live out the rest of his days following his own sensibility towards life. Oketani's essay, then, offers a new theory on Kafū, which highlights the distinction between his thought and his artistic sensibility and taste.

Kyōka zenshū (The Collected Works of Izumi Kyōka) has been reprinted and although an additional volume of his writing which for various reasons could not be gathered during World War II did not appear until March 1976, the reprinting is beginning to stimulate studies on Kyōka. Kasahara Nobuo's article in *Bungaku* (July 1975), "Kyōka-teki biishiki no genkei" (The Archetype of Izumi Kyōka's Esthetic Sense) [VI-05] demonstrates by citing a number of Kyōka's novels that the source of his esthetic consciousness, which is consistent from early on in life to his death, was the nostalgia for his hometown which had long been lost to him.

Again making a great leap in time, we come to the most controversial work on Natsume Sōseki, Etō Jun's doctoral thesis (September 1975), *Sōseki to Āsā-Ō densetsu* (Sōseki and the Legend of King Arthur) [VI-06]. He compares Sōseki's "Kairokō" (Eulogy) with the Legend of King Arthur and argues that the short story was meant to be a eulogy to his sister-in-law. This essay emerges from the motifs Etō has been pursuing in his book *Sōseki to sono jidai* (The Life and Times of Natsume Sōseki), and the debate over the interpretation of the story of King Arthur, with Ōoka Shōhei began in late 1975. It will certainly be some time before this controversy is settled.

Higuchi Ichiyō is the subject of Maeda Ai's essay "Kodomotachi no jikan" (*Tenbō*, June 1975) [VI-07]. This article juxtaposes the games of the children in *Takekurabe* against the utilitarianism of the Meiji period. His thesis, showing how Japan's modernization destroyed innocent, childish pleasures such as Ichiyō portrayed, brings in the larger insights of sociological perspective.

Miyoshi Yukio, "Mumyō no yami" (Darkness of the Spirit) (*Kokugo to kokubungaku*, April 1975) [VI-08], concerns Akutagawa Ryūnosuke's *Rashōmon* and his genius for injecting into his short stories the darkness and anguish of his own life. Miyoshi verifies that this talent had already emerged by the time Akutagawa wrote his first historical novel. By delving for the internal logic of the work, Miyoshi seeks to reveal Akutagawa's genius and the implications of that logic. His methodology is truly admirable.

With reference to Tanizaki Jun'ichirō, I should like to mention Kōno Taeko's "Tanizaki bungaku to kōtei no yokubō" (Tanizaki and His Craving for the Affirmative) (*Bungakukai*, January 1975–February 1976) [VI-09]. As the title suggests, this essay proposes that Tanizaki's great wish was that paradise be found in this world and that it is this craving for such affirmation that was the well-spring of his creative activity. Kōno herself is a writer and her personal experiences are visible in her astute analyses. What is more important, she traces back to the original manuscripts and editions of all his writings. This essay reconfirms the value of the fundamental technique of literary research of going back, wherever possible, to the earliest edition or even to the original manuscripts despite the availability of the author's *zenshū* (complete works), which are so much more accessible.

文　献

I-01　加藤周一 Katō Shūichi『日本文学史序説』(上) *Introduction to the History of Japanese Literature*, Vol. I, 322 pp., 筑摩書房, 1975.

02　村松　剛 Muramatsu Takeshi『死の日本文学史』 *Death in Japan's Literary Traditions*, 315 pp., 新潮社, 1975.

03　秋山　虔・神保五弥・佐竹昭広 Akiyama Ken, Jinbo Kazuya and Satake Akihiro『日本古典文学史の基礎知識』 *The Fundamentals of the History of Classical Japanese Literature*, 533 pp., 有斐閣, 1975.

04　山岸徳平 (編) Yamagishi Tokuhei (ed.)『日本漢文学史論考』 *Essays on the History of Japan's Kanbun Literature*, 624 pp., 岩波書店, 1974.

05　福田秀一, プルチョウ・ヘルベルト (編) Fukuda Hideichi and P. Herbert (eds.)『日本紀行文学便覧　──紀行文学から見た日本人の旅の足跡──』 *Handbook of Japan's Literary Travelogues: Footprints of the Traveler in Diary Literature*, 271 pp., 武蔵野書院, 1975.

06　片野達郎 Katano Tatsurō『日本文芸と絵画の相関性の研究』 *The Correlation between Literature and Painting in Japan* [笠間叢書] 404 pp., 笠間書院, 1975.

07　伊原　昭 Ihara Aki『日本文学色彩用語集成 ──中世──』 *A Catalogue of Color Words in Japanese Literature: The Medieval Period*, 420, pp., 笠間書院, 1975.

08　大森志郎 Ōmori Shirō『日本文化史論考』 *Studies in Japanese Cultural History*, 211 pp., 創文社, 1975.

II-01　西宮一民 Nishimiya Kazutami 古事記行文注釈二題──「禊祓」条と「天孫降臨」段── "Two Problems in *Kojiki* Notation"『倉野憲司先生古稀記念古代文学論集』pp. 200-44, 桜楓社, 1974.

02　西宮一民 Nishimiya Kazutami「古事記語釈三題」 "Three Problems in Kojiki Semantics"『境田教授喜寿記念論文集 上代の文学と言語』pp. 89-110, 境田教授喜寿記念論文集刊行会, 1974.

03　万葉七曜会 (編) Man'yō Shichiyōkai (ed.)『論集上代文学』(第5冊) *Studies of Early Japanese Literature*, Vol. 5, 197 pp., 笠間書院, 1975.

04　日本文学研究資料刊行会 (編) Committee for the Publication of Research Materials in Japanese Literature (ed.)『古事記・日本書紀 II』 *The "Kojiki" and "Nihonshoki,"* Vol. 2 [日本文学研究資料叢書] 319 pp., 有精堂, 1975.

05　大林太良 (司会)・伊藤清司, 岡田精司・松前　健・森　浩一・吉井　巌 Ōbayashi Taryō (moderator), Itō Seiji, Okada Seishi, Matsumae Takeshi, Mori Kōichi and Yoshii Iwao『日向神話』 *The Myths of Hyūga Province* [シンポジウム 日本の神話 4] 268 pp., 学生社, 1974.

06　伊藤清司 (司会)・上田正昭・大林太良・松前　健・森　浩一・吉田敦彦 Itō Seiji (moderator), Ueda Masaaki, Ōbayashi Taryō, Matsumae Takeshi, Mori

Kōichi and Yoshida Atsuhiko 『日本神話の原形』 *The Original Form of Japanese Myths* [シンポジウム 日本の神語 5] 245 pp., 学生社, 1975.

07 松前 健 Matsumae Takeshi 『古代伝承と宮廷祭祀──日本神話の周辺──』 *Ancient Legends and Shinto Ceremonies of the Court: The World of Japan's Mythology*, 397 pp., 塙書房, 1974.

08 三谷栄一 Mitani Eiichi 『日本神話の基盤 ──風土記の神々と神話文学──』 *The Foundation of Japan's Mythology: the Gods of the Fudoki and Mythological Literature*, 630 pp., 塙書房, 1974.

09 佐藤四信 Satō Shinobu 『出雲国風土記の神話』 *The Myths of the Fudoki of the Province of Izumo*, 538 pp., 笠間書院, 1974·

10 志田諄一 Shida Jun'ichi 『常陸風土記とその社会』 *Society as Depicted in the Hitachi Fudoki*, 248 pp., 雄山閣, 1974.

11 倉野憲司 Kurano Kenji 『古事記全註釈』 第二巻 上巻篇（上） *A Complete Commentary on the "Kojiki,"* Vol. 2, 344 pp., 三省堂, 1974.

12 倉野憲司 Kurano Kenji 『古事記全註釈』 第三巻 上巻篇（下） *A Complete Commentary on the "Kojiki,"* Vol. 3, 376 pp., 三省堂, 1975.

13 西郷信綱 Saigō Nobutsuna 『古事記注釈』 第一巻 *Commentary on the "Kojiki,"* Vol. 1, 405 pp., 平凡社, 1975.

14 林 勉 (編) Hayashi Tsutomu (ed.) 『万葉代匠記 三』 *Man'yōdaishōki*, Vol. 3 [契沖全集 第三巻 （久松潜一 監修）] 579 pp., 岩波書店, 1974.

15 久保田淳 (編) Kubota Jun (ed.) 『万葉代匠記 四』 *Man'yōdaishōki*, Vol. 4 [契沖全集 第四巻 （久松潜一 監修）] 652 pp., 岩波書店, 1975.

16 池田利夫 (編) Ikeda Toshio (ed.) 『万葉代匠記 五』 *Man'yōdaishōki*, Vol. 5 [契沖全集 第五巻 （久松潜一 監修）] 626 pp., 岩波書店, 1975.

17 筑島 裕 (編) Tsukishima Hiroshi (ed.) 『万葉代匠記 六』 *Man'yōdaishōki*, Vol. 6 [契沖全集 第六巻 （久松潜一 監修）] 540 pp., 岩波書店, 1975.

18 筑島 裕・林 勉 (編) Tsukishima Hiroshi and Hayashi Tsutomu (eds.) 『万葉代匠記 七・厚顔抄』 *Man'yōdaishōki (Vol. 7) and Kōganshō* [契沖全集 第七巻 （久松潜一 監修）] 651 pp., 岩波書店, 1974.

19 小島憲之・木下正俊・佐竹昭広 (校注・訳) Kojima Noriyuki, Kinoshita Masatoshi and Satake Akihiro (eds.) 『萬葉集』 (四) *The "Man'yōshū,"* Vol. 4 [日本古典文学全集] 546 pp., 小学館, 1975.

20 正宗敦夫 (編) Masamune Atsuo (ed.) 『萬葉集総索引, 単語篇』 *General Index to the "Man'yōshū": Vocabulary*, 1344 pp., 平凡社, 1974 (復刊).

21 正宗敦夫 (編) Masamune Atsuo (ed.) 『萬葉集総索引, 漢字篇』 *General Index to the "Man'yōshū": Character Readings*, 322 pp., 平凡社, 1974 (復刊).

22 五味智英・小島憲之 (編) Gomi Tomohide and Kojima Noriyuki (eds.) 『万葉集研究 第三集』 *Studies on the "Man'yōshū,"* Vol. 3, 298 pp., 塙書房, 1974.

23 伊藤 博 Itō Hiroshi 『万葉集の構造と成立』 (上) *The Structure and Creation*

of the "Man'yōshū," Vol. 1, [古代和歌史研究 1] 434 pp., 塙書房, 1974.

24 伊藤　博 Itō Hiroshi 『万葉集の構造と成立』(下) *The Structure and Creation of the "Man'yōshū,"* Vol. 2 [古代和歌史研究 2] 471 pp., 塙書房, 1974.

25 伊藤　博 Itō Hiroshi 『万葉集の歌人と作品』(上) *The Man'yō Poets and Their Work"*, Vol. 1 [古代和歌史研究 3] 385 pp., 塙書房, 1975.

26 伊藤　博Itō Hiroshi 『万葉集の歌人と作品』(下) *The Man'yō Poets and Their Work*, Vol. 2 [古代和歌史研究 4] 457 pp., 塙書房, 1975.

27 伊藤　博 Itō Hiroshi 『万葉集の表現と方法』(上) *Poetic Expression and Technique in the "Man'yōshū,"* Vol. 1 [古代和歌史研究 5] 462 pp., 塙書房, 1975.

28 橋本達雄 Hashimoto Tatsuo 『万葉宮廷歌人の研究』 *The Man'yō Court Poets*, 521 pp., 笠間書院, 1975.

29 梅原　猛 Umehara Takeshi 『さまよえる歌集 赤人の世界』 *The Elusive Poem Collection—the World of Yamabe no Akahito*, 365 pp., 集英社, 1974.

30 尾崎暢殃 Ozaki Nobuo 『大伴家持論攷』 *A Study of Ōtomo no Yakamochi*, 496 pp., 笠間書院, 1975.

31 寺田　透 Terada Tōru 『万葉の女流歌人』 *The Women Poets of the "Man'yōshū"* [岩波新書 928] 226 pp., 岩波書店, 1975.

32 北山茂夫 Kitayama Shigeo 『続万葉の世紀』 *The Man'yō Era*, II, 471 pp., 東京大学出版会, 1975.

33 森脇一夫 Moriwaki Kazuo 『万葉の美意識』 *Sense of Beauty in the "Man'yōshū,"* 332 pp., 桜楓社, 1974.

34 瀬古　確 Seko Katashi 『万葉集の表現』 *Literary Expression in the "Man'yōshū,"* 431 pp., 教育出版センター, 1974.

35 滝川政次郎 Takigawa Masajirō 『万葉律令考』 *Ritsuryō in the World of the "Man'yōshū"* 698 pp., 東京堂, 1974.

36 稲岡耕二 (司会)・五味智英・阿蘇瑞枝・曾倉　岑・鈴木日出男 Inaoka Kōji (moderator), Gomi Tomohide, Aso Mizue, Sokura Takeshi and Suzuki Hideo 『万葉集』 *The "Man'yōshū* [シンポジウム日本文学 1] 259 pp., 学生社, 1975.

37 西宮一民 Nishimiya Kazutami　古事記訓詁二題 ——修理固成・開天石屋戸而刺許母理坐也——"Two Problems of Interpretation in the *Kojiki*" 「国文学」(吉永登先生古稀記念上代文学特集) 52 号, pp. 25–34, 関西大学国文学会, 1975 年 9 月.

38 「国文学　解釈と教材の研究」——万葉の抒情——(特集) *Kokubungaku: kaishaku to kyōzai no kenkyū* (Special Edition on Lyricism in the *Man'yōshū*), 263 号 (19 巻 6 号), 学燈社, 1974 年 5 月.

39 「国文学　解釈と教材の研究」——日本の神々——(特集) *Kokubungaku: kaishaku to kyōzai no kenkyū* (Special Edition on the Gods of Japan), 273 号 (20 巻 1 号), 学燈社, 1975 年 1 月.

40 「国文学　解釈と教材の研究」——日本文学史の構想——(特集) *Kokubungaku:*

kaishaku to kyōzai no kenkyū (Special Edition on the Framework of Japanese Literary History), 279 号 (20 巻 7 号), 学燈社, 1975 年 6 月.

41　「国文学 解釈と鑑賞」──古代歌謡・その夢と秘儀──(特集) *Kokubungaku: kaishaku to kanshō* (Special Edition on Visions and Esoteric Rites of the Ancient Ballads), 515 号 (40 巻 10 号), 至文堂, 1975 年 9 月.

42　「上代文学」──追悼 高木市之助先生── *Jōdaibungaku* (Special Edition in Memory of Professor Takagi Ichinosuke), 36 号, 上代文学会, 1975 年 7 月.

43　「美夫君志」 *Mifukushi*, 19 号, 美夫君志会, 1975 年 7 月.

44　吉井　巌 Yoshii Iwao 崇神王朝の始祖伝承とその変遷 "The Founding of Emperor Sujin's Court: Versions of the Legend"「萬葉」86 号, pp. 14–37, 萬葉学会 (大地), 1974 年 12 月.

45　倉塚曄子 Kuratsuka Akiko オキナガタラシヒメの物語 (上) "The Tale of Okinagatarashi-hime," Part 1「文学」42 巻 8 号, pp. 961–79 (55–73), 岩波書店, 1974 年 9 月.

46　倉塚曄子 Kuratsuka Akiko オキナガタラシヒメの物語 (下) "The Tale of Okinagatarashi-hime," Part 2「文学」42 巻 9 号, pp. 1076–91 (58–73), 岩波書店, 1974年 9 月.

47　ハーラ・イシュトウヴァン Halla István 『萬葉集』名義の謎 "The Riddle of the Naming of the *Man'yōshū*"「萬葉」84 号, pp. 1–32, 萬葉学会, 1974 年 6 月.

48　渡瀬昌忠 Watase Masatada 志賀白水郎歌の場──歌群の構造論として──"The Settings of Shika no Ama's Poetry: The Structure of Poem Groupings"「萬葉」87 号, pp. 1–21, 萬葉学会, 1975 年 3 月.

49　益田勝実 Masuda Katsumi 文学のひろば "The Literary Forum"「文学」43 巻 4 号, pp. 402–403 (46–47), 岩波書店, 1975 年 4 月.

50　梅原　猛 Umehara Takeshi 『『水底の歌』のアポロギア──益田勝実氏に──』 "Apologia on My Book, *Suitei no Uta*, to Masuda Katsumi"「文学」13 巻 10 号, pp. 1154–74 (14–34), 岩波書店, 1975 年 10 月.

51　益田勝実 Masuda Katsumi アポロギアとアポリアと──梅原猛氏に──"Apologia and Aporia, to Umehara Takeshi"「文学」43 巻 12 号, pp. 1404–1412 (40–48), 岩波書店, 1975 年 12 月.

III-01　山中　裕 Yamanaka Yutaka 『平安朝文学の史的研究』 *A Historical Study of Heian Literature*, 482 pp., 吉川弘文館, 1974.

02　上村悦子 Uemura Etsuko 『平安女流作家の研究』 *The Women Authors of the Heian Period* [笠間叢書] 424 pp., 笠間書院, 1975.

03　川口久雄 Kawaguchi Hisao 『西域の虎──平安朝比較文学論集』 *Tiger of Western Asia: Comparative Studies of Heian Literature*, 392 pp., 吉川弘文館, 1974.

04　小沢正夫 (編) Ozawa Masao (ed.) 『作者別・年代順 古今和歌集』 *"Kokinwa-*

214

kashū" Rearranged by Author and Chronological Sequence, 284 pp., 明治書院, 1975.

05 佐々木孝二 Sasaki Kōji 『猿丸集と猿丸大夫説話』 *The Sarumarushū and Saru-marudayū Legends*, 498 pp., 旭川, 1974.

06 横田幸哉 Yokota Yukiya 『小野小町伝記研究』 *Biographical Studies of Ono no Komachi*, 426 pp., 風間書房, 1974.

07 神作光一 Kansaku Kōichi 『曾禰好忠集の研究』 *A Study of the "Sone no Yoshi-tada-shū*," 822 pp., 笠間書院, 1974.

08 神作光一・島田良二 Kansaku Kōichi and Shimada Ryōji 『曾禰好忠集全釈』 *A Complete Commentary on the "Sone no Yoshitada-shū*," 666 pp., 笠間書院, 1975.

09 清水 彰 Shimizu Akira 『四条宮下野集全釈』 *A Commentary on the "Shijōno-miya Shimotsuke-shū*," [笠間注釈叢刊] 376 pp., 笠間書院, 1975.

10 安田章生 Yasuda Ayao 『王朝の歌人たち』 *Poets of the Heian Court* [NHK ブックス] 240 pp., 日本放送出版協会, 1974.

11 三谷栄一 Mitani Eiichi 『物語文学の世界』 *The World of Monogatari Literature* [有精堂選書] 299 pp., 有精堂, 1975.

12 池田 勉 Ikeda Tsutomu 『源氏物語試論』 *An Essay on "The Tale of Genji"* 古川書房, 1974.

13 阿部秋生 (編) Abe Akio (ed.) 『源氏物語の研究』 *A Study of "The Tale of Genji*," 300 pp., 東京大学出版会, 1974.

14 目加田さくを Mekata Sakuo 『源氏物語論』 *On "The Tale of Genji*," 664 pp., 笠間書院, 1975.

15 小山敦子 Koyama Atsuko 『源氏物語の研究——創作過程の探求——』 *Re-search on "The Tale of Genji" : A Study of the Process of Its Creation*, 488 pp., 武蔵野書院, 1975.

16 大朝雄二 Ōasa Yūji 『源氏物語正篇の研究』 *A Study of the Principal Portions of The Tale of Genji*," 652 pp., 桜楓社, 1975.

17 伊井春樹 (編) Ii Haruki (ed.) 『内閣文庫本 細流抄』 *The "Sairyūshō*," *a Re-print of the Cabnet Libreary Text*, 522 pp., 桜楓社, 1975.

18 鈴木弘道 Suzuki Hiromichi 『平安末期物語研究史 寝覚浜松編』 *A History of Research on Late Heian Monogatari: the "Yoru no Nezame" and "Hamamatsu chū-nagon Monogatari*," 570 pp., 大学堂書店 (京都), 1974.

19 磯部貞子 Isobe Sadako 『尾州徳川家本住吉物語とその研究』 *Research on the Owari Tokugawa Family Text of "The Tale of Sumiyoshi"* [笠間叢書] 216 pp., 笠間書院, 1975.

20 工藤進思郎・伊奈あつ子・川嶋春枝・高見沢狭子 Kudō Shinjirō, Ina Atsu-ko, Kawashima Harue and Takamisawa Kyōko 『夢の通ひ路物語』 *Tales of the Dream Trail*, 381 pp., 福武書店 (岡山), 1975.

21 関根慶子教授退官記念会 (編) Committee for the Commemoration of Pro-fessor Sekine Yoshiko's Retirement (ed.) 『関根慶子教授退官記念寝覚物語対

校・平安文学論集』 *A Textual Critique of "Nezame Monogatari" ; Essays on Heian Literature*, 522 pp., 風間書店, 1975.

22 高橋　貢 Takahashi Mitsugu『中古説話文学研究序説』*Introductory Studies in Medieval "Setsuwa" Literature*, 402 pp., 桜楓社, 1974.

23 守屋俊彦 Moriya Toshihiko『日本霊異記の研究』*Research on "The Tales of Wonder,"* 198 pp., 三弥井書店, 1974.

24 守屋省吾 Moriya Shōgo『蜻蛉日記形成論』*On the Formation of "The Gossamer Years,"* 400 pp., 笠間書院, 1975.

25 目加田さくを Mekata Sakuo『枕草子論』*On "The Pillow Book,"* 528 pp., 笠間書院, 1975.

26 有精堂編集部 Yūseidō Editorial Staff『枕草子講座』(全4巻) *Lectures on "The Pillow Book"* (4 vols.), 348 pp.; 360 pp.; 324 pp.; 356 pp., 有精堂, 1975–76.

IV-01 伊藤博之 Itō Hiroyuki 『隠遁の文学——妄念と覚醒——』*The Writings of the Recluses: Delusion and Enlightenment* [笠間選書] 272 pp., 笠間書院, 1975.

02 小林智昭 Kobayashi Tomoaki 『続中世文学の思想』 *Thoughts on Medieval Literature*, II [笠間叢書] 390 pp., 笠間書院, 1974.

03 福田秀一 Fukuda Hideichi『中世文学論考』*Studies of Medieval Literature*, 554 pp., 明治書院, 1975.

04 福田雄作 Fukuda Yūsaku『定家歌論とその周辺』*Fujiwara Teika's Prosody and Related Questions* [笠間叢書] 299 pp., 笠間書院, 1974.

05 森本元子 Morimoto Motoko『私家集と新古今集』*The Shikashū and the Shin-kokinshū*, 494 pp., 明治書院, 1974.

06 半田公平 Handa Kōhei 『寂蓮法師全歌集とその研究』*Research on the Poetry of the Priest Jakuren*, 726 pp., 笠間書院, 1975.

07 間中冨士子 Manaka Fujiko『慈鎮和尚及び拾玉集の研究』*Studies of the Priest Jichin and "The Shūgyokushū,"* 566 pp., ミツル文庫 (川崎), 1974.

08 鎌田五郎 Kamata Gorō『源実朝の作家論的研究』*A Study of Minamoto no Sa-netomo as a Poet*, 1052 pp., 風間書房, 1974.

09 岩佐美代子 Iwasa Miyoko 『京極派歌人の研究』*A Study of the Poets of the Kyōgoku School*, 512 pp., 笠間書院, 1974.

10 石村雍子 Ishimura Yasuko 『和歌連歌の研究』 *Waka and Renga Poetry*, 306 pp., 武蔵野書院, 1975.

11 奥野純一 Okuno Jun'ichi 『伊勢神宮神官連歌の研究』*A Study of Ise Shrine Renga*, 652 pp., 日本学術振興会, 1975.

12 角川源義 Kadokawa Gen'yoshi 『語り物文芸の発生』 *The Emergence of the Genre of Narrative Tales*, 623 pp., 東京堂, 1975.

13 平家正節刊行会 (編) 渥美かをる (解説) Committee for Publication of the *Heike Mabushi* (ed.) with an introduction by Atsumi Kaoru『平家正節』(上巻, 下巻) *Heike mabushi* (2 vols.), 712 pp.; 749 pp., 大学堂書店 (京都), 1974.

14 北川　弘・B.T. ツチダ(訳) Kitagawa Hiroshi and Bruce T. Tsuchida (trans.), *The Tale of the Heike,* 807 pp., 東京大学出版会 (University of Tokyo Press), 1975.

15 山内潤三 Yamanouchi Junzō『平松家本平家物語の研究』*A Study of the Hiramatsu Family Version of "The Tale of the Heike,"* 570 pp., 清文堂出版 (大阪), 1975.

16 佐々木八郎 Sasaki Hachirō『平家物語の達成』*The Completion of "The Tale of the Heike,"* 244 pp., 明治書院, 1974.

17 大隅和雄 (編) Ōsumi Kazuo (ed.)『太平記人名索引』*Index of Names in "The Taiheiki,"* 279 pp., 北海道大学図書刊行会 (札幌) 1974.

18 志村有弘 Shimura Kunihiro『中世説話文学研究序説』*Introductory Studies of "Setsuwa" Literature of the Medieval Period,* 308 pp., 桜楓社, 1974.

19 春田　宣 Haruta Akira『中世説話文学論序説』*An Introductory Analysis of "Setsuwa" as a Literary Genre,* 425 pp., 桜楓社, 1975.

20 有精堂編集部 Yūseidō Editorial Staff「徒然草講座」*Lectures on the "Tsurezuregusa"* (5 vols.), 296 pp.; 264 pp.; 272 pp.; 288 pp.; 288 pp., 有精堂, 1974.

21 中川徳之助 Nakagawa Tokunosuke『兼好の人と思想』*Yoshida Kenkō: The Man and His Thought,* 439 pp., 古川書房, 1975.

22 小林　責 Kobayashi Seki『狂言史研究』*A History of Kyōgen,* 311 pp., わんや書店, 1974.

23 平川祐弘 Hirakawa Sukehiro『謡曲の詩と西洋の詩』*The Poetry of Noh Drama and Western Poetry* [朝日選書] 282 pp., 朝日新聞社, 1975.

V-01 中村幸彦 Nakamura Yukihiko『近世文芸思潮 攷』*Early Modern Trends in Literary Thought,* 402 pp., 岩波書店, 1975.

02 守随憲治 (編) Shuzui Kenji (ed.)『近世文芸の研究——資料編——』*Research on Early Modern Literature: Basic Documents,* 272 pp., 笠間書院, 1974.

03 宮本三郎 Miyamoto Saburō『蕉風俳諧論考』*A Study of Bashō-style Haiku* [笠間叢書] 447 pp., 笠間書院, 1974.

04 赤羽　学 Akabane Manabu『芭蕉の更科紀行の研究』*A Study of Bashō's "Sarashina Journey,"* 424 pp., 教育出版センター, 1974.

05 阿部正美 Abe Masami『芭蕉連句 抄』*Selected Linked Verse by Bashō* (4 vols.), 432 pp.; 540 pp.; 400 pp.; 524 pp., 明治書院, 1965, 1969, 1974, 1976.

06 宮脇昌三・田子　檀・亀村　宏・矢羽勝幸 Miyawaki Shōzō, Tago Mayumi, Kamemura Hiroshi and Yaba Katsuyuki『加舎白雄全集』(上巻・下巻) *The Complete Collection of Kaya Shirao's Poetry* (2 vols.), 500 pp.; 585 pp., 国文社, 1974–75.

07 石田吉貞 Ishida Yoshisada『良寛 その全貌と原像』*Ryōkan: The Man and His Image,* 512 pp., 塙書房, 1975.

08 日野龍夫 Hino Tatsuo『徂徠学派』*The Ogyū Sorai School,* 232 pp., 筑摩書房,

1975.

09 田中　伸 Tanaka Shin 『仮名草子の研究』 *A Study of "Kanazōshi,"* 393 pp., 桜楓社, 1974.

10 田中　伸・深沢秋男・小川武彦 (編) Tanaka Shin, Fukazawa Akio and Ogawa Takehiko (eds.) 『可笑記大成 影印・校異・研究』 *The Complete "Kashōki": Photocopies of Original Editions, Textual Critique, Analysis,* 770 pp., 笠間書院, 1974.

11 岸　得蔵 Kishi Tokuzō 『仮名草子と西鶴』 *Ihara Saikaku and Kanazōshi,* 518 pp., 成文堂, 1974.

12 野間光辰 (編) Noma Kōshin (ed.) 『西鶴論叢』 *Essays on Saikaku,* 562 pp., 中央公論社, 1975.

13 水野　稔 Mizuno Minoru 『江戸小説論叢』 *Essays on the Fiction of the Edo Period,* 416 pp., 中央公論社, 1974.

14 横山邦治 Yokoyama Kuniharu 『読本の研究──江戸と上方と──』 *Tokugawa Period Novelettes of Edo and Osaka,* 876 pp., 風間書房, 1974.

15 武藤禎夫・岡　雅彦 Mutō Sadao and Oka Masahiko (eds.) 『噺本大系』(全 8 巻) *Series on the Light Fiction of the Edo Period* (8 vols.), 320 pp. each, 東京堂, 1970–71.

16 武藤禎夫 Mutō Sadao 『江戸小咄の比較研究』 *A Comparative Study of Humorous Edo Literature,* 310 pp., 東京堂, 1970.

17 祐田善雄 Yuda Yoshio 『浄瑠璃史論考』 *Essays on the History of Jōruri,* 651 pp., 中央公論社, 1975.

18 祐田善雄 Yūda Yoshio 『全講心中天の網島』 *A Comprehensive Commentary on the "Love Suicide at Amijima,"* 444 pp., 至文堂, 1975.

19 諏訪春雄 Suwa Haruo 『近松世話浄瑠璃の研究』 *A Study of Chikamatsu's Jōruri,* 579 pp., 笠間書院, 1974.

20 諏訪春雄 Suwa Haruo 『歌舞伎史の画証的研究』 *A Pictorial Study of Kabuki History,* 482 pp., 飛鳥書房, 1974.

21 服部幸雄 Hattori Yukio 『変化論 歌舞伎の精神史』 *Ghost Plays: A History of the Kabuki Spirit* 「平凡社選書」 269 pp., 平凡社, 1975.

22 今尾哲也 Imao Tetsuya 『ほかひびとの末裔』 *Descendants of Beggars,* 240 pp., 飛鳥書房, 1974.

VI-01 前田　愛 Maeda Ai 成島柳北の日記 "The Diary of Narushima Ryūhoku" 「文学」 43 巻 2 号, 3 号, pp. 221–32; pp. 293–303, 岩波書店, 1975 年 2–3 月.

02 平岡敏夫 Hiraoka Toshio 殺戮する露伴──長篇「いさなとり」試論 "Rohan, the Hunter: His Major Work, *The Whalers*" 「文学」 43 巻 11 号, pp. 1261–75, 岩波書店, 1975 年 11 月.

03 蒲生芳郎 Gamō Yoshirō 「阿部一族」論──「阿部衆事談」と初稿本「阿部

一族」との関係 "Essay on *Abe Ichizoku*"「文学」43 巻 11 号, pp. 1288–1304, 岩波書店, 1975 年 11 月.

04 桶谷秀昭 Oketani Hideaki「断腸亭日乗」覚書——文明の変質と感受性の運命 "Notes on Kafū's *Dyspepsia House Days*"「海」6 巻 4 号, pp. 186–210, 中央公論社, 1974 年 4 月.

05 笠原伸夫 Kasahara Nobuo 鏡花的美意識の原型 "The Archetype of Izumi Kyōka's Esthetic Sense"「文学」43 巻 7 号, pp. 808–18, 岩波書店, 1975 年 7 月.

06 江藤 淳 Etō Jun 『漱石とアーサー王伝説——薤露行の比較文学的研究』 *Sōseki and the Legend of King Arthur: A Comparative Study of "Kairokō,"* 342 pp., 東大出版会, 1975.

07 前田 愛 Maeda Ai 子どもたちの時間——「たけくらべ」試論 "Children at Play: A Study of *Takekurabe*"「展望」198 号, pp. 16–34, 筑摩書房, 1975 年 6 月号.

08 三好行雄 Miyoshi Yukio 無明の闇——「羅生門」再説 "Darkness of the Spirit: A Reappraisal of *Rashōmon*"「国語と国文学」52 巻 4 号, pp. 52–60, 至文堂, 1975 年 4 月.

09 河野多恵子 Kōno Taeko 谷崎文学と肯定の欲望 "Tanizaki and His Craving for the Affirmative"「文学界」29 巻 1 号〜30 巻 2 号, 文芸春秋, 1975 年 1 月〜1976 年 2 月.

10 越智治雄 Ochi Haruo 『近代文学の誕生』 *The Birth of Modern Literature* 「講談社現代新書」222 pp., 講談社, 1975.

11 長谷川泉 Hasegawa Izumi『近代日本文学の位相』 *Phases of Modern Japanese Literature*, Vol. 1, 354 pp.; Vol. 2, 268 pp. 桜楓社, 1974.

12 村松定孝・紅野敏郎・吉田凞生 (編) Muramatsu Sadataka, Kōno Toshirō, and Yoshida Hiroo (eds.) 『近代日本文学における中国像』 *The Image of China in Modern Japanese Literature*, 300 pp., 有斐閣, 1975.

13 瀬沼茂樹 Senuma Shigeki 『明治文学研究』 *Studies in Meiji Literature*, 530 pp., 法政大学出版局, 1974.

14 木村 毅 Kimura Ki『明治文学夜話 新文学の霧笛』 *Anecdotes on the Search for a New Style in Meiji Literature* [至文堂選書] 232 pp., 至文堂, 1975.

15 木村 毅 Kimura Ki 『比較文学新視界』 *New Perspectives on Comparative Literature*, 554 pp., 八木書店, 1975.

16 大岡 信 Ōoka Makoto 『岡倉天心』 *Okakura Tenshin* [朝日評伝選] 299 pp., 朝日新聞社, 1975.

17 永井荷風 Nagai Kafū『荷風全集』第 29 巻 (拾遺・続参考篇) *The Complete Works of Nagai Kafū*, Vol. 29, 896 pp., 岩波書店, 1974.

18 夏目漱石 Natsume Sōseki『漱石文学全集』(別巻) *The Complete Works of Natsume Sōseki*, supplementary volume, 770 pp., 集英社, 1974.

19　太田文平 Ōta Bunpei『寺田寅彦の周辺』*Terada Torahiko's Milieu*, 328 pp., 日本放送出版協会，1975.

20　『志賀直哉宛書簡』*Letters to Shiga Naoya* [志賀直哉全集別巻] 822 pp., 岩波書店，1974.

21　吉田精一・渡辺正彦（編）Yoshida Seiichi and Watanabe Masahiko (eds.)『平林初之輔文芸評論全集』（上・中・下）*Complete Collection of Literary Critiques by Hirabayashi Hatsunosuke* (1892–1931), 3 vols., 420 pp.; 754 pp.; 950 pp., 文泉堂書店，1975.

22　川村二郎 Kawamura Jirō『懐古のトポス』*Topos of Nostalgia*, 230 pp., 河出書房新社，1975.

23　野山嘉正 Noyama Yoshimasa 北村透谷の散文 "Kitamura Tōkoku's Prose Writings"「文学」42 巻 8 号，pp. 26–41, 岩波書店，1974 年 8 月.

24　山崎正和 Yamazaki Masakazu 不機嫌の時代 "The Sullen Age"「新潮」71 巻 10 号，12 号；72 巻 7 号，11 号，pp. 193–225; pp. 141–68; pp. 135–51; pp. 170–90, 新潮社，1974 年 10, 12 月；1975 年 7, 11 月.

25　饗庭孝男 Aeba Takao 龍之介における "敗北,, の意味 "The Meaning of 'Defeat' in Akutagawa's Writings"「国文学 解釈と鑑賞」39 巻 10 号，pp. 63–68, 至文堂，1974 年 8 月.

26　森山重雄 Moriyama Shigeo 日本マルクス主義文学への道――コップ結成と蔵原理論への展開 "The Road to Japanese Marxist Literature: The Establishment of KOPF [Federacio de Proletaj Kulturaj—Organizoj Japanaj] and Kurahara Korehito's Theory of Proletarian Culture"「日本文学」23 巻 7 号，pp. 32–50, 日本文学協会，1974 年 7 月.

27　羽鳥徹哉 Hatori Tetsuya 川端康成・母の秘密と身替りの母 "Kawabata Yasunari: Maternal Secrets and Substitutes"「国語と国文学」51 巻 6 号，pp. 42–58, 至文堂，1974 年 6 月.

28　清水孝純 Shimizu Takayoshi 小林秀雄における自由の問題――ベルグソンとの関連において "The Problem of Freedom for Kobayashi Hideo: The Influence of Bergson's Philosophy"「日本近代文学」第 21 号，pp. 90–104, 日本近代文学会，1974 年 10 月.

29　奥野健男 Okuno Takeo 太宰治文学の基層――津軽の土着性と普遍性について "The Root of Dazai Osamu's Literature: The Uniqueness and Universality of the Tsugaru Area"「国文学解釈と鑑賞」39 巻 15 号，pp. 6–12, 至文堂，1974 年 12 月.

ART HISTORY

AKIYAMA Terukazu and TAGUCHI Eiichi
University of Tokyo

Translated by Peggy Miller

In 1974 and 1975 publications relating to Japanese art history have flourished. The sheer number of separate studies, as well as periodical articles, presents a problem in discussing research trends in art history during these years. The following discussion concentrates on the more scholarly publications concerning the arts before the Meiji period. And for convenience, we have divided it into categories: I. Noteworthy Events in Art History (A. Exhibitions, B. Art Series, C. Basic Research); II. Painting; III. Sculpture, and IV. Decorative Arts.

I. NOTEWORTHY EVENTS

A. Exhibitions

While research and appreciation in art history begins with direct experience and observation, permanent exhibition of Japan's priceless, but fragile, art works (particularly National Treasures and Important Cultural Properties) is difficult. Researchers have regrettably few chances to view objects directly. For this reason art historians are particularly pleased with the special yearly exhibitions of the three big National Museums in Tokyo, Kyoto and Nara. Besides a catalog at the time of the exhibition, usually some time after the exhibition closes, a scholarly study or report with large-format plates is published. The following are prominent examples of such catalogs, reports, and related studies published during this two-year period.

As mentioned in Volume I, Part 2, in conjunction with a special exhibit in 1972 a detailed study of the paintings of the Heike sutras (donated to the Itsukushima Shrine) was published in 1973. Various other studies relating to the *Heike nō-kyō* include two by Kameda Tsutomu [II-03, 05], who examines the letters (especially of Taira no Kiyomori) at the time of the donations in 1164; and a stylistic analysis of the sutra paintings by Sasaki Kōzō [II-04].

The following year, in the fall of 1973, the Kyoto National Museum held a more general exhibit, Pure Land Buddhist Paintings (*Jōdo-kyō kaiga*). During the exhibition, representative scholars in the field gathered in a symposium to discuss this most characteristic genre of Japanese religious painting. Their report appeared in 1974 [II-06]. Another study on Pure Land paintings that includes large-format plates was published in 1975 [II-07].

In 1971, the Nara National Museum held an exhibit called "Founding and Miracles of Temples and Shrines," that gathered together hanging and hand scrolls, murals and other paintings depicting the history and legends of Buddhist temples and Shinto shrines. A compendium of studies on these religious narrative paintings, *Shaji-engi-e*, by Nakano Genzō, et al. [II-08], was published in 1975.

In the fall of 1974 at the Tokyo National Museum, an extensive narrative scroll-painting exhibition was organized. While only short explanations accompany the plates in *Emaki* [II-13], the extent of the exhibit, with representative hand scrolls from all periods up until contemporary times, makes this publication useful for its reproductions. On the other hand, the first volumes of a revised edition, with detailed text, of *Nippon emakimono zenshū* (The Complete Collection of Illustrated Scrolls) [II-15], have appeared. These volumes contain the findings of research conducted since the initial edition began publication in 1958.

The Kyoto National Museum held an exhibition in the fall of 1975 of illustrations in various styles and media (including the decorative arts) based on the literary classic, *The Tale of Genji*. The research report from the exhibition has not yet been published, but the catalog [II-14] is useful for its reproductions of works from the Heian to Edo periods.

In 1974 a comprehensive study, by Mitsumori Masashi (Curator of Sculpture), of the objects in the Nara National Museum's 1972

"Statues of Amida" exhibit, was published [III-01]. Research is also continuing, inspired in part by a more specialized exhibition held at the Tokyo National Museum in 1973, and its accompanying publication *Buddhist Images Inscribed on Mirrors* [IV-02].

B. Art Series

During 1974–75, many volumes in several art series (*zenshū*) were published that are particularly useful for the beginning art researcher. The series *Temples of Nara* [I-03] published by Iwanami Shoten deals with art of the early and medieval periods. An earlier series by the same publisher, the large-format *Six Important Temples of Nara* (cf. Vol. I, Part 2), has been rearranged under more specific themes, rewritten and expanded into this handier *Temples of Nara* series. New and more detailed plates have also been added. Published by Shōgakkan, *Bukku obu bukkusu Nihon no bijutsu* (Book of Books: The Art of Japan) [I-04] is another handy-size series based on a previously published series, *Japanese Art in Color* (cf. Vol. I, Part 2). The new series includes books on subjects not dealt with in the original set, as well as some that, though they have the same title, have been revised. The color reproductions continue to be excellent. Another very useful series is Shibundō's *Japanese Art* [I-05]. At first each volume covered a rather broad topic, but recent volumes have become more specialized. As scholarly works, the value of the latter is higher. Selected books from this series are being translated and published in an English edition. Kodansha International has recently taken on this project originally begun by Weatherhill. Heibonsha took an Italian art series by Fabri as the model for the *Heibonsha Gallery* series [I-06]. The large-format reproductions are excellent, but the quality of the texts varies with the interests of the authors. Those by specialists writing in their fields tend to be good.

C. Basic Research Materials

A catalog in several volumes, *Jūyō bunkazai* (Important Cultural Properties) [I-01], published by Mainichi Shinbunsha, includes tiny, but comprehensive, black-and-white reproductions, with brief explanations arranged by general category (subdivided iconographically). Sculpture IV–VI, Architecture IV–VI, Painting IV and V, and

Calligraphy and Documents III, were published in 1974–75. Yet another series, edited by the Nara National Museum, deals exclusively with Buddhist art works that are National Treasures or Important Cultural Properties. The volumes are divided according to region, with a very detailed text accompanied by excellent plates. Volume II (on Kyushu, excluding Fukuoka) is the most recent [I-02].

Volume II of *Literary Documents in the Study of Art History* [I-07] appeared in 1975. The selection and commentary on these primary sources (usually from temples) relating to Buddhist art is the invaluable life work of Fujita Tsuneyo. The *Mikkyō jiten* (Dictionary of Esoteric Buddhism) [I-08] edited by Sawa Ryūken, despite its theological orientation, includes many items relating to art. The iconographic explanations, in particular, make it a very useful handbook.

II. PAINTING

As mentioned in Volume I, Part 2 of this bibliography, the unexpected discovery in 1972 of the Takamatsuzuka Tumulus murals generated a flurry of publications. Among these studies, an indispensable work is the official report, *Mural Paintings in the Takamatsuzuka Tumulus* [II-01]. It presents the findings of the *in situ* research and very detailed photographic examination conducted by members of the government-sponsored committee. The report dates the paintings between the end of the seventh and the first decade of the eighth century. The separate folio of reproductions, which includes not only large color plates, but detail and infrared photos, is an invaluable resource. Of the several publications by historians concerning the murals, that of Arisaka [II-02] stands out as being an informed opinion based, unlike some, on careful examination of the paintings. Saitō Tadashi's general survey of *kofun* mural paintings in the Shibundō series [I-05, Vol. 110] is another useful perspective on Japanese painting before the introduction of Buddhism in the fifth and sixth centuries.

Akiyama examines [I-03, Vol. 6] two of the earliest extant Buddhist paintings, on the Tamamushi and Lady Tachibana tabernacles, both preserved in Hōryūji. He concludes that the paintings on the earlier Tamamushi tabernacle are the collaboration of two painters. The color paintings that decorate the sides of the Lady Tachibana tabernacle are in the style of the end of the seventh century, but the fine, goldline drawings, against a black lacquer ground, of the doors date from the early eighth century. Akiyama thus suggests that the doors of the Tachibana tabernacle were later ordered by Lady Tachibana's daughter, Empress Kōmyō.

Yanagisawa's new study in the same series [I-03, Vol. 8] discusses the wall paintings of the Golden Hall at Hōryūji. In a close stylistic and iconographic examination of each of the main murals, Yanagisawa argues that the paintings were the collaboration of eight people. Comparing details of the people's features and the brocade patterns with the style of murals at such places as Tun-huang, she dates the murals to the same early Nara period (late seventh century) as the Takamatsuzuka murals and the Lady Tachibana tabernacle. The above-mentioned official report on the *Mural Paintings in the Takamatsu-zuka Tumulus* [II-01] is also valuable for its examination of the close relationship between the tumulus murals and the paintings at Hōryūji.

Takada and Yanagisawa's *Buddhist Painting* [I-04, Vol. 9] is a distinguished general introduction to the subject. *The Ryōkai Mandala* [II-09] by Ishida Hisatoyo, is an invaluable theological and icono-graphical study in the specialized field of esoteric Buddhist art. Ishida examines the prototypical type of mandala, called the *taizokai mandara* (*garbhadhātu* mandala) of the early Heian period (9th century). His identification of each of the numerous deities is accompanied by extensive charts and detailed black-and-white reproductions. He also traces the historic development of these mandala and their relation to other examples of esoteric art. There is a brief summary in English.

Ariga Yoshitaka has written an article about his discovery through infrared photography, of an inscription (including the date 1088) on the back of one of the scroll paintings of the Five Myō-ō in Kiburuji [II-10]. His research is important in establishing a chronology in Heian esoteric painting. Another valuable article discusses the iconographical classification and development of various types of *Ninnokyō* (Jên-wang-ching) mandala [II-11].

Yanagisawa has published the first two articles [II-12], in a projected series about the eight-scroll painting, *Shingon hasso gyōjōzu* (Legends of the Eight Shingon Patriarchs). She discovered that this previously unappreciated work was formerly in the Shingondō of

Eikyūji. Although it was greatly retouched, her dating the painting to 1136, when the Shingondō was built, means that it is now established as a major work of Heian times.

In connection with the special exhibition and symposium at the Kyoto National Museum, in addition to an official report, *The Painting of Pure Land Buddhism* [II-07] was published in 1975 under the supervision of Yamamoto Kōji, Curator of Paintings. The text is divided into a comprehensive discussion of two types of painting, one depicting the Western Paradise and the other the *raigō* ("welcoming descent"). It is accompanied by large color plates and many black-and-white reproductions which include close-up details.

Emakimono by Akiyama [I-04, Vol. 10] is a useful introduction to the development of scroll painting. It includes color plates of representative examples. The first three volumes have also appeared in the revised and expanded edition of the excellent series *Japanese Scroll Painting*. *Genji monogatari emaki* [II-15, Vol. 2] discusses this early twelfth century scroll illustrating the *Tale of Genji;* another volume covers the scrolls of the *Heiji monogatari* and the *Mōko shūrai ekotoba* [II-15, Vol. 10] (both works dating from the last half of the thirteenth century); and *Ippen-hijiri-e* [II-15, Vol. 11] deals with the scroll, dated 1299, which depicts the life and miracles of the priest Ippen. The number of color plates has increased, along with the material covered, reflecting the results of research since the original series was published ten years ago.

Komatsu Shigemi, in his *Hikohohodemi-no-mikoto emaki* (Study of the Hikohohodemi-no-mikoto Scroll) [II-16] examines a hitherto ignored Edo period copy of this no longer extant scroll painting. Through a comparison of the copy and such works as the *Bandainagon emaki*, he has tried to show that the original must have been done in the latter half of the twelfth century. Among the many articles about scroll painting, those by the following researchers are particularly noteworthy: Tamagami [II-17], Miya [II-18, 19, 20], Umezu [II-21], and Yoshida [II-22]. Finally, Akiyama discusses in an article [II-23] his discovery of the mate (though a copy) to the *Amawakahiko sōshi emaki*, by Tosa Hirochika (15th century), now in the Berlin East Asian Art Museum.

The series *Suiboku bijutsu taikei* (Mainstreams in the Art of Ink

Painting) [II-24] is an important and scholarly contribution to the study of monochrome ink painting. Of the four volumes published in 1974–75, Volume V focuses on the earliest period of Japanese ink painting, the fourteenth to early fifteenth centuries. It includes a general introduction by Tanaka Ichimatsu, as well as chapters by other authors on the three early masters, Kaō, Mokuan, and Minchō. Each discussion is supplemented by historical documents and color reproductions of all the extant works of each artist. The next period in the development of ink painting, dominated by Josetsu, Shūbun, and the Ami school, is dealt with in Volume VI [II-24, Vol. 6]. The authors, Matsushita and Tamamura, have organized documents and reproductions in an excellent presentation, comparable to Volume V.

Matsushita has also written a book [I-05, Vol. 100] about the greatest master of ink painting, Sesshū (1420–1506). Number 970 of the art history journal, *Kokka* [II-25] is a special issue devoted to Sesshū's "Bird and Flower" paintings. And in connection with an exhibition on Sesson, a distinguished painter influenced by Sesshū's style, several articles were published [II-26, 27, 28].

From the Momoyama to the early Edo period (late sixteenth to early seventeenth centuries) is a particularly important time in the development of Japanese painting. Among the most monumental works of this period are the paintings decorating Nijō Castle in Kyoto. Although the main quarters of the castle are no longer extant, Takeda Tsuneo, with the aid of architectural historians [I-09], examines the *Ninomaru-goten* (secondary quarters), with its gorgeous wall and door paintings by Kanō Tan'yū and his school. This large-format book has excellent reproductions of these paintings that were ordered by the Tokugawa shogun to honor the visit by Emperor Go-mizuno-o in 1626. Takeda has also published a study of the life and work of Kanō Eitoku (1543–90) [I-05, Vol. 94], and a discussion of the fascinating folding screens depicting the large festival held in 1604 to mark the seventh anniversary of Toyotomi Hideyoshi's death (*Hōkoku-sai*) [I-06, Vol. 21].

For an analysis of the decorative style of Tawaraya Sōtatsu, active in the early 1700s, Volume X of the *Suiboku bijutsu taikei* series, entitled *Kōetsu, Sōtatsu and Kōrin* [II-24, Vol. 10] is especially good. In this work, Yamane tries to make a clear distinction between paintings by Sōtatsu himself and the numerous paintings of his studio and followers. The section by Kōno on Sōtatsu's successor, Ogata Kōrin (1658–1716), expands the discussion of the process whereby the style of Sōtatsu and Kōrin, originating in Chinese ink-painting, came to have a very different, Japanese feeling. Yamane has also written two articles [II-29, 30] about the audacious decorative quality Sōtatsu imparts to his colored paintings, even though the subjects, often derived from classic Heian literature, are set in traditional compositions.

In 1974–75, six volumes of the continuing series *Bunjinga sui* (The Essence of Literati Painting) devoted to individual artists of the eighteenth and nineteenth centuries were published. Each volume contains a biographical study, with related literary documents, and a thorough examination of each painter's artistic output. Recent volumes include one on Ikeno Taiga [II-31, Vol. 12], Yosa Buson [II-31, Vol. 13] and Uragami Gyokudō [II-31, Vol. 14], the three most original artists of this group. A more comprehensive discussion of Gyokudō's monochrome ink paintings may be found in Volume XIII of the *Suiboku* series: *Gyokudō and Mokubei* [II-24, Vol. 13] by Yoshizawa. Haga, in *Watanabe Kazan: A Footloose Traveler*, has written an interesting study about the life and travel sketches of another literati artist, Kazan [II-32]. An important study on the life and paintings of Itō Jakuchū was published by Tsuji Nobuo [II-33].

Many publications relating to *ukiyo-e* continue to appear. On the whole, most of them are attractive picture-books with color reproductions that are a pleasure to look at but lack any substantive analysis. The eight volumes of the big series *Ukiyo-e taikei* [II-34] and two volumes, *Kiyonaga, Utamaro and Sharaku* and *Hiroshige*, from the series on prints in the Takahashi Sei'ichirō collection [II-35, Vols. 2 and 5] are among the few scholarly studies. There is also an interesting book about the paintings and drawings, but not the prints, of Katsushika Hokusai [II-36].

Recently interest has developed in the influence of Western painting styles and techniques on pre-Meiji Japanese painting. This artistic development can be divided into two main periods. During the first (late sixteenth to early seventeenth centuries), Japanese copied and studied European paintings, especially Catholic religious paintings, brought by Portuguese and Spanish merchants and missionaries.

In religious schools, missionaries undertook to systematically teach Western painting techniques. As a result, not only were European-style oil-paintings produced for the first time, but the Japanese soon created a new style—*nanbanga* (painting of the "Southern Barbarians")—which combined Western techniques (such as shading and perspective) and European subject matter with traditional Japanese mineral pigments and paper. This new art form lasted until the Tokugawa government began its campaign to eradicate Christianity and closed the country to foreign contact in the 1640s. The few paintings that survived the persecutions tend to be of subjects with no (or carefully hidden) Christian connections. *Nanban Art* [I-04, Vol. 34] is an excellent introduction to this first period. Sakamoto's research in Europe and in Japan has found many of the European works that were probably taken as models for particular *nanban* paintings. His coauthor, Yoshimura, a specialist in decorative arts, traces Western motifs in Japanese crafts, particularly on lacquer and *maki-e* objects.

The paintings of the second period are often called *ranga* ("Dutch paintings"). They began to be produced in the mid-eighteenth century, when the bakufu permitted increased scholarly contacts through the port of Nagasaki. European, especially Dutch, books were imported and eagerly studied. Through the copper-plate illustrations of these books, Japanese were once again exposed to Western painting styles and techniques. Even the technique of copper-plate engraving itself was studied. In this second period Western painting was closely associated with Japanese study of the natural sciences and other fields of Western learning. Sakamoto has published an interesting article about this second period, "Rubens and Western-style Painting in the Edo period" in *Bijutsu kenkyū* [II-37]. Sugano's *Study of Copper-plate Engraving in Japan: The Early Modern Period* [II-38], and two studies [II-39, 40] on a representative *ranga* artist, Shiba Kōkan (1740–1818), are also good. Another publication, *Akita ranga* [II-41], discusses an offshoot of "Dutch painting" that flourished throughout the nineteenth century, under the patronage of the feudal lords of Akita in northern Japan. An informative study of the influence of European art on literati painting is found in *Watanabe Kazan: Landscapes of Four Provinces* [II-42].

III. Sculpture

About fifteen years ago excavations revealed the foundation plan of Asukadera (Gangōji), one of the earliest Buddhist temples. Using documentary sources, art historians have long debated whether the Asukadera Great Buddha (*Shaka nyoraizō*), now in the central Golden Hall, dates from the late sixth century, when the central hall was built under the patronage of the Soga family (592), or whether the image dates from the time of Shōtoku Taishi's enlargement of the temple in the early seventh century. François Berthier's article, "Asukadera mondai no saiginmi" [III-02], not only reexamines the excavation reports and documents, but presents a detailed stylistic examination of the *Daibutsu* that suggests the image was done by Tori, in 606. This stimulating research evoked several rebuttals and confirmations by Japanese scholars. Machida's article, "In Answer to the Criticism of M. François Berthier" and Kuno's "The Great Buddha of Asukadera," are the most important [III-03, 04].

The series *Temples of Nara* [I-03] contains several useful volumes dealing with the sculpture of the Asuka and Nara periods (seventh-eighth centuries). *Yakushiji: The Kondō Yakushi and Shō-Kannon* (Vol. 9) is an important work on the renowned Yakushi trinity. Although some scholars have argued that the images were done when Yakushiji was rebuilt at its present location in 718 (when the court moved to the new capital at Nara), author Hasegawa demonstrates that the triptych dates from the late seventh century, when the temple was originally founded.

Machida Kōichi, in *Tōdaiji: The Dry Lacquer Images in the Hokke-dō* [I-03, Vol. 15] concludes that the Hokke-dō's main image, the *Fukū-kensaku* Kannon (Amoghapāśa) and its accompanying eight, hollow dry-lacquer figures were made as a set, in the mature classical Tenpyō (late Nara) style of about 746–48. In a similar format to most in the series, Maeda Yasuji, in Volume 14, uses both historical documents and the results of careful examination of the image to describe how the Great Buddha (Vairocana) at Tōdaiji was first cast in the mid-eighth century and then repaired twice, after being damaged by fires, in 1180 and 1567.

Nishikawa, in *Tōshōdaiji: The Image of Ganjin and Wooden Sculptural*

Groups [I-03, Vol. 20], classifies the many Tōshōdaiji sculptures, which continue to resist firm dating, into three general periods. He writes that the wooden statues—Yakushi and two Kannon originally called *Fukūkensaku* but now known as *Shu-bō-ō-bosatsu* and *Shishiku-bosatsu* respectively, date from an early period (about 759–64) when Ganjin came from China bringing artists with him. After Ganjin's death the Kondō main image, a hollow dry-lacquer Vairocana, and the wooden *Bonten, Taishakuten,* and Four Guardian Kings, were created during a second period (770–80). Finally a third period (782–805) encompasses the dry-lacquer (over wooden body) images of Yakushi and the Thousand-armed Kannon, as well as wooden images in the Lecture Hall (*Kōdō*).

Several studies about seventh- and eighth-century small bronze Buddhist statues have also been published. A particular focus of research has been the collection of small bronzes, traditionally known as the "Forty-eight statues of Buddha" (although actually numbering fifty-three in all), now preserved in a special building of Hōryūji treasures at the Tokyo National Museum. In 1878, this important collection was offered by the financially strapped Hōryūji to the imperial family, from whom it passed to the museum after the war. Noma did the pioneering research on these objects and a series of his articles, along with those of Kobayashi, were gathered (after their recent deaths) into *Studies of Small Bronze Buddha Statues in the Imperial Collection* [III-05]. In a similar work, also including many reproductions, Satō expands on the basis laid by Noma, and presents new dating attributions that are especially convincing [III-06]. Volume 7, in the *Temples of Nara* series, *Hōryūji: Miniature Bronze Buddhas* [I-03, Vol. 7] also discusses the Tokyo National Museum's collection, though it is, as mentioned, no longer at Hōryūji. The author has his own rather unique system for dating the bronzes, in which he compares the lotus-petal designs on the image pedestals with the lotus-petal designs of temple roof tiles that have been dated through archaelogical excavation.

The Heian period (9th–12th centuries) saw the development of a characteristically Japanese style in sculpture. Kuno Takeshi's large-format *Studies on the Sculpture of the Early Heian Period* [III-07] is very good. It presents the results of the author's thirty years of research centered on the origin in the earlier Nara period and early trends of Heian sculpture. The historical discussion is accompanied by a volume of black-and-white reproductions, with numerous photographs of details. A fresh conclusion he draws is that the earliest Heian wooden sculpture grew out of the tradition of simple, wooden images created as acts of faith and religious training by individual monks, often in isolated mountain temples. The austerely simple image of Yakushi at Jingoji is an example he cites. Such an image contrasts with the works, in dry lacquer, stucco, or bronze, produced in the workshops of the great national temples, such as Tōdaiji. But as the ninth century progressed, Kuno writes, the two traditions combined into a mature Heian style.

Ikawa Kazuko has also compiled the research of many years into a single volume, *Studies on Japanese Sculpture* [III-08]. She concentrates on the Heian period, but the Kamakura period (13th–early 14th centuries) is also included. Her study is especially good for its comparison of stylistic variations and its iconographical research into types of Kannon and other heavenly-being images.

Developments in Heian sculpture are also discussed in the Nara National Museum publication, *Statues of Amida Buddha* [III-01]. Finally, in Volume 12 of the *Temples of Nara* series, *Kōfukuji: Images in the Eastern Kondō* [I-03, Vol. 12], Inoue examines such famous Heian works as the Twelve Guardian Deities of Yakushi (*Jūni shinshōzō*).

For a scholarly study of Unkei (early 13th century), the leading sculptor of the Kamakura period, there is *Sculpture of Unkei* [III-09] by Kuno. It includes excellent plates, a detailed biography and a discussion of Unkei's stylistic development supported with original documents and inscriptions. *Kōfukuji: Images in the North and South Octagonal Halls* [I-03, Vol. 13] and *Tōdaiji: The Great South Gate and Its Two Guardian Figures* [I-03, Vol. 17] also focus on Unkei and discuss the formation of a Kamakura period style. Various articles, many published before 1940, have been collected together in *Studies in the History of Kamakura Sculpture*, published posthumously for the late Shibue Jirō. Although postwar research has produced new conclusions about Kamakura sculpture, this book is interesting for its glimpse of developments in the field of art history [III-10].

The creative period of Japanese sculpture was virtually over by the mid-Kamakura period (about 1300), but the production of Buddhist images continued to flourish until the Meiji era. Recently, researchers have shown quickened interest in the Muromachi period (15th–16th centuries), when many images, unlike earlier works, bear inscriptions of dates and artists' names, thus lending themselves to systematic classification. *Muromachi Sculpture* [I-05, Vol. 98] assembles the important works of the period into a systematic and useful survey.

Finally, for anyone interested in Buddhist sculpture, a handbook has been brought out under the direction of Kuno Takeshi, *A Dictionary of Buddha Images* [III-11]. Explanations of technical terms are assembled, together with short biographies of artists, in a glossary. There is also a detailed list of important extant works, including their inscriptions. Many images are reproduced in small, black-and-white reproductions arranged by iconographical type: standing Kannon, seated Shaka, etc. Kuno asked many researchers to write entries, and while some are not up to standard, overall the book is indeed very useful.

IV.   DECORATIVE ARTS

In the decorative arts, which includes ceramics, lacquer, metalwork, and textiles, there has been a tendency for specialists to become so involved in the technical vocabulary and details of their particular field that they cannot communicate with other art historians. We mention here only a few books of excellence and broad interest.

In ceramics, Nakagawa's *Kutani Ware* [I-05, Vol. 103] gives an excellent perspective on the development of this ware, with its distinctive color and bold design. He includes the results of recent excavations of the kiln sites.

Japanese Lacquerware [I-04, Vol. 38], by Okada, is a fine historical survey by the renowned scholar in this field. Okada, Curator at the Tokyo National Museum, leads a group of five, including a practicing lacquer craftsman, Matsuda, in presenting their comprehensive report on the lacquer treasures (dating from the 7th and 8th centuries) in the Shōsōin collection [IV-01]. It includes not only color plates and many reproductions of enlarged detail showing techniques and design motifs, but line drawings and diagrams of shapes, and X-ray photos showing the interior structures of most pieces.

For an overview of the many types of Japanese metalwork, Kurata and Nakano's *Metalwork* [I-04, Vol. 39] is an excellent introduction. Nakano joins Ishida, a specialist in esoteric Buddhist iconography, in writing *Buddhist Images Inscribed on Mirrors* [IV-02]. These bronze mirrors (*kyōzō*) were objects of worship during the Heian and Kamakura periods. Their book carefully attempts to date the mirrors by comparing the decoration on the mirror backs with the designs and style of the finely incised Buddhist figures on the actual mirror surfaces. The elaborate Saidaiji metalwork reliquaries from the early Kamakura period (early 13th century) are discussed in Okada's volume in the *Temples of Nara* series [I-03, Vol. 21].

Three volumes in the *Japanese Textile Arts* series have been published. Although the presentations are highly technical, clear explanations, and above all, the color reproductions reveal a beauty that appeals even to the nonspecialist. Yamanobe, in *Kasuri* [IV-03, Vol. 7] discusses fabrics whose pre-dyed threads reveal a pattern during weaving. *Mon'ori* [IV-03, Vol. 8] is about fabrics with repeated woven patterns in the background, and *Katazome* [IV-03, Vol. 9] surveys stencil and wax-resist method dyeing. Two other books of interest are the publication about the ancient textiles in the Shōsōin [I-05, Vol. 102] and the general introduction [I-05, Vol. 106] to the gorgeous hand-painted fabrics of *yūzen* dyeing, which developed in the eighteenth century.

文　献

I-01　毎日新聞社「重要文化財」委員会事務局 Mainichi Newspapers, Secretariat, Committee on Important Cultural Properties『彫刻』IV *Sculpture*, Vol. 4 [重要文化財 4] 128 pp., 毎日新聞社, 1974.

『彫刻』V *Sculpture*, Vol. 5 [重要文化財 5] 140 pp., 毎日新聞社, 1974.

『彫刻』VI *Sculpture*, Vol. 6 [重要文化財 6] 127 pp., 毎日新聞社, 1975.

『建造物』IV *Architecture*, Vol. 4 [重要文化財 15] 137 pp., 毎日新聞社, 1974.

『建造物』V *Architecture*, Vol. 5 [重要文化財 16] 148 pp., 毎日新聞社, 1975.

『建造物』VI *Architecture*, Vol. 6 [重要文化財 17] 154 pp., 毎日新聞社, 1975.

『絵画』IV *Painting*, Vol. 4 [重要文化財 10] 137 pp., 毎日新聞社, 1974.

『絵画』V *Painting*, Vol. 5 [重要文化財 11] 146 pp., 毎日新聞社, 1975.

『書跡・書籍・古文書』III *Calligraphy, Books and Ancient Documents*, Vol. III, [重要文化財 20] 145 pp., 毎日新聞社, 1975.

02 奈良国立博物館 (編) Nara National Museum (ed.)『国宝・重要文化財・仏
教美術 九州』2. *National Treasures and Important Cultural Properties of Buddhist
Art—Kyushu*, Vol. 2, 263 pp. (うち図版 192 pp.), 小学館, 1975.

03 鈴木嘉吉 Suzuki Kakichi『法隆寺・東院伽藍と西院諸堂』*Hōryūji—Buildings
of the Eastern and Western Quarters* [奈良の寺 2] 68 pp., (図 48 pp., 本文 20
pp.), 岩波書店, 1974.

長廣敏雄 Nagahiro Toshio 『法隆寺 五重塔の塑像』*Hōryūji Stucco Images in
the Five-story Pagoda* [奈良の寺 4] 70 pp. (図 52 pp., 本文 18 pp.), 岩波書店,
1974.

秋山光和 Akiyama Terukazu『法隆寺・玉虫厨子と橘夫人厨子』*Hōryūji—
Tamamushi Tabernale and Lady Tachibana's Tabernacle* [奈良の寺 6] 70 pp., (図
48 pp., 本文 22 pp.), 岩波書店, 1975.

石田尚豊 Ishida Hisatoyo『法隆寺・小金銅仏』*Hōryūji-Miniature Bronze Buddhas* [奈良の寺 7] 62 pp. (図 44 pp., 本文 18 pp.), 岩波書店, 1974.

柳沢 孝 Yanagisawa Taka『法隆寺・金堂壁画』*Hōryūji—Wall Paintings in
the Kondō* [奈良の寺 8] 72 pp., (図 52 pp. 本文 20 pp.), 岩波書店, 1975.

長谷川 誠 Hasegawa Makoto『薬師寺・金堂薬師三尊と聖観音』*Yakushiji
—The Kondō Yakushi and Shō-Kannon* [奈良の寺 9] 65 pp. (図 48 pp., 本文 17
pp.), 岩波書店, 1974年.

沢村 仁 Sawamura Hitoshi『薬師寺・東塔』*The Yakushiji Eastern Pagoda*
[奈良の寺 10] 66 pp., (図 48 pp., 本文 18 pp.), 岩波書店, 1974.

井上 正 Inoue Tadashi『興福寺・東金堂の諸像』*Kōfukuji—Images in the
Eastern Kondō* [奈良の寺 12] 66 pp. (図 48 pp., 本文 18 pp.), 岩波書店, 1975.

西川杏太郎 Nishikawa Kyōtarō『興福寺・北円堂と南円堂の諸像』*Kōfukuji
—Images in the North and South Octagonal Halls* [奈良の寺 13] 66 pp. (図 48 pp.,
本文 18 pp.), 岩波書店, 1974.

前田泰次 Maeda Yasuji 『東大寺・大仏と大仏殿』*Tōdaiji—The Great
Buddha and the Great Buddha Hall* [奈良の寺 11] 66 pp. (図 40 pp., 本文 0 pp.),
岩波書店, 1974.

町田甲一 Machida Kōichi『東大寺・法華堂の乾漆像』*Tōdaiji—Dry Lacquer
Images in Hokke-dō* [奈良の寺 15] 66 pp. (図 48 pp., 本文 8 pp.), 岩波書店,
1974.

太田博太郎 Ōta Hirotarō『東大寺・南大門と二王』*Tōdaiji—The Great South
Gate and Its Two Guardian Figures* [奈良の寺 17] 66 pp., (図 48 pp., 本文
18 pp.), 岩波書店, 1975.

工藤圭章 Kudō Keishō 『唐招提寺・金堂と講堂』*Tōshōdaiji—Kondō and
Kōdō* [奈良の寺 18] 66 pp. (図 48 pp., 本文 18 pp.), 岩波書店, 1974.

西川新次 Nishikawa Shinji 『唐招提寺・鑑真像と木彫群』*Tōshōdaiji—The
Image of Ganjin and Wooden Sculptural Groups* [奈良の寺 20] 66 pp. (図 48 pp.,

本文 18 pp.),岩波書店，1975.

岡田　譲 Okada Jō『西大寺・舎利塔 十二天』*Saidaiji—The Twelve Devas of the Shari* [奈良の寺 21] 66 pp. (図 48 pp.，本文 18 pp)，岩波書店，1974.

04　江坂輝弥 Esaka Teruya『縄文式土器』*Jōmon Pottery* [日本の美術 2 ブック・オブ・ブックス] 209 pp. (図共)，小学館，1975.

土井　弘 Doi Hiromu『正倉院』*The Shōsōin*『日本の美術 6 ブック・オブ・ブックス』203 pp. (図共)，小学館，1974.

高田　修・柳沢　孝 Takada Osamu and Yanagisawa Taka『仏画』*Buddhist Painting* [日本の美術 9 ブック・オブ・ブックス] 219 pp. (図共)，小学館，1974.

秋山光和 Akiyama Terukazu『絵巻物』*Emakimono* [日本の美術 10 ブック・オブ・ブックス] 215 pp. (図共)，小学館，1975.

宮　次男 Miya Tsugio『肖像画』*Portrait Painting* [日本の美術 33 ブック・オブ・ブックス] 211 pp. (図共)，小学館，1975.

坂本　満・吉村元雄 Sakamoto Mitsuru and Yoshimura Motoo『南蛮美術』*Nanban Art*, [日本の美術 34 ブック・オブ・ブックス] 211 pp. (図共)，小学館，1974.

本間正義 Honma Masayoshi『円空と木喰』*Enkū and Mokujiki* [日本の美術 35 ブック・オブ・ブックス] 215 pp. (図共)，小学館，1974.

久野　健 Kuno Takeshi『石　仏』Stone Buddhas [日本の美術 36 ブック・オブ・ブックス] 221 pp. (図共)，小学館，1975.

鈴木　充 Suzuki Mitsuru『民　家』*Minka* (Houses of the People) [日本の美術 37 ブック・オブ・ブックス] 209 pp. (図共)，小学館，1975.

岡田　譲 Okada Jō『日本の漆工』*Japanese Lacquerware* [日本の美術 38 ブック・オブ・ブックス] 208 pp. (図共)，小学館，1975.

蔵田　蔵・中野政樹 Kurata Osamu and Nakano Masaki『金工』*Metalwork* [日本の美術 39 ブック・オブ・ブックス] 211 pp. (図共)，小学館，1974.

杉原荘介・神沢勇一・工楽善通 Sugihara Sōsuke, Kanzawa Yūichi, Kuraku Yoshiyuki『弥生式土器』*Yayoi Pottery* [日本の美術 44 ブック・オブ・ブックス] 207 pp. (図共)，小学館，1975.

05　真保　享 Shinpo Tōru『法然上人絵伝』*The Illustrated Biography of Hōnen Shōnin* [日本の美術 95] 96 pp. (図共)，至文堂，1974.

白畑よし Shirahata Yoshi『歌仙絵』*Imaginary Portraits of Immortal Poets* [日本の美術 96], 98 pp. (図共)，至文堂，1974.

長谷部楽爾 Hasebe Rakuji『染　付』*Blue and White Ware* [日本の美術 97] 98 pp. (図共)，至文堂，1974.

上原昭一 Uehara Shōichi『室町彫刻』*Muromachi Sculpture* [日本の美術 98] 102 pp. (図共)，至文堂，1974.

藤岡通夫 Fujioka Michio『京都御所と仙洞御所』*The Kyoto Imperial Palace*

and the Sentō Palace [日本の美術 99] 98 pp. (図共)，至文堂，1974.

松下隆章 Matsushita Takaaki『雪　舟』*Sesshū* [日本の美術 100] 102 pp. (図共)，至文堂，1974.

林屋晴三 Hayashiya Seizō『光悦』*Kōetsu* [日本の美術 101] 至文堂，1974.

松本包夫 Matsumoto Kaneo『正倉院の染織』*Textiles from the Shōsōin* [日本の美術 102] 94 pp. (図共)，至文堂，1974.

中川千咲 Nakagawa Sensaku『九谷焼』*Kutani Ware* [日本の美術 103] 94 pp. (図共)，至文堂，1974.

楢崎宗重 Narasaki Muneshige『広　重』*Hiroshige* [日本の美術 104] 102 pp. (図共)，至文堂，1975.

松島順正 Matsushima Junsei『正倉院の書跡』*Calligraphy in the Shōsōin* [日本の美術 105] 94 pp. (図共)，至文堂，1975.

北村哲郎 Kitamura Tetsuo『友禅染』*Yūzen Dyeing* [日本の美術 106] 98 pp. (図共)，至文堂，1975.

佐藤寒山 Satō Kanzan『山城鍛冶』*Sword Forging of Yamashiro* [日本の美術 107] 102 pp. (図共)，至文堂，1975.

金子良運 Kaneko Ryōun『能狂言面』*Nō and Kyōgen Masks* [日本の美術 108] 100 pp. (図共)，至文堂，1975.

佐々木丞平 Sasaki Jōhei『與謝蕪村』*Yosa Buson* [日本の美術 109] 110 pp. (図共)，至文堂，1975.

斎藤　忠 Saitō Tadashi『古墳の絵画』*Kofun Mural Painting* [日本の美術 110] 110 pp. (図共)，至文堂，1975.

長谷川栄 Hasegawa Sakae『夏雄と勝珉』*Natuo and Shōmin* [日本の美術 111] 102 pp. (図共)，至文堂，1975.

森　　蘊 Mori Osamu『修学院離宮』*Shūgakuin Detached Palace* [日本の美術 112] 94 pp. (図共)，至文堂，1975.

今永清士 Imanaga Seishi『辻が花染』*Tsuji-ga-hana Dyeing* [日本の美術 113] 98 pp. (図共)，至文堂，1975.

鈴木　進 Suzuki Susumu『池大雅』*Ikeno Taiga* [日本の美術 114] 106 pp. (図共)，至文堂，1975.

坪井清足 Tsuboi Kiyotari『平城宮跡』*The Remains of the Heijō Palace* [日本の美術 115] 94 pp.，(図共)，至文堂，1975.

06　澤野久雄 Sawano Hisao『びいどろ・ぎやまん』*Glass of the Edo Period* [平凡社 ギャラリー 16] 24 pp. (図共)，平凡社，1974.

観世寿夫 Kanze Hisao and Ishimoto Yasuhiro『能面』*Nō Masks* [平凡社 ギャラリー 17] 24 pp. (図共)，平凡社，1974.

金子光晴 Kaneko Mitsuharu『英　泉』*Eisen* [平凡社 ギャラリー 18] 24 pp. (図共)，平凡社，1974.

渋澤龍彦 Shibusawa Tatsuhiko『地獄絵』*Paintings of Hell Scenes* [平凡社 ギ

ャラリー 19] 24 pp. (図共), 平凡社, 1974.

北小路功 Kitakōji Isao『京都御所』 *Kyoto Imperial Palace* [平凡社 ギャラリー 20] 24 pp. (図共), 平凡社, 1974.

武田恒夫 Takeda Tsuneo『豊国祭礼』 *The Festival Illustrations of Hōkoku Shrine* [平凡社 ギャラリー 21] 24 pp. (図共), 平凡社, 1974.

坂本 満 Sakamoto Mitsuru『北斎漫画』 *Caricatures by Hokusai* [平凡社 ギャラリー 23] 24 pp. (図共), 平凡社, 1974.

芳賀 徹 Haga Tōru「崋山—四州真景」 *Watanabe Kazan's "Landscapes in Four Provinces"* [平凡社 ギャラリー 22] 24 pp. (図共), 平凡社, 1974.

東野芳明 Tōno Yoshiaki『出雲大社』 *Izumo Shrine* [平凡社 ギャラリー 24] 24 pp. (図共), 平凡社, 1974.

円地文子 Enchi Fumiko 『室生寺』 *Murōji* [平凡社 ギャラリー 25] 24 pp. (図共), 平凡社, 1974.

谷川徹三 Tanigawa Tetsuzō『埴 輪』 *Haniwa* [平凡社 ギャラリー 26] 24 pp. (図共), 平凡社, 1974.

小松茂美 Komatsu Shigemi 『平等院』 *Byōdōin* [平凡社 ギャラリー 27] 24 pp. (図共), 平凡社, 1974.

寺田 透 Terada Tōru『鉄 斉』 *Tessai* [平凡社 ギャラリー 28] 24 pp. (図共), 平凡社, 1974.

秋山光和 Akiyama Terukazu『源氏物語絵巻』 *Genji monogatari emaki* (Scroll-paintings of the *Tale of Genji*) [平凡社 ギャラリー 29] 28 pp. (図共), 平凡社, 1974.

白洲正子 Shirasu Masako『小 袖』 *Kosode* (padded outer kimono) [平凡社 ギャラリー 30] 24 pp. (図共), 平凡社, 1974.

07 藤田経世 Fujita Tsuneyo『校刊 美術史料・寺院篇』中巻 *Literary Documents in the Study of Art History: Temples*, Vol. II, 517 pp., 中央公論美術出版, 1975.

08 佐和隆研 (編) Sawa Ryūken (ed.)『密教辞典』全 *Dictionary of Esoteric Buddhism*, 906 pp., 法蔵館, 1975.

09 林屋辰三郎・吉永義信・武田恒夫・土居次義・大森健二・川上貢・藤岡通夫 Hayashiya Tatsusaburō, Yoshinaga Yoshinobu, Takeda Tsuneo, Doi Tsugiyoshi, Ōmori Kenji, Kawakami Mitsugu, and Fujioka Michio『二条城』 *Nijō Castle*, 472 pp. (うち図 207 pp.), 小学館, 1974.

II-01 高松塚古墳総合学術調査会 Committee for Interdisciplinary Scientific Research on the Takamatsuzuka Tumulus『高松塚古墳壁画』 *Official Report of the Mural Paintings in the Takamatsuzuka Tumulus* (Edition for Public Purchase) 図版 71 葉, 附図 7 葉, 本文 40 pp., 便利堂, 1974.

02 有坂隆道 Arisaka Takamichi 高松塚の壁画とその年代 "The Murals of the Takamatsuzuka Kofun and Their Dating"『高松塚論批判』 pp. 178–258, 創

元社, 1974.

03 亀田 孜 Kameda Tsutomu 厳島願経と平清盛 "Heike Nōkyō and Taira no Kiyomori" 「古美術」Vol. 45, pp. 33–40, 三彩社, 1974 年 7 月.

04 佐々木剛三 Sasaki Kōzō 平家納経の一雑感 "A Question of Heike Nōkyō" 「古美術」Vol. 45, pp. 41–45, 三彩社, 1974 年 7 月.

05 亀田 孜 Kameda Tsutomu 平家納経の絵と今様の歌 "Paintings in the Illustrated Sutra Known as Heike Nōkyō and the Poems Known as Imayō" 「仏教芸術」100 号, pp. 105–119, 毎日新聞社, 1975 年 2 月.

06 松下隆章 (編) Matsushita Takaaki (ed.) 『研究発表と座談会 浄土教美術の展開報告書』 Symposium: The Development of the Art of Jōdo Buddhism 67 pp., 仏教美術研究上野記念財団助成研究会, 1974.

07 京都国立博物館 (編) Kyoto National Museum (ed.) 『浄土教絵画』(特別展図録) Paintings of the Jōdo Sect, Catalogue of Special Exhibition, 288 pp. (うち図 176 pp.), 平凡社, 1975.

08 奈良国立博物館 (監修) Nara National Museum (Supervisor) 『社寺縁起絵』 Illustrated Legends of Temples and Shrines, 235 pp. (図版 334 pp.), 角川書店, 1975.

09 石田尚豊 Ishida Hisatoyo 『曼荼羅の研究』(研究篇 図版篇) The Ryōkai Mandala (Studies and Plates), 研究篇 255 pp., 図版 128 pp., 東京美術, 1975.

10 有賀祥隆 Ariga Yoshitaka 来振寺本五大尊像 (図版解説) "Paintings of Five Great Vidyārājas Owned by the Kiburuji" 「美術研究」293 号, pp. 18–26, 東京国立文化財研究所, 1974 年 11 月.

11 錦織亮介 Nishigori Kyōsuke 仁王経曼荼羅図の形式——儀軌と図像の間—— "Style of Painting in Jên-wang-ching Mandala" 「仏教芸術」101 号, pp. 61 95, 毎日新聞社, 1975 年 1 月.

12 柳澤 孝 Yanagisawa Taka 真言八祖行状図と廃寺永久寺真言堂障了絵 (一, 二) "Paintings Depicting the Lives of Eight Patriarchs of the Shingon Sect Originally Owned by the Eikyuji" (Parts 1 and 11) 「美術研究」300 号, 302 号, pp. 14–35; pp. 11–32, 東京国立文化財研究所, 1975 年 7 月.

13 東京国立博物館 (編) The Tokyo National Museum (ed.) 『絵巻』 Emaki, 便利堂, 1975·

14 京都国立博物館 (編) The Kyoto National Museum (ed.) 『特別展 源氏物語の美術カタログ』 Art Inspired by the "Tale of Genji" (Catalogue of the Special Exhibition) 138 図, 京都国立博物館, 1975.

15 秋山光和 (編) Akiyama Terukazu, Itō Takuji, Suzuki Keizō, Abe Tokio, Ienaga Saburō and Nakamura Yoshio (eds.) 源氏物語繪巻 Genji Monogatari Emaki [新修 日本繪巻物全集 第 2 巻], はり込図 21 枚, 図版 65 pp., 本文 125 pp., 角川書店, 1975.

松下隆章 (編) Matsushita Takaaki (ed.) 『平治物語絵巻・蒙古襲来絵詞』 The

240

Heiji Monogatari Emaki and the Mōko Shūrai Ekotoba, [新修 日本繪卷物全集 第 10 巻] はり込図版 8 枚, 図版 68 pp., 本文 130 pp. 角川書店, 1975
望月信成 (編) Mochizuki Shinzei (ed.)『一遍聖繪』*Ippen Hijiri-e* [新修日本繪 卷物全集 第 11 巻] はり込図 7 枚, 図版 128 pp., 本文 116 pp., 角川書店, 1975.

16 小松茂美 Komatsu Shigemi『彦火々出見尊絵巻の研究』*Study of the Hikohoho-demi-no-mikoto Emaki*, 図版 108 pp., 本文 171 pp., 東京美術, 1974.

17 玉上琢弥 Tamagami Takuya 物語の享受と絵巻 "Emaki and Enjoyment of Literary Romances" 「Museum」 No. 283 (特集・繪卷研究 (1)), pp. 16–25, 東京国立博物館, 1974 年 10 月.

18 宮 次男 Miya Tsugio 矢取地蔵縁起について "Illustrated Scroll of the Story of 'Yatori Jizō'" 「美術研究」298 号, pp. 1–12, 東京国立文化財研究 所, 1975 年 3 月.

19 宮 次男 Miya Tsugio 東寺本弘法大師行状絵巻——特に第十一巻第一段の 成立をめぐって——"The Tōji Version of the Scroll Painting of the Story of Priest Kūkai" 「美術研究」 No. 299, pp, 1–23, 東京国立文化財研究所, 1975 年 12 月.

20 宮 次男 Miya Tsugio 地蔵霊験絵巻について "On the Picture Scroll De-picting the Tale of the Miracle of Ksitigarbha Known as *Jizō Reigen-ki*" 「仏 教芸術」97 号, pp. 65–83, 毎日新聞社, 1974 年 7 月.

21 梅津次郎 Umezu Jirō 山王霊験記絵巻雑記 "About the Sannō Reigen-ki Emaki" 「国華」 No. 984, pp. 7–23, 国華社, 1975 年 9 月.

22 吉田友之 Yoshida Tomoyuki 天神縁起絵初期の問題——メトロポリタン美 術館本道賢巡歴の巻をめぐって "Problems Concerning Early Illustrations of the Tenjin Engi Stories: Concerning the Scroll of Dōken's Pilgrimage in the Collection of the Metropolitan Museum of Art" 「Museum」 No. 284 (特集 絵巻研究 (2)), pp. 14–21, 東京国立博物館, 1974 年 11 月.

23 秋山光和 Akiyama Terukazu 天稚彦草紙絵巻をめぐる諸問題——上巻図様 の新出を機に——"Several Problems Concerning the Amawakahiko Sōshi Emaki—On the Occasion of the Discovery of a Complete Version" 「国華」 No. 985, pp. 9–25, 国華社, 1975 年 12 月.

24 田中一松 Tanaka Ichimatsu『可翁・黙庵・明兆』*Kaō, Mokuan and Minchō* [水墨美術大系 5] 205 pp. (図版 128 pp.), 講談社, 1974,
山根有三 (編) Yamane Yūzō (ed.)『光悦・宗達・光琳』*Kōetsu, Sōtatsu, and Kōrin* [水墨美術大系 10] 205 pp. (うち図版 132 pp.) 講談社, 1975.
松下隆章・玉村竹三 Matsushita Takaaki and Tamamura Takezō『如拙・周 文・三阿弥』*Josetsu, Shūbun, and San'ami* [水墨美術大系 6] 211 pp. (うち図 版 116 pp.) 講談社, 1974.
吉澤 忠 (編) Yoshizawa Chū『玉堂・木米』*Gyokudō and Mokubei* [水墨美

術大系 13] 196 pp.（うち図版 130 pp.），講談社，1975.

25 田中一松・米澤嘉圃・(司会) 吉澤　忠・水尾比呂志 Tanaka Ichimatsu, Yo-nezawa Yoshiho, Yoshizawa Chū (moderator), and Mizuo Hiroshi 座談会: 雪舟の花鳥画 "Dialogue: The Bird and Flower Paintings of Sesshū" 「国華」No. 970, pp. 17–26, 国華社，1974 年 7 月.

26 衛藤　駿 Etō Shun 雪村の花鳥画 "Sesson's Bird and Flower Paintings" 「Museum」No. 281 (特集 雪村), pp. 4–13, 東京国立博物館，1974 年 8 月.

27 中村溪男 Nakamura Tanio 雪村関係資料——資料から見た雪村のおもかげ "Sesson's Paintings in Foreign Collections" 「Museum」No. 281 (特集 雪村), pp. 27–34, 東京国立博物館，1974 年 8 月.

28 赤沢英二 Akazawa Eiji 雪村の人物画における様式展開の一つのケース——用筆法の問題に関連して—— "The Problem of Brushwork in the Develop-ment of Sesson's Figure Painting" 「東京学芸大学紀要」No. 26, 東京学芸大学，1975.

29 山根有三 Yamane Yūzō 伝宗達筆 伊勢物語図色紙について "Study on the Ise Monogatari Shikishi, attributed to Sōtatsu" 「大和文華」No. 59 (伊勢物語図色紙特輯), pp. 1–27, 大和文華館，1974 年 3 月.

30 山根有三 Yamane Yūzō 俵屋宗達と異本伊勢物語絵および執金剛神縁起絵——新出の伊勢物語図屏風を中心に—— "Tawaraya Sōtatsu and Illustrated Scrolls of Ise Monogatari and Shūkongōjin Engi" 「国華」No. 977, pp. 11–33, 国華社，1975 年 2 月.

31 加藤周一・脇田秀太郎・中田勇次郎・入矢義高 Katō Shūichi, Wakita Hide-tarō, Nakata Yūjirō, and Iriya Yoshitaka 『祇園南海・柳沢淇園』 Gion Nankai, Yanagizawa Kien [文人画粋編 11] 155 pp.（うち図版 96 pp.），中央公論社，1975.

寺田透・細野正信・中田勇次郎・入矢義高 Terada Tōru, Hosono Masanobu, Nakata Yūjirō and Iriya Yoshitaka 『池大雅』 Ikeno Taiga [文人画粋編 12] 161 pp.（うち図版 100 pp.），中央公論社，1974.

安岡章太郎・佐々木丞平・中田勇次郎・清水孝之 Yasuoka Shōtarō, Sasaki Jōhei, Nakata Yūjirō and Shimizu Takayuki 蕪村の山水画 "The Landscapes of Buson" 『与謝蕪村』 Yasa Buson [文人画粋編 13] 158 pp.（うち図版 100 pp.），中央公論社，1974.

石川淳・鈴木進・中田勇次郎・入矢義高 Ishikawa Jun, Suzuki Susumu, Nakata Yūjirō and Iriya Yoshitaka 『浦上玉堂』 Uragami Gyokudō [文人画粋編 14] 168 pp.（うち図版 98 pp.），中央公論社，1974.

篠田一士・飯島勇・中田勇次郎・入矢義高 Shinoda Hajime, Iijima Isamu, Nakata Yūjirō and Iriya Yoshitaka 『田能村 竹田』 Tanomura Chikuden [文人画粋編 17] 171 pp.（うち図版 100 pp.），中央公論社，1975.

杉浦明平・菅沼貞三・中田勇次郎・入矢義高 Sugiura Minpei, Suganuma

242

Teizō, Nakata Yūjirō and Iriya Yoshitaka 『渡辺崋山』 *Watanabe Kazan* [文人画粋編 19] 150 pp. (うち図版 100 pp.), 中央公論社, 1975.

桑原武夫・小高根太郎・中田勇次郎・入矢義高 Kuwabara Takeo, Odakane Tarō, Nakata Yūjirō, Iriya Yoshitaka 『富岡鉄斎』 *Tomioka Tessai* [文人画粋編 20] 178 pp. (うち図 100 pp.), 中央公論社, 1974.

32　芳賀　徹 Haga Tōru 『渡辺崋山——優しい旅人——』 *Watanabe Kazan: A Footloose Traveler* [日本の旅人 13] 248 pp. (図共), 淡交社, 1974.

33　辻　惟雄 Tsuji Nobuo 『若冲』 *Jakuchū*, 262 pp., 美術出版社, 1974.

34　楢崎宗重 Narasaki Muneshige 『師宣』 *Moronobu* [浮世絵大系 1] 143 pp. (原色図版 72 pp., 単色図版 23 pp.), 集英社, 1974.

楢崎宗重 Narasaki Muneshige 『春章』 *Shunshō* [浮世絵大系 3] 143 pp. (原色図版 72 pp., 単色図版 23 pp.), 集英社, 1974.

岡　畏三郎 Oka Isaburō 『清長』 *Kiyonaga* [浮世絵大系 4] 143 pp. (原色図版 72 pp., 単色図版 23 pp.), 集英社, 1975.

岡　畏三郎 Oka Isaburō 『北斎』 *Hokusai* [浮世絵大系 8] 143 pp. (原色図版 pp., 単色図版 23 pp.), 集英社, 1974.

鈴木重三 Suzuki Jūzō 『豊国』 *Toyokuni* [浮世絵大系 9] 143 pp. (原色図版 72 72 pp., 単色図版 23 pp.), 集英社, 1975.

鈴木重三 Suzuki Jūzō (総説) 末期浮世絵 "Introduction: Late Ukiyoe" 『国貞・国芳・英泉』 [浮世絵大系 10] pp. 74–88, 集英社, 1974.

高橋誠一郎・吉田　漱 Takahashi Seiichirō and Yoshida Sō 『清親』 *Kiyochika* [浮世絵大系 12] 143 pp. (原色図版 72 pp., 単色図版 23 pp.), 集英社, 1974.

小林　忠 Kobayashi Tadashi 『富嶽三十六景』 *Thirty-six Scenes of Mt. Fuji* [浮世絵大系 13] 123 pp. (原色図版 56 pp., 単色図版 39 pp.), 集英社, 1975.

吉田　漱 Yoshida Sō 東海道五拾三次 "The Fifty-three Stations of the Tōkaidō" 『東海道五拾三次』 [浮世絵大系 14] pp. 66–72, 集英社, 1975.

菊地貞夫 Kikuchi Sadao 『木曾街道六拾九次』 *The Sixty-nine Stations of the Kiso Kaidō* [浮世絵大系 15] 123 pp. (原色図版 80 pp., 単色図版 7 pp.), 集英社, 1975.

宮尾しげを Miyao Shigeo 『名所絵戸百景 (一)』 *A Hundred Famous Places in Edo*, Part 1 [浮世絵大系 16] 123 pp., (原色図版 72 pp., 単色図版 15 pp.), 集英社, 1975.

35　楢崎宗重 Narasaki Muneshige 『清長・歌麿・写楽』 *Kiyonaga, Utamaro and Sharaku* [高橋誠一郎コレクション浮世絵 2], 中央公論社, 1975.

楢崎宗重 Narasaki Muneshige 『広重』 *Hiroshige* [高橋誠一郎コレクション浮世絵 5] 218 pp., 中央公論社, 1975.

36　小山寛二・青木進三朗 (編) Koyama Kanji and Aoki Shinzaburō (eds.) 『肉筆葛飾北斎』 *Brushstyle—Katsushika Hokusai*, 313 pp. (おもに図), 毎日新聞社, 1975.

37 坂本　満 Sakamoto Mitsuru　江戸時代の洋風画とリューベンス "Rubens and Western-style Painting in the Edo Period"「美術研究」295 号，pp. 26–34，東京国立文化財研究所，1975 年 2 月.

38 菅野　陽 Sugano Akira『日本銅版画の研究・近世』 Study of Copper-plate Engraving in Japan: The Early Modern Period, 580 pp. (図版 121 pp.)，美術出版社，1974.

39 成瀬不二雄 Naruse Fujio　司馬江漢筆『帆布職人図』をめぐって "On the 'Craftsman Mending the Sail' by Shiba Kōkan"「国華」No. 976, pp. 5–13，国華社，1975 年 1 月.

40 細野正信 Hosono Masanobu『司馬江漢——江戸洋風画の悲劇的先駆者——』 Shiba Kōkan: A Tragic Pioneer of Edo Western-Style Paintiug [読売選書 29] 262 pp. (うち図 4 pp.)，読売新聞社，1974.

41 太田桃介・武塙林太郎・成瀬不二雄 Ōta Tōsuke, Takehana Rintarō and Naruse Fujio『図録・秋田蘭画』 Illustrated Catalogue of Dutch Paintings in Akita, はり込図版 30 枚，図版 16 枚，別冊解説 42 pp.，三一書房，1974.

42 鈴木　進・森　銑三 Suzuki Susumu, Mori Senzō and Higuchi Hideo『四州真景』 Landscapes of Four Provinces [覆刻渡辺崋山真景・写生帖集成 1] 巻子四巻，解説 62 pp.，平凡社教育産業センター，1974.
鈴木進・森銑三・樋口秀雄 Suzuki Susumu, Mori Senzō, and Higuchi Hideo『両國橋図稿・辛巳画稿他』 Sketches of the Ryōgoku Bridge and Sketches Done in 1821 [覆刻渡辺崋山真景・写生帖集成 2] 図版五冊，解説 86 pp.，平凡社教育産業センター，1975.

III-01 奈良国立博物館 (編) Nara National Museum (ed.)『阿弥陀仏彫像』 Statues of Amida Buddha, 352 pp. (うち図版 171 p)，東京美術，1975.

02 フランソワ・ベルチエ François Berthier　飛鳥寺問題の再吟味——その本尊を中心として—— "A Reexamination of the Asukadera Buddha"「仏教芸術」96 号，pp. 55–73，毎日新聞社，1974 年 5 月.

03 町田甲一 Machida Kōichi　飛鳥大仏について——ベルチエ氏の批判にこたえる—— "The Great Buddha of Asukadera. In Answer to the Criticism of M. François Berthier"「仏教芸術」98 号，pp. 98–105，毎日新聞社，1974 年 9 月.

04 久野　健 Kuno Takeshi　飛鳥大仏論 (上) "The Great Buddha of Asukadera" (Parts 1 and 2)「美術研究」300 号; 301 号，pp. 1–13; pp. 16–26，東京国立文化財研究所，1975 年 7 月.

05 小林　剛・野間清六 Kobayashi Takeshi and Noma Seiroku『目録・御物金銅仏』 Studies of Small Bronze Buddha Statues in the Imperial Collection, 1975.

06 佐藤昭夫 Satō Akio『法隆寺献納金銅仏』 An Illustrated Catalogue of Bronze Statues from Hōryūji, 270 pp. (うち図版 182 pp.)，講談社，1975.

07 久野　健 Kuno Takeshi『平安初期彫刻史の研究』 Studies on the Sculpture of the Early Heian Period, 2 巻仕立 (本文・図版)，本文 372 pp.，図版 434 pp.，吉川弘文堂，1974.

244

08 猪川和子 Ikawa Kazuko『日本古彫刻史論』*Studies of Ancient Japanese Sculpture*, 381 pp. (うち図版 6 p.), 講談社, 1975.

09 久野 健 Kuno Takeshi『運慶の彫刻』*Sculpture of Unkei*, 202 pp. (うち図版 100 pp). 平凡社, 1974.

10 渋江二郎 Shibue Jirō『鎌倉彫刻史の研究』*Studies in the History of Kamakura Sculpture*, 280 pp., 図 16 pp., 有隣堂, 1974.

11 久野 健 (編) Kuno Takeshi (ed.)『仏像事典』*A Dictionary of Buddha Images*, 603 pp. (図共), 東京堂出版, 1975.

IV-01 正倉院事務所 (編集) Shōsōin Offices (ed.), with Matsuda Gonroku, Okada Jō, Kitamura Ōmichi, and Arakawa Hirokazu『正倉院の漆工』*Lacquer in the Shōsōin*, Plates 384, X 線写真 86, 本文 180 pp., 平凡社, 1975.

02 石田尚豊・中野政樹 Ishida Hisatoyo and Nakano Masaki『鏡像』*Buddhist Images Inscribed on Mirrors*, 180 pp. (うち図版 75 図), 東京博物館, 1975.

03 山辺知行 Yamanobe Tomoyuki『絣』*Kasuri* [日本染織芸術叢書 7] はり込図 40 枚, 27 pp., 芸艸堂, 1975.
西村兵部 Nishimura Hyōbu『紋織 1』*Mon'ori* 1 [日本染織芸術叢書 8] はり込図 25 枚, 図 28 枚, 15 pp., 芸艸堂, 1975.
神谷栄子 Kamiya Eiko『型染』*Katazome* (Stencil Dyeing) [日本染織芸術叢書 9] はり込図 40 枚, 図 10 枚, 28 pp., 芸艸堂, 1975.

AUTHOR INDEX

260

SUBJECT INDEX

270